the hope and the glory of

Catholic History

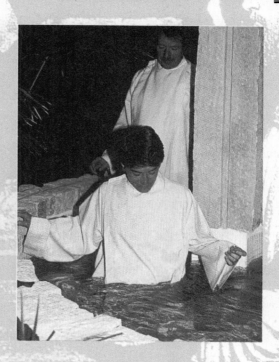

Rev. William A. Anderson, D. Min., Ph.D.

BROWN-ROA

A Division of Harcourt Brace & Company

Nihil Obstat
Rev. Joseph O'Reilly, D. Min.

Imprimatur
Most Rev. Bernard W. Schmitt
Bishop of Wheeling-Charleston
January 5, 1996

This Imprimatur is an official declaration that a book or pamphlet is free of doctrinal or moral error. No implication is contained therein that anyone who granted the Imprimatur agrees with the contents, opinions, or statements expressed.

Book Team
President—Matthew J. Thibeau
Managing Editor—Marge Krawczuk
Product Development Manager—Lynn Burds-Molony
Developmental Editors—Gina L. Burkart, Marilyn Bowers Gorun
Consultant—Anne Francis Bartus, S.S.J., D. Min.
Design—Susan T. Staron
Production layout—Springraphics

Print Credits
Scripture quotations indicated NRSV are from the New Revised Standard Version Bible: Catholic Edition copyright © 1993 and 1989 by the Division of Christian Education of the National Council of Churches of Christ in the U.S.A. All rights reserved.

Scripture quotations indicated CEV are from Contemporary English Version, Catholic Edition. Copyright © American Bible Society 1991, 1992, 1995. All rights reserved.

Excerpts from the English translation of the Catechism of the Catholic Church for the United States of America, copyright © 1994, United States Catholic Conference, Inc.-Libreria Editrice Vaticana. All rights reserved.

Photo Credits
Gene Plaisted, OSC
James L. Shaffer
Skjold Photography
Editorial Development

Printed in the United States of America

ISBN 0-15-950332-9

Table of Contents

Preparing for the Journey

A high school football team was playing its second game of the season when one of its players had his leg broken by an angry player on the other team. The fans and players shouted in vain for a penalty for the opposing team, but the referees refused to acknowledge that the player had violated any rules.

When the team's player had his leg broken, the high school was losing by two touchdowns. The team became so inflamed by the accident that they fought back, scoring four touchdowns during the rest of the game while they kept the opposing team from scoring again.

The next day, in the town newspaper, a reporter simply told of some of the outstanding plays of the game and reported the score of the game. The students became enraged that the newspaper told nothing of the broken leg as the incentive behind the team's stunning victory. They felt that the newspaper related only a portion of the story.

Since a newspaper is limited to reporting facts, it often reveals only part of the story. Like the students attending the high school game in the opening story, we all eventually realize that a newspaper rarely reports the personalities, the life situations, or the motives behind the events it describes.

Without a knowledge of our Catholic history, reading the Bible can be like reading the newspaper. You get only the facts, and often the facts can be distorted or misunderstood if you don't know the rest of the story.

As you piece together the story, you will see how many of the practices of the Catholic Church have evolved, and how we became the Church that we are today.

In this book you will study our Catholic heritage, and in doing so, will see the events of Church in a whole new way.

Throughout the text you will find some information presented as though it were appearing in the newspaper during the time it took place. The title of our ageless newspaper is The Christian Times. Presenting the information this way gives you a sense of the time in which it occurred.

At the end of each article, you will find a **Notepad** section containing a box of questions to challenge you, the reader. Your answers will determine what you have learned from the article and what further questions you may have about the story. The Notepad will then be followed by **The Rest of the Story**. In The Rest of the Story you will get the background information necessary to fully understand the story as a whole. This information will include a brief synopsis of the culture's values, practices, and politics.

As you proceed through the section entitled The Rest of the Story, you will also find **Clipboards** which contain questions and reflections that get to the heart of the story. When answering and responding to these, think of yourself as a reporter preparing to report the inside scoop of a front page story.

On occasion, you will find a **Map Search**. The Map Search is designed to give you an idea of what the countries looked like and where they were located during the time of the story. The maps are intended to enhance your understanding of the story.

You are now ready to begin your journey.

chapter one

Shaping the Community Of Disciples

Roberto's high school religion teacher assigned each student in class a Bible story. Each student was instructed to retell the story as though he or she had witnessed the events of the story. In telling the story the students were to include the feelings and personalities of the characters. This is how Roberto retold the story of Doubting Thomas.

"The disciples laughed again as they spoke about poor Thomas. Thomas was not with them on that first Sunday, when Jesus appeared to them. He foolishly and brazenly declared that he would not believe that Jesus had been raised from the dead unless he could put his finger in the wounds in Jesus' hands and place his hand in Jesus' side.

On that second Sunday, Thomas was with them when Jesus appeared. His faced reddened, and he tried to hide behind Peter when Jesus appeared. He choked as Jesus invited him to touch his wounds, and Peter had to push Thomas forward to Jesus.

Thomas spluttered something about 'My Lord and my God,' and even Jesus seemed to look amused at Thomas's loss for words. That was what made the disciples laugh. Thomas was always so sure of himself, and now, here he was, seeing Christ's face, staring at his wounds, touching him, and feeling foolish about not believing.

Time has passed now and the disciples retell the story over and over again. Thomas is able to laugh at his foolishness. The story reminds them of Jesus' encouraging words at the time, 'Blessed are those who do not see, but believe.'"

Without realizing it, Roberto had all the ingredients of history in his story. In retelling the gospel story, Roberto had captured the memory, told the story, and presented an historical foundation for future readers of the Scriptures.

Ingredients for History

Many times we fail to see history as what it really is—a story. Too often history becomes a conglomeration of facts and dates. This causes history to become impersonal and boring. To fully appreciate history, it is necessary to understand its main ingredients.

Because the students in Roberto's history class had been complaining that Church history was boring, the teacher assigned each of the students a Bible story to retell so that they would understand that Church history was more than facts and dates. She wanted them to envision Church history as a living story which they themselves continue to live each day.

In retelling the story of Doubting Thomas, Roberto gained an understanding of history's main ingredients. By giving the characters in the story personalities and feelings, he brought the story to life. The students were able to meet these same characters over and over again as they retold their stories to each other. They felt the pain and sadness of the crucifixion of Christ, and the joy in his resurrection. For the first time they saw how they were Jesus' current apostles, and for the first time they felt the call to discipleship. In telling their stories the students were able to *see* how all of the stories were connected to form one continuing story—a story that was continuing with them. This is the first main ingredient of history—**telling a story**.

The students found the second main ingredient of history when they saw how all of their stories connected. They were able to **remember** the friendship that formed between Jesus and the apostles, the despair and abandonment that the apostles felt when Jesus was crucified, and the disbelief and excitement that the apostles felt in Jesus' resurrection. To fully appreciate history, we must use our gift of memory. This second ingredient is what brings history to life. It allows us to see how the characters have changed, failed, succeeded, and grown. Remembering the past is what connects the stories together and brings them into the present.

In connecting the stories together, the students arrived at the third main ingredient for history—**a context for present life**. In connecting the stories, the students were able to understand how they are Jesus' present-day disciples. And by understanding the struggles and challenges that the disciples went through in continuing Jesus' work after he ascended, they were better able to face their everyday struggles and challenges. In discovering their Catholic heritage, the students understood the full meaning of their call to discipleship. In understanding the past, they were better able to understand the present and thus, better equipped to work toward their goals for the future.

History as a Context for Life

Like the students of Roberto's class you may also think that Church history is boring. You also may wonder why you even need to study it. After all, the past already happened. Why should you waste your time learning about something that happened years ago? There are more important things to worry about, such as the present. Right?!?!

Unfortunately this is the attitude of a lot of people. And this attitude stems from the inability to understand that everything that we do depends on history. What you do today depends on the knowledge of what you did yesterday. For example, if you miss a day of class you have to find out what the class studied the day you were gone in order to understand what the class is currently studying. You may be able to get by OK without the knowledge of what happened in the previous class, but it will be much more difficult. Or, on a simpler note, in getting dressed for school, you have to know where you put your shoes when you last took them off, or you may waste a lot of time looking for them—time that could have been spent doing other things.

In the same way, knowing the history of our nationality, our race, and our religion may help us to identify who we are. Knowing the past helps us to recognize how we share a common history with others. We are students who belong to particular families, live in a specific nation, profess a definite religion, and claim a certain heritage and nationality. Recognizing how we share this common history with others will show us how we are unique.

Without studying history, we may still find out who we are, but the process will be much more challenging, and the knowledge we discover about ourselves will not be as complete.

Church History as a Context for Life

If we lost our memory of civil history, we would not know why we obey the laws of our country or act with freedom. Likewise, if we lost our memory of Church history, we would not know the purpose of acting in the world as Church. To explain what we are doing today, we need to remember what we did in the yesterdays of our lives.

We study Church history to broaden our context of history and to understand more clearly our mission as Church. Shortly after the Second Vatican Council, in the 1960s, many people became alarmed because the Catholic Church was going through a period of change. When the council changed the language of the Eucharistic liturgy from Latin to English, many felt that we were being unfaithful to the past. Some, however, welcomed the change because they knew that the Church did not always worship in Latin, and they could now understand what was taking place during worship. Those who knew the history of the Catholic Church were able to see beyond the limited context of our current era. They were able to welcome and fully appreciate the changes of the Second Vatican Council.

In studying Church history we need to focus on three main ingredients: storytelling, memory, and a context for living and understanding our faith today.

History Needs Maps

A journey of the past is no different from a journey of the present—it requires a good map. Using maps, in your study of history, can help you better visualize what actually happened. Many times the maps can even give you clues as to why certain events happened as they did. The maps will show you what the country looked like and where it was located. They will help you to better understand the journeys of the characters, and the politics of the day. Occasionally, we will use maps in this text to better understand exactly what happened and why.

Our Jewish Heritage

The Christian Times

First Century   **Vol. 1   No. 1**

Jerusalem Awaits Jesus' Visit

As the celebration of the Feast of Passover nears, the city of Jerusalem tensely awaits the arrival of Jesus and his disciples. The Romans have doubled their patrol for this feast, expecting that Jesus and his disciples, as good Jews, will certainly arrive in Jerusalem.

Over the past few years, Jesus has occasionally embarrassed some of the religious leaders by challenging their interpretation of the Scriptures. The Romans do not like the idea that Jesus' disciples are calling him the Messiah.

Many of the Jewish population fear that the Romans will punish the whole nation for Jesus' crimes. They fear that the

Romans will force the Jewish people to worship Roman gods. Until now, the Romans have allowed Jews to worship the one true God instead of the Roman gods.

Since Jesus began his preaching, he has become suspect of inciting the people to rebellion. Jesus speaks of a reign of God. The Romans wonder if this means that he will lead a rebellion against the reign of the Roman emperor, whom they honor as a god.

Although Jesus is unpopular with many religious and political leaders, thousands of Jews from colonies outside Palestine are swarming into the city, clamoring to see Jesus. With tensions rising in the holy city, both Roman and

religious leaders express hope that the celebration of Passover will end peacefully.

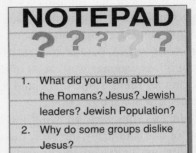

NOTEPAD ? ? ? ? ?

1. What did you learn about the Romans? Jesus? Jewish leaders? Jewish Population?
2. Why do some groups dislike Jesus?
3. Why is it likely that Jesus will appear in the city with his disciples?

The Rest of the Story

Although Jesus' life would end on that fateful Friday when the Roman authorities and many religious leaders joined together in crucifying Jesus, we should not make the mistake of blaming the Jewish population for the death of Jesus. Jesus was a devout Jew who had

chosen Jewish disciples, followed Jewish laws, customs, and feast days. Since the Catholic Church builds its history on the life and person of Jesus, who was a Jew, we also need to learn about the Jewish heritage in relationship to our Catholic history.

Jewish Heritage

Although the newspaper story tells of the impending visit of Jesus to Jerusalem, the "rest of the story" begins approximately three years before Jesus' fatal trip to that city. As the newspaper reported, Jesus and his disciples were devout Jews. Jesus gathered his followers from among the Jewish population. This means that our Christian heritage has its roots in the Jewish faith.

After Jesus was baptized at the Jordan by John the Baptist, he walked along the shores of the Sea of Galilee in Palestine and beckoned four Jewish fishermen to follow him. We can picture the sun setting as the men—Peter, Andrew, James and John—lugged their heavy nets up on the shore to clean them. The magnetism of Jesus' personality and his invitation led the men to leave their nets and families and to follow him.

During the next few days, Jesus summoned other women and men from the Jewish population to follow him. Jesus himself was a loyal Jew who shared a common ancestry with his disciples. They were all descendants of Abraham and Sarah, and therefore held common beliefs. Because of God's promise to Abraham and later to Moses, the disciples could boast that they were God's chosen people.

In his preaching, Jesus remained faithful to God's promise to the chosen people. They were the ones chosen to share God's message with all nations. He showed greater favor toward his Jewish audience than those of foreign lands. He would tell the Jewish people of the mission they had to spread his message throughout the foreign lands. Jesus claimed that he came for the fulfillment of Judaism.

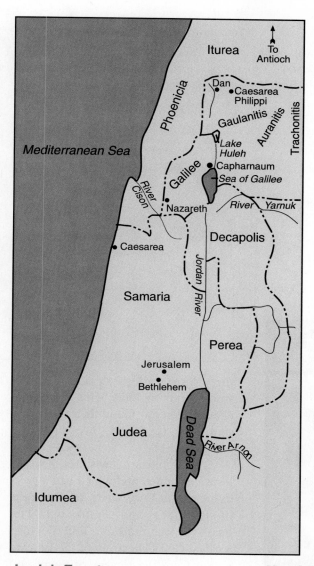

Jewish Feasts

Since Jesus and his disciples lived in a more religious atmosphere than many of us do today, the people could expect them to arrive at Jerusalem on a solemn feast such as the Passover. As devout Jews, Jesus and his disciples would do all in their power to celebrate major Jewish feasts in Jerusalem.

In Jesus' day, each religious holiday was a special festival which marked some memorial during which God showered blessings on the Jewish people. On these feasts, the holy city of Jerusalem would fill with Jews coming to worship for the feast. Since there was never enough homes to provide for all

Map Search

Before proceeding any further, it would be well to plan our trip by looking at the map below to become familiar with the land of Palestine. Find the following on the map.

• The Mediterranean Sea
• Jerusalem
• Samaria
• Nazareth
• Galilee
• Bethlehem
• Jordan River
• Sea of Galilee

Map Search

Study the map and make a note of the extensiveness of the Roman Empire. Find the following.

- On the west: Spain, Gaul, Britain
- On the north: Gaul, Macedonia, Asia Minor
- On the south: Egypt
- On the east: Jerusalem, Palestine

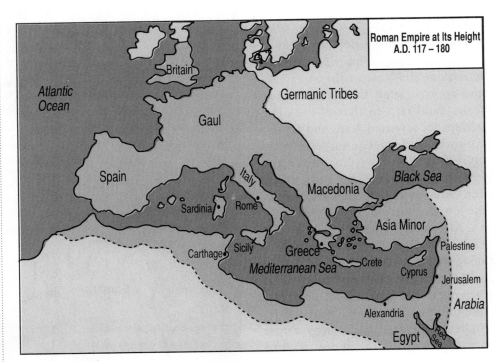

Roman Empire at Its Height A.D. 117 – 180

KEY TERMS

Passover: a religious feast recalling God's liberation of the Israelite nation from the slavery of Egypt and the Israelites' eventual escape to the Promised Land.

Pentecost: (a Greek word meaning fifty) a feast which celebrates the fiftieth day after the liberation of the people from Egypt, when their leader, Moses, received the commandments in their name, as their part in the covenant with God.

the visitors to Jerusalem, the people would sleep outdoors. Jesus and his disciples apparently found their customary spot in the Garden of Olives, known as Gethsemane.

Two significant Jewish feasts which Jesus celebrated and which had a great influence on Christianity are the feasts of Passover and Pentecost. The **Passover** was a religious festival which recalled God's liberation of the Israelite nation from the slavery of Egypt and the Israelites' eventual escape to the Promised Land. On the night that the Israelites fled from Egypt, each household within the Hebrew community sacrificed a lamb, painted its blood on their doorposts, and ate the lamb. They were a people ready for a journey.

The story in Exodus tells the story of the angel of death passing over the doors painted with the blood. The doors not painted in blood belonged to the Egyptians. According to Scripture, the angel of death brought death to the firstborn male child and animals of the Egyptians.

Each year, the Hebrew people would celebrate the feast of the Passover as the time of liberation and freedom. It was a time to recall that

God was still present with the Israelite people. Jesus and his disciples, as devout Jews, would celebrate this feast together with their families, or with each other.

The feast of **Pentecost** was also a major Jewish feast. The word Pentecost comes from a Greek word meaning fifty. According to the story, fifty days after God freed the Israelites from the powerful Egyptian army, Moses climbed Mount Sinai in the desert and received the commandments from God. Thus, the feast celebrates the fiftieth day after the liberation of the people from Egypt, when their leader, Moses, received the commandments in their name.

Roman Occupation of the Land

The news article reported that Roman soldiers had doubled their patrols in preparation for the arrival of Jesus and his disciples. Although the Jewish people learned to accept the presence of Roman soldiers in their land, they looked upon the Roman occupation of Palestine with sadness and disgust. They had received the land from God, and believed that no foreign power had the right to possess it.

A little more than sixty years before the birth of Christ, Roman soldiers took control of Palestine and joined it to the Roman Empire. Although the Jewish people were angered by this, they did receive some benefits from Roman rule. With Roman guards on patrol to protect the people from bandits, the people knew that they could travel throughout Palestine with relative safety from robbers or murderers, however, it sometimes brought unexpected and unjust suffering to the people. Crucifixion of robbers, murderers, and leaders of rebellions had become common, and many of the people feared the Roman guards as much as they felt a need for their protection. The presence of the Roman Guards reminded the people that their land was in the hands of foreign rulers.

One fervent group of Jews within Palestine believed that God wanted them to fight to regain Jewish control of Palestine. This group, known as the **Zealots**, believed that God would give them the strength necessary to overcome the powerful Roman armies.

Since the Jewish people sometimes found themselves punished for the minor skirmishes incited by the Zealots, the group had become unpopular with the religious leaders and many of the people. Some of the people, however, were afraid that if they spoke out against the Zealots they would find themselves victims of their attacks.

Jesus did not support the endeavors of the Zealots. He proclaimed a spiritual reign, not a worldly one. He ate and drank with the hated Jewish tax collectors who collected taxes from their own people for the Roman government. He cured servants and family members of Roman soldiers and preached to them. He showed that God loved them as much as God loved the Jews and he preached the forgiveness of enemies. The Zealots could not understand this.

Worship of Roman Gods

The news article spoke of the people's fear that the Roman authorities would force them to worship Roman gods. This fear stemmed from the fact that the Roman armies forced conquered nations to worship Roman gods in addition to their own gods. Usually the emperor was included in the list of Roman gods. In doing this, the Roman emperor assured the allegiance of the conquered people. After all, who wanted to fight against a god?

Since the conquered nations (except the Jews) already worshipped a number of gods, they had no problem worshiping the additional Roman gods. In fact these people believed that the Roman gods, who protected the powerful empire of Rome, must indeed be the most powerful of all gods.

Unlike other conquered nations, the Jewish people worshiped only one God. Since the Jews did not accept worship of many gods, Roman authorities did not force them to worship other gods. This unusual exception for the Jewish people applied to every Jewish colony throughout the Empire.

In exchange for the release of the Jewish people from the obligation of worshiping Roman gods, the Roman emperor took it upon himself to appoint the major religious leader for the Jews, known as the **High Priest**. This gave the emperor some control over the religious life of the people as he would appoint someone who would protect the interests of Rome in Palestine. Likewise, the corrupt high priest could use his office, to have his enemies put to death by accusing them of threatening Roman leadership.

Religious Leaders

As the article stated, Jesus often embarrassed many of the religious leaders by challenging their interpretations of the Scriptures. He had become so popular with people that the religious leaders grew jealous of him. As many people

JOURNAL

If Jesus were a student in your school, with whom would he eat and drink? Do you eat and drink with these people? Why or why not?

KEY TERMS

Pharisees: laymen dedicated to adapting the religious law to the everyday life of the Jews.

Sadducees: a priestly class centering their authority on the Temple.

Sanhedrin: a powerful religious group, led by the high priest, consisting of seventy men chosen from among the Pharisees and Saduceees.

Jesus Christ: an expression meaning that Jesus is the Christ or Messiah.

Christ: a title; the Greek translation for the Jewish word Messiah, also translates as the anointed one.

Diaspora: Jewish groups living outside Palestine

For a child has been born for us, a son given to us; authority rests upon his shoulders; and he is named Wonderful Counselor, Mighty God, Everlasting Father, Prince of Peace. His authority shall grow continually, and there shall be endless peace for the throne of David and his kingdom.

Isaiah 9:6–7, NRSV

awaited Jesus' visit to Jerusalem to hear his message, some religious leaders awaited his visit with the intention of having him killed by Roman soldiers.

Jesus respected the rights of the religious leaders of his day, but he did not hesitate to confront them when they did not live up to God's law, or when they changed the law to fit their own designs. Among these leaders was a group known as the **Pharisees** who were laymen dedicated to adapting the religious law to the everyday life of the Jews. Another group, known as the **Sadducees**, was a priestly class centering their authority on the Temple. As a wealthy class not wishing to have their wealth threatened, they tended to align themselves with the high priest and the Roman rulers in Palestine.

The Gospels tell us that the day before Jesus died, soldiers found him in the Garden of Olives and dragged him to a gathering of the most powerful religious group in Palestine, known as the **Sanhedrin**. This group, with the high priest as its leader, consisted of seventy men chosen from among the Pharisees and Saducees. According to the Gospel accounts, the high priest presided over this group, which in their name, condemned Jesus to death.

Messianic Hope

The news report recognized the great fear the Roman authorities had for anyone the people acclaimed as messiah. There had been times in the history of this people when the people put their hopes in a messiah who was to be a warrior leader. The Romans may have feared that Jesus was such a military messiah, intent on recapturing Palestine from Rome. Because of earlier experiences, they sometimes sought to control the situation by killing a leader who claimed to be the Messiah.

Central to Jewish belief was the expectation that God would always be their liberator. Now and then this expectation, at least for some groups

among the people, included a human, like Moses, through whom God would liberate the people. The prophets understood that such a messiah was to be a spiritual leader who would bring the people back to God. They did not expect a messiah who would lead the Israelites into battle with their enemies. In Jesus' day, however, some of the people may have expected a warrior Messiah, who would free the country from its foreign rulers.

Although, as Christians, we believe that Jesus is truly the Messiah, Jesus forbade the people to use this term for him. Today we use the expression **Jesus Christ**, as though Christ were Jesus' last name. The expression really means that Jesus is the Christ or Messiah. **Christ** is a title, the Greek translation for the Jewish word Messiah, which can also translate as the Anointed One.

Although the people knew that a messiah's power would come from God, they never dreamed of a messiah who would be God. They never imagined a messiah who would die on a cross to redeem them for a spiritual, rather than a political, reign. Jesus is the Christ, the Messiah, and he is human and divine. This belief stands at the center of the history of the Catholic Church.

The Dispersion

As the newspaper article stated, many Jews from outside Jerusalem had come to Jerusalem for the celebration of the Passover. During Jesus' time, a number of Jewish colonies existed outside of Palestine. These Jewish colonies date back centuries, when many Jews fled from the country to avoid an invasion and when countries carried the Jewish people off to their own countries as slaves. These groups living outside Palestine are referred to as the Jews of the Dispersion, or the **Diaspora**.

These diaspora Jews had to learn the language and customs of the people of the host country in which they settled. Greek and Latin were the common languages of the empire, while the Jews of Palestine spoke Aramaic. Many of the people of the diaspora no longer spoke Aramaic.

Three centuries before the birth of Christ, some scholars became concerned about the struggles of these Greek speaking Jews of the diaspora and translated the Bible into Greek. The name of this Greek translation of the Bible is the **Septuagint**, which is a Greek word meaning seventy. It has its origins in the legend that seventy scholars translated the Bible into Greek and all seventy of them, without checking with each other while they worked, had translated the text exactly the same.

The diaspora Jews struggled to keep their Jewish customs alive in these foreign lands. When Jesus and his disciples encountered them on major feasts, the diaspora Jews would be fulfilling their constant longing to return to Jerusalem as often as possible during their lifetime. The Roman roads and the protection of the Roman patrols provided relatively safe highways for traveling throughout the empire.

At the time when Jesus and his disciples were spreading Jesus' message in the Holy Land, there were four to five million Jews living outside of Palestine. Almost every major city in the Roman Empire had a Jewish colony. The Jewish settlements of the diaspora lived at the center of a Greek culture which had a great influence on their daily lives. Although they remained faithful to their basic Jewish beliefs, they adapted many of their customs to the culture in which they lived.

The diaspora Jews accepted converts into their fold from those who were not Jews without imposing many of the Jewish laws and practices on these converts. They called these converts **God-fearers**. Some of the more rigid Jewish communities in Palestine rejected these adaptations and refused to acknowledge these God-fearers as true converts.

Reign of God

Because Jesus preached the **reign of God**, the Romans would naturally suspect him of laying the foundations for a rebellion. Since they believed that the emperor was a god and that he ruled the Roman Empire, anyone who spoke of a different reign of God could only have the intention of overthrowing the government. When Jesus spoke of the reign of God, the Roman authorities thought that he was speaking of replacing the reign of the emperor god.

Jesus, however, was not speaking of a worldly reign when he spoke of the reign of God. He did proclaim that the reign of God had come into the world, but he also proclaimed that it would reach its fulfillment in eternity. The reign of God was the presence of Jesus and his message. It is a message of love of God, neighbor, and self. Jesus did not proclaim hatred and conquest, but justice and peace.

When Jesus spoke with his disciples about the reign of God, he gave to them the mission to share the gifts and knowledge of this reign with others. Preaching the presence of the reign of God would be the mission of Jesus' disciples.

KEY TERMS

Septuagint: Greek word meaning seventy; the Greek translation of the Bible.

God-fearers: converts accepted by the Diaspora Jews.

reign of God: the presence of Jesus and his message of love of God, neighbor, and self.

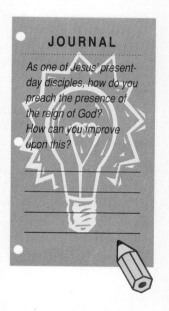

JOURNAL

As one of Jesus' present-day disciples, how do you preach the presence of the reign of God? How can you improve upon this?

CLIPBOARD

1. List and discuss some elements from the Jewish faith that we use in Christianity today.
2. Discuss the three elements of history as found in the Messianic hope of the Jewish People.
3. Discuss the three elements of history as found in the diaspora.

Community of Disciples

The Christian Times

First Century   Vol. 1   No. 1

Rumors Spread: Jesus Still Lives

Early this morning, in the streets of Jerusalem, one of our investigative reporters encountered a jubilant disciple of Jesus named Thomas. When asked for the reason behind this joy, Thomas made the absurd claim that Jesus, who was crucified by Roman soldiers more than seven weeks ago, is still alive.

Thomas claims to have seen Jesus and put his hand in Jesus' wounds. He also claims that Jesus has been visiting with his disciples over the past seven weeks. During his short interview, Thomas refused to disclose the hiding place of the other followers of Jesus.

Thomas made another absurd statement which really challenges the minds of thinking people. He claims that he and a band of Jesus' followers saw Jesus raised from earth. He added that Jesus had commanded them to re-evaluate their understanding of Jesus and his message.

After the interview, our reporter felt that we would be hearing a great deal from this community of disciples.

NOTEPAD

? ? ? ? ?

1. What did you learn about Thomas? Jesus? the other disciples?
2. How would the fact of Jesus' rising from the dead affect the disciples' understanding of Jesus' message?
3. How do you think the Roman soldiers reacted to Thomas's claim of Jesus' rising from the dead?

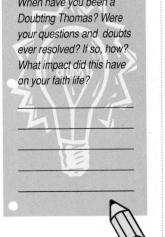

JOURNAL

When have you been a Doubting Thomas? Were your questions and doubts ever resolved? If so, how? What impact did this have on your faith life?

_____

_____

_____

_____

The Rest of the Story

Three days after his death, Jesus appeared to his disciples in glory. They recognized that this was Jesus who had died and had now come back from the dead. We can imagine them becoming frightened at first and then, realizing that it truly was Jesus and that he was alive, bursting out in laughter and joy. Their friend, their teacher, and their hope had been raised from the dead. When Jesus disappeared from their midst that Sunday night, they knew that he had returned.

Thomas was with them a week later when Jesus appeared. He had doubted Jesus' resurrection, but when he put his fingers in Jesus' wounds and his hand in the wound in Jesus' side, he knew it was Jesus. With the rest of the disciples, he would now reflect on Jesus' life and message in light of the resurrection.

During the days following Jesus' appearance, the disciples reflected on his message and drew closer together as a community. Without realizing it, they were beginning to shape the foundation for the future of the Church. A number of days after his resurrection, Jesus met his disciples on a hillside, promised to be with them until the end of the world, told them to preach and baptize people of all nations, and ascended out of their sight.

In the Spotlight

St. Thomas was a Jew and probably a Galilean of humble birth. His name is Syriac, which means the 'twin.' Didymus, as we know he was also called, is the Greek equivalent. Tradition has it that after the descent of the Holy Spirit, Thomas preached the gospel in India. This is supported from several seemingly independent sources, of which the chief source is the *Acta Thomae*, a document dating apparently from the first quarter of the third century. The story told in the *Acta* characterizes St. Thomas as a slave to King Gundafor in India. As Gundafor's slave, St. Thomas was ordered to use his carpentry skills to build King Gundafor a palace. Instead, St. Thomas helped the poor and spread the message of Christ. When Gundafor asked to see his palace, St. Thomas responded, "You cannot see it now, but only when you have left this world."

It is agreed that there is no truth behind this legendary story. There is, however, evidence that St. Thomas preached in India. Along the Malabar Coast, in the states of Cochin and Travancore, there is a large population of native Christians who call themselves the Christians of St. Thomas. In their liturgies, these Christians used forms and a language (Syriac) that undoubtedly were derived from Mesopotamia and Persia. They claim, as their name indicates, to have been originally evangelized by St. Thomas in person. They have an ancient oral tradition that he landed at Crangamore on the west coast, established seven churches in Malabar, and then passed eastward to the Coromandel

Coast, where he was martyred, by spearing, on the "Big Hill," eight miles from Madras.

In 1522 the Portugese discovered the alleged tomb of St. Thomas in Mylapore, now a suburb of Madras. Some of his relics have been preserved there in the cathedral of St. Thomas of Mylapore.

*S*ince, like all the
faithful, lay
*Christians are entrusted
by God with the aposto-
late by virtue of their
Baptism and
Confirmation, they
have the right and duty,
individually or grouped
in associations, to work
so that the divine mes-
sage of salvation may
be known and accepted
by all...*

Catechism of the Catholic
Church, #900

The ascension of Jesus

Community of Disciples

As Thomas stated in the article, the followers of Jesus had gathered together
to reflect on his message in light of his
resurrection. The followers of Jesus realized that Jesus, during his lifetime, had
knit them into a community. He had
them follow him, live and eat with him,
listen to his message, and witness his
healings. They were sharing a common
experience and a common message.

At the death of Jesus, the community
of Jesus' disciples scattered, but eventually gathered back together in a commonly used meeting place. Jesus had appeared to them on the evening of his
resurrection, and they gradually regained
their courage by encouraging each other
and reflecting on Jesus' message.

One of the early features of the
Christian Church was that it was a community of disciples. During his public
life, Jesus had shaped them into a community of disciples, and, after his death
and resurrection, they would continue
to live as a community shaped by Jesus.

As the community of disciples pondered together under the guidance of
the Holy Spirit, they became aware that
Jesus was truly the Messiah and God.
They realized that they had received a
mission from Jesus, to spread the good
news to all ends of the earth. They gradually recognized the importance of baptism and knew that this would be the
path for others to follow in joining the
community of disciples. They kept pondering and reflecting on Jesus' message
until they received the fire of wisdom,
courage, and love which sent them out
to spread the message.

A Community of Saints
and Sinners

From the beginning, the community of
disciples recognized that they were a
fragile lot. They could look around the
room at a disciple such as Peter, who
had denied Jesus and trusted Jesus
enough to seek forgiveness. They could
look at Nathaniel who cynically wondered if anything good could come
from the lowly town of Nazareth.
Thomas refused to believe in Jesus unless he saw him with his own eyes.

As they pondered the various personalities in their small community, they
could also remember Judas who was not
present. He had betrayed Jesus and did
not show the trust and humility necessary to return to him. Judas had good intentions at the beginning, but he allowed
his desire for wealth to overcome him.

Without realizing it, the community
of disciples were witnessing in each
other a miniature of the personalities
who would make up the future of the
Church. The Church would have its
leaders like Peter, its skeptics like
Nathaniel, its doubters like Thomas, and
its sinners like Judas. Belonging to the
community of disciples did not assure
that every disciple would be a saint.
The history of the community of disciples would be a history of sinful, repen-
tant, and saintly people.

A Pilgrim Church

Prophetically, the news reporter predicted that we would hear more from this community of disciples. When Jesus was shaping his community, he reminded them that they must live in the world with all of its temptations. He told them that they must be in the world, but not of the world. This meant that the world is not their final destiny, but only part of their journey. Like Jesus, the community of disciples would be on a journey through place and time.

Throughout the history of the Church, the community of disciples continued to live in a changing world, attempting to adapt the message of Jesus to every age. At times, they had to face death rather than deny Christ, and at times experience the allurement of wealth and power without succumbing. Through each of these periods, some would fail, desiring to become part of the world in which they live, while others will remain faithful, accepting death or hardship.

As a community on a pilgrimage through time, the community of disciples continues to apply Jesus' message to each new age. Jesus spoke to shepherds, not to factory workers. He did not speak to the nuclear age, but to an age when sowing seed was most common. The community of disciples must travel through the tunnel of time, from one culture and age to the next, remaining faithful to Jesus' life and message by applying the message to each new age.

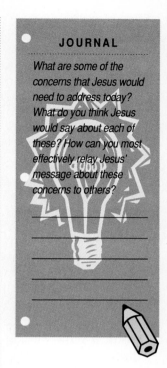

JOURNAL

What are some of the concerns that Jesus would need to address today? What do you think Jesus would say about each of these? How can you most effectively relay Jesus' message about these concerns to others?

CLIPBOARD

1. What stories and memories of Jesus enabled the disciples to form a community?

2. Name some saints and sinners you may recall in your current knowledge of Church history.

3. What are some of the major changes which have taken place in the world since Jesus first preached his message? How do you think these changes affected our understanding of Jesus' message?

KEY TERMS

Zealots	Septuagint
Pentecost	Sanhedrin
Passover	Christ
High Priest	Jesus Christ
Pharisees	Diaspora
Sadducees	God-fearers
Reign of God	

A Voice from the Past

As a persevering and dedicated reporter, you have studied the factors which led up to the Crucifixion of Christ. You know what happened and have a pretty good understanding of why. You are also aware of how the resurrection of Christ affected the disciples and Romans. Now it is time for you to relay what you have uncovered in your own editorial column. Write an article to your readers recapping the history that you have uncovered thus far. Use at least eight of the key terms from the chapter in your article. Conclude your article with a discussion of the community of disciples and our role in that community today. Be sure to show your readers how the events of the past affect our daily lives. As you write your article, it may be helpful to refer to your Clipboard notes.

REVIEWING THE ERA

BC AND AD—Writers will sometimes use the letters BC when referring to the era Before the birth of Christ and AD when referring to the era After the birth of Christ. In this text, we will not use AD with dates after Christ unless we are contrasting it with an event which took place before the birth of Christ.

- **800 BC**

DIASPORA. Those Israelites who were exiled or fled from the Assyrian invasion of northern Israel in the 700s before Christ and the Babylonian invasion of southern Israel in the 500s before Christ make up the Diaspora. The people of the Diaspora settled outside the Holy Land and learned the customs and language of their neighbors without giving up their Israelite beliefs.

- **70 BC**

ROMAN EMPIRE TAKES CONTROL OF PALESTINE. The Romans took control of the Empire approximately 60 years before the birth of Jesus and controlled the country throughout Jesus' life.

- **25 AD**

JESUS CHOOSES JEWISH DISCIPLES. Jesus was a Jew who chose Jewish disciples, celebrated Jewish feasts with them, and preached his message mainly to Jews. After his death and resurrection, Jesus appeared to his Jewish followers and gave them the mission of spreading his message.

- JESUS FORMS A COMMUNITY OF DISCIPLES. Throughout his public life, Jesus shaped his disciples into a community. Although the early followers of Jesus would not use this title for themselves, they acted as a community from the moment of Jesus' resurrection, pondering his life and message together in light of the resurrection. It would be a pilgrim community through time with its saints and sinners.

Then and Now

Jesus left his disciples with the story of his life, a memory of him and his message, and the context for living as a community of disciples. The community of disciples was originally a Jewish community of sinners and saints who faced the challenge of living in this world with faith in Christ.

Today we continue to live as a community of disciples. We place the foundation of our Catholic history in the life and times of Jesus, the Jew. We belong to a community of disciples who live in a context of history shaped by the memories and stories of the saints and sinners who have gone before us.

NEWS IN REVIEW

1. Why is history central to our lives?
2. List and explain how the three elements of history affect Church history.
3. Why does Church history need to recall the life of Jesus?
4. Why is knowledge of our Jewish heritage important for Church history?
5. What are two major Jewish feasts which have a special place in later Christian life?
6. What was the effect of the Roman presence on Jewish life during the days of Jesus?
7. What is the diaspora and why is it important?
8. Why did Jesus deny that he was the Messiah?
9. What do we mean by the Community of Disciples?
10. What are some elements of the Community of Disciples?

chapter two

The Early Stories Of Church History

Imagine yourself as one of Jesus' disciples. Jesus has ascended. You and the other disciples are recalling the many memories that you shared with Jesus. You realize that the meaning of many of these memories has changed in light of Jesus' death and resurrection.

If we lived as disciples right after the ascension of Jesus, we would have our stories and memories of Jesus' public life, but we would also have our stories and memories of Jesus visiting us occasionally after his resurrection. Because we knew he was raised from the dead, we would be recalling the story and memories of his public life in a different way. The context of history in which we would be living would be a context of pondering all that had happened and trying to make sense out of it.

If we were disciples of Jesus after his ascension, we would most likely be Jews, wondering how we were going to tell the rest of the Jewish community that Jesus, the expected Messiah, has already come. We could recognize that we now had the dangerous task of sharing his message with people who put him to death. We would be willing, but we would also be very frightened about the mission ahead.

As Jesus' disciples you have the responsibility to share his message with others.

The New Testament as a Source for History

The Christian Times

First Century   Vol. 1 No. 3

Fragments of Early Writings Discovered

One of our reporters made an important discovery this past week in the ruins of an old building recently used by a group of Christians. The reporter found notes referring to some writings called Gospels, apparently written by men named Mark, Matthew, Luke, and John. There were also a few fragments of some letters written by Paul, Peter, James, and John along with a short reference to a work called The Book of Revelations.

The longest fragments found contained reflections from a work entitled The Acts of the Apostles. If we are to believe these last notes, we must conclude that God certainly has blessed this community of Jesus' followers. The reporter found the following story of Pentecost most interesting.

It seems that shortly after the death of Jesus, an unexplained and noisy gust of wind roared through the crowded streets of Jerusalem where people were celebrating the Jewish feast of Pentecost. Many of the Jews of the Diaspora had arrived in Jerusalem for the feast. The wind literally herded them along to the dwelling of Jesus' disciples.

Witnesses inside the dwelling claimed that they saw tiny tongues that looked like fire rest on the heads of each of Jesus' disciples, like flames on candles. These witnesses marveled as the once cowardly disciples of Jesus stood up with courage and determination to follow Peter out to meet the crowds. They were muttering that they felt the presence of the Holy Spirit in their hearts.

Although most of the crowd could not speak Aramaic, they surprisingly understood Peter's sermon as though he spoke it in their own language. Peter preached of Jesus who, he claimed, was the Christ.

When Peter finished, the people clamored to be baptized.

According to the *Acts of the Apostles*, almost three thousand people were baptized. It was indeed an astounding and unforgettable experience for those who witnessed it.

These fragments seem to indicate that writing holds an important place in the Christian Community.

NOTEPAD
? ? ? ? ?

1. What did you learn about the disciples? the crowd?
2. What does the article tell you about the New Testament?
3. What does the article tell you about Pentecost?

The Rest of the Story

The New Testament

When we speak about the history of the early Church, we must use the New Testament as a source for our history. The New Testament is the Christian Scriptures, and it is the book that guides Christians in their faith. To understand the history of the Catholic Church, we must understand the New Testament.

In reading the New Testament we need to remember that it is not intended to be a history book, but rather a religious book. It does have a large amount of history, but the writers often adapted the history to respond to questions and situations existing at the time of the writing. In doing this, the writers were not distorting Jesus' message, but actually making it more understandable to their audiences. The development of the New Testament is one of the early stories of Church history.

Passing on the Message

After the resurrection and ascension of Jesus, the community of disciples hovered together in some type of dining room, reflecting on the life and message of Jesus Christ in light of his resurrection. They now knew the end of the story. This Jesus who lived with them was actually the Son of God. He was human and divine, their Messiah and Savior.

In their desire to pass on Jesus' message to the people of their own day, the community of disciples devised a clever technique for their preaching. They divided Jesus' message into segments which preachers could memorize and preach as they traveled from town to town. Since the people of Jesus' day had few books and no notepads, they had to rely on their memories to recall and pass on Jesus' message.

Some of the missionaries would memorize and preach one segment of the wisdom sayings of Jesus. Others would preach some of Jesus' parables, while some memorized and preached about Jesus' passion or other events in his life. These preachers would travel from town to town, preaching the segment they had memorized. The people would listen to the message, and pass it on from memory, as accurately as possible.

The Gospel of Mark

Around the year 65, a young man named Mark made an ingenious decision. He listened as different preachers preached about different segments of Jesus' life and message. He then decided to put them together, using a format similar to that of someone writing a biography. The difference was that he knew the story did not end with Jesus' death, but with his resurrection and ascension. He knew that Jesus was human and divine.

Mark lined up the events of Jesus' life, placed the sayings and miracles of Jesus in places where he felt they belonged, paid special attention to the passion and death of Jesus, and wrote the first Gospel. Without realizing it, Mark could have received a Nobel prize for inventing a new type of writing called Gospel. It was a religious book based on the community's reflections on the actual events and messages in Jesus' life. Mark adapted his presentation to a particular need felt by a certain community of disciples around the year 65, thirty-five years after the death and resurrection of Jesus.

Mark knew that Christians were suffering and dying in Rome, and many were asking why they had to endure these hardships. If Jesus brought salvation, why did suffering continue? Mark wanted to answer this question in his Gospel. He stressed that Christians were disciples of Jesus Christ. Just as Jesus, our Lord and Master, suffered and died, so must Christians. Mark stressed the idea that a disciple must take up his or her cross and follow Jesus.

The possibility of a reporter finding notes referring to all the books of the New Testament could happen only late in the first century or early in the second century or even later. Some commentators think that the Gospel of John was not written until the year 100, which places it in the second century. Others feel that it was written shortly before the year 100.

Pentecost

The Gospel of Matthew

Approximately twenty years after Mark wrote his Gospel, an unknown author learned of other sayings and stories from Jesus which Mark had not heard. The name mistakenly given to this unknown author is that of Matthew, so that we now call the book *The Gospel of Matthew*. He was an educated Jew who decided to add the stories and sayings he had heard to Mark's original Gospel.

The author of the Gospel of Matthew had a written manuscript which contained some sayings of Jesus that Mark did not have. He also learned of some sayings, stories, and events in Jesus' life from the community in which lived. He added the sayings of Jesus found in the manuscript, as well as the sayings and stories he heard from his community, to the Gospel of Mark. This collection shaped the Gospel of Matthew.

Like Mark, Matthew also wanted to answer some questions in his Gospel. Jewish Christians wondered why the Jewish nation had not rallied to Jesus. They believed that the Messiah was to come for the Jewish people, but Christian Jews marveled that the Jewish nation missed him. Matthew explains that it was the Jews who rejected Christ, not Christ who rejected the Jews. Jesus preached among the Jewish people, but the religious leaders rejected his message.

The Gospel of Luke

Another author, known as Luke, wrote about the same time as Matthew, although he did not know Matthew. Just as we know little about the lives of Mark and Matthew, so we know little about the life of Luke. He knew nothing of the Gospel of Matthew, but he did have a copy of Mark's Gospel.

Luke also had a copy of the written manuscript of sayings which the author of Matthew had. He himself had learned some sayings and stories not found in Mark or Matthew. Like Matthew, Luke added the sayings from the written manuscript to Mark's Gospel, but he also added the sayings and stories which he alone knew. This shaped the Gospel of Luke.

Luke wrote for a non-Jewish audience. He explained how Jesus' message was not just for the Jewish nation, but for all people of the world. He also wanted to tell the poor, the suffering, the outcast, and women that Jesus had special concern for them. He structured his Gospel according to the message he wished to convey.

The Acts of the Apostles

Luke also wrote The Acts of the Apostles. He wrote the story of Pentecost almost fifty years after it happened. Since he was not present at Pentecost, he gathered his material together from witnesses who either heard about the story or were actually present when it happened.

When Luke wrote the Acts of the Apostles, he was more concerned about inspiring his readers than he was about reporting events with accuracy. In Luke's day, writers idealized the heros of their stories and sometimes exaggerated events. Since Luke was writing an idealized picture of Pentecost, we cannot determine exactly what happened on the first Christian Pentecost. We can say that some extraordinary event took place which enabled the early community of disciples to know that the Holy Spirit was visibly at work.

A large portion of the Acts of the Apostles depicts the missionary activities of Peter and Paul. In the Gospel of Luke, Jesus heads toward Jerusalem where he dies and is raised. In the Acts of the Apostles, the early Church begins from Jerusalem and moves out to the world.

The Holy Spirit and the Church

The story of Pentecost found in the Acts of the Apostles offers a devotional presentation of the coming of the Holy Spirit upon the Church. Through dramatic stories of soaring winds and tongues of fire, the Acts of the Apostles teaches the historical truth that the Holy Spirit guides and protects the Church throughout its history. This is an important foundation for the study of Church history.

The Acts of the Apostles compresses the many stories of miraculous conversions into the one story of Pentecost. It reports that three thousand people accepted baptism on that day. Since the book does not present accurate history, we cannot say with historical certainty that this is exactly what happened. The story does teach, however, the historical fact that the early community of disciples converted a large number of people to Christ.

Christians now celebrate the Jewish feast of Pentecost as a Christian feast. The feast commemorates the beginning of the ministry of the community of disciples under the guidance of the Holy Spirit. Christians celebrate the Feast of Pentecost fifty days after Easter. The community of disciples has the mission to preach the message of Christ to the world. Pentecost reminds us that the Holy Spirit, who is God, enables the Church to attempt this seemingly impossible task throughout its history.

The Letters of Paul, Peter, James, Jude, and John

During his missionary journeys, Paul the apostle wrote a number of letters to the communities he visited. Later writers, believing that they were faithful to the spirit of Paul, also wrote letters found in the New Testament and signed Paul's name to them.

There were also other writers who, feeling that they were following in the spirit of earlier apostles, wrote letters signing other apostles' names to them. The New Testament has letters attributed to Peter, James, Jude, and John. Whether they were written by these authors or not, the Church has accepted these letters as inspired writings making up part of the New Testament.

The Book of Revelation

A New Testament book which still causes some confusion and misunderstanding is the Book of Revelation, or as it is also known, the Apocalypse. Some preachers today read predictions of disaster into the Book of Revelations, which the author never intended. Some see the book as a prediction of the worlds last days and the end of the world, which is far from the intention of the author.

JOURNAL

In your notebook, write a motivational letter to your classmates addressing some of the world concerns that you have as a class. Choose one of your favorite authors from the letters of Paul, Peter, James, Jude, or John. Emmulate this author's style in your letter and sign his name to it.

_____

_____

_____

_____

_____

I am the Alpha and the Omega, the beginning and the end. To the thirsty I will give water as a gift from the spring of life. Those who conquer will inherit these things, and I will be their God and they will be my children.
Revelation 21:6-7, NRSV

The writers of the Book of Revelation used the Apocalyptic form which was commonly used by Jewish writers. This form of writing was used by writers, during difficult times, to secretly share the message of God's total involvement in the world, with people who understood this form of writing. It contains codes, numbers, poetry, and hidden words of encouragement.

The Book of Revelation had the intention of encouraging Christians who were undergoing persecution at the time it was written. It teaches that God has control of the world. No matter how powerful evil may appear, God is stronger and will win in the end. Those who do evil in the world must eventually face punishment, while the faithful who suffer for holiness in the world will reach eternal happiness with Christ.

The Gospel of John

Another unknown author wrote the Gospel attributed to John around the year 100. This author wrote a highly theological book which emphasized the disciples growing awareness of the divinity of Jesus Christ. Where the other Gospel writers stress the human side of Jesus, John stresses the divine side of Jesus. He writes about the fact that Jesus is human and divine.

CLIPBOARD

1. If you had to explain how Jesus loves us to a friend who feels blessed by God, to another who feels rejected, and to one who was crippled in a car accident, how would your explanations differ? Discuss how your different explanations to your friends compare to the differences among the Gospels of Matthew, Mark, Luke, and John.

2. Why is it important to recognize the role of memory in the writings of the Gospels?

3. Why is it important to recognize the role of the Holy Spirit in the study of Church history?

Peter and the Early Community

The Christian Times

First Century   **Vol. 1   No. 4**

Peter Shows No Fear

Peter, who denied Jesus of Nazareth at the time of his crucifixion, was thrown into jail yesterday for preaching about the same Jesus. Peter shows a change of heart and now believes firmly that sharing Jesus' message is worth the hardship and imprisonment it brings.

Peter apparently heads a new sect within Judaism known as *The Way*. Sect members are Jews who claim that the Messiah has already come in the person of Jesus. They continue to worship with their Jewish brothers and sisters, but they teach that Jesus fulfills the prophecies of the Hebrew Scriptures.

Recently, some orthodox Jews have rumbled against this new sect within their ranks. They cheered Herod when he put James, Peter's companion, to death. Although Peter and his followers are converting more Jews to Christ, sentiment is rapidly growing in opposition to this new sect.

Despite the opposition, Peter remains fearless. He defies the religious leaders, by refusing to cease his preaching about Christ. Officials fear that Peter will soon meet the same end as his companion, James the Apostle.

NOTEPAD
? ? ? ? ?

1. What did you learn about Peter? James? Jewish leaders? Herod?

2. What did you learn about this new movement called The Way?

3. Why does the author of this article call Peter fearless?

The Rest of the Story

Much of our information about Peter comes from the Gospels and the Acts of the Apostles. Because the early community admired Peter, we can suspect that some of the stories about Peter have been expanded to legendary proportions. The books, however, capture the spirit of Peter.

Peter and the early converts to Jesus did not consider themselves as beginning a new religion. They saw themselves as faithful Jews who believed that the Messiah has come in the person of Jesus. They believed that their mission was first to the Jewish people of the world with the expectation of a mass conversion of Jews to Jesus. After that, they expected that the Jewish people would carry the message of Jesus as the Christ to the rest of the world.

In the Spotlight

St. Peter, first pope of the Church, was the first of the apostles to perform miracles in the name of Our Lord. Of the disciples he was the greatest miracle worker.

St. Peter, accompanied by St. James, led the Council of Jerusalem where the prohibition of preaching to Gentiles was reversed, which allowed the Church to become universal.

It is known with certainty that St. Peter was martyred in Rome under the reign of Emperor Nero, probably around 64. The testimony of the early Church

reports that St. Peter was crucified upside down, at his own request.

St. Peter's years prior to his martyrdom are obscure. Although, there is a long and accepted tradition of connecting him with Rome.

The traditional symbols used to represent St. Peter are the keys of the kingdom, depicting his primacy over the Church. Although, he is also represented by an inverted Cross, a boat (for the barque of Christ, which he guides), and the cock (for the triple denial of Christ).

JOURNAL

Although the Gospels and the Acts of the Apostles describe the strength and courage of Peter, they also portray him as a man of contradictions. While sometimes Peter is courageous, strong, and trusting, other times he is boastful, cowardly, and indecisive. He was very human, like us. Describe how you are, at times, a person of contradictions. How can you change this? Be specific.

_____

_____

_____

_____

_____

The Power and Frailty of Peter

The constant teaching of the New Testament is that Jesus and the early Christian community saw Peter as serving in a leadership role. Despite Peter's impetuous nature, Jesus favored him with a leadership position over the other disciples. The Gospels tell us that Jesus changed Simon's name to Peter, a name which means rock. Later, writers would proclaim that it was on this rock that Jesus built his Church.

During Jesus' life, Peter shows many sides to his personality. Many times he speaks without thinking, making a fool of himself. Sometimes he is a passionate defender of Jesus, and yet at other times he is submissive or cowardly.

The events surrounding Jesus' passion give us glimpses of Peter at both his best and his worst. At the Last Supper, Peter staunchly bragged that he would willingly die with Christ. He loved Jesus and sincerely believed that he would give his life for his master. Later, however, when Jesus was taken prisoner and brought to a large hall for trial, Peter cringed with fear in a courtyard outside the hall. Three times someone asked

Peter if he was a follower of Jesus, and each time Peter strongly denied it.

The Gospel writers catch one of the rapid changes in Peter's personality when they describe Peter's remorse following his third denial of Jesus. After Peter denied Jesus for the third time, the guards lead Jesus past him in the courtyard. When Peter looks at Jesus, he feels pain at his betrayal and flees from the scene in tears.

In the Gospel of Matthew, Peter again plays the role of a leader and a fool. When Jesus asks his disciples who they think he is, Peter is the first to respond, proclaiming that Jesus is the Messiah, the Son of God. Jesus praises Peter for his answer, proclaiming that he does not have this knowledge on his own, but that God has given it to him. Peter, however, after receiving praise from Jesus, manages to ruin the day by not knowing when to remain silent.

As the story continues, Jesus tells Peter and his disciples that he will suffer, die, and be raised on the third day. When Peter hears Jesus speaking of his suffering and death, he openly rejects any such thought as unacceptable. He reprimands Jesus, and Jesus retaliates with a harsh criticism of Peter, calling him "Satan." The story has value in presenting an insight into the personality of the person chosen to lead the early community of disciples.

Peter After the Resurrection

After the resurrection, Peter continues to play a leading role among the disciples. In one story found in the Gospel of John, Jesus meets with Peter and other disciples after his resurrection, and three times he asks Peter if he loves him. Each time, as Peter tells Jesus that he loves him, Jesus tells Peter to feed his flock of lambs and sheep. Jesus' flock in this story seems to be the Church. The story suggests that Jesus is calling Peter to shepherd the Church, while at the same time allowing him to repent of his three denials of Christ during the passion.

On the day of the resurrection, the Gospels note that Peter and John ran to the tomb of Jesus when they heard it was empty. Although John arrived first, he stepped aside to let Peter enter the tomb first. Paul, a later disciple, recognized Peter's role of primacy at the resurrection when he declared that Christ appeared first to Peter, then to the other disciples. The Gospels portray Peter as having a special leadership role in the community of disciples.

After Jesus' death, Peter calls a gathering of the eleven apostles, in the upper room, to announce the need to replace Judas. This event points to Peter's accepted role as leader of the chosen apostles, the Twelve.

Since Peter and the others believed in life after death, they recognized that a member of the Twelve does not lose his place by dying. That person continues to live in eternity. When someone betrays Jesus, however, he forfeits his position. Since Judas betrayed Christ, the eleven had to choose someone to take Judas's place. Under the guidance of the Holy Spirit, the eleven chose a faithful disciple named Matthias who had been a follower of Jesus since the beginning of his public ministry.

As mentioned earlier, the Acts of the Apostles has Peter preach to the Jews of the Diaspora, on the day of Pentecost. In his discourse, Peter speaks with firmness and courage about Jesus and the fact that he is the Messiah. Because of Peter's words here and throughout his ministry, many Jews turn to Christ.

Faithful Jews

The early converts to Christ showed no inclinations toward beginning a new religion. They considered themselves faithful Jews with no reason to believe that they would have to face persecution at the hands of their own nation. Although the early converts formed a community of disciples, they saw themselves as one of many different sects within Judaism.

The early Jewish followers of Jesus went to the synagogue to pray and followed all the Jewish customs and laws. They differed only in their belief that the Messiah had come in the person of Jesus. They expected to awaken one day to find that all of Jerusalem now recognized Jesus as the true Messiah. History, however, tells a different story.

The community at Jerusalem chose James, a relative of Jesus, as the head of their community. This Jewish community became the central community of the early Church, since it was the first community established. The disciples at Jerusalem sent out missionaries to other areas of the empire to spread the good news of Jesus Christ.

Persecution by Herod

The persecutions of the followers of Jesus in Jerusalem began with Herod Agrippa, a local ruler who governed Jerusalem in the name of the Roman Emperor. He strongly supported Jewish interests within the territories he governed. As long as he kept the religious leaders content, he knew that they would keep the people from rebelling.

A Jewish synagogue

Therefore let the entire house of Israel know with certainty that God has made him both Lord and Messiah, this Jesus whom you crucified.
Acts 2:36, NRSV

This fullness of the Spirit was not to remain uniquely the Messiah's, but was to be communicated to the whole messianic people. On several occasions Christ promised this outpouring of the Spirit, a promise which he fulfilled first on Easter Sunday and then more strikingly at Pentecost. Filled with the Holy Spirit the apostles began to proclaim "the mighty works of God," and Peter declared this outpouring of the Spirit to be the sign of the messianic age. Those who believed in the apostolic preaching and were baptized received the gift of the Holy Spirit in their turn.

Catechism of the Catholic Church, #1287

When Herod witnessed the rapid growth of Christ's followers, he became alarmed, fearing that they were becoming too powerful. He knew that the Roman government had crucified Jesus, and he felt that his followers were using Jesus' death to incite the people to rebellion. He felt a need to subdue this new sect within Judaism.

In the year 40, Herod ordered the execution of James the apostle. This James was not the head of the Jerusalem community, but one of the Twelve. To Herod's surprise and delight, he found that many of the people of Jerusalem celebrated his decision to persecute the Christians. The Jewish leaders had begun to view the followers of Jesus as heretics who were preaching a new message contrary to Judaism. They hoped that Herod would purify Judaism of these followers of Jesus.

As a result of the popular approval of Herod's attack on Christians, the persecution spread more rapidly. The religious leaders imprisoned Peter along with many other Christians. Later, when released from prison, Peter had to flee from Jerusalem with other Christians to avoid death. Since the persecutions lasted only a short time, Peter and others returned to Jerusalem and continued their preaching.

Peter and the Holy Spirit

The early chapters of the Acts of the Apostles followed the saga of Peter, as he continued to spread Christ's message. Through the power of the Holy Spirit, Peter performed healings in the name of Jesus. The once timid disciple began to speak in a bold and fearless manner. He frustrated the religious leaders in Palestine by declaring that it was more important for him to follow the mission given to him by Christ than to obey human law.

According to the Acts of the Apostles, Peter had the power of recognizing the activity of the Holy Spirit in people. On several occasions, Peter was determined to baptize converts, because he recognized that the Holy Spirit was already working in them. The Holy Spirit continued to surprise Peter throughout his ministry, giving him a new understanding of God's blessings in the hearts of these new converts.

CLIPBOARD

1. Would you have chosen someone like Peter to be the head of the apostles? Why?

2. What should be our attitude toward Judaism today as we recognize our Jewish roots?

3. Why is the plight of Peter so important in our understanding of the early Church?

The Church Spreads

The Christian Times

First Century   Vol. 1   No. 5

Deacon Stephen Stoned to Death

Earlier in the week, an angry mob dragged a Greek Jew named Stephen out into the street and stoned him to death. As the stones fell on him like an avalanche on a hillside, Stephen lay in a pool of blood, praising Jesus and warning his tormentors to be faithful to Judaism.

Stephen belonged to the new sect within Judaism known to many as "The Way." He was preaching about Jesus being the Christ when the crowd became enraged, threw their cloaks to a young man named Saul, and hurled stones at Stephen until he died.

Roman soldiers stood calmly nearby, watching the stoning. They refused to interfere, claiming that it was the result of a religious argument among Jews.

One of the Roman guards told our reporter that the followers of Christ had made Stephen a deacon along with a man named Philip and five others. He did not know the significance of the title, although he knew that Stephen was a Greek-speaking Jew, who came from outside Jerusalem.

Reports reached our Antioch office yesterday that many of the Greek-speaking followers of

Christ have fled from Jerusalem to cities as far away as Antioch.

NOTEPAD
? ? ? ? ?

1. What did you learn about Stephen? the crowd? the Roman soldiers?
2. What did a deacon do during Stephen's era?
3. What did you learn about the spread of Christ's message in this article?

The Rest of the Story

The story of Stephen has its source in the Acts of the Apostles. Although we are again reading an idealized story of an event which took place in the early Church, we can still recognize in the story some historical needs of the day. One of the needs arising early in the community of disciples concerned the need to care for the Jews of the Diaspora, known in the Acts of the Apostles as the Hellenists.

The Need for Deacons

Although the Jewish religious leaders feared the influence of the Jews in Jerusalem who were turning to Jesus as the Christ, they feared even more the influence of the Jews of the Diaspora who had turned to Christ. The Diaspora Jews tended to be less rigid in their beliefs and practices. The Jewish leaders knew that the population would more easily accept the death of these Greek speaking Jews than that of a Jew from Judea.

Even within the community of disciples, some prejudice existed against the Diaspora Jews. As a large number of the Jews from the Diaspora joined the community of disciples in Jerusalem, they found that they did not always receive the same attention as the more orthodox Jews who converted to Christ.

The leaders of the community recognized the need to assure that the Jews from outside Jerusalem received care equal to that of the more strict Jews of Jerusalem. They chose seven men, whom they called **deacons**, from among the Greek-speaking Jews, to serve the needs of the converts from the Diaspora.

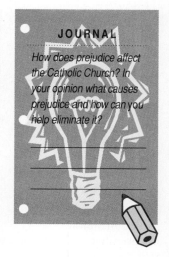

JOURNAL

How does prejudice affect the Catholic Church? In your opinion what causes prejudice and how can you help eliminate it?

KEY TERMS

Deacons: men chosen by the leaders of the community of disciples, to serve the Jews of the Diaspora.

St. Stephen

In addition to caring for the Greek-speaking Jewish converts during liturgy, the deacons also had the duty of preaching Christ's message to the Diaspora Jews. Because they could speak Greek, some of them traveled outside Jerusalem to preach. The two deacons mentioned by name in early Church writings, as dedicated preachers in the early community, are Stephen and Philip.

According to the Acts of the Apostles, Stephen became the first martyr for Christianity. As we read in the article, he was stoned to death, and those who stoned him entrusted their cloaks to the care of a young man named Saul. Saul would later play a major role in the spread of Christianity. With the acceptance of the death of Stephen on the part of the populace, the Jewish leaders could now vent their anger against this new group within Judaism and at the same time attack the Jews of the Diaspora.

Philip the Deacon

After Stephen's death, many Christian Jews from the Diaspora fled from Jerusalem to avoid the mobs. A deacon named Philip journeyed to Samaria, where he successfully taught about the faith. When Peter and other Jerusalem Christians heard of Philip's success, they came to Samaria and conferred the Holy Spirit on the new converts by laying hands on them.

When Peter arrived at Samaria to confer the Holy Spirit on Philip's converts, he realized that God was already reaching outside of pure Judaism to invite races with partial Israelite ancestry to join the community of disciples. Through the missionary work of Philip, the community of disciples had taken a new step outside of pure Jewish ancestry.

Philip's Conversions

One of Philip's converts was a magician named Simon who became astounded at Philip's spiritual powers. When Simon saw Peter offering the Holy Spirit by laying hands on the new converts, he offered to pay for the power to do the same. Peter became enraged and accused Simon of having an unrepentant spirit and urged him to pray for forgiveness.

As well as describing Philip's conversion of the Samaritans, the author of the Acts of the Apostles credits Philip with converting the first non-Jewish person to Christ. Following the directions given by the Holy Spirit, Philip approached an Ethiopian, a non-Jew, and joined him in his chariot. He interpreted the Scriptures for the Ethiopian and preached to him about Jesus.

When the chariot arrived at a river, the Ethiopian asked Philip to baptize him. Philip did so without imposing Jewish laws and practice on the Ethiopian. Philip was immediately whisked away to new missionary fields to preach to non-Jews, whom the Jews referred to as Gentiles. Philip's action of baptizing a new convert without imposing Jewish laws and practices would become a major conflict within the early Church.

Although the Judean converts to Christ did not have to fear an early persecution, the Greek-speaking Jewish converts could not ignore the dark mood in Jerusalem. They realized that they would become targets of persecution if they did not flee immediately from the city. After the persecution of Stephen, many of the Jews of the Diaspora fled to Samaria and other areas outside Palestine. This persecution helped spread Christianity outside of Palestine by forcing Christians to flee for their lives.

Because of the persecution, a community began to develop at Antioch, which is in modern day Turkey. This community began to reach out to the Gentiles and was rapidly becoming as large a Christian community as that at Jerusalem. It was at Antioch that the Christians first used the name Christian. Although Jerusalem still remained as the center of Christianity, Antioch was quickly becoming a center of Christianity for the Gentile converts.

CLIPBOARD

1. How does prejudice affect the lives of people in religion even today?

2. How does the story of Philip show that God can draw good out of evil?

3. Why do you think the Christian Jews of Jerusalem were so surprised when Christ's message became so widely accepted outside of Jerusalem?

REVIEWING THE ERA

• 30

PENTECOST. On the Jewish feast of Pentecost, which celebrates the fiftieth day after the Israelites left Egypt and the day Moses received the commandments from God, the community of disciples received a special gift of the Holy Spirit which filled them with the courage and understanding needed to spread the word of God.

PETER PROCLAIMS THE MESSAGE OF JESUS. Peter, who once denied Christ, courageously dedicated his life to the spread of Christ's message. The community of disciples recognized Peter as their leader.

STEPHEN MARTYRED. Stephen, the deacon, becomes the first martyr among the community of disciples.

PHILIP CONVERTS SAMARITANS AND GENTILES. Philip, the deacon, takes the message of Christ outside of Jerusalem to the people of Samaria and to the Gentiles.

PAUL WRITES HIS LETTERS TO THE COMMUNITIES HE VISITED. Paul wrote his letters (epistles) which became part of the New Testament to the Churches he founded or visited. Some later New Testament writers signed Paul's name in writing to their letters, believing that they were properly representing the thoughts of Paul.

• 65

THE GOSPEL OF MARK WRITTEN. Mark gathered together all that he heard in the preaching about Jesus' life, sayings, and passion and wrote the first Gospel.

• 85

THE GOSPEL OF MATTHEW WRITTEN. An unknown Jewish scribe gathered together Mark's Gospel, a written source of Jesus' sayings, and some material (M) he apparently heard from preachers who visited his community and shaped the Gospel of Matthew.

THE GOSPEL OF LUKE WRITTEN. An unknown writer gathered together Mark's Gospel, the written source of Jesus' sayings known to Matthew, and some material (L) he apparently heard from preachers who visited his community and shaped Luke's Gospel.

LETTERS OF PETER, JAMES, JUDE, AND JOHN WRITTEN. Later New Testament letters showing the development of the organization and thought of the community of disciples.

THE BOOK OF REVELATION. A later writing by someone named John, who was in exile and who wrote symbolically to suffering Christians, reminding them that God has control of the world.

THE GOSPEL OF JOHN WRITTEN. An author, using the name John, wrote a highly symbolic and theological Gospel which begins with the existence of Jesus before creation.

A Voice from the Past

This week in your column you are going to address the call to discipleship. Summarize what you have learned about the disciples in this chapter. Address the challenges that they encountered as a result of spreading the message of Jesus. Be sure to mention the issues of persecution and discrimination. Show your readers how the issues of the past are present in society today. Compare and contrast the responsibilities of the disciples of the early Church with the responsibilities of disciples of the Church today.

Then and Now

The message of the early Church was that the Holy Spirit was active in the Church. Martyrs like Stephen offered their lives for this community of disciples. Peter was the first spiritual leader, while James served as a type of administrative and spiritual leader in Jerusalem, and the Holy Spirit touched the hearts of the Gentiles. On Pentecost, through the special influence of the Holy Spirit, the community of disciples initiated the mission of proclaiming Jesus' life and message to the world.

Today, we continue to recognize that the Holy Spirit is active in the Church, that the successor of Peter is the spiritual head of the Church, that martyrs still offer their lives for Christ's message, and that Christ came for all the world, Jews as well as Gentiles. We also recognize that the New Testament writings play an important part in the tradition of the Church, and we celebrate Pentecost as a Christian feast which recognizes the active role of the Holy Spirit in the Church.

As Christians, we shape our historical context from the stories and memories of the Jewish people and the early community of disciples.

NEWS IN REVIEW

1. How does each of the books of the New Testament influence our study of Church history?
2. Why is it important to consider the role of the Holy Spirit in our study of Church History?
3. List some strengths and weaknesses of Peter before and after the resurrection?
4. Why does the Church consider Peter to be the first head of the Church?
5. Did the early converts to Christ consider themselves to be beginning a new religion? Explain your answer.
6. What do the lives of Stephen and Philip tell us about the role of deacons in the early Church?
7. What is Simony and where does the name come from?
8. How did Christianity begin to spread outside Jerusalem?
9. Describe how some of the practices in the Catholic Church today link us with the Church of the apostles.
10. What names were given to the early community of disciples, and where did they originate?

chapter three

Becoming Church

If we were followers of Jesus at the time of the early Church, we would likely be Jews who prayed on the Sabbath, by attending the synagogue service, and gathered on the day after the Sabbath to celebrate the day of Christ's resurrection from the dead. The Sunday celebration would recall Jesus' resurrection. The celebration would consist in a meal at which we would recall the living memorial of Jesus' Last Supper with his disciples. We would call our gathering the Breaking of the Bread, the Table of the Lord, or The Lord's Supper.

As Jews, we would also be wondering about the new converts from outside Judaism. We would be disturbed by the rumors that these new converts were not following Jewish laws. We would believe that Christ came for the Jewish people, and that they would all accept Christ and be the ones to share his message with the world.

Jesus' Last Supper is still the focus of our Catholic celebration.

Paul the Apostle

The Christian Times

First Century   Vol. 1   No. 6

Saul Spreads the Word of Christ

It was reported today that Saul of Tarsus, who once flushed out Christians and persecuted them, has now become one of their leading missionaries.

In an astounding about-face, Saul, the persecutor, has suddenly become the great champion of Christianity. He had persecuted so many Christians in the past that Christians cringed in fear at the mere mention of his name.

According to eye witnesses, Saul had a major conversion on his way to Damascus. Bystanders saw Paul speaking in the direction of a dazzling light. Saul claims that Jesus of the Christians has spoken to him.

Those closest to Paul claim that he went into seclusion for a long period of time after this experience. He then traveled to Jerusalem to meet with some Christian leaders, and from there, he went on to Antioch. A disciple, named Barnabas, joined him at Antioch. The one-time persecutor of Christians, now spends his time traveling to areas inside and outside of Palestine.

Paul has become so dedicated to his mission, that he is willing to face any danger in spreading the message of Christ. He has already lived through a shipwreck.

Ironically, Paul claims that his greatest antagonists seem to be Jewish Christians, rather than non-Christians.

Since he preaches so often to Greek audiences, he has changed his name from the Hebrew name of Saul to its Greek equivalent, which is Paul.

NOTEPAD
? ? ? ? ?

1. What did you learn about Saul? Jewish Christians?

2. What places are mentioned in this article? How do they relate to the story?

3. Why do you think that Paul's greatest antagonists are Jewish Christians? Explain.

The Rest of the Story

One of the more dynamic and intriguing people of the early Church is Paul, the apostle who first appears on the scene as Saul of Tarsus. In an earlier episode, we learned that Saul held the garments of those who stoned Stephen to death. We know nothing about Saul's reaction to the event, but we do know that Saul dedicated his early adult life to persecuting Christians.

Saul of Tarsus

At one time, the people of Tarsus defended Julius Caesar in a civil war. Because of their support, the emperor conferred Roman citizenship on the people of that area and on their offspring. Others who lived in lands conquered by Rome did not receive citizenship. As a citizen of Tarsus, Saul had the rare privilege of being a devout Jew and a citizen of the Roman Empire.

Saul belonged to a diaspora Jewish colony that resided a little north of Palestine. He was a dedicated Jew, intent on cleansing Judaism of any contamination by false messiahs. Before his conversion Saul believed Jesus to be one of the false messiahs.

Saul the Persecutor

Saul had a great love for his Jewish roots and chose to follow the more rigid approach to Judaism. Because of his desire to protect the Jewish faith, Saul found the disciples of Christ to be a misguided group who threatened the purity of Judaism. He pursued these Christians with the same energy he would later use in spreading the faith. The community of disciples uttered his name in terror. He would later admit with sorrow that he hounded Christians to the point of personal exhaustion, intent on destroying those who preached the message of Christ.

The Acts of the Apostles tells the story of Saul's conversion. On one of his trips to Damascus, where he was planning to persecute Christians, Jesus appeared to Saul in a blazing light which sent him stumbling to the ground. From this burning light came the words, "Saul, Saul, why do you persecute me?" Saul understood that Christ was identifying himself with the Christians whom he was persecuting. Through this vision, Saul immediately recognized that he was fighting against God.

By identifying Christ in his followers Saul later developed a teaching which identified the Church as the Body of Christ. He reflected that the Church was actually Christ active in the world, with each member of the Church carrying out the mission of Christ in a specific manner.

Just as the human body needs its parts to function, so Christ needs individuals within the Body of Christ to fulfill his mission on earth. Christ is the head, and the baptized make up the members of the body. Each one is important to the proper functioning of the body, which is Christ, the Church.

Paul the Missionary

Although Saul became an energetic, persistent, and passionate disciple of Christ, some of the followers of Christ mis-

Saul of Tarsus

trusted him because of his past actions. It would take some time for them to accept Paul. According to the Acts of the Apostles, Paul went off by himself for three years after his conversion, most likely to reflect on his experience.

After three years in his chosen exile, Paul spent two weeks in Jerusalem where he met Peter and other Christian leaders. Paul later spoke of the brevity of his stay in Jerusalem and emphasized that he did not receive the content of his teaching from the community, but from Christ. In time, Paul went to Antioch where he did some preaching and missionary work.

Antioch became the center for Paul's missionary activity. In the early Church, Jerusalem stood as the original center of the faith. Jerusalem sent out missionaries throughout and eventually beyond Palestine. The major Christian center outside Jerusalem became Antioch. The majority of Jewish converts in this town came from the diaspora group who spoke Greek and mixed freely with others of the Greek-speaking world.

JOURNAL

Whom do you persecute? Judging others' actions, and making accusations about others based on our judgments is a form of persecution. Oftentimes, like Saul we find that we have judged wrongly. Describe a time that you judged someone wrongly? How did you feel afterwards? What did you learn from that experience and how can you avoid doing this in the future?

_____

_____

_____

_____

For just as the body is one and has many members, and all the members of the body, though many, are one body, so it is with Christ. For in one Spirit we were all baptized into one body—Jews or Greeks, slaves or free— and we were all made to drink of one Spirit.
1 Corinthians 12:12–13, NRSV

In the Spotlight

St. Barnabas was a Jew from Cyprus. When the early Christian community was beginning, Barnabas dedicated himself totally to the community by selling all he had and turning his funds over to the community. Because of actions such as this, the early community of disciples changed his name, which was originally Joseph, to Barnabas, which St. Luke translates as "son of consolation."

It was Barnabas who introduced Paul to the apostles and defended him to the Christians of Jerusalem. Barnabas continually stood beside Paul, while many of the Christians questioned the authenticity of his conversion.

Together Barnabas and Paul embarked on a missionary journey, beginning with Cyprus. Barnabas is considered the founder of the Cypriot Church. According to legend Barnabas continued his travels and was martyred in 61 at Salamis, but nothing of this is recorded in the New Testament.

Paul's Travels

Over the next several years, Paul traveled throughout most of the known world, especially in areas around the Mediterranean Sea. He traveled to Asia Minor and to cities such as Ephesus, Philippi, Athens, Corinth, Thessalonica, and Rome. Paul was the first missionary to preach Christ in some of these cities.

During his travels, Paul endured crushing hardship. He himself reports that he endured eight whippings, extreme hunger, thirst, heat, cold, a stoning in which he was left for dead, and three shipwrecks. Where other missionaries with less stamina would have abandoned the missions, Paul just rested long enough to regain a little of his strength and continued to preach.

Paul's problems did not come only from religious leaders. On one occasion, a silversmith who made miniature statues of popular gods saw Paul's preaching about the one true God as a threat to his business. He gathered together the other silversmiths of the area and warned them that Paul would ruin their business if they did not stop him. A riot broke out which involved a large number of people in the town. When it threatened to become violent, a town clerk intervened and persuaded the mob to settle their differences in court. Paul and his disciples quietly left the town.

On one occasion, a young man named Mark began a journey with Barnabas and Paul, but, due to homesickness, he abandoned the mission and returned home. Mark, at a more mature age, wanted to rejoin them on a later journey, but Paul refused to take Mark with them. Barnabas, remaining true to his name, agreed to separate from Paul and to encourage Mark in his missionary activity. Paul took a new companion known as Silas with him. Although Barnabas and Paul had occasional disagreements, Paul later praised Barnabas, portraying him as an example of apostolic behavior (I Corinthians, 9:6).

In addition to his missionary travels, Paul was a zealous letter writer to the communities where he established himself, and to several Christian communities which he visited. In these powerful letters, Paul revealed his understanding of Christ's life and message, while reprimanding or praising the communities to which he was writing. These letters laid the foundation for the development of Christian theology in later ages.

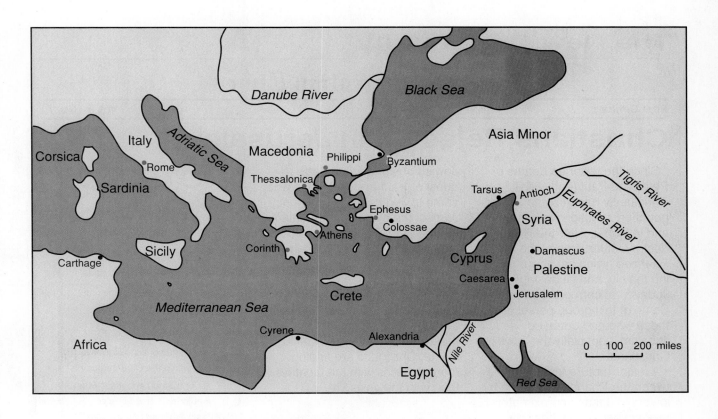

CLIPBOARD

1. What messages come through to the Church today from Paul's experiences with Christian Jews?
2. Would you prefer to have Paul or Barnabas as your friend (or both)? Why?
3. Discuss the importance of the story and memory of Paul's life in shaping our historical context today.

Map Search

Study the map and locate the following:

The Mediterranean Sea

Tarsus

Philippi

Jerusalem/ Palestine

Athens

Corinth

Asia Minor

Rome

Thessalonica

Ephesus

Antioch

Cyprus

The New Community

The Christian Times

First Century   Vol. 1 No. 7

Christians Rejected in Jerusalem

Since the reported deaths of Peter and Paul [early 60s], Christianity has become the target of persecutions in Jerusalem and in Rome. After the Romans destroyed Jerusalem, the Pharisee group set about rebuilding the city and cleansing Judaism of corrupting influences. Some of this group persecuted those who had betrayed Judaism, especially the Jewish Christians.

A major rupture took place between the Pharisees and the followers of Jesus approximately twenty years ago when Jewish Christian leaders exempted Gentile converts from some Jewish observances. At the request of Paul and Barnabas who came to Jerusalem from Antioch, James, the bishop of Jerusalem, decreed that the Gentile converts did not have to follow certain Jewish observances.

This move, on the part of the Jerusalem Christians, angered some of the Pharisees. Now, with the rebuilding of Jerusalem and the death of Peter and Paul in Rome, Christians are finding more success with the Gentiles than with the Jews.

NOTEPAD

? ? ? ? ?

1. What did you learn about the Pharisees? Romans? Peter and Paul? Paul and Barnabas? Jewish Christians?Gentiles?

2. What seems to be the biggest source of conflict? Are there conflicts similar to this within the Church today?

3. As one of the apostles, what would have been one of your main concerns? How would you have addressed this concern?

The Rest of the Story

When Paul joined the community of disciples at Antioch, he began to preach not only to Jewish audiences, but also to Greek audiences. Jews generally referred to all those who were not Jews as Gentiles. In receiving converts from among the Gentiles, however, Paul encountered new problems. Some of the demands of Jewish law, such as circumcision and refraining from certain "unclean" food, were too difficult for Gentiles.

New Conflicts

During Paul's time, Jews who converted to Christ saw themselves as good Jews who believed in Christ. The problem confronted by Paul and other members of the early Church was the need for Gentile converts to live Jewish laws and customs. The community at Antioch eventually came to believe that baptism had replaced the need for practicing certain Jewish customs such as circumcision. They proclaimed that Jesus Christ had called for a new form of initiation rite.

When some Jewish Christians from Jerusalem visited Antioch, they became alarmed that the Jewish leaders had not circumcised the new male converts, nor did these leaders teach their converts to refrain from "unclean" foods.

The Jewish Christians from Jerusalem caused such havoc in Antioch and other areas outside of Palestine that the community at Antioch sent Paul and Barnabas to Jerusalem to meet with the leaders of the community of disciples.

Although Antioch had become a vibrant and strong community, the early Christians still considered Jerusalem the center of Christianity. It was important to Paul, Barnabas, and the others at Antioch to receive the approval of the Jerusalem Church in releasing the new Gentile converts from these Jewish obligations. When Paul and Barnabas arrived at Jerusalem, they met with James, a relative of Jesus, who was the bishop of the Jerusalem Church. They also found Peter present along with other leading members of the church at Jerusalem.

Peter and Cornelius

A story told in the Acts of the Apostles explained why Peter was willing to support the request of Paul and Barnabas at the Jerusalem meeting. According to the story, Peter received a vision of a large sheet covered with food considered unclean and repugnant by the Jews. When Peter protested that he could not eat the food, God replied that anything God made cannot be considered unclean.

The day after receiving his vision, Peter followed a group of Gentiles to the home of their master, whose name was Cornelius. When Peter saw Cornelius and the large crowd gathered with him, he noted aloud and regretfully that it was unlawful for a Jewish person such as himself to visit or associate with Gentiles. He then recalled that God had told him in the previous vision that no person is unclean, so he visited with Cornelius.

Peter later preached to a Gentile audience gathered together by Cornelius. To his astonishment and that of the other Jewish Christians who accompanied him, the Gentiles, prompted by the Holy Spirit, began to speak in tongues and to praise God. Peter saw in this a sign that the Jewish Christians should accept the Gentiles into the community of disciples through baptism.

When Peter returned to Jerusalem, a party of Jewish Christians confronted him concerning his baptism of Gentiles. Peter explained his vision and meeting with Cornelius, and the visible outpouring of the Holy Spirit on the Gentiles. Upon hearing the news, the Jewish Christians relented and agreed that Peter had indeed acted correctly.

Although the story of Peter and Cornelius may not have happened exactly as described by the Acts of the Apostles, it does teach the historical message that Peter had to struggle with the question concerning the place of Jewish laws and customs within Christianity. It also teaches that Peter recognized that God called Gentile Christians to become followers of Christ without imposing Jewish laws on them. For this reason, he supported the request of Paul and Barnabas.

The Council of Jerusalem

After a long and apparently heated debate, the leaders of the Church at Jerusalem agreed not to impose circumcision and certain dietary laws on the Gentiles. James, speaking on behalf of the community of disciples at Jerusalem, announced the decision which would forever change the future direction of Christianity. Later history would name this meeting of Church leaders at Jerusalem as the **Council of Jerusalem,** the first council of the Church.

Paul and Barnabas returned to Antioch with the joyful news, hoping the decision made at Jerusalem would end the controversy. They expected that they would be able to peacefully accept Gentile converts into the community through baptism.

Some Jews, however, refused to accept the decree given at Jerusalem. For the next several years, they tormented Paul wherever he spoke about baptism as the ritual which made one a

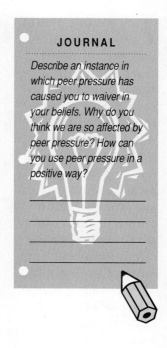

JOURNAL

Describe an instance in which peer pressure has caused you to waiver in your beliefs. Why do you think we are so affected by peer pressure? How can you use peer pressure in a positive way?

_____

_____

_____

KEY TERMS

Council of Jerusalem: the first council of the Church; established that Gentiles would not be required to be circumcised or accept the dietary restrictions of the Jewish faith.

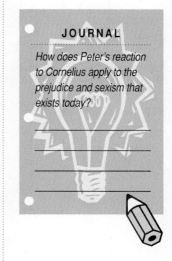

JOURNAL

How does Peter's reaction to Cornelius apply to the prejudice and sexism that exists today?

_____

_____

_____

I am a debtor both to Greek and to barbarians, both to the wise and to the foolish—hence my eagerness to proclaim the gospel to you also who are in Rome. For I am not ashamed of the gospel; it is the power of God for salvation to everyone who has faith, to the Jew first and also to the Greek. For in it the righteousness of God is revealed through faith for faith; as it is written, "The one who is righteous will live by faith."

Romans 1:14–16

St. Paul and St. Peter

Christian. They taunted and insulted him, often provoking the Jews in synagogues to cast Paul out. Paul refused to cower under this mistreatment and eventually turned his greatest efforts to converting Gentiles to Christianity.

Christian Jews who supported the rights of Gentile converts sometimes found themselves slipping back into their past prejudices when confronted with peer pressure. On one occasion, after the Council of Jerusalem, Peter was eating with Paul, Barnabas, and some Gentiles. When some Jewish Christians arrived from Jerusalem, they were horrified that Jews would eat with Gentiles. Peter and Barnabas quietly slipped away from the Gentile tables to eat with the Jewish Christians.

When Paul saw Peter and Barnabas snubbing the Gentile converts, he became angry and rebuked Peter. Although his actions showed the intensity of his beliefs, they also showed the importance of Peter. Because of Peter's position in the community of disciples,

it was important for Paul to convince him not to reject the Gentiles. The event stresses the problems associated with change taking place in the history of the Church.

Paul was eventually recognized as the missionary of the Gentiles. He could claim a leading role in the rapid spread of Christianity outside of Jerusalem. Although other missionaries shared in this rapid spread of the faith, Paul's dedication to his mission had an enduring impact on the future of Christianity. His energy, courage, and dedication brought many Gentiles into Christianity. His letters greatly influenced the development of the Church through the ages.

The Death of Paul

Despite the problems caused by Jewish Christians, Paul retained a great respect for Jerusalem as the center of Christianity. Toward the end of his life, he sought to help the Christians in Jerusalem who were living in poverty. He accepted the task of delivering the collection from the Gentile communities to the Jerusalem community.

Besides his high respect for the Church at Jerusalem, Paul also believed in the significance of unity in Christianity. Christianity was not a group of individual communities with their own laws and customs, but a united group making up a single Church. For Paul, the collection among all the churches for the church at Jerusalem not only helped a community faced with poverty, but it became a sign of Church unity and of the importance of the community of disciples in Jerusalem.

When Paul arrived at Jerusalem with the collection, James and the other Jewish Christian leaders persuaded him to take part in a ceremony in the Temple. They believed that such an action would convince Paul's enemies of his faithfulness to Judaism. In the

Temple, however, some people clamored that Paul was a traitor to Judaism. A riot ensued and a Roman tribune had to fight through the crowd to arrest Paul and drag him away from the angry mob.

After spending two years in prison in Jerusalem, Paul declared his right as a Roman citizen to have his case appealed to Rome. The authorities shipped Paul to Rome where he spent another two years under house arrest. The story of Paul ends here. No records exist which tell of Paul's trial and eventual death. Most believe that he died in the year 64, during the persecution of the Christians by the Emperor Nero.

The Death of Peter

We know nothing of Peter's history after he left Jerusalem. Christian tradition proclaims that he was crucified under Nero, dying around the same time as Paul. Roman law forbade the crucifying of a Roman citizen, and since Paul was a Roman citizen, he was most likely beheaded and not crucified. Peter, however, was not a Roman citizen, but a Roman subject, and as such, he was eligible to face death by crucifixion.

As the death place of both Peter and Paul, Rome holds a special place of significance in Christianity. In the Church today, the bishop of Rome, the **pope**, is considered the successor of Peter and the visible leader of the Catholic Church.

Although Peter showed no signs of any awareness of being a first pope, history places him at the beginning of a long line of popes. The life of Peter is far different from that of our present-day popes. Our current understanding of the office of pope developed gradually.

Later Persecution in Jerusalem

In the year 66, a rebellion on the part of some Jews in Jerusalem triggered a Roman reaction against Jerusalem. The Zealots had always caused trouble for the Romans, but by the year 66 they were becoming more successful and bothersome for the Romans. In their effort to recover Palestine from the Romans, they were ambushing and killing small groups of Roman soldiers. Roman losses were increasing and Roman anger was rising.

The Romans at first attempted to subdue these minor rebellions by killing the rebels and those who harbored them, but when the attacks became more numerous and more bloody, Roman armies marched into Jerusalem to crush the rebellion. In the year 70, the Roman army ravaged the city, slaughtering many of the inhabitants and completely demolishing the magnificent temple.

When the Roman armies felt that they had taught a proper lesson to the Jews of Jerusalem, they lifted the seige and left the remaining population with a devastated city and no Temple. Without the Temple, priests were no longer needed. Since the priestly party formed the group known as the Sadducees, this group disappeared from Judaism.

With the destruction of the Temple, synagogue worship became the dominant form of worship in Judaism. The Pharisees now led worship in the synagogues, and the people began to refer to them more often as rabbi. Besides attempting to rebuild the city of Jerusalem, the Pharisees also sought to cleanse Judaism of outside influences. They saw the Jews who believed in Jesus in this light.

The followers of Christ faced a major persecution in Jerusalem at this time. Besides being accused of contaminating Judaism, Christians also faced the frustration, fear, and anger of the orthodox Jews who remained in Jerusalem during the Roman invasion. Because many Christians had left Jerusalem to avoid an earlier persecution, some of the

Jews thought they abandoned the city to escape the Romans. To the Jewish inhabitants, Christians fled the country when they were needed the most.

To the surprise of the Jewish followers of Jesus, they found themselves being ousted from synagogues. This rejection by the beleaguered Judaism con-fused many Jewish Christians who now had to rethink their faith in Jesus and his message. Instead of bringing about a renewal of Judaism, the early Christians found themselves rejected by Judaism. Surprisingly, they found that they had developed a community of disciples with their own practices and beliefs.

CLIPBOARD

1. Imagine you are Paul or Barnabas at the meeting with James and Peter. Explain how you would argue your case in favor of the Gentile converts.
2. How did the Council of Jerusalem affect the context of our history as Christians today?
3. How did the destruction of Jerusalem affect the context of our history today?

Christianity Becomes a Distinct Religion

The Christian Times

First Century   Vol. 1   No. 8

Rome Refuses to Grant Privileges to Christians

The Roman Empire today declared that the followers of Christ do not belong to Judaism, and therefore, do not share in the privileges granted to the Jewish people. A representative of the Roman government informed us that those who profess to be Christian are mostly non-Jews from other villages outside of Jerusalem.

The representative also noted that converts became Christian through an immersion in water called baptism. They see themselves as a community of disciples, united as though they form a single body. They show extraordinary love not only for each other, but also for their enemies. They go out of their way to serve the needs of the poor and outcast.

Whenever they gather together, they read from the Scriptures and from missionary letters and share in a meal known as the *Eucharist*. They refer to themselves as the *New Israel*.

"In reality," stated the spokesman, "They could hardly be identified with current day Judaism. They do not follow the old Jewish laws and customs. Therefore, they do not share in the privileges granted Judaism by the Roman Empire."

NOTEPAD

? ? ? ?

1. What did you learn about the Jewish Christians? the Jews? Roman government?
2. List the customs and practices of Christians as found in this article.
3. How do the Jewish Christians differ from traditional Jews?

The Rest of the Story

Signs of a New Church

With the destruction of Jerusalem, Christianity no longer saw the city as its center. Cities such as Alexandria and Antioch became centers of Christianity. Instead of the Jerusalem community sending missionaries out to convert people to Christ, the new Gentile communities began sending missionaries out to all corners of the known world. With this Gentile influence, the Jewish influence on Christianity was far less visible.

By the time Christians realized that their bond with Judaism no longer existed, although the deep roots remained strong, they had already established a number of practices and beliefs which were strictly Christian. Christ had left the community of disciples with the necessary means for the establishment of a Church. The letters and preaching of Paul and other leading missionaries built on the structure of this community of disciples.

By the end of the first century, the Church had established some identifiable elements which still exist today. The community of disciples saw themselves as a new people of God, a chosen race. They also saw themselves as the unified Body of Christ living and working in the world. The Church gathered for worship and for the celebration of other rituals,

POINTS TO PONDER

In the early days after the resurrection of Christ, the largest number of converts to Christianity were Jewish. By the time Paul died in Rome, the number of Gentile converts far outnumbered the Jews who were Christian. With these changes, the Jewish practices found at the beginning of the community of disciples disappeared and new practices became more central.

Jesus teaching

chosen people, the People of God. He wrote that Jewish and Gentile Christians "who in times past were not a people, are now the people of God" (1 Peter 2:10). The Church, the People of God, received from Christ the mission of bringing Christ's gifts and message to all nations of the world.

The Body of Christ

The community of disciples recalled Paul's conversion on the road to Damascus. When Christ asked Paul why he persecuted him, Christ was identifying himself with all Christians. Paul developed this concept even further, using the image of a body. He saw the Church as a visible image of Christ present in the world today. For Paul, the Church is the Body of Christ.

Paul developed an understanding of Church which has become dominant even today. He said that the Church, as the Body of Christ, needed each member. He stated, "If a foot should say, 'Because I am not a hand I do not belong to the body,' it does not belong any less to the body" (1 Corinthians 12:15). The Body of Christ needs each member to fulfill his or her function here on earth.

When we speak of the Church as the Body of Christ, we must realize that our gifts come to us through the power of the Holy Spirit. Every gift we receive comes as a gift for the common good, and not for ourselves. Paul again writes, "To one is given through the Spirit the expression of wisdom, to another the expression of knowledge according to the same Spirit, to another faith by the same Spirit, to another gifts of healing by the same Spirit, to another mighty deeds, to another prophecy, to another discernment of spirits, to another varieties of tongues, to another the interpretation of tongues (1 Corinthians 12:8–10)."

On our Journey, we will meet prophets, healers, people of great faith, wise rulers, people of prayer, and sinners. They all belong to the Body of Christ.

and they sought to serve those in need. Following the direction of Christ, the Church saw preaching as central to its mission of sharing Christ's message.

The New People of God

The Israelites of the Old Testament era were the chosen race, the People of God. They were the People of God because they were ancestors of Abraham. Christ taught that it was not physical relationship that linked a people with Abraham, but a relationship in faith. Christians believed that the followers of Christ were the new People of God.

The author of a later letter called *First Peter* spoke of Christians as a

A Common Worship

One day, Paul heard a report from the community of disciples at Corinth concerning the celebration of the Lord's Supper. This was the celebration of the Eucharist which was also known as the Breaking of the Bread. It was the central form of worship in the early Church community and continues to be the central form of worship in the Church today.

Paul heard that some of the people who gathered for the Eucharistic celebration at Corinth had brought large quantities of food and drink while the poor had nothing to bring. The celebration of the Eucharist ordinarily took place at the end of a meal. The richer people ate without sharing their food with the poor, and some of them became drunk on too much wine.

When the time came for the celebration of the Eucharist, those who had acted selfishly and those who were drunk joined together in worship. The hungry poor had to sit idly by, waiting for the celebration of the Eucharist at the end of the meal. When Paul heard about the situation, he became enraged that a celebration intended for worship had become a celebration of divisiveness. He commanded the Corinthians, hereafter, to eat and drink at home and then to join together for worship.

In time, all communities separated the regular meal from the celebration of the Eucharist. The community would come together, listen to the Word of God and the letters of the early missionaries, and then take part in the Lord's Supper. From these early days, the format for the celebration of our Eucharistic liturgy had already begun.

By the time the community lost its close ties with Judaism, it had a form of worship that needed neither a synagogue nor a Temple. The community gathered together at the home of some leading Christian to celebrate the Eucharist.

In time, Christians viewed every sacrament as centering in the Eucharist. Through the Sacrament of Baptism, people share in the priesthood of Jesus Christ. Through this share in Christ's priesthood, Christians receive the power to participate in worship. The First Letter of Peter proclaims that Christians are a "chosen race, a royal priesthood" (1 Peter 2:9). In time, Christians came to recognize the distinction between the ordained or ministerial priesthood and the priestly power given in baptism.

A Church of Service

In the Gospel of John, the author describes the celebration of the Last Supper as a celebration of service. Instead of describing the events of eating and drinking, the author of the Gospel of John describes Jesus performing the lowly tasks of a servant. In Jesus' day, a host would ordinarily have a servant wash the feet of each of his guest. At the Last Supper described in John's Gospel, Jesus performs this task.

Jesus stands up among his disciples during the meal, wraps a towel around his waist, and begins to wash the feet of his disciples. They naturally protest, but Jesus continues to wash their feet. After he washed their feet, he reminded them that they rightly called him "Master," and "Lord," for that he is. Then he tells them that if he, as Master and Lord, was willing to wash their feet, so they should wash the feet of one another.

The Church today continues to remind us that we must be a Church of service. Jesus told us to love God, our neighbor, and ourselves. Such a command of love demands service to those in need. We must have concern for the poor, the outcast, the suffering, and the lonely. From the earliest days of the Church, this call to service stood at the center of the Christian message.

KEY TERMS

Homily: a message which applies the readings of the day to situations in our lives.

Bishops: successors of the office of the apostles; in governing a diocese a bishop has the responsibility of teaching the faith, celebrating divine worship, and guiding his parishes.

College of bishops: the group of bishops that help govern the Church; they report directly to the Pope.

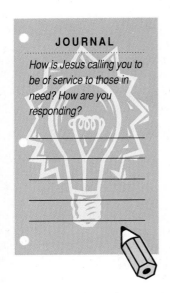

JOURNAL

How is Jesus calling you to be of service to those in need? How are you responding?

Preaching the Message

Jesus traveled throughout Palestine preaching. On the day of his ascension, he commanded his disciples to continue his mission. He asked them to preach his message and baptize. Paul traveled to many cities preaching the message of Jesus. The story of Christianity, from the days of Christ to the present, tells the importance of preaching.

As we share in the celebration of the Eucharist in our pesent day, readers proclaim the Scriptures by reading from the Old and New Testaments. The Presider at the liturgy has the duty of preaching a message called a **homily**. A homily is a message which applies the readings of the day to situations in our lives. It has the role of making Scripture passages speak to us today, as they did to the people of the day in which they were written.

The Organization of the Church

Toward the end of the first century, Rome recognized that Christians had developed a structure for governing the community. They had elders and presbyters to lead the communities. These elders and presbyters eventually became the bishops, ordained priests, and deacons.

After the destruction of Jerusalem and the rapid spread of the faith among the Gentiles, Christians no longer looked to the Pharisees in Jerusalem as their leaders or interpreters of the law. The new structure in Christianity came to be seen as a definite sign that Christianity had become a Church distinct from Judaism. Today, we refer to the leaders of the Church as the hierarchy, a term which designates those at the head of an organization.

The Pope

Around the year 100, the people who belonged to the Church at Corinth received a letter from a bishop named Clement who was the fourth bishop of Rome. Some members of the Church at Corinth had removed their bishops and deacons from office and intended to replace them with others. Although Clement was not the bishop of Corinth, he ordered the people of Corinth to reinstate the deposed bishops and deacons.

From this piece of evidence, we conclude that Christians saw the bishop of Rome as having authority over the Church in areas outside of Rome. Clement saw himself as the successor of Peter, whom Christians considered to be the head of the community of disciples. As Peter's successor in Rome, Clement believed he inherited Peter's authority in the Church. He showed his authority in ordering the Church at Corinth to reinstate deposed bishops.

Christians in the early centuries did not view the pope as we do today. Thousands of people would not come out to see him if they heard he was coming to town. Christians accepted that he had a special role in the Church, but they also had a great regard for the authority of all bishops. The pope was not as well known in the early Church as he is today.

Bishops

Members of the early Church and the Church today see **bishops** as the successors of the office of the apostles. Except for their recognition that the bishop of Rome was a successor of Peter, Christians did not view other bishops as successors to specific apostles. They saw them as successors of the group of apostles known today as the college of apostles. The Church today refers to the bishops as belonging to the **college of bishops**.

From earliest times, bishops taught the faithful, celebrated the Eucharist and other sacraments with them, and made decisions for those in their care. Bishops today continue to teach, to sanctify, and to govern the Church. They have a responsibility to the total Church throughout the world, but their immediate responsibility is often to a large area called a **diocese**. A diocese covers a number of towns, and cities, and rural areas which contain many parishes. The parishes usually have an ordained priest as its pastor.

Ordained Priests

As many converts began to come into Christianity, bishops needed help in providing for the spiritual needs of the growing Christian communities. Since bishops could not preside over the number of Eucharistic celebrations taking place in their area, they ordained certain Christians to lead the communities in worship. These ordained **priests**, often called presbyters, recognized the authority of the bishop and presided at the Eucharist in place of the bishop.

Today, these presbyters preside at worship and serve as pastors of parishes. They celebrate the sacraments for those in their care and act in union with the bishop of the diocese in matters pertaining to their particular parish.

Deacons

Besides presbyters for worship, bishops also found a need for assistance in the performance of many other ministries and liturgical functions. The office of **deacon** and deaconess developed to assist the bishop in caring for the needs of the poor and the outcast, as well as assisting with liturgical functions.

Today a presbyter first shares in the office of deacon on his journey toward the ordained priesthood. In the early Church, bishops sometimes had need for a presbyter to lead the Eucharistic liturgy. As the need increased, they tended to ordain the deacons who were assisting them and sent them to care for the faithful in a particular area.

This procedure led to the eventual practice of ordaining candidates as deacons before ordaining them as presbyters.

The Church and Its Mission

By the year 100, Christianity had definitly become a Church distinct from Judaism. Jewish Christians, who thought that the Jewish nation would accept Jesus as the Messiah, became disillusioned when they found themselves rejected by the Jewish leaders because of their beliefs. The Jewish converts to Christianity not only accepted Jesus as the Messiah, but they also came to accept a Church which had become in many ways non-Jewish.

As Christianity headed into the second century, it had developed into a specificially organized and unified Church with very specific beliefs and forms of worship.

KEY TERMS

Diocese: large area covering a number of towns, cities, and rural areas which contains many parishes; governed by a bishop.

Priests: often called presbyters; preside at worship and serve as pastors of parishes; they celebrate the sacraments and act in union with the bishop of the diocese in matters pertaining to their particular parish.

Deacon: developed to assist the bishop in caring for the needs of the poor and outcast; today a presbyter first shares in the office of deacon on his journey toward ordained priesthood.

When Christ instituted the Twelve, "he constituted [them] in the form of a college or permanent assembly, at the head of which he placed Peter, chosen from among them." Just as "by the Lord's institution, St. Peter and the rest of the apostles constitute a single apostolic college, so in like fashion the Roman Pontiff, Peter's successor, and the bishops, the successors of the apostles, are related with and united to one another."

Catechism of the Catholic Church, #880

CLIPBOARD

1. How does the image of Church as the People of God and the Body of Christ affect our understanding of Church today?
2. How does the image of Church as a Church of Service influence the mission of Church today?
3. How important do you think the institutional elements of the Church are today?

A Voice from the Past

This week in your column you are going to report on the events that led up to the break of the Catholic Church from the Jewish Church. Be sure to include the key terms in your article. Also, show your reader how our Jewish heritage still affects and influences our faith today.

REVIEWING THE ERA

• **50**

THE COUNCIL OF JERUSALEM. Decreed that Gentile converts to Christianity do not have to follow certain Jewish practices and observances of the law.

PETER AND PAUL KILLED IN ROME. Under Nero's persecution, Peter was apparently crucified (since he was not a Roman citizen), and Paul was most likely beheaded.

• **70**

DESTRUCTION OF JERUSALEM. The Roman army invaded Jerusalem, destroying the Temple, killing many of the inhabitants, and ravaging the city. The Pharisees rebuilt the city and the Jewish faith after this destruction.

Then and Now

During this period, Christianity became distinct from Judaism. The Council of Jerusalem had already laid the groundwork for a break with Judaism, while the destruction of Jerusalem and its resulting conditions in Palestine influenced the complete break.

The fact that both Peter and Paul were killed at Rome makes this city a sacred and major city in Christianity. The bishops who followed Peter, as bishops of Rome, also became recognized as the visible head of the community of disciples.

Paul explained much of the theology of Church taught today. He used the image of the Body of Christ and emphasized that the Church had a structure, a call to service and preaching. He called it a Church of sacrament, and recognized it as a community.

A later writer, using the name of Peter, stressed that the community of disciples is a people of God, a chosen people and a royal priesthood. As a royal priesthood, we recognize, as the early community did, that our life as followers of Christ centers on the Eucharist.

Today, we recognize in the Church all the characteristics found in the letters of the New Testament. Popes have lived predominantly in Rome, the place where Peter and Paul died.

NEWS IN REVIEW

1. How did Paul prove his dedication to Christ?
2. What was Luke's purpose in telling the story of Peter and Cornelius in the Acts of the Apostles?
3. What led up to the Council of Jerusalem, and how did it help the future of Christianity?
4. How did the destruction of Jerusalem help the spread of Christianity?
5. How did Paul receive his Roman citizenship, and what difference did it make when he and Peter were put to death?
6. How do the images of the Church as a people of God and as the Body of Christ work together in our understanding of Church?
7. Why are the sacraments important for the Church?
8. How important is it that the Church serve the poor and needy in the world?
9. Why is the Church as a visible organization important for the ministry of the Church in the world?
10. Why is preaching important for the Church?

chapter four

From Persecution to Acceptance

If we lived around the year 100, the context of our faith would differ greatly from that of Christians fifty years earlier. We would have lost most of our memory of the Jewish roots of Christianity and viewed Christianity as very different from Judaism. Our stories would center on Jesus Christ, Paul the apostle, and other missionaries who came from Antioch and other major cities to preach the faith.

We would know our bishops as teachers, leaders of worship, and guides for daily living. The bishops, presbyters, and deacons would wear the same type of clothing as everyone else. We would worship in small groups, usually around a table, using ordinary bread and wine for the celebration of the Eucharist. Baptism would take place in a river or pond.

We would pride ourselves in being a community united in love for one another. We would hear rumors of persecutions and live in fear that someday government authorities would challenge us to deny our faith in Christ or face death. We would have stories and memories of martyrs that would greatly affect the context of history in which we lived.

Bishops are still teachers, leaders of worship, and guides for daily living.

The World of the Roman Empire

The Christian Times

Second Century   **Vol. 2   No. 1**

Demonstrators Protest Persecutions

A group of demonstrators from the empire are carrying signs outside the emperor's palace protesting Decius's sickening persecution of Christians. A group of educators have joined the demonstrators to protest the number of persecutions of educated Christians, such as Justin Martyr.

Since the time of Nero, Christians have periodically undergone persecution in the empire. Rome considers Christians to be an atheistic secret society that refuses to worship the Roman gods, and thus the practice of Christianity has been made illegal.

The painful martyrdom of people such as Ignatius, the bishop of Antioch, and Polycarp, the bishop of Smyrna, has only served to increase the number of those embracing Christianity rather than destroying it.

A governor named Pliny has recently written to Emperor Trajan concerning the persecution of Christians, asking whether he should seek them out to kill them. Trajan suggests waiting until someone accuses them of being Christian. This seems to be the mood of the empire at this time.

NOTEPAD

? ? ? ?

1. What did you learn about Rome? the Christians? the martyrs? Decius?
2. What did you learn about the Roman people of this era?
3. How effective do the persecutions seem to be? Why?

The Rest of the Story

When armies captured new territory, they would force the conquered people to accept their gods. Roman armies followed this custom, but they exempted the Jews who worshipped only one God. Christians, however, posed a new problem for Roman authorities.

Christian Rejection of Roman Gods

At the beginning of Christianity's missionary movement, Roman authorities viewed the followers of Christ as simply another sect within Judaism. In time, however, as large numbers of Gentiles throughout the empire became Christian, the Roman authorities decided not to allow Christians to share in the benefits of Judaism. They saw this new group as a religion different from Judaism. A bishop named Ignatius of Antioch gives an example of the Roman response to the Christian's refusal to worship false gods.

Around the year 107, Ignatius, an elderly bishop of Antioch, stood in a Roman arena awaiting his death. The occasion was a Roman festival, and the authorities had planned the slaughter of Ignatius to amuse the crowds. Many Christians in the crowd wept as this very popular bishop bravely and defiantly welcomed death for his faith.

Ignatius's ordeal began back at Antioch when some of his enemies accused him of tyranny and heresy against Roman gods. He had dedicated himself to living the Christian message, and he boldly condemned those who attempted to change Christ's message to make it less demanding. His enemies easily convinced the authorities that Ignatius was undermining Roman rule by refusing to worship Roman gods.

After being condemned, Ignatius began a long and difficult journey toward his execution in Rome. During his journey, the Roman guards permitted Christians to visit with him. Through these visits, Ignatius discovered that some Christians in Rome were plotting to free him. Not wishing to cause further trouble and well prepared for death, he rejected this plot.

During his journey to his martyrdom, Ignatius wrote seven letters which offered encouragement to members of the early Church. In his writings, he begs the Christians of Rome to pray for him, rather than attempt to free him. He willingly accepts his martyrdom in union with Christ who also suffered, died, and was raised from the dead. In one of his letters, Ignatius is the first one to apply the term Catholic, meaning universal, to the Church. In using this term, he was referring to all Christians.

Ignatius and his letters quickly became the model for others who would be facing persecution and death for their faith in the centuries to follow. His courage in dying for the faith would inspire others to willingly join their sacrifice to that of Jesus Christ.

When Christians refused to worship false gods, Roman authorities condemned them as traitors to the Roman Empire. They also considered them atheists, since Christians rejected the gods worshipped by so many others.

The refusal of Christians to worship the gods caused problems for the Roman population as well as for Roman authorities. Romans feared that the gods would punish everyone because Christians stubbornly refused to offer worship. During times of natural or military disasters, the non-Christians blamed Christians for stirring up the gods' wrath. The mobs began to believe that the only way to appease the gods was to destroy Christianity.

Misunderstanding Christianity

Some Christians, believing that the world would soon end, prepared for the expected coming of Christ by withdrawing from the activities of daily life. Another reason they withdrew from the daily life of the people was their abhorrence of bloodshed. Many of the people of the era, however, delighted in seeing blood shed and thus attended the games in the arena, which consisted in gladiators killing each other, or criminals being mauled by ferocious animals.

Fearing the hatred and anger of the people, Christians began to worship in secret. They would greet each other with secret signs for fear that the non-Christians would betray them to the authorities. Because of their secrecy, some people who heard Christians speaking of the sacrifice of the Eucharist thought they were talking about human sacrifice. Rumors spread that Christians were eating human flesh in their worship.

Some merchants selling images of the gods for pagan worship found their business threatened by Christians. They used every rumor they heard to incite riots against Christianity. As a result of all these issues, people began to view Christians as aloof and hostile. They began to clamor for their death.

The Persecutions Begin

The Roman persecutions of Christians began one fatal day, shortly after the year 60, when a disastrous fire raced through Rome, ravaging a large portion of the city. When early rumors reported that the Emperor Nero started the fire, Nero distracted the people from this accusation by blaming the Christians for the devastation of Rome. In supposed retaliation for the burning of Rome, Nero began a massive persecution of Christians.

The persecution under Nero became the first major persecution of

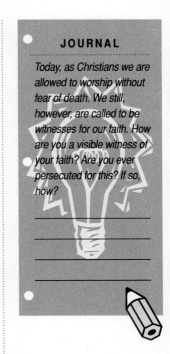

JOURNAL

Today, as Christians we are allowed to worship without fear of death. We still, however, are called to be witnesses for our faith. How are you a visible witness of your faith? Are you ever persecuted for this? If so, how?

_____

_____

_____

_____

Christians in the Roman Empire. The multitude, always ready to hear accusations against Christians, chose to believe Nero's accusation and supported his decision to persecute Christians. The crowds were soon enjoying the sight of animals tearing Christians apart in the arena, Christians being skinned alive, and Christians being burned at the stake.

Not all Christians accepted death as easily as Sts. Peter and Paul. Some weakened in the face of persecution and renounced their faith in Christ. Most, however, refused to abandon their faith in Christ and faced death with courage. As mentioned in the last chapter, many historians believe that Peter and Paul were killed during the persecution under Nero.

Persecutions Continue

The persecution of Christians under Nero did not destroy Christianity. Surprisingly, in some cases, it helped Christianity to prosper. The courageous

resolve of the Christians in the face of death inflamed many pagans with a desire to know more about the faith of these fearless martyrs. After Nero's death, the remaining emperors throughout the rest of the first century refused to pursue any organized persecution of Christians.

Despite the lack of persecution of Christians in Rome, persecutions of Christians did continue in some areas throughout the empire. Although the Roman authorities did nothing to encourage these persecutions, they also did nothing to prevent them. Whenever news reached Rome of persecutions in other areas within the empire, the emperors, with no reason to support Christianity, quietly ignored these reports.

Second Century Persecutions

At the beginning of the second century, Pliny, a governor of one of the cities in the Roman Empire wrote to emperor Trajan. Recognizing that Christianity

In the Spotlight

St. Ignatius (c. 35–107) was probably a Syrian and a disciple of Sts. Peter and Paul or St. John. It has been proposed that he was the child whom Christ placed among the apostles in Matthew 18:1-6. There is some debate whether he was the second or third Bishop of Antioch.

Upon being arrested and placed in the custody of Roman soldiers, St. Ignatius began writing epistles (letters) to the Christian communities of Ephesus, Magnesia, Tralles, Rome, Philadelphia, and Smyrna. He is also well known for his farewell letter to Bishop Polycarp. His letters tell of the state of the Church at that time, and throughout Church history they have been held in great esteem.

St. Ignatius was an important martyr of the early Church and is remembered for proclaiming "Let me follow the example of the suffering of my God" as he was thrown to the wild animals of the Roman circus.

was still forbidden, Pliny asked Trajan what he should do about the Christians in his territory. Trajan admitted that the Roman Empire still supported the death penalty for Christians, but he directed the governor not to search for Christians. He wrote that rulers should act against Christians only if someone brought an accusation against them. His reply set the tone for many emperors during the second century.

Trajan expanded on his directive when he added that Christians should receive an opportunity to seek freedom. They would simply have to renounce their Christian beliefs or face death. Throughout the remainder of the second century, Christians professed their faith secretly, fearing that a neighbor or friend would accuse them before the authorities.

Bishop Polycarp, a friend of Ignatius, gave the early Christians another example of courage in the middle of the second century. When Polycarp appeared before a judge, the judge tried to convince Polycarp to worship the emperor as a god, but the bishop refused. The judge then ordered him to betray his Christian comrades by crying out, "Death to the atheists." Instead of calling Christians atheists, Polycarp defiantly pointed to the judge and those accusing him and called them atheists instead.

Polycarp continued to frustrate and anger the judge during his trial. When the judge threatened to burn him alive, Polycarp showed no fear of the consuming flames. He declared that a few moments of pain would bring him eternal glory. The judge condemned Polycarp to death by burning.

As the flames engulfed Polycarp, he seemed to welcome them. He believed, along with other Christians, that the greatest gift they could receive was to die for Christ. Only minutes after he died, Christians were already calling the bishop by the title, "St. Polycarp."

Justin Martyr and the Apologists

Many of the Gentile converts in the early Church came from among the common people who were not well educated. With the exception of Paul and the writers of the New Testament, many of the early disciples had a minimum of education.

Shortly after the year 100, educated non-Jews began to challenge the message of Christ. They rejected Christianity, regarding it a pointless and absurd religion, directed only toward the superstitious and uneducated. They used philosophy to prove that Christianity offered nothing to one's life. Some even saw Christianity as destructive of a healthy attitude toward daily living.

Justin was a teacher who became frustrated with the empty answers to

Bishop Polycarp

KEY TERMS

Apologists: the educated Christians of Justin's era; justified their beliefs by explaining them to unbelievers in philosophical language.

life found in the non-Christian teachings of the day. He felt an emptiness in his life and began to search for meaning in the religions of his day. He noted that Christians bravely faced persecution and death rather than deny their faith, and he wanted to discover the beliefs that allowed them to accept death so easily. He began to investigate Christ's teachings from the viewpoint of philosophy.

In his study of Christianity, Justin found, to his excitement, a logical answer to his many questions about life. He discovered the meaning Christ gave to life, a meaning which motivated Christians to courageously face death. He recognized that Christ was a well educated Jew who dedicated his life to saving others. Once he accepted Christianity, he followed the example of Christ by dedicating himself to serving others with courage.

Justin became so dedicated to the Christian message that he chose the dangerous path of teaching philosophy courses about Christianity in pagan Rome. This would bring him to the attention of some powerful enemies. In his teaching, he stressed the power of Christian life and ritual, while boldly challenging the foolishness of pagan worship.

The Church refers to educated Christians of Justin's era as **Apologists**. Justin himself was not aware that history would list him among the Apologists, but he defended the faith with an intellectual level, before educated non-Christians. The title Apologist comes from a Greek word meaning justification. The Apologists justified their beliefs by explaining them to unbelievers in philosophical language. Justin, like other Apologists, sought to explain his teachings in a language understandable to the uneducated.

Other educated Christians besides Justin used the science of philosophy in their explanation of Christianity. The Church lists sixteen Apologists who defended the faith as Justin did. Each day they faced the possibility of having someone publicly accuse them of being Christian, or of spreading the teachings of Christ. The fear of death failed to deter the Apologists from their open defense of the faith.

At one point, a non-Christian rival became enraged at Justin's teachings and accused him of being a Christian. Since he lived in an era when Christians would only face trial if someone accused them, Justin had to defend himself once his non-Christian rival accused him. In the face of death, Justin continued to defend his belief in Christ. Because he willingly accepted death rather than deny his faith in Christ, Christian history has given to him the name, Justin Martyr.

Emperor Decius

Shortly after the year 200, when the Roman Empire showed signs of decay, an emperor named Decius resolved to revive its spirit. Following the example of emperors who ruled during the peak of the early Roman Empire, he aimed to unite the empire under a common pagan religion. He knew that rulers of the powerful Roman Empire demanded worship of common gods to secure political unity and power in the empire. He intended to do the same.

Decius began his reform with a decree that all people of the Empire should publicly worship Roman gods. When they did so, they were to receive certificates testifying that they had performed this public worship. The people had to carry these certificates and show them to any authority who demanded to see them. If they could not produce a certificate, the authorities would take this as a sign that they had refused to worship Roman gods in public.

Whenever the soldiers discovered someone without a certificate, they would torture the offender until he or she agreed to offer public worship. The soldiers would inflict such horrible tortures that many unwillingly made these mandated offerings. Those who could endure these atrocious tortures without denying Christ often died from the pain of the torture alone. The bloodiest and most horrible executions of the second century took place under Decius.

Decius's persecution had become so intense and painful that the emper-

ors who followed him showed greater toleration for Christians to avoid upsetting the population with such an overwhelming bloodshed. The persecutions ceased in most areas. With a growing feeling of peace, Christians began to express their beliefs openly and gained a feeling of security. Some emperors even granted a short reprieve to Christians by restoring their cemeteries and places of worship.

You will be hated by all because of my name. But not a hair of your head will perish. By your endurance you will gain your souls.
Luke 21: 17-19, NRSV

CLIPBOARD

1. Jews and Christians believe that there is *one* God who created everything and who has concern for creation. How does your belief in *one* God and your knowledge of God's actions, through Jews and Christians, throughout history shape your attitudes about life today? How do these attitudes differ from the attitudes of Society?

2. Explain what changed in the memory and stories of Christians to make the Romans view them as living in a context of history different from that of Judaism.

3. Is your faith strong enough right now that you would undergo persecution rather than deny God?

The Christian Empire

The Christian Times

Fourth Century   **Vol. 4 No. 1**

Christians Mourn a Dedicated Emperor

Christians throughout the empire mourn the death of Constantine, whom many already honor as a saint. Since the retirement of the notorious Emperor Diocletian, the persecution of Christians has almost ceased. Constantine refused to persecute Christians.

Constantine was the son of Constantius, one of the four leaders chosen by Diocletian to rule a segment of the empire. Constantine had to fight for the right to be the sole emperor. Christians believe that God blessed Constantine, especially since his victory at Milvian Bridge in which he miraculously defeated a far more powerful army.

As emperor, Constantine remained faithful to his decree of toleration known as the Edict of Milan. During his reign, Christianity moved from a persecuted religion to the most powerful and favored religion in the empire.

The thousands of people mourning Constantine's death show how revered he was. With many bishops serving in civil courts under Constantine, his funeral was a mixture of political and religious leaders, often represented by the same person.

NOTEPAD

? ? ? ? ?

1. What did you learn about Constantine? the Christians?
2. What does the article tell you about Christianity?
3. What does the article tell you about the relationship between the Church and the political system?

The Rest of the Story

The Roman Empire was continually declining and every new emperor scrambled to return it to its early days of glory. The desire for uniting the empire under one religion continued to bring affliction to the Christians who resisted worshiping false gods.

Diocletian (284–305)

When Diocletian became emperor, he found the Roman Empire mired in weakness, slowly disintegrating as a great force in the world. Faced with the same type of crisis Decius found a century earlier, Diocletian, after reigning for twenty years, followed Decius in seeking to unite the people through worship of the common gods.

Since Diocletian had allowed Christians to live in peace for two decades, Christians moved easily and openly around the empire. Their newly discovered freedom and trust of the Roman authorities had lulled them into a false feeling of security.

With an unexpected and vicious reversal, Diocletian suddenly turned his fury on the Christians. Many were so well known that Diocletian's soldiers could easily capture and imprison them. Within a short period of time, his soldiers tortured and killed thousands of Christians.

Diocletian murdered many more Christians than Decius did. Those who did not perish during the persecution found themselves cut off from society, slowly dying from lack of food and drink. The emperor dismissed all Christians from imperial service, destroyed their Churches, and burned their books. He imprisoned the clergy and ordered death for those who refused to offer sacrifice to the gods. Following Decius, he decreed that all citizens must offer sacrifice to the gods as a visible proof of their paganism.

Like the people of Decius day, the population became sickened at the spectacle of persecution and torture. They were soon risking their lives to shelter Christians. Like the many people who dared to offer shelter to the Jews during the period of the Holocaust, those who aided Christians during the time of Diocletian faced death if discovered. Diocletian's persecution stands out as the bloodiest in the early history of the Church.

Diocletian's desire to destroy Christianity in the empire failed because many of his own people found the persecution too savage. Besides attempting to wipe out Christianity to preserve the Roman Empire, he also decided to divide the empire into four areas. Unknown to Diocletian, his decision to divide the empire would later prove to be beneficial for the Christians.

Division of the Empire

As part of his desire to reform the empire, Diocletian divided it into four areas. He appointed a ruler for each area. He himself ruled a large area and he appointed three others to rule the remaining areas. Two of the rulers willingly followed Diocletian's example in persecuting Christians, while a third, Constantius reluctantly allowed limited persecutions.

Despite the horrible persecutions under Diocletian, Christianity continued to flourish. When Diocletian finally resigned his position in 305, Constantius declared an end to the persecutions in the West. In the East, however, the persecutions continued for approximately five more years.

JOURNAL

Who is persecuted in your school? How do you offer shelter?

_____

_____

_____

_____

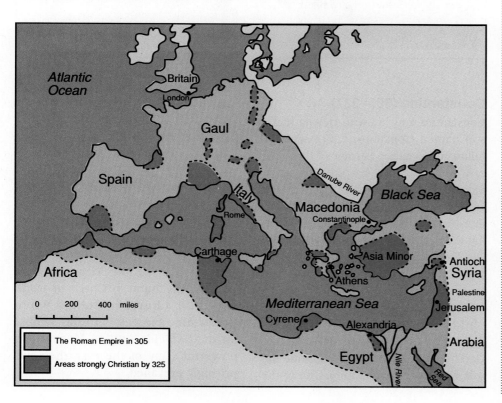

The Roman Empire in 305

Areas strongly Christian by 325

Map Search

The map presents a picture of the Roman Empire around the time Constantine became Emperor. Find the following on the map:

- Roman Empire
- Constantinople
- Rome
- Gaul
- Spain
- Britain

Make special note of:

the area covered by the Roman Empire

distance between Constantinople and Rome

distance between Constantinople and Gaul, Spain, and Britain

In the Spotlight

St. Helena (c. 250–330) was born to a poor family of little social status in Bithynia. She was working as a servant when she met Constantius I Chlorus (d 306). As Constantius was not yet politically prominent, their relationship was not discouraged. They were married and had a son named Constantine.

When Constantius became Caeser in 293, however, he found it politically necessary to divorce Helena and marry Theodora, stepdaughter of Emperor Maximian. After the divorce, Helena withdrew from public until 306 when her son succeeded Constantius.

Helena converted to Christianity and enjoyed much prestige throughout the empire during her son's reign. She was given the honorific title *Augusta* and weilded much influence in the government. Having control of the imperial treasury, Helena went on a pilgrimage to the Holy Land where she helped build churches with her money, especially the *Holy Sepulchre*, the *Nativity*, and the *Ascension*. Legend has it that while she was in the Holy Land she found the True Cross.

Constantine (306–337)

Constantius and his wife Helena had a son named Constantine. Constantine followed his father as ruler of the western portion of the Empire. The three emperors in the East continued to persecute Christians, while Constantine, like his father, did not relish persecuting them. The four rulers would eventually fight each other until Constantine would triumph as the Emperor of the Roman Empire.

Since Constantine showed favor to Christianity during his reign, Christians developed many legends, reporting that God helped Constantine to become the sole emperor of the empire. One of the legends concerned a battle between Constantine and one of the powerful rulers of the East, Maxentius. They fought at a place called Milvian Bridge.

According to the legend, Constantine, who had the weaker army, had a vision in a dream in which God bade him to emblazon the Greek letters Chi Rho on the shields of his soldiers. In the Greek alphabet, the letters would look like XP, a Christian symbol still found in Christian paintings and churches today. When Constantine's forces, with this symbol on their shields, battled Maxentius's powerful army of the east, they surprisingly prevailed.

Constantine had already showed signs of favoring Christianity before the battle, but after the battle, he became the great champion of Christianity. Intoxicated by his victory, he ordered the restoration of Christian property, freed the clergy from certain civil obligations, and sought more opportunities to strengthen the role of Christianity in the empire. Under Constantine, Christianity in the West had moved from a persecuted religion to one of favor.

Constantine's Roman Empire

With one of the emperors defeated, the empire now had three rulers. One of the three remaining rulers of the Empire met with Constantine in the year 313 at Milan to discuss the role of Christianity in the Empire. Shortly after this meeting, the two remaining emperors fought until only one survived. Now there was only one other emperor besides Constantine.

The remaining emperor issued a decree known as the **Edict of Milan**, which contained the basics of the agreement made between himself and Constantine. The decree allowed for toleration of all religious beliefs, non-Christian as well as Christian, and granted the return of property, that had been seized, to Christians.

Although Constantine favored Christianity, he also allowed the continuation of some non-Christian customs in his portion of the empire. He retained the title of Supreme Pontiff, a title given to non-Christian rulers. He allowed the imprinting of images of the sun god on the official coins of his empire, and he treated the non-Christians of the empire with profound respect. Although Constantine turned to Christianity by the year 312, he did not accept baptism until his death in 337.

In 324, when the other emperor attempted to renew his persecution of Christians, Constantine saw himself as the champion of Christianity in the em-

pire. He fought the remaining emperor with religious fervor and defeated him, thus becoming the sole emperor of the entire empire.

As the emperors did in the past, Constantine wanted the empire to be united and powerful under a single religion. Instead of uniting it under a non-Christian religion, however, he chose to unite it under Christianity. Later, under Charlemagne, the empire became known as the Holy Roman Empire.

Favors for the Church

Under Constantine, rapid changes began to take place in Christianity. He not only transferred basilicas (official buildings) and palaces to the Church, but he also built new places of worship. He gave the Church permission to accept and keep gifts, established Sunday as a public holiday, and had a basilica built over the tomb of St. Peter in Rome.

Besides providing places for worship, Constantine also strengthened the role of the clergy in his empire. He freed them from all taxation, a favor enjoyed in the past only by the pagan

Constatine is considered a saint by the Church in the East.

priests, and exempted them from military service and forced labor. The clergy, who once had to hide in fear of discovery, now held positions of honor in the Holy Roman Empire.

Constantine had a great effect on the role of bishops in the Church. He placed bishops in positions of political authority, making them the local judges and civil officials. Their powers were not only religious, but also political. Bishops became the governors in many areas of the empire. Some of the liturgical garb worn by bishops today have their origin in this era, as it resembles the clothing worn by judges and governors in Constantine's time.

Constantine laid the foundation for a dramatic change for Christianity when he decided to move his throne from Rome to Byzantium, a major city in the east. He turned his home in Rome, the majestic Lateran Palace, over to the Pope and his successors. The popes lived in the Lateran Palace until the 1300s.

By the time of Constantine's death, the Church had become a central force in the empire. For the first time, the clergy had become a separate class from the common people. The bishops, who now dressed in the garb of government officials, stood out as political and spiritual leaders.

CLIPBOARD

1. Why do many countries today allow freedom of choice in religion, while the leaders of ancient Rome felt a need to unify the empire under one religion?

2. What was the significance of Constantine's victory at Milvian Bridge. Compare and contrast the significance of this event with one from today.

3. Do you think that Constantine's choice of placing bishops in positions of political authority has left any effect on the Church today? Give examples to support your answer.

The Emperor and Church Matters

The Christian Times

Fourth Century   Vol. 4 No. 2

Athanasius Returns in Triumph

The people of Alexandria filled the streets yesterday, as their beloved bishop Athanasius returned from exile for the fifth time. When asked how he felt about his return, Athanasius smiled and said, "I hope I can stay among my people without being forced into exile again."

An ecumenical council held at Nicea some years ago condemned Arius, who taught that Jesus did not exist from all eternity. Although the ecumenical council involved almost all the bishops of the world, some bishops from the East rejected the conclusion of the council. They forced Athanasius, the council's strongest supporter, into exile.

As strong as Emperor Constantine and his son were, the plight of Athanasius and the inability of the emperor to enforce the decrees of councils underlined the weakness of most emperors in matters of religion. The emperor unsuccessfully attempted to fight the Donatist heresy which denied that a sinful bishop could ordain another bishop. Constantine's later failure at squelching the Arian heresy presents one of the problems of allowing government to solve Church matters.

NOTEPAD

? ? ? ? ?

1. What did you learn about Constantine? Athanasius?

2. What did you learn about the heresies mentioned?

3. What did you learn about the effectiveness of government in Church matters?

The Rest of the Story

As Christianity gained more freedom, religious thinkers could openly discuss some basic teachings of the Church. Christians began to ask what the Church meant when it said that Jesus Christ was God. How could a person be both divine and human at the same time? They were also asking how a person could deny Christ, repent, and then return to the Church? The answers to these questions threatened to split Christianity and the empire.

Donatist Heresy (311)

One of Constantine's first attempts at settling disagreements within Christianity ended in disaster. Jesus did not answer all questions which would arise centuries later. Since the Church was confronting new problems, not addressed by Christ in the Gospels, it often faced differences of opinions. The emperors viewed these differences as a threat to the unity of the empire. Throughout most of history, church and state were so closely aligned that religious problems often ignited political problems.

A major controversy of Constantine's era concerned the forgiveness of sin. Jesus spoke of the forgiveness of sins and of baptism, but he never made any statements concerning the forgiveness of sins of people after baptism, especially if that sin included denial of the faith. Under torture, some Christians would deny Christ and later seek forgiveness for this denial.

POINTS TO PONDER

Since the empire depended on religious unity as a foundation for political unity, Constantine believed that he had a duty equal to that of the apostles or bishops to intervene in Church matters. Non-Christians used the title Supreme Pontiff for their ruler. Constantine, in accepting this title for himself, saw himself as a Supreme Pontiff in all Church matters.

KEY TERMS

heresy: teachings that depart from the accepted official beliefs of the Church

KEY TERMS

Schism: a term used to signify a break in the church.

Donatism: a schism in the Church resulting from the teaching that a minister in sin did not have the power to confer a valid sacrament.

Arianism: a heresy that stated only the Father is truly God, that Christ the Son is not.

Excommunication: highest form of penalty in the Church; cuts a person off from the community of the Church.

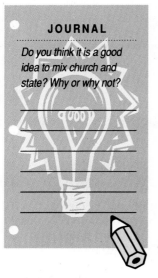

JOURNAL

Do you think it is a good idea to mix church and state? Why or why not?

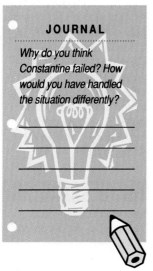

JOURNAL

Why do you think Constantine failed? How would you have handled the situation differently?

Catholics today have no difficulty believing Christ gave the Church the power to forgive all sins, even those committed after baptism. The Church also believes that those who received forgiveness could share in the privileges they had before they committed this sin. This teaching, however, was not as clearly understood during the time of Constantine.

During the era of Constantine, a bishop in the town of Carthage in Africa died. A leading bishop of the area, who once renounced his faith during the persecutions under Diocletian and later repented, consecrated a new bishop for Carthage. Although many bishops accepted the new bishop, others refused to believe that a bishop who once denied the faith could regain his powers to consecrate a new bishop. These bishops saw him as unworthy and believed that an unworthy minister lost the power to celebrate any of the sacraments.

A group of bishops defied the appointment at Carthage by appointing their own bishop named Donatus. A conflict ensued and became heated enough to involve the emperor. Constantine convened two councils which both condemned Donatus. A number of Christians, however, refused to accept the condemnation and declared themselves free from all Church authority.

A **schism**, which signifies a break in the Church, resulted from this controversy. The schism received the name of **Donatism**, a name derived from that of Donatus. Many schisms and heresies carry the name of the person who proposes or plays a leading role in the schism or heresy. The basic teaching of Donatism was that a minister in sin did not have the power to confer a valid sacrament.

As the controversy spread, Constantine feared that his empire would become divided. Religious issues were so closely linked with political unity that Constantine sent troops to Africa to protect the empire from turmoil. His intentions were to expel the Donatist heretics from the Churches they had taken, but this move only incited the Donatists to fight more boldly.

In time, Constantine realized that his armies were not solving the problem, but only making it worse. With no other solution, he ordered a decree of toleration for the Donatists. Constantine had failed miserably in his first intervention in Church matters.

Arianism

Arius (250–336), a presbyter in Alexandria, was a popular preacher who taught that Jesus was not really God. He was created by God before God created the world, but he was not eternal. Arius stated that Jesus was created, and once created, he created everything else. Christians, however, believe that Jesus Christ is God from all eternity. Arius was teaching heresy in denying the divine nature of Jesus.

Alexander, the bishop of Alexandria, commanded Arius to cease preaching his heresy. When Arius refused, Alexander called a council of bishops from nearby dioceses to settle the problem. At the gathering in Alexandria, the bishops voted to **excommunicate** Arius, which means that they cut him off from the life of the Church. Cutting a person off from the life of the community is the highest form of penalty in the Church. When Arius heard the news of his condemnation, he fled from the country, fearing that someone would kill him.

Arius went to Palestine and pleaded his cause before a council of bishops who supported his teaching. Armed with the support of the council at Palestine, he boldly returned to Alexandria to continue spreading his message. As people took sides between Arius and the bishop of Alexandria, riots erupted in the streets.

Constantine decided to intervene in the crisis, but he misjudged the intensity of the controversy. He regarded it as a trivial dispute between Arius and his bishop. To his surprise, he again failed to solve the problem. He resolved to bring about a solution and summoned all the bishops of the Church to meet in council at a place called Nicea.

The council at Nicea was called an **ecumenical council**, a title which means that it included all the bishops of the world. It was the first ecumenical council of the Church and is known as the **Council of Nicea**.

Council of Nicea (325)

In the year 325, nearly three hundred bishops came to Nicea to take part in the historic council at Nicea. Since the Pope was too elderly to attend the meeting, he sent two delegates to represent him. A young deacon named Athanasius also attended this council. At the time, no one realized that Athanasius would later become the staunch and tormented champion of the council's decision against Arianism.

During the Council, the bishops composed a creed which later became the foundation for the creed which Catholics pray today during the Eucharistic liturgy on Sundays. A line from the creed declares that the Son of God is "one in being with the Father." This rejected Arius' teaching by clearly stating that the Son of God is one with God, truly eternal and divine, and not someone created by God.

The majority of the bishops at the Council came from the eastern part of the empire. Although the eastern bishops supported the statements of the council while it was in session, they returned home and began to rethink their vote. They protested that they had difficulty with the Greek word, Homoousios, used to express the unity of the Son with the Father and, as a result, refused to support the Nicene Creed.

Despite the condemnation of Arianism at the Council of Nicea, many bishops from the East refused to reject the heresy. The controversy would become a major issue for decades to come, as many of the eastern bishops accepted Arianism and the western bishops did not.

Athanasius (d. 373)

Three years after the Council of Nicea, Athanasius became bishop of Alexandria, but he found that his position did not guarantee safety against the forces of Arianism. Some influential eastern bishops began to support Arius and torment Athanasius. They even questioned the validity of Athanasius's election as bishop.

When Constantine witnessed the growing support for Arianism, he decided to avoid disunity in the empire by supporting the eastern bishops and recalling Arius from exile. When Athanasius refused to accept Arius back into Alexandria, some Arian eastern bishops persuaded Constantine to force Athanasius into exile.

After Constantine died, Athanasius returned to Alexandria. Constantius, Constantine's son and successor, became an Arian believer, and Athanasius had to flee to the West where the pope offered him protection. Before the heresy of Arianism ended, Athanasius would have to flee into exile five times. After his fifth exile, the emperor had to invite him back because of the overwhelming respect the people of Alexandria had for Athanasius.

Although Athanasius wrote some insightful works on theology, his most notable achievements centered on his defense of the divinity of Jesus against the teachings of the Arians. His stubborn and courageous opposition to Arianism weakened the force of this heresy in the empire, but the heresy continued to exist. It would prove to be one of the major points of conflict between the East and the West in the centuries ahead.

KEY TERMS

Ecumenical council: a council involving all the bishops of the world.

Council of Nicea: (325) first ecumenical council of the Church; called by Constantine to resolve the Arian heresy crisis; resulted in the composition of the Nicene Creed.

"The results of the incarnation of the Savior are such and so many, that anyone attempting to enumerate them should be compared to a person looking upon the vastness of the sea and attempting to count its waves."

St. Athanasius of Alexandria

The Incarnation of God's son reveals that God is the eternal Father and that the son is consubstantial with the Father, which means that, in the Father, and with the Father, the Son is one and the same God.

Catechism of the Catholic Church, #262

JOURNAL

St. Ambrose once said, "This Creed is the spiritual seal, our heart's meditation and an ever-present guardian; it is, unquestionably, the treasure of our soul." What does this mean to you? Explain it in your own words, and then state whether or not you agree with St. Ambrose. Support your opinions.

_____

_____

We believe in one God, the Father, the Almighty, maker of heaven and earth, of all that is seen and unseen. We believe in one Lord, Jesus Christ, the only Son of God, eternally begotten of the Father, God from God, Light from Light, true God from true God, begotten, not made, one in Being with the Father. Through him all things were made. For us and for our salvation he came down from heaven: by the power of the Holy Spirit he was born of the Virgin Mary, and became man. For our sake he was crucified under Pontius Pilate; he suffered, died, and was buried. On the third day he rose again in fulfillment of the Scriptures; he ascended into heaven and is seated at the right hand of the Father. He will come again in glory to judge the living and the dead, and his kingdom will have no end. We believe in the Holy Spirit the Lord, the giver of life, who proceeds from the Father and the Son. With the Father and the Son he is worshiped and glorified. He has spoken through the Prophets. We believe in one holy catholic apostolic Church. We acknowledge one baptism for the forgiveness of sins. We look for the resurrection of the dead, and the life of the world to come. Amen.

Nicene Creed

CLIPBOARD

1. What are some problems that would arise today if the president made decisions for the Church?

2. How do Arians differ from people today who believe that Jesus is just a good human being?

3. What differences and similarities do you find between the treatment of St. Athanasius and the treatment of bishops today who disagree with political decisions of the government?

REVIEWING THE ERA

- **100**

IGNATIUS OF ANTIOCH. He accepted martyrdom willingly; noted for the letters he wrote on his journey to martyrdom.
ST. POLYCARP OF SMYRNA. Bishop Polycarp was burned at the stake as a result of his refusal to reject Christianity.
JUSTIN MARTYR. He was put to death for his philosophical defense of Christianity; one of the Apologists, who were educated Christians defending Christianity in a scholarly fashion.

- **200**

DECIUS REIGNS AS EMPEROR. Decius directed a horrible persecution against a large number of Christians during the third century.

- **300**

DIOCLETIAN REIGNS AS EMPEROR. Diocletian directed the most savage persecution against Christians during the early part of the fourth century.
CONSTANTINE REIGNS AS EMPEROR. Constantine made Christianity a favored religion in the empire, causing a rapid growth in the number of Christians; under Constantine, many bishops served in government positions; the persecutions of Christians end.
DONATIST HERESY. The belief that an unworthy minister cannot validly celebrate a sacrament; it began when Donatus was made bishop of Carthage.
ARIUS. He began the heresy known as Arianism. He taught that Jesus was not divine, but rather the greatest of God's creatures, created before the world was created.
COUNCIL OF NICEA (325). The first ecumenical council which condemned the heresy of Arianism; began composition of the Nicene Creed.
ATHANASIUS. The great defender of the decisions of the Council of Nicea who, despite being bishop, had to flee into exile five times when Arians influenced the emperors.

KEY TERMS

Apologists

Edict of Milan

Schism

Donatism

Excommunication

Ecumenical council

Council of Nicea

 A Voice from the Past

This week in your column you will be reporting on the persecutions of the Christians, and the early heresies of the Church. Give your readers a brief synopsis of what happened, and then show them how these events affect the Church today.

Close your article with a discussion on church and state. Explain what problems arose from the unity of church and state, and also how it still affects the Church today. Be sure to include your own opinions on the subject. Discuss how some issues in the Church would be affected if the President was head of the Church today.

Then and Now

When Constantine made Christianity a favored religion, it flourished and grew rapidly. The emperor made bishops his judges and government officials, leading to their habit of wearing the garb of government officials. Because of their civic duties and robes of office, bishops became more separated from the common people.

During this period, some Christians fell into heresies attempting to offer a clearer understanding of the faith. The Council of Nicea met and explained that Jesus Christ is "one in being with the Father." Some, like the eastern bishops, rejected the teachings of the council, while others, like St. Athanasius, dedicated their lives to defending the council.

Today, Christianity is one of the largest single groups of believers throughout the world. Bishops continue to wear distinctive garb, some of it resembling the garb of civic office held by bishops in Constantine's day.

Most Christian denominations pray the Nicene Creed in their worship and share the common belief against Arianism that Jesus is "of one being with the father." Some of the Eastern Churches, although believing that Jesus is divine, still refuse to accept the Greek word, Homoousios, used to express the unity between the first two persons of the Trinity.

NEWS IN REVIEW

1. What was the reason for Rome forcing the worship of its gods on conquered nations, and why were the Jews exempt?

2. What are some underlying reasons for the Roman persecution of Christians?

3. What is the significance of Trajan's reply to Pliny the Younger concerning the persecution of Christians?

4. Citing examples from the life of Justin Martyr, describe the importance of Apologists in the history of the Church.

5. When did Emperor Decius live and what is noteworthy about his persecution of Christians?

6. Who was Diocletian and why was he able to persecute such a large number of Christians?

7. In what ways did Constantine favor Christianity over other religious beliefs in the empire?

8. Why do some people call Donatism a schism as well as a heresy?

9. What did the Ecumenical Council of Nicea declare concerning Arianism?

10. What do we learn about the problem of Arianism from the treatment of St. Athanasius?

chapter five

Monasticism

If we lived as Christians around the middle of the fourth century, we would be living in a context of history very different from that of the first three centuries. We would have vague memories of persecutions, but more dominant memories of worshiping freely in a society that favors us as Christian. We would glory in the legends and stories surrounding Constantine, and like most people of the day, we would consider him a saint.

As Christians living in the mid-fourth century, we would worship in large buildings given to us by Constantine. We would no longer meet in small groups, but, because of the large numbers of converts coming into the faith under Constantine, we would meet in large gatherings with the bishop presiding over our Eucharistic celebration. We would stand in awe of these bishops, who stood above us in their government robes.

Baptism would take place in a pool inside the Church, or in a pool in a special building attached to the Church. With the luxury allowed Christians, we would use expensive chalices in our worship. The spirit of sacrifice that marked the lives of the early Christians would be noticeably lacking. Some of us would accept the new luxury found in being favored by the government, while others in our community would seek solitude in the desert for a life of hardship, sacrifice, and prayer.

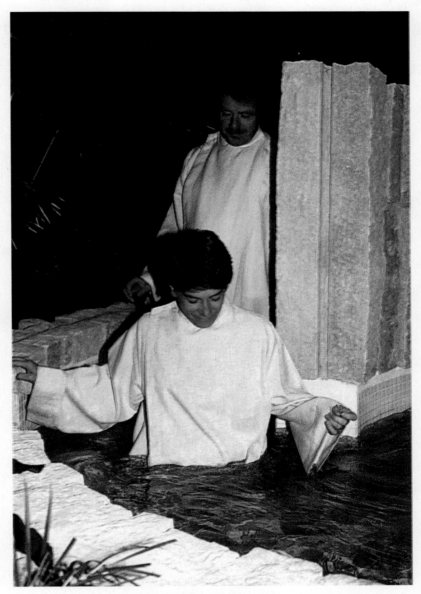

Baptism by immersion is still practiced in some parishes.

The Birth of Monasticism

The Christian Times

Fourth Century   Vol. 4   No. 3

New Monastery Established

A new monastery opened yesterday near Cappadocia under the guidance of the monk named Basil. Reports indicate that Basil has published a list of practices for the monks to follow in their pursuit of God.

Basil, following in the footsteps of great monks like Anthony of Egypt, and Anthony's friend, Pachomius, went to Egypt at the urging of his sister Macrina to learn more about life in the desert, commonly called monastic life. During his time there, he scribbled some notes about monastic life which he brought back to Cappadocia with him.

The trend of living in the desert seems to have its roots in the favoritism shown to Christianity by Constantine and those who followed him. Only one of Constantine's successors, his nephew Julian the Apostate, persecuted Christians for a brief period. A later emperor, Theodosius I, made amends by making Christianity the official religion of the empire.

Monasticism has indeed taken firm root in the empire.

NOTEPAD
? ? ? ? ?

1. What did you learn about Basil? Macrina? Constantine? Julian the Apostate? Theodosius I?
2. What did you learn about monastic life from this article?
3. What did you learn about Christianity?

The Rest of the Story

The sudden change of Christianity, from a persecuted faith to a highly favored faith by the emperor, did not affect all Christians in the same fashion. Some rejoiced, while others lamented the loss of opportunities to offer their lives for God through martyrdom. In reaction to the new life of luxury, safety, and comfort, found in the empire, some Christians sought their own form of sacrifice by going into the desert to live and pray.

The Successors of Constantine
After Constantine's death, his son Constantius followed Constantine's example of favoring Christians throughout the empire, although he could not always control what was happening far from Constantinople. Christians continued to hold a high place in government and shared in privileges previously granted to non-Christians.

From 361 to 363, a nephew of Constantine, Julian, became emperor. Julian had a seething anger toward Christians, since Christian emperors had condemned most of his family members to death. He began to persecute Christians by making life difficult for them. Under Julian's reign Christians were not allowed to teach in schools or serve in the army.

Although he was raised Christian, Julian gained a great love for Greek culture and the religion of the past, sometimes referred to as paganism. He introduced innovations into the pre-Christian culture which he learned about in his studies of the ancient Greeks. Although he attempted to support pre-Christian thinking, most non-Christians of his own day were unfamiliar with their cultural past. As a result, they rejected his new innovations and foiled his attempts to return the empire to a pre-Christian religion.

Julian died after only two years as emperor. Since Julian rejected his Christian faith and caused so much pain for Christians, he was seen by Christians as an **apostate**. An apostate is one who once professed the faith, but later denied it. Because of this, Christian history refers to him as Julian the Apostate.

For the next sixteen years, the emperors followed the lead of Constantine, favoring Christianity over other beliefs. One emperor, Gratian (375-395), rejected the pre-Christian title of Supreme Pontiff, thus ending any visible link between the emperor and non-Christian religions and cultures.

In 379, Theodosius I became emperor and made Christianity the official religion of the empire. He persecuted some leading non-believers, ordered the people to accept the Nicene Creed and condemned Arianism.

Since the time of Constantine, the general trend in the empire toward favoring Christianity led to the birth of a new movement in which Christians like Anthony, Pachomius, Basil, and others dedicated their lives to God in a new manner.

Anthony of Egypt (251–356)

A young man of twenty, named Anthony, experienced several major changes in his life. Shortly after the death of his parents, he sold all he owned, gave his wealth to poor people, and headed out to the desert to dedicate his life to prayer and contemplation of God. Since he lived in Egypt, he had no problem finding large expanses of desert where he could live in solitude and prayer. He became a **hermit,** a word which has its roots in a Greek word meaning *desert*.

Anthony was not original in his idea of seeking God in the silence of the desert. We know from the Scriptures that John the Baptist also lived in the desert, and that Jesus went on a long retreat in the wastelands of the desert. Anthony chose a life called **monasticism**, which also comes from a Greek word which means *to live alone*. Those who chose to live a monastic life were called monks, or if women, nuns.

Anthony reflected the spirit of many holy people of his own day who watched the Church move from an era of persecution to an era of favor with the government. Life had become too luxurious for him. Since martyrdom was no longer a possibility as a way of offering one's life to God, Anthony chose a life of **asceticism**. This word, ascetic, comes from the Greek and has as its root the idea of *training*, such as soldiers endure in preparation for service. The ascetical life was a life of hardship and sacrifice as a form of prayer.

Anthony had a younger sister who chose to enter a community of nuns. Once she made this choice, Anthony was no longer financially responsible for her and so felt free to move out to the desert, owning nothing and trusting completely in God. Monks living in the desert depended on the meager food they could find there and on the generosity of the people of nearby villages. The people revered the monks and nuns as holy men and women and sought their advice on many occasions.

Anthony as a Spiritual Guide

In time, Anthony's fame grew as people admired his piety and dedication. Other men and women who wanted to dedicate their lives to God in the desert sought direction from Anthony. Although Anthony continued to live alone, he met with these other men and women in the desert, recognizing their need for direction. Anthony worshiped with them and studied the Scriptures with them. Each of the men and women in the desert still lived alone with no common rule to guide them.

KEY TERMS

Apostate: someone who denies the Christian faith after having once professed it.

Hermit: a person who cuts him/herself off from society to live in solitude; has its roots in a Greek word meaning desert.

Monasticism: comes from a Greek word which means to live alone; those choosing to live a monastic life were called monks/nuns.

Asceticism: comes from the Greek and has its root in the idea of training; those in the ascetic life dedicated themselves to lives of hardship and sacrifice as a form of prayer.

JOURNAL

Do you think that Theodosius I actions were Christian? Why or why not? Are your actions always Christian? Give an example of a recent occasion where you weren't very Christian-like? How can you act more Christian in the future?

I am the voice of one crying out in the wilderness, 'Make straight the way of the Lord.'

John 1:22, NRSV

If you wish to be perfect, go, sell your possessions, and give the money to the poor, and you will have treasure in heaven; then come, follow me.

Matthew 19:21

JOURNAL

What role does prayer and sacrifice have in your life? What are some benefits of living a life of prayer and sacrifice?

For more than ten years, Anthony served as a guide for a large number of hermits in their desire to dedicate their life to God. He guided them through the use of the Scriptures, which he viewed as directives from Christ. Armed with Jesus' message, each hermit had the freedom to determine how he or she would respond to that message in the desert.

After ten years of directing others, Anthony still had a longing to live alone in complete silence and dedication. He eventually moved further into the desert, distancing himself from everyone. There, surrounded by silence and alone with God, he found comfort in prayer.

Anthony's life had attracted many other people into the desert, and some chose, as he did, to move further away from all human relationships. By the time Anthony died, the deserts and hills surrounding Egypt flourished with thousands of hermits who had followed Anthony into this new lifestyle.

Hermits, who lived alone as Anthony did, became known as **anchorites**. This term refers to a person who lives a life of solitude and penance. The anchorite hermit lived alone, often near a village where people would provide food, with no specific rule except the Gospels. Some hermits lived in a type of **semi-anchoritic** form of life. In this case, they lived alone, but they would meet with other hermits for prayer or support. Anthony began his life as an anchorite, became a semi-anchorite while he directed others, and escaped further into the desert to return to his life alone as an anchorite.

St. Pachomius (290–347)

Pachomius grew up in Egypt as a son of non-Christian parents. His first real encounter with Christianity came while he was in the army. He and some other soldiers came across a village of Christians who fed and comforted them in their need. Inspired by the selfless example of the people of the village, he became a Christian after his departure from the army. Like Anthony, he went into the desert to dedicate his life to God as a hermit, and there he became a friend of Anthony.

For a period of time, Pachomius lived in the desert with another hermit until he left to live alone. His brother soon joined him, but Pachomius became restless, desiring more than mere solitude. He longed for a life of service as well as a life of prayer. As a result, he and his brother gathered other hermits together to form a community. His first attempt at forming a community failed, but his later attempts became successful.

Pachomius recognized that many hermits living alone retained a healthy attitude and balance in their lives, but there were others who began to choose strange forms of discipline. Some even became competitive with others, sometimes choosing more absurd and imprudent forms of discipline. Since they had no rule to guide them, each of the anchorites had the freedom to choose his or her own form of asceticism. One hermit, for instance, sat at the top of a long pole for many years, depending on others to pass food up to him.

Pachomius, realizing the value and benefits of life in a community, in which a common rule could be shared, formed and established the first organized monastery in Egypt. Those who made vows (solemn promises) to life in the monastery became known as **monks**. Pachomius introduced the idea that monks should provide service for others.

In Pachomius' rule, each monk had to serve the others and live in obedience to his superior. The superior, who was Pachomius himself, became known as an **abbot**, a name derived from the Hebrew word Abba, which means father. Although the other monks vowed obedience to the superior, the superior was bound by the same rules of service. In addition to serving as leader, he also dedicated his life to serving the needs of others in the community.

Although Pachomius's rules were very strict by today's standards, the requirements were not as difficult as some of the penances individual hermits had previously placed upon themselves. Prayer, of course, became the center of the monks' lives. They prayed continuously, either privately, while they worked, or in community prayer. They also performed a multitude of tasks which supported the monastery and served the people of the surrounding areas. None of the monks were ordained priests, nor could they seek any special office in the Church.

Instead of living alone in the desert, they lived together in an enclosure surrounded by a wall with a single doorway. Inside the enclosure were several buildings—the chapel, a hall for meals, the sleeping quarters, the storeroom, and the gathering hall. They vowed never to marry and chose a life of poverty. Despite their vow of poverty, Pachomius ordered his monks to eat enough to protect their health. He refused to allow them to take part in unhealthy penances.

Twenty years after Pachomius established his rule, his sister organized a house for women and wrote a rule which she based on that of Pachomius's. During Pachomius's lifetime, nine monasteries of men and two of women used his rule. The spirituality of the monasteries had become so well-known, that many people begging for entry into the community were non-Christians. They were not only seeking a life of dedication to God, but they wanted to learn about the faith which led these monks and nuns to such deep dedication. They sought to become Christians as well as monks or nuns.

By the time of Pachomius's death, monasticism had grown to include monks and nuns who lived alone as well as those who lived in a community. The anchorites mentioned earlier were monks who lived alone. Those who lived in a community, such as that established by Pachomius, received the name **cenobites** which comes from the Greek word for *common*. Despite Pachomius's emphasis on community life, the monks and nuns still spent a major part of their day alone with God.

St. Macrina (327–379)

During the 300s, a young woman named Macrina dedicated her life and wealth to God. She was the daughter of prominent parents who had planned her marriage to a young lawyer.

Shortly before the marriage, Macrina's intended husband died suddenly, and she dedicated herself to a life consecrated to God. Despite her parents' protests, she staunchly refused to consider anyone else for marriage.

Macrina had a number of brothers. Two of them, Basil and Gregory, would have great influence on the Church. Basil received his education in Athens and returned home to use his education for his own interests. When Macrina saw him using his education to support his own pride, she became irritated and scolded him. Basil resisted her taunting, claiming she was uneducated, too religious, and not able to understand him.

JOURNAL

In your notebook write a few paragraphs addressing the following questions: How has the monastic life changed? Why do you think the monastic life has lost its popularity? What do you think would lead to an increased interest in the monastic life among today's youth? What would be a benefit of an increased participation of the monastic life?

KEY TERMS

Cenobites: comes from the Greek word meaning common; term used to describe monks and nuns who lived within a community.

Men religious gathered for communal parayer

In the Spotlight

St. Macrina was born the eldest of ten children to St. Basil the Elder and St. Emmelia, in Cappadocia about the year 330. She was raised with particular care by her mother, who taught her to read. At twelve years old she was betrothed, but the young man whom she was betrothed to died unexpectedly. After his death Macrina refused all other suitors and assisted her mother in educating her younger brothers and sisters. St. Basil the Great, St. Peter of Sebastea, St. Gregory of Nyssa and the rest of her brothers and sisters learned from her contempt of the world, dread of its dangers, and application to prayer and the Word of God.

Macrina particularly influenced her brothers St. Basil and St. Peter.

Macrina and her mother lived on an estate, that St. Basil established for them by the river Iris in Pontus, together with other women in an ascetic communal life. After her mother's death, Macrina turned the estate over to the poor and lived on what she earned with her own hands.

She fell ill nine months after the death of her brother St. Basil, in 379. When her brother St. Gregory visited her, he found her sick, lying on two boards for her bed. He was deeply impressed by the encouragement and cheerfulness which she offered him, as she prepared for her death. She died very happily.

Macrina had lived in such poverty that after her death nothing could be found to cover her body. St. Gregory, therefore, provided a special linen rove. He and the bishop, Araxius, carried her body to her grave, with a crowd of people following.

Basil's life changed abruptly and dramatically when an older brother died unexpectedly. He turned to Macrina and sought to learn about religious life. Macrina, recognizing Basil's genius and newly discovered piety, suggested that he go to Egypt to learn more about monastic life.

Macrina then turned her attention to her widowed mother. She persuaded her to turn their estate into a monastery for women. Macrina became superior of the monastery and held that position until she died.

When Macrina lay dying, her brother Gregory visited her and became deeply upset with her condition. She consoled him and instructed him concerning life as a journey toward God. Gregory learned so much from Macrina that he wrote a pious account of her life, in which he gives her the title Teacher.

Macrina was an example of the spiritual attitudes of the age. She was one of many rich people of the age who rejected a life of luxury to dedicate herself to God. She not only founded a monastery of nuns, but also influenced her two brothers to use their genius for God.

St. Basil (330–379)

As a result of the influence of his sister, Macrina, Basil himself became interested in monasticism. He traveled to Egypt where monks like Anthony and Pachomius had developed various forms of monastic life, and he searched other areas of the empire to broaden his understanding of monasticism.

When Basil returned home from his travels, he followed the example of Pachomius and formed a community. He did not write strict rules for his community, but responded to questions about values and principles involved in living monastic life in community. Although later writers would refer to these responses as *The Rule of Saint Basil*, they are actually a list of responses to spiritual questions.

Basil believed that living in a community was a higher calling than living alone. He recognized that community living provided opportunities for charitable acts, such as caring for a brother or sister in need.

Basil's principles regulated times for meals, work, and prayer. He established a lifestyle dedicated to a life of poverty, obedience, and celibacy, and urged his community to provide for the needs of the poor and the sick. Although he expected discipline in eating and drinking, he sought balance in the practice of such sacrifices.

Before Basil, many monks questioned the value of studying, but Basil introduced scholarly pursuit into monastic life. Basil himself was a great scholar and prolific writer. In the future, many scholarly monks would play a major role in the defense and development of Church teachings. Eventually, many of those chosen as bishops would come from the monasteries.

CLIPBOARD

1. Anthony went into the desert to escape from the luxuries of the world in which he lived and to dedicate himself to prayer and penance. Why would anyone choose to live a life of prayer and dedication today?

2. List the names of some current communities of monks or nuns dedicated to solitude and prayer.

3. How would your friends react to Macrina if she attended your high school?

Monasticism and Church Pastors

The Christian Times

Fourth Century   Vol. 4   No. 5

Chrysostom Reported Dead

Rumors, from the Black Sea, report that the great pastor and powerful preacher, John Chrysostom, died while in exile. At one time, Chrysostom hoped to live his life as a monk, freed from the cares of the world. Instead, he was made bishop of Constantinople and became a thorn in the side of the weak emperor, Arcadius.

The death of Chrysostom underlines the growing power of the Church over the emperor. This power seems most powerful when used by former monks like Martin, the bishop of Tours, Chrysostom, the bishop of Constantinople, and Ambrose, the bishop of Milan.

Many people of the empire still recall how Ambrose excommunicated Emperor Theodosius from the Christian Church and how the emperor was forced to humbly seek forgiveness from Ambrose.

Only time will tell which will prevail in the long run, the Church or the government.

NOTEPAD

? ? ? ? ?

1. What did you learn about Chrysostom? Ambrose? Emperor Theodosius? Martin?

2. What conflict seems to be occurring between church and state?

3. What affect does this conflict have on the Church? on the empire?

The Rest of the Story

Although monasticism arose from a desire to flee from the temptations and luxuries of life, many monks found themselves leaving the monasteries to serve as pastors and bishops. While a great number of them quietly performed their tasks in local villages and towns, some became more widely known. Martin of Tours, Ambrose, and John Chrysostom, all saints and all chosen to be bishops, had monastic foundations which seemed to give them the dedication needed to lead in the face of difficulties.

St. Martin of Tours (317–397)

While Martin of Tours is credited with educating the people on the importance of a monastic background for those serving as bishops, history also recognizes him as the founder of western monasticism. Egypt had become the center of training for many people interested in monasticism, and Martin brought monasticism to the western part of the empire.

When Martin, a son of a non-Christian soldier, wanted to become Christian, his father enrolled him in the army, hoping to distract him from the influence of his Christian friends. Although Martin served in the army for a number of years, he never forgot his desire to be a Christian.

According to an ancient biography of Martin, he once met up with a beggar who sought his help. Since Martin had no money to give him, he took off his cloak, cut it in half, kept half for himself, and gave the other half to the beggar. In a dream that night, he saw Jesus in half a soldier's cape. Jesus said, "As long as you did it to one of these least ones, you did it to me." Martin soon received baptism and later left the army.

After years of traveling throughout the empire, Martin settled just outside the French city of Tours, where he devoted himself to living the monastic life. Although he lived a life of humility and poverty, the people who met him saw the hand of God at work through his prayers and healings.

After the death of the bishop of Tours, the people wanted Martin elected as bishop. Understandably, the bishops felt that his dirty and ragged appearance would hurt the image of the office of bishop. During the bishops' period of prayer, however, the reader read a passage from the Bible which had fallen open to the words, "Out of the mouths of babes and sucklings you have fashioned praise because of your foes, to silence the hostile and the vengeful" (Psalm 8:3). The bishops felt this was a sign from God, they decided to listen to the voices of the people, and Martin became bishop of Tours.

Martin tried to live a monastic life after being made bishop. He built a small room next to the cathedral where he devoted himself to the monastic life. Pastoral tasks eventually called him from his monastic solitude, but he did manage to incorporate many monastic ideals into his pastoral duties. Because of Martin, charitable and missionary works ordinarily performed by monks now became recognized as the mission of everyone in the Church.

In viewing monastic life as a fitting preparation for pastoral ministry, especially in the fulfillment of one's duties as a bishop, Martin contributed to the growing tendency of the age.

St. Ambrose (339–397)

Ambrose was the son of Christian parents, and his father held a position in service to the government. Thus, Ambrose had grown up familiar with public service. He attended the best Roman schools and was educated in literature and law. In time, he became governor of the city of Milan in Italy, which was the center of the Roman government at the time. The emperors resided at Milan when they were in the western part of the empire.

While Ambrose governed Milan, the Arian heresy still held influence over some of the emperors. When it appeared that an Arian would become bishop of Milan, the people rioted and refused to accept an Arian bishop. Ambrose, a staunch defender of the Church against Arianism, rushed to the cathedral with an armed guard and calmed the crowds.

As he firmly stood his ground against an Arian bishop, someone shouted out, "Ambrose for bishop!" The crowd began to chant his name, and Ambrose, who was not yet baptized, panicked. He tried to refuse and even flee, but eventually he succumbed to the will of the people. Ambrose was baptized, confirmed, and celebrated his first Eucharist. Then he was ordained a priest and a bishop.

Ambrose dedicated himself totally to his new charge, as he had dedicated himself to being governor. He studied, taught, preached, and ruled with a new determination. His background as a statesman later helped him in his dealings with the government.

Church and State

To fulfill his role as bishop, Ambrose embraced an intensive study of the Scriptures and theology. His intelligence permitted him not only to grasp his subject clearly, but it led him to compose many creative essays on theology. The Church still uses some of these today.

POINTS TO PONDER

Many centuries after Martin's death, a half cloak, which the people claimed came from Martin, was kept in a small church. The word for cloak was capella, and people referred to the little church by the name of capella, or later as the chapel. From this cloak, we have the origin of the word chapel. Monks who served there became known as chaplains.

St. Ambrose

... go, sell what you own, and give the money to the poor, and you will have treasure in heaven; then come follow me.

Mark 10:21, NRSV

Ambrose became a fearless bishop, confronting the emperors when they supported any issue harmful to the Church. For example, when an Arian emperor attempted to impose an Arian bishop on the cathedral of Milan, Ambrose, again with the support of the people, defied the emperor. Ambrose courageously insisted on a principle which has remained firm since his day: "The emperor is within the Church, not above the Church."

Ambrose and Emperor Theodosius apparently had many occasions to meet. They became friends, but neither of them would easily submit to the other. Ambrose had strong feelings about his role as bishop, and Theodosius, with a quick temper, had equally strong feelings regarding his role as emperor in relation to the Church.

Theodosius's quick temper led him to order the troops at Thessalonica to massacre thousands of the rebellious people who had killed some government officials. Viewing the emperor's order as mass murder, Ambrose begged the emperor to reconsider his order. Although Theodosius did reconsider his order, his recall of it did not travel from Milan to Thessalonica before the troops had slaughtered several hundred people.

Ambrose reacted strongly to the massacre. He surprised the emperor by excommunicating him, thus denying him the sacraments. Theodosius at first defied Ambrose's excommunication, but he eventually relented and yielded. After he performed a public penance, Theodosius was received back into communion with the Church by Ambrose. Later, when Ambrose preached at the emperor's funeral, he spoke admirably of the emperor's willingness to humble himself before the discipline of the Church.

Through his courage and deep faith, Ambrose was able to establish limits of the rule of the emperor. He demonstrated that the emperor had no right to rule the Church as though it were simply a civil organization. The conflict between Ambrose and Theodosius concerning the role of the Church would continue down through history as popes and national leaders entered into numberless conflicts between church and state.

St. John Chrysostom (349–407)

John had already proven himself an able lawyer when, at the age of twenty-three, he accepted Baptism as a Christian. After his Baptism, Chrysostom decided to become a monk, but he had to rethink his decision when he recognized his mother's need for his support. Chrysostom responded by turning his home into a monastery. After his mother's death, he joined a group of monks in Syria.

After six grueling years of living an ascetical life as a monk, John's health began to deteriorate, and he had to return to Antioch where he was later ordained a deacon, and then a presbyter. John immersed himself in his pastoral duties, especially into his preaching. Due to his wide education in philosophy and preaching, he became a highly acclaimed educator and preacher.

John became famous in Antioch as a saintly preacher and pastor. The emperor then ordered the bishops to take John to Constantinople and make him bishop of that capital city. The authorities, fearing that the people of Antioch would revolt if they discovered they were losing this famous pastor, forcefully and secretly whisked him away from the city.

Although some of the leaders of Constantinople had influenced the emperor in his choice of John as bishop of the capital, John soon antagonized many people in leadership position by denouncing the mire of luxury which infiltrated the city. He reformed the clergy by calling them to dedicate their lives to all the people, the poor as well as the rich. He sold valuable items from the bishop's home to help the poor and ordered the clergy to do the same. The common people rallied to this new bishop, but many in the wealthy class turned against him.

When a group of people fled from the cruelty of a close advisor to the emperor, they sought asylum in Saint Sophia's church, the largest Christian church of the capital city and of the world. As bishop, Chrysostom controlled the church and forbade the emperor's closest adviser from forcing the refugees out of the church. The emperor's advisor threatened the bishop with his powerful army, but John's firm preaching drew the multitude and the emperor to his support.

When the emperor's advisor lost power, the mob turned on him, and ironically he fled to Saint Sophia for safety. John protected the advisor's right of asylum, as he had earlier protected the people against the same man's armies. One night, the advisor to the emperor tried to sneak away, but the crowd caught and killed him.

Chrysostom and the Emperor

The emperor's wife, Acadia had a growing hatred for John's preaching, especially since he preached against the foolishness and selfishness of the rich. Acadia convinced a small group of bishops to renounce John and convinced the emperor to exile him from the city. A larger group of bishops and presbyters, along with a large number of the population, offered their support to John, but he refused to accept it. Not wishing to cause a riot, he quietly went into exile.

After an earthquake, which was taken as a sign of God's wrath, and a threatening gathering of the people of the city, the emperor allowed John to return. A few months later, the emperor had him exiled again to a remote village. John went quietly, but he wrote letters which incited the pope and a number of other religious leaders against the emperor.

The emperor ordered his soldiers to take John to the cold shores of the Black Sea. John did not withstand the grueling trip. Recognizing that he had done all he could to give glory to God through his life, he accepted his death.

Because of John's great power of preaching, two centuries after his death, writers gave him the name Chrysostom, which means *golden mouth*. He is better known by this name today than by his family name. In addition to his work as a pastor and the power of his preaching, he is also famous for his insightful writings on topics related to Scripture and theology. John Chrysostom, like Ambrose, developed his courageous attitudes while in the monastic life. He used these attitudes as he bravely faced the power of the government and defended the message of the Church.

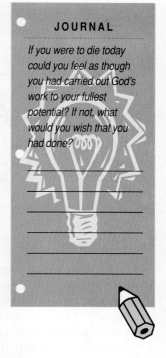

JOURNAL

If you were to die today could you feel as though you had carried out God's work to your fullest potential? If not, what would you wish that you had done?

CLIPBOARD

1. While many bishops today are chosen from monastic backgrounds, others bishops are chosen from a pastoral background. Why is a pastoral background (especially work in parishes) a good preparation for bishops?

2. How does the election of Ambrose as bishop differ from the choosing of bishops today?

3. What can we learn from the conflict between Ambrose and Theodosius about the role of the state and the church in the world?

The Educated Monks

The Christian Times

Fifth Century   **Vol. 5   No. 1**

Jerome Attacks Augustine

Reports, from our religious editor's desk, indicate that Jerome has chosen to ignore a letter from Augustine which is critical of Jerome's translation of the Bible into Latin.

Augustine, who had proven himself an able scholar in his works such as *The Confessions* and *The City of God,* disagrees with Jerome's expressed intention of using both the Hebrew and the Greek Bible as a source for his translation of the Bible into Latin.

Jerome, who has often proven himself a scathing critic of his opponents, implied that Augustine was competent in many areas, but

he had no business interfering in the area of scriptural translations.

In recent months, Jerome used Augustine's arguments against Pelagianism to refute those who deny the necessity of God's grace in performing good acts.

Jerome also seems to recognize that Augustine has offered some strong arguments against the Donatists when he stated that the minister of a sacrament can validly confer a sacrament, even when the minister is in sin.

Jerome, who has established a monastery and convent with the help of the saintly Paula, often grates on his opponents with his

quick, sharp, and insulting tongue. He has dedicated himself to Christ with the same intensity he uses in refuting his enemies.

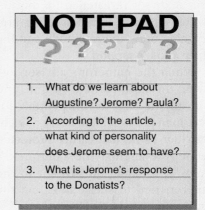

NOTEPAD

1. What do we learn about Augustine? Jerome? Paula?

2. According to the article, what kind of personality does Jerome seem to have?

3. What is Jerome's response to the Donatists?

POINTS TO PONDER

Besides providing pastors and scholars for the Church, the monastic life also provided a foundation for many of the theological writers of the Church. These writings not only confronted the major heresies of the day, but they also provided theological and scriptural foundations for the future. St. Augustine and St. Ambrose were two such men.

The Rest of the Story

St. Augustine (354–430)

Augustine was the son of a Christian mother named Monica and a non-Christian father named Patricius. Like Ambrose, Augustine had a keen intelligence, which enabled him to attend school in the best Roman tradition, far from any real Christian learning. At sixteen, he changed schools and reveled in a life filled with sexual pleasures and heavy drinking and gambling. Like others of his day, Augustine took a mistress and eventually had a son by her.

After returning to school and finishing his studies, Augustine became a renowned teacher of literature and taught at major schools within the empire. His teaching career eventually brought him to a prestigious school in Milan, where he moved with his mistress and son. At Milan, Augustine met Ambrose who challenged him to turn his life over to God.

A few years before his conversion, Augustine began to experience an emptiness in his life. Shortly after he arrived at

Milan, he joined a group which followed the **Manichaeism** heresy.

Manichaeism believed that one god created the good, which is the spiritual, and a second god created the evil, which is the material world. Manichaeism viewed sin as nearly unavoidable, and offered the only solution as an avoidance of everything offering pleasure. This included those things that Christianity considers acceptable and good, such as marriage, and the bearing of children. It also taught that those unable to avoid things offering pleasure might as well indulge in all forms of pleasure, since they were already sinful.

Finding little comfort in Manichaeism, Augustine studied the Greek philosopher, Plato, who claimed that human beings have a spiritual, as well as, a physical side to their existence. Plato emphasized the role of the spiritual life in human existence, something far different from many other philosophers of ancient Greece, who emphasized the material world and the seeking of fulfillment in pleasure.

Augustine's study of Plato had a great influence on his conversion and his later writings. In Christianity, he found strong belief in the spiritual side of one's life. He firmly believed that the one true God wanted humans to develop the spiritual side as well as the physical side of their nature.

According to Augustine, his real conversion of heart took place when he heard some children calling out, "Take and read." As though in response to this call, Augustine picked up his Bible and turned to a passage in Paul which directs the Romans to put aside earthly pleasures and jealousies and to live in union with Jesus Christ (Romans 13:13–14; 14:1). Augustine accepted these words as a directive from God for his own life.

After his baptism, Augustine resigned his teaching position, left his mistress and child, and went to North Africa, where he lived a life of poverty and prayer as a monk. At the urging of his followers, he was ordained and five years later became bishop of Hippo. For the next thirty-five years, he not only served as bishop of Hippo, but he confronted many heresies of his period and wrote many treatises which have had a lasting effect on Christian theology.

Donatism

Since Augustine was bishop of Hippo, in North Africa, he was living close to the area where the **Donatist heresy** had originated and had not yet been totally rejected. At Carthage in North Africa, some bishops had chosen Donatus in place of a bishop ordained by a one-time unworthy bishop. The pressing question of the Donatists centered on the worthiness of a minister in the celebration of a sacrament. Could an unworthy minister celebrate a valid sacrament?

Augustine taught that the validity of a sacrament does not depend on the worthiness of the minister. He explained that one obvious reason for the answer comes from the goodness of God and the weakness of human beings. If the validity of a sacrament depends on the worthiness of a minister, who is human then the validity of a Sacrament would almost always be in question.

Pelagianism

Pelagius, a British monk, who lived near Augustine, proposed the belief that human beings could secure salvation through the unaided power of their own will and personal toil. He denied the effects of original sin on human nature and rejected the teaching that a person needed any special help from God in achieving salvation. The heresy initiated by Pelagius received the name **Pelagianism** after its originator.

Pelagius noted that people had become careless in their practice of faith and morals, and he wanted to stress individual responsibility in overcoming

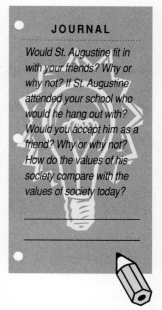

JOURNAL

Would St. Augustine fit in with your friends? Why or why not? If St. Augustine attended your school who would he hang out with? Would you accept him as a friend? Why or why not? How do the values of his society compare with the values of society today?

_____

_____

L et us live honorably as in the day, not in reveling and drunkenness, not in debauchery and licentiousness, not in quarreling and jealousy.
Romans 13:13–14, NRSV

JOURNAL

How can we apply St. Augustine's conversion to our own lives?

sin. He especially wanted to oppose those who denied that they could overcome sin in their lives. He denied that people needed God's help to avoid sin. In an effort to call people to personal responsibility, Pelagius rejected the need for God's help and placed total responsibility on the individual.

As Pelagianism spread, Augustine became the chief opponent of the heresy, noting that it not only denied the effects of original sin on human nature, but it also denied the need of God's grace in overcoming evil and sin. Augustine wrote a treatise on the grace of God.

Augustine's teaching on original sin centered on the loss of God's blessings (grace) through the sin of Adam and Eve. The effects of this sin were passed on to each human being and instilled in each person as a tendency to sin. Because of this sin, human beings need God's help, gained through Jesus Christ, in overcoming sin and their sinful tendencies. This help comes in the form of grace, i.e., God's special blessing regained through Jesus Christ. Without this help, the world would have many more experiences of sin.

Although Pelagius's teachings were condemned in North Africa, they still reached Palestine where Jerome attacked them. They also reached Rome where Pope Innocent immediately condemned them. Celestius, a lawyer and friend of Pelagius, however, was able to convince Pope Innocent's successor, Pope Zosimus, to reconsider the Church's stance against Pelagianism. At the council of Carthage in 418, over two hundred bishops gathered. They were able to convince Pope Zosimus of the heresies present in Pelagianism. Nine canons, based on St. Augustine's doctrine of original sin, denounced Pelagianism. After the Council, the pope released a "Brief Statement of Faith," reversing his original thoughts concerning Pelagianism, reiterating Pope Innocent's position. Pelagius subsequently disappeared from history,

although Celestius continued to advocate his heresies with his followers. Although, Pelagianism was once again condemned by the Council of Ephesus in 431, it endured in parts of the West, most notably in Britain and Gaul.

Writings of Augustine

Augustine wrote a number of essays and books offering spiritual commentaries and opinions on various topics. He wrote scriptural commentaries on topics such as the Trinity and personal reflections. Many of his writings are still read today.

One of St. Augustine's great literary achievements, *Confessions*, is a type of spiritual autobiography. The book was written as a prayer to God, expressing how God led him along a difficult and painful path into the faith. The book is an outstanding spiritual work and a literary achievement. It reflects on St. Augustine's sinful youth and details his struggle to find God.

In the *Confessions*, Augustine talks about his mother, Monica, and her mystical insights. She apparently could have a sharp tongue when needed and a stubborn temperament. She spent many years praying for Augustine, who found her a nuisance during his years of searching for meaning in his life.

Once, when Augustine tried to elude her and traveled to Milan alone, she caught up with him. At this time, she found that he no longer practiced beliefs that hindered him from accepting Christianity.

From that period in Milan onwards, Augustine and Monica became close companions, sharing their deep religious experiences. Monica met Ambrose, who directed her spiritually and had a part in the conversion of Augustine. When Ambrose baptized Augustine, Monica joyfully witnessed the event. Augustine credited his conversion to Monica's persistent prayers for him. She spent her last years believing that she had accomplished her mission in life.

In the Spotlight

St. Monica, probably born in Thagaste, was raised a Christian and married a local official named Patricius. During the course of their marriage, they bore three children, the eldest being Augustine.

St. Monica was greatly upset and concerned about Augustine's contempt for Christianity, and his affair with an unknown woman. She prayed earnestly for his conversion, finding solace in the advice of a clergyman to whom she had confided her troubles, "It is impossible that the son of so many tears will be lost."

Monica followed her son on his journey to Rome, first to the Eternal City, and then Milan. It was in Milan where they came under St. Ambrose's influence. Her son's conversion brought her great joy and peace, and she retired to Cassiciacum. She, later, decided to return to Africa and died during the journey, in Ostia. St. Augustine recorded many of his dialogues with her.

MAKE REMEMBRANCE

In the year 410, Rome fell to invaders, and some non-Christians claimed that Rome had fallen because of the rejection of the ancient gods and the turn to Christianity. Augustine wrote *The City of God* in response to these accusations. Augustine taught that there are two cities, the city of God and the earthly city. From our viewpoint in human history, these two cities seem to be mingled with each other, but, according to Augustine, there is an irreconcilable difference between them.

Augustine taught that, in the end, only the city of God will remain. Meanwhile, nations and kingdoms are transient earthly cities built on self-love. No matter how powerful they are now, they will perish. God allowed Rome and its empire to flourish, but now that its purpose had been fulfilled, God let Rome be destroyed to follow the destiny of all human kingdoms.

St. Jerome (348–420)

As Latin became the common language of the empire, a need arose for a translation of the Bible into the Latin language. Such a work demanded a man of genius and dedication. Jerome was that man, but his coarse personality almost clouded his remarkable contribution to Church history.

JOURNAL

What aspects of your personality get in the way? How do you deal with these personality traits?

He had a great love for classical Greek and devoted himself to the study of Scripture and Christian literature. In his desire to dedicate himself to Christ, he became a monk. But because of the rigorous demands of his life as a monk and his own self-inflicted sacrifices, Jerome chose to leave his life as a monk within three years. The experiences he had as a monk, however, had a deep effect on his future attitudes.

Jerome eventually went to Constantinople to continue his studies, and then went to Rome, where he served as a secretary to the pope. Although he lived a life fully dedicated to Christ, Jerome was an austere person who made rigid demands on himself and others. He was quick tempered and brusque with others. Whether debating with dignitaries or the saintly, he had no difficulty insulting and scolding them.

When Jerome moved to Rome, he met some saintly and scholarly women, among them was the sister of Ambrose. These women had a great love for learning, especially for the study of Greek and Hebrew, the languages of the Scriptures. Years later, Jerome and one of the women, Paula, established two monasteries in Palestine, one for women and the other for men. They demanded less severity from the monks and nuns in their monastery and convent. These monks and nuns dedicated themselves to praying and learning.

In addition to leading the monks in his own monastery, Jerome taught Hebrew and Greek to Paula and her nuns. These nuns proved to be a great support and balance for Jerome. They were able to confront him about his terrible temper and insulting brusqueness, without losing his friendship.

The Latin Vulgate

Jerome's greatest contribution to the Church was his translation of the Bible into Latin. Many people believed that the Greek translation of the Bible, known as the Septuagint, was the unchangeable translation. Jerome defied them by choosing to translate a large part of the Bible that had originally been written in Hebrew from that original language. Many people became angry that their favorite texts sounded different. The Church has encountered, and still encounters, similar conflicts anytime a new, official translation has appeared.

Even the great scholar Augustine found fault with Jerome's desire to translate the Bible from the Hebrew. Despite his great learning, Augustine did not have the insight of Jerome when it came to translating the Scriptures. He believed that the Scriptures should be translated from the Greek Septuagint and not from the Hebrew.

Augustine wrote to Jerome, chiding him on his arrogance in believing he could find new insights in the Hebrew words, which previous translators missed and urged him not to make a translation of the Scriptures from the Hebrew. Although Jerome would later show his approval of Augustine's scholarship in other areas of theology, he felt that Augustine did not understand fully what he was talking about when it came to translating the Scriptures.

For fifteen years, Jerome and his students translated the Bible from the original Greek and Hebrew into Latin. Almost ten centuries later, Jerome's translation acquired the name, *The Latin Vulgate*. In addition to this exceptional work, Jerome added commentaries on many books of the Hebrew Scriptures. He also dedicated his energies to refuting views of other theologians and heretics of his own day. Unfortunately, Jerome's difficult personality hindered many of his contemporaries from recognizing his genius and saintliness.

CLIPBOARD

1. Write a paragraph about a famous person who has had a complete turnaround, after having lived a wild lifestyle. In your paragraph compare and contrast the person with St. Augustine.

2. Today we have an abundance of self-help books telling us how to improve our lives. Many of these books say nothing about the need for prayer or spiritual guidance in personal development. In light of the Pelagian heresy, what do you think St. Augustine would say about these books? Would you agree with him? Why or why not?

3. The Church recognizes Jerome as a saint. Why do you think the Church would declare someone with such an insulting and quick temper a saint?

JOURNAL

Today, there are many versions of the Bible. What version do you prefer? Why? How does it differ from other versions?

_____

_____

_____

_____

_____

REVIEWING THE ERA

• **300**

REIGN OF CONSTANTIUS. Constantius, Constantine's son, followed Constantine in his favoring of Christianity.

ST. ANTHONY OF EGYPT. Anthony went off into the desert to live a life of asceticism. Others eventually followed him. Monasticism became a popular form of life for those wishing to flee the luxury given some Christians, in their newly accepted roles in the empire.

ST. PACHOMIUS. Pachomius began a life known as cenobian monasticism, which was a monastic life lived in community.

• **350**

JULIAN THE APOSTATE. Julian was a nephew of Constantine who became emperor and persecuted Christians.

EMPEROR GRATIAN. Gratian rejected the pagan title of Supreme Pontiff, thus ending any visible link between the emperor and paganism.

THEODOSIUS I. Theodosius became emperor in 379, and made Christianity the official religion of the empire.

ST. BASIL. Basil became known for his monastic rule, although he really did not author a set of rules. His rules were actually a collection of responses he made to queries concerning monastic life. He led a monastic community and contributed many writings on spirituality and theology to the history of the Church.

ST. MARTIN OF TOURS. Martin brought monasticism to the West. His foundations as a monk made him an exemplary bishop.

ST. AMBROSE. Ambrose was a monk who became a great statesman and then a bishop by the popular acclamation of the people. He excommunicated Emperor Theodosius I for his massacre of a large number of innocent people. The emperor had to seek forgiveness from Ambrose. This was an early confrontation concerning the separation of the powers of the church and state.

ST. JOHN CHRYSOSTOM. John was an eloquent speaker and theologian who became bishop of Milan and later faced exile because of his preaching against the luxuries of the emperor and his wife. His early life as a monk shaped his dedication and courage in later life.

• **400**

ST. JEROME. Jerome had a highly intense personality. He translated the Greek and Hebrew Scriptures into the Latin translation of the Bible known as the Latin Vulgate, which was used as an official translation by the Church for many centuries. He was a monk who founded a monastery and had the support and guidance of a nun named Paula.

ST. AUGUSTINE. Augustine has had a great influence on the theology of the Church from his own time to the present. He shared his soul in his reflections on his sinful life and conversion in his *Confessions*, and he explained the struggle between the city of God and the earthly city in his *City of God*. He wrote treatises against Donatism and Pelagianism.

KEY TERMS

Apostate

Hermit

Monasticism

Asceticism

Anchorites

Semi-anchorite

Abbot

Manichaeism

Donatist heresy

Pelagianism

A Voice from the Past

This week in your article you are going to highlight some of the important saints from Catholic history. Relay to your writers what you have learned about the saints in this chapter, and show how their contributions to the Church still affect the Catholic Church. Finally, challenge your readers to use their gifts and talents in the Church today.

Then and Now

The Monastic movement and the saints it produced had a deep effect on the Church in the fourth and fifth centuries. Monks provided saints to lead the Church and to challenge leaders attempting to make decisions in Church matters. It was a time when major theologians helped in the fight against heresies. They explained the faith more clearly to the people of their own age.

Today monasticism lives on. In a world which extols the lives of the rich and famous, monks today continue to dedicate themselves to a simple life of prayer, study, and work. The Church today can also boast of some outstanding theologians who continue to make use of discoveries in many sciences to explain our faith to the people of our age.

NEWS IN REVIEW

1. Why is Emperor Julian known as the Apostate, while Theodosius who also sinned is not?

2. What were the differences between Anthony's life in the desert and the monastic life established by Pachomius?

3. What contributions did St. Macrina make to the Church?

4. How did St. Basil's introduction of scholarly pursuit help the future of monasticism and the Church?

5. What does Martin of Tours teach us about monasticism? How did the word chapel originate with him?

6. What did Ambrose do to stress the role of the Church in the time of the Roman emperors?

7. Give a short account of the accomplishments of St. Augustine.

8. How does Augustine's *City of God* explain the sacking of Rome in the early fifth century?

9. What was the *Latin Vulgate*, and why did some people want to reject it?

10. Why is it surprising to find that the Church recognizes Jerome as a saint?

chapter six

Light and Darkness

If we were living at the beginning of the fifth century, we would recall the great beginnings of the monastic movement. We would be telling stories of the monks who went into the desert to pray as well as stories of a new group of spiritual leaders, whose spirituality led them to become great scholars and defenders of the faith. We would be conscious that we were living in a context of history dominated by monasteries and monks.

The men religious are still an important part of the Christian Community.

The Development of the Papacy

The Christian Times

Fifth Century   Vol. 5   No. 2

Pope Leo the Great Changes Papacy

The people of the world mourn the loss of Pope Leo I, who has changed the image of the papacy forever. Before Leo's election as pope, a large number of people did not recognize the Bishop of Rome as the leader of the Church. Leo leaves the world with no doubt that the pope is indeed the visible head of the Church.

Leo established his power as pope, by becoming the first pope to head an ecumenical council. The bishops at the Council of Chalcedon echoed his teachings on Jesus being both human and divine. When he rejected the city of Constantinople in the East as equal to Rome, many people were disgruntled, but the decision strengthened his place as the head of Christianity.

On the political level, Leo courageously met with Attila the Hun and King Gaiseric, the leader of the Vandals. His influence over these two powerful armies increased his strength as a temporal as well as a spiritual leader.

Leo strongly supported the monastic movement and urged monks to become missionaries to non-Christian lands. He favored monks like St. Patrick who left England to convert Ireland.

The world recognizes that because of Leo, the papacy will never be the same. He has raised this office to one of high prestige.

NOTEPAD

? ? ? ? ?

1. What did you learn about Pope Leo? St. Patrick? Attila the Hun?
2. What did you learn about the papacy in this article?
3. What evidence does this reporter cite in giving Pope Leo credit for visibly establishing the pope as the head of the Church?
4. What important changes were happening in the Roman Empire at this time?

The Rest of the Story

With the disintegration of the empire, civilization needed new leaders to protect the development of civilization against the Germanic migrations. The Church responded to this need.

Lines Drawn Between the East and the West

Shortly after the beginning of the fifth century, the mighty Roman Empire was showing signs of collapse. The emperor lived in Constantinople in the East, far from Rome and even farther from the western frontiers of the empire which were under siege by various invading tribes from the north. The split between the East, with its capital at Constantinople, and the West, with its capital at Rome, was becoming wider.

The original reasons for dividing the empire were for the sake of administering such a large expanse of land. Today, with our means for instant communication, it's hard to imagine communication that took months or years in this vast empire. After Constantine united the kingdom under one emperor, emperors attempted to keep the rule of the entire empire under the power of the single emperor. The political and military situation of the empire would not permit this.

In time, there were again two emperors, one in the East and one in the West. The emperors in the East believed that they were the true emperors of the whole Roman Empire, and they hoped that one day they would unite the empires of the East and the West under their leadership.

In 410, with weak emperors ruling in the West, Germanic tribes invaded and captured Rome. The emperor in the East refused to endanger his own position by helping the situation in the West. As a result of the disintegration of the political power of the weak emperor in the West, the Church emerged as the unifying force in the West. Through its saints and popes, the Church had a great effect on history when the empire gave way to the Germanic migrations.

St. Patrick (390–461)

One of the major influences in spreading the faith, in the midst of the disintegrating empire, was the work of the monks who became missionaries to lands that had previously not been Christianized. These monks brought the word of Christ and education to the people. One such monk was St. Patrick.

Patrick's story begins in the early part of the fifth century, when invaders from Ireland captured him in his homeland of Britain and carried him off to Ireland, where he worked as a slave for six years. By the time Patrick had escaped from his slavery in Ireland, he had learned some of the customs, religious practices, superstitions, and language of the tribes of Ireland.

Patrick went to Gaul and lived there many years as a monk. He went from Gaul to England where he became an ordained priest. He then begged his superiors to send him to Ireland to convert to Christianity the people who once held him in slavery. Very few of the people of Ireland had converted to Christianity at the time.

St. Patrick

After being made a bishop, he traveled to Ireland and established a number of monasteries. These monasteries became the centers of Christianity wherever he had established them. Using this method of spreading the Christian faith, by establishing monasteries as centers of communities, Patrick and his successors were able to convert most of the inhabitants of Ireland to Christianity. Patrick's ministry in Ireland had a major effect on the spread of Christianity in that land and eventually throughout other parts of the world.

KEY TERMS

Pope: a word meaning father; originally used as a title of respect for bishops and presbyters; now the exclusive title of the bishop of Rome.

Supreme Pontiff: the title that Leo the Great chose for the papacy; at one time it was the title used to designate the head of the pre-Christian religion in Rome.

Monophysitism: a heresy which taught that Jesus was only divine, and not human.

Following the holy Fathers, we unanimously teach and confess one and the same Son, our Lord Jesus Christ: the same perfect in divinity and perfect in humanity, the same truly God and truly man, composed of rational soul and body; consubstantial with the Father as to his divinity and consubstantial with us as to his humanity; "like us in all things but sin."

Catechism of the Catholic Church, # 467

Because Patrick's ministry had such miraculous results, many legends became mixed with facts of his missionary activity, and it became difficult to separate the two. Stories abounded from one village to the next and grew into larger legends after he died. In reality, he was a great man, dedicated to spreading God's word and educating the people he learned to love.

Pope Leo the Great (440–461)

While the monks worked to evangelize and educate in far-flung lands, the pope was becoming a new force in the empire. Previously, Christians respected the pope, but the position of the bishop of Rome did not have the prestige it was to have at the end of the fifth century.

The term **pope** was originally a title of respect given to important bishops and even to presbyters. It means "father" and was used not only for the bishop of Rome, but for all bishops, especially in the East. A Spanish council was apparently the first to use the term pope in reference to the bishop of Rome in the year 400. Gradually, the use of the term pope became limited to the bishop of Rome who was recognized as the successor of Peter the Apostle.

Prior to the papacy of Pope Leo I, there were many debates about the authority of the pope in the Church. In the West, Christians strongly supported the idea that the bishop of Rome, as a successor of Peter, held the highest place in the Church. At the Council of Chalcedon, some bishops wanted to pass a statement that Rome and Constantinople were equal in dignity. Fearing that such a proposal would infer that the patriarch of Constantinople was equal to the pope, Pope Leo rejected this proposal.

The real power of the Roman bishop as pope over the whole Church became more fully realized under Leo, whom history later called Leo the Great. Leo had no doubt that the pope held a position equal to none in the Church, and he chose the title of **Supreme Pontiff** for the papacy, a title once used to designate the head of the pre-Christian religion in Rome. Popes after Leo continued to use the title of Supreme Pontiff.

Theological Crises

Shortly before Leo I became pope in 440, a new form of heresy took hold in the empire, a heresy which was the opposite of Arianism. The heresy, known as **Monophysitism**, taught that Jesus' divinity absorbed his humanness so that he had only one nature, which was divine. While Arianism denied the divinity of Jesus, this new heresy denied that Jesus was human.

When a number of people began to accept the heresy that Jesus Christ had a divine nature, but not a human nature, the emperor became concerned and suggested a council to settle the issue. Leo convened the Council of Chalcedon in 451 and sent two delegates to represent him at the council. This was the first time a pope actually presided over an ecumenical council, although he did so through two representatives.

In a public letter, called Leo's Tome, the pope had insisted that Jesus Christ was both human and divine. When the bishops at the Council of Chalcedon declared that Jesus Christ was both human and divine, they proclaimed, "Peter has spoken through Leo." This proclamation was agreeable to those who believed that the pope, as bishop of Rome and successor of Peter, was the visible head of the Church.

Political Crises

One of Leo's major political challenges came when there was an obvious need for a leader to defend Rome against Germanic invaders. By the middle of the fifth century, western leaders had become too weak to protect the people against more powerful armies coming across the borders of the empire. Since the powerful emperor of the East had no interest in helping Rome with its problems, the people of Rome braced themselves for further anguish as powerful forces gathered at its borders. They had already suffered during the sack of Rome in 410, and now they feared more attacks on their city.

In 452, one powerful group of invaders, known as the Huns, stormed through northern areas in Italy and stood ready to sack Rome itself. With no army available for support, Leo courageously traveled unarmed to meet with Attila, the leader of the barbarian Huns. No one knows what happened when Leo and Attila talked, but after the meeting, Attila agreed not to invade Rome.

Three years later, Leo had to face another invading army, the Vandals. They had already overtaken parts of Africa and were planning to pillage Rome. Leo again journeyed unarmed to meet the Vandal leader, Geiseric, hoping to deter him from attacking Rome. Although Leo could not persuade the Vandals not to plunder the wealth and people of Rome, he persuaded them not to burn the city and not to kill the entire population.

After his successful meeting with Attila the Hun, Leo became an immediate champion and hero to the inhabitants of Rome. They saw him as the powerful and visible agent of God before the enemy. When Leo negotiated a partial peace with the Vandals, his stature grew in the eyes of the people so that many saw him as a new and awe-inspiring leader.

A New Recognition

Leo's genius and power of leadership earned him the title Leo the Great. Leo believed that the pope was the principal leader, teacher, and judge in the Church. He not only spoke about the authority of the papacy, he lived it by making decisions for the Church throughout the empire. He also broadened the role of the pope in political matters by meeting with the leaders of invading Germanic groups.

When Leo the Great died, he left behind a new image of the papacy. The Christian world now had a greater regard for the bishop of Rome and saw him as the true successor of Peter and the visible head of the Church. Leo the Great, in shaping the attitudes toward the papacy in his own day, also helped establish the role of pope in our present era, as the visible head of the Church.

JOURNAL

How do you think the Church would be different today if it did not have one main leader in Rome?

CLIPBOARD

1. Should popes today take the same role in the political lives of the people, as Leo the Great did?

2. How does the role of our present pope compare with that of Leo the Great in making spiritual decisions for the Church?

3. How do the events of Leo the Great's times relate to the issues of our own age?

Shifts in the Roman Empire

The Christian Times

Sixth Century   **Vol. 6   No. 1**

Monks Spreading the Faith

A new hope for civilization in the western empire came earlier this year from an unexpected source. Monks from Ireland are flooding the empire with the Word of God. These monks, along with others who have kept civilization alive through learning, are our hope for the future.

Reports from the monasteries note that most of these monks follow a rule written by a Benedict of Nursia. This rule has found its way into monasteries in Germany, France, and other areas.

Monasticism has a long history, but the monks seem to have a new mission. They no longer remain enclosed in their monasteries, but travel instead to every land conceivable.

Rumor has it that Clovis, the king of the Franks, attributes his conversion to monks. Although Clovis has had many military triumphs, he readily admits that Christianity has been the most powerful force for unity in his kingdom. His sons, although not as strong as Clovis, continue to practice Christianity.

Emperor Justinian will most likely be calling on the monks in his efforts to unite the empire under Christianity. He believes that he has a right to control the Church with as much authority as he controls the empire.

NOTEPAD

? ? ? ?

1. What did you learn about Clovis? Justinian?

2. What does the article tell us about the value of monasticism?

3. To what does Clovis attribute the unity in his kingdom?

4. Why do you think many monks moved from life in the monastery to missionary work?

The Rest of the Story

With the fall of the last emperor of the West in 476, Germanic chieftains ruled in the name of the eastern emperor. One of these leaders was Theodoric, who took over the rule of Italy around the beginning of the sixth century. He managed to keep peace between the barbarian Goths and the Italians, despite their mutual dislike for each other.

Since the Italians were allied to the Church of Rome, the Northerners, including Theodoric himself, as Arians (Christians who believed that Jesus was human, but not divine), had to allow for religious tolerance. Theodoric realized that the Church alone offered the unity in Italy that he needed to keep the peace. His political wisdom often drove him to seek help from Catholic bishops in Italy. This led to a period of relative calm for Italy.

Clovis and the Franks (466–511)

Clovis followed the practice of his grandfather by uniting the different tribes known as the Franks into one powerful group. To the people of Gaul, who inhabited a large portion of present day France, the Franks were an uncivilized hoard from northern Europe that swept down into Gaul and began to capture land along the northern border of the empire. The Franks so thoroughly overran the northwestern portion of Europe that it eventually bore their name, becoming France.

Clovis was a non-Christian leader who was conquering a land dominated by Arians. He swept across Gaul, subduing one tribe after another. Although he learned about Christianity and married a Christian, he did not immediately accept the faith. Since he ruled a number of tribes and not a united nation, he needed some common ground such as religious beliefs to gain the support of the tribes living in Gaul. He believed that his profession of non-Christian leadership enabled him to enlist non-Christian soldiers.

In 496, Clovis faced a powerful enemy who threatened to destroy him. He promised the God of the Christians that he would accept Christianity if he won the battle. After a defeat of his enemy which he considered miraculous, Clovis declared that the Christian God had brought him to victory. As a result, he accepted baptism, and three thousand men in his army became Christian along with him.

By the time of his death, Clovis had subdued most of present-day France. Although his military forces were not as large as other armies in the West, he worked to build up his power by overpowering weaker armies and enlisting them in his forces. His success also came from the attitude of Christian bishops in Gaul. They abhorred Arianism and opened their gates for the army of Clovis, thus allowing him to overrun the supporters of Arianism.

Like other rulers before him, Clovis recognized the necessity of using religion to unify the tribes under his control. Since his conversion to Christianity, he forced these Christian beliefs on the tribes he conquered. With the support of the bishops of the area, he gained control over many areas of Church life, including the appointment of bishops. The control of the Frankish rulers over the Church became so strong that it would lead to a later conflict between the kings and the pope.

Emperor Justinian (527–565)

A little more than fifteen years after the death of Clovis, an emperor in the East, Justinian, dreamed of restoring the glory of the Roman Empire by reuniting the East and West. Since Germanic groups from the north had invaded the West and destroyed Rome in the early 400s, the West had lost its line of emperors. In order to bring the empire under a single emperor, Justinian had to battle the Germanic groups who had invaded the might of the western emperors.

In order to finance his armies for the battles ahead, Justinian imposed heavy taxes on the people of the eastern empire. His soldiers won a series of battles in the West, but the people of the East were becoming unhappy under his heavy taxation. He was also weakening the defenses in the East by sending his powerful armies to crush the Germanic groups in the West. With the armies away fighting in the West, Germanic tribes swept down from the north and seized large tracts of land in the eastern empire.

Besides the growing unrest of the people, Justinian also faced conflict with the Church. Like rulers before him, Justinian practiced **Caesero-Papism**, the custom of the emperor giving himself rights that belonged to the Church, especially those rights which belonged to the pope. He claimed the right to appoint and depose patriarchs and bishops, and to administer practical matters

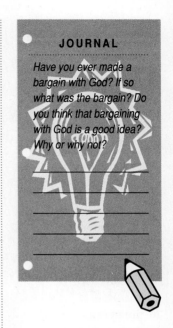

JOURNAL

Have you ever made a bargain with God? If so what was the bargain? Do you think that bargaining with God is a good idea? Why or why not?

KEY TERMS

Caesero-Papism: the custom of the emperor giving himself rights that belonged to the Church, especially those rights which belonged to the pope.

POINTS TO PONDER

Justinian built the magnificent Hagia Sophia (Holy Wisdom) church which stands as a masterpiece of Byzantine architecture. An earthquake had destroyed the previous church, and Justinian built the new monument as a symbol of the unity and harmony he hoped to accomplish between the East and the West.

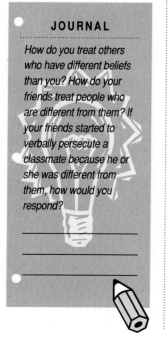

JOURNAL

How do you treat others who have different beliefs than you? How do your friends treat people who are different from them? If your friends started to verbally persecute a classmate because he or she was different from them, how would you respond?

_____

_____

_____

pertaining to the Church. Church leaders protested strongly against this practice of emperors interfering in Church matters.

In his desire to unite the empire, Justinian provided a set of rules, called a code. The word code comes from a Latin word which implies "ruler" or "guide." He commissioned a group of educated subjects to compile this code. When published, these laws became known as the **Justinian Code**. Although the code proposed to offer Christian directions for living one's daily life in the empire, it presented some practices which today would be clearly contrary to Christianity.

Persecution by Christians

Recognizing the value of an empire united under a single religion, Justinian attempted to crush all rebellious religious groups and to build his empire on Christianity. He weakened the power of pre-Christian religion by closing its powerful and popular school at Athens. He supported any attempt to bridle the influence of Jews and heretical groups within Christianity. Taking their cue from Justinian, Christian rulers made life difficult for the Jews living in their areas, often pressuring them to convert to Christianity.

At this time, Christians were forbidden by Church law to loan money for interest. Because the Jews could loan money and receive interest on their loan, many Christians borrowed money from them when they needed capitol. Despite this service provided by the Jews, many Christians still took part in torturing or killing them for the least or greediest of reasons. This period of persecution of the Jews hangs like a dark shadow over the history of Christianity.

After Justinian died, a series of weak emperors followed him, and the eastern empire, like that in the West, began to crumble. Within three years of Justinian's death, some Germanic tribes invaded the area we know today

as Italy and by the end of the century, these tribes had gained control of most of the country.

The Influence of Irish Monks

While the empire was falling apart on the temporal scene, missionaries continued to bring hope to Christianity in the East as they moved beyond the eastern boundaries of the Roman Empire to convert people as far away as Russia. The monks especially had a significant effect on the religious history of the world.

Fifty years after the death of St. Patrick, monasteries had spread rapidly throughout the Irish countryside, significantly linking the Church of Ireland to monastic spirituality. For a number of centuries, most of the Irish saints came from monastic life.

St. Brigid (453–525) became as famous to many in Ireland as had St. Patrick. She was a nun who founded monasteries and performed a number of miraculous deeds throughout the country. She founded a **double monastery**, which was a monastery for both men and women. Thousands of women dedicated themselves to the monastic life in monasteries linked with that of St. Brigid.

The Irish monks and nuns gained a love and respect for learning from their culture and carried it into the monasteries. Irish monasticism placed great emphasis on spiritual literature, although they did not ignore a study of significant secular writings. Along with their love for learning, the Irish monasteries also became known for the austere life led by the monks and nuns. This way of life reflected many of the acts of sacrifice and deprivation followed by the early hermits of the desert.

A major contribution of Irish monasticism consisted in missionary endeavors. Traveling throughout the world to spread the message of Christianity, even to unchartered and unexplored areas of the world, they not only brought Christianity with them, but

In the Spotlight

St. Brigid (The Mary of the Gael) was born into a peasant family near Dundalk in Ireland. Her mother, a slave woman, and her father, a nobleman, were both baptized by St. Patrick.

She became a nun at an early age, under the direction of the Bishop of St. Mel of Armagh. The king of Leinster became so impressed with her that he gave her a parcel of land in Kildaire, where she established the first convent of Ireland. The foundation was a double monastery, with Brigid as abbess of the convent, and in time it became the center for Irish spirituality and learning for the community of Kildaire. Brigid is also credited with founding a school of art in that same community.

In her miracle stories many find the qualities of compassion, charity, and strength. Some of the stories emphasize the theme of multiplication of food. She is known for giving butter to the poor, changing her bath-water into beer to satisfy the thirst of unexpected clerical visitors, and having her cows produce milk three times a day, to enable some bishops to have enough to drink.

There is also a legend that Bishop Ibor had a vision which personified St. Brigid as the Blessed Virgin, thus she is often called 'Mary of the Gael.'

Brigid died at Kildare and was buried there, but her relics were reburied at Downpatrick, along with those of St. Patrick, during invasions by the Danes. Place names and churches throughout Britain testify to the extent of her cult, most notable St. Bride's Bay in Dyfed, Wales, and the Church on Fleet Street in London.

Accroding to Gerald of Wales (d.c. 1220) a fire was kept burining continuously at her shrine for centuries, tended by the twenty nuns of her community. The fire was surrounded by a circle of bushes, which no one was allowed to enter. This shrine, along with the following passage from the *Book of Lismore*, give us some insight into her special position in the Irish religious tradition: "It is she that helpeth everyone who is in danger: it is she that abateth the pestilences: it is she that quelleth the rage and the storm of the sea. She is the prophetess of Christ: she is the Queen of the South: she is the Mary of the Gael."

In art she is depicted as an abbess, usually holding a lamp or candle with a cow lying at her feet, which recalls her phase as a nun-cowgirl. An interesting relic of her shoe, made of silver and brass, set with jewels, survives, in the National Museum at Dublin.

She was formally named a patron saint of Ireland in 1962. She is also the patron saint of poets, blacksmiths, healers, cattle, dairymaids, midwives, newborn babies, and fugitives. Her feast day is February 1.

---

they also brought some of the customs practiced in their monasteries. One of these customs was the practice of individual confession of sins to a presbyter. Before this, serious sins demanded public confession and penance.

St. Benedict (480–547) and His Rule

A young man named Benedict followed the example of monks before him, as he sought out a remote area about forty miles from Rome and lived alone as a hermit. In time, news about this saintly hermit began to spread, and others who wished to dedicate themselves to a life of prayer and solitude came to him for spiritual guidance.

Benedict became so well-known for his holiness and prayer that a group of monks in a nearby monastery asked him to be their abbot. He accepted, but his demands on the monks became so rigid that they attempted to poison him. Benedict returned to his solitude and formed his own monastery.

As Benedict's popularity grew, some of the local clergy became jealous of him. One presbyter caused him so much difficulty that Benedict had to

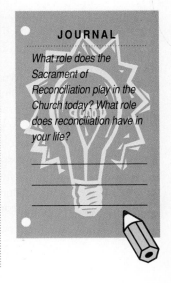

JOURNAL

What role does the Sacrament of Reconciliation play in the Church today? What role does reconciliation have in your life?

_____

_____

_____

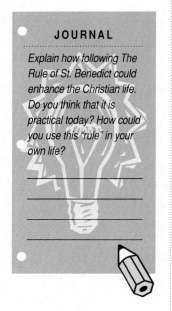

JOURNAL

Explain how following The Rule of St. Benedict could enhance the Christian life. Do you think that it is practical today? How could you use this "rule" in your own life?

leave the area. He and his monks went to Monte Cassino, which was midway between Rome and Naples, and there erected a **motherhouse**, as the central house for his monasteries.

Life at Monte Cassino stressed the three obligations of prayer, manual labor, and spiritual reading. Prayer, the central work of the day which took approximately five hours, included praying the daily prayers of the Church called the Divine Office. Work consisted in working on crafts, art, building, gardening, and other pursuits. The monastery was to be self-sustaining.

The Rule of St. Benedict

At Monte Cassino, Benedict composed his famous Rule, which was eventually used in many other monasteries. Because of the success and wide use of this Rule, Benedict received the historical title of Patriarch of the Monks of the West. His rule monitored the daily life of the monks, placing special emphasis on moderation and balance.

St. Scholastica (480–453), a sister of St. Benedict, founded a monastery for nuns near Monte Cassino. She used **The Rule of St. Benedict** in her monastery and is credited with bringing Benedict's Rule to monastic communities for women.

Although The Rule of St. Benedict was austere, he felt that it did not go beyond the capabilities of the ordinary person. He urged the monks to read the older monastic literature along with the Scriptures, to eat sparingly but adequately, to sleep as needed (up to eight hours), and to abstain from meat. Reading of the Scriptures, the early theologians of the Church, and early monastic literature occupied four or more hours of each day.

In reality, The Rule of St. Benedict did not add anything new to monastic life in terms of content. His emphasis on moderation offered a new, balanced approach to monastic dedication. Unlike rules of the past, which were commentaries or treatises on monastic life, St. Benedict's Rule was more orderly and explicit. He regulated the duties of superiors, occupations for every hour of the day, and procedures for training and punishing members.

Benedict did not include any directions for intellectual pursuits in his Rule except spiritual reading and reflection. Later, monks combined their copying and studying of the Scriptures with the more devotional directives of The Rule of St. Benedict. The copying of sacred and secular writings was a major historical contribution to come out of monastic life.

Although many monasteries used The Rule of St. Benedict, each monastery was an independent, self-sufficient unit, entirely separate from other houses. For a period of time, Benedict's followers remained at Monte Cassino. Ironically, the destruction of the monastery by a Germanic group in 581 forced the monks to flee in different directions, thus helping to spread The Rule of St. Benedict to other areas.

CLIPBOARD

1. What cautions can we take from the Church's experience with Clovis and the Franks?

2. What would happen if rulers in our country attempted to practice caeseropapism, as Justinian did?

3. Why do you think The Rule of St. Benedict was so beneficial to monastic life?

A Stronger Papacy

The Christian Times

Seventh Century   Vol. 7 No. 1

Pope Gregory the Great Leaves a Legacy

With sadness, we announce the death of Pope Gregory, called "the Great" by many who followed all he had done for the empire.

Many have compared the reign of Pope Gregory with that of Pope Leo the Great. Gregory showed a greatness equal to that of Leo who served as pope almost two centuries ago.

Besides his innovative leadership in liturgy, Gregory has shown outstanding concern for the poor and for the spread of Christianity. Prior to becoming pope, he was a monk, and, as pope, he has sent monks throughout the empire to convert those people who were not yet Christian. He was also a great political leader.

Gregory is responsible for sending Bishop Augustine of Canterbury to convert the Anglo-Saxons to the Christian faith. Augustine has had great success in his missionary endeavors.

A spokesperson in Rome stated that Gregory the Great had as strong an impact on imparting a positive image of the pope as Leo the Great did. We will miss him.

NOTEPAD
? ? ? ? ?

1. What did you learn about Pope Gregory? St. Augustine?

2. What does this article say about monastic life in the time of Gregory?

3. How does the article compare Pope Leo the Great to Pope Gregory the Great?

The Rest of the Story

Gregory the Great (590–604)

One hundred and fifty years after the election of Pope Leo the Great, the Church again needed a pope as powerful and zealous as Leo. The people responded to the needs of the time by electing Pope Gregory I, who would later become known to historians as Gregory the Great. He came from a highly respected Roman family, received an excellent education, and had personal qualities which suited him well to serve as pope at this time.

Long before he became pope, Gregory held the position of prefect of Rome and had an important role in shaping other polices for the government. He had a special concern for the people of Rome who were poor, attending to their needs and organizing the food supplies of Italy and Rome to provide for the suffering people of the country.

After the death of his father, Gregory resigned his position in Rome, gave away much of his land and money, and, like other rich nobles before him, turned his family mansion into a monastery in which he then lived. When the monks elected him as their abbot, he refused to accept this position. He served others in the monastery and intended to spend the rest of his life living in a monastic community.

Since the pope knew of Gregory's past experience in government, he commanded Gregory to leave the monastery and accept the delicate position of representing the pope at Constantinople, the capital of the East. For the next eight years, Gregory filled this position with dignity. The people recognized his deep spirituality and sought his help whenever necessary.

When the pope died, the people of Rome immediately chose Gregory as his successor. Not wishing to be pope, Gregory went into hiding for several days, hoping that the people would elect another in his place. When he realized that the people had no intentions of selecting another, he came out of hiding to accept the role he believed God had chosen for him.

St. Gregory

Although he did not wish to be pope, Gregory was well prepared for his role as leader of the Church. He had many years of experience in diplomatic service and knew how to deal with leaders of countries. He had already proven his deep faith, outstanding courage, and care for those who were needy and poor, traits which made him a great pope in the history of the Church.

Reform in the Church

Gregory the Great, like Leo the Great, strengthened the prestige of the papacy. The bishop of Constantinople had begun to call himself the universal patriarch, viewing himself as having power second only to that of the pope. Due to the continuing struggle between East and West, Gregory, like Leo, did not wish Constantinople to seize for itself any special position of prestige over other areas of the Church. Despite the influence of the bishop of Constantinople, Gregory strongly rebuked him.

Gregory left a legacy of reform and development in the Church during his time as pope. He challenged bishops to remain obedient and faithful to the Church and to fight heresy and schism. He urged them to establish schools for those preparing for the ministerial priesthood. He entreated all those dedicated to service in the Church to offer themselves entirely to those they served.

Gregory wrote extensively. Besides composing commentaries on the Bible, he wrote a number of letters on living well as a Christian and on the goodness and duties of the clergy. His works, translated into many languages, became a basis for training presbyters and bishops. His biographies of the saints became a model for writers of the lives of the saints.

Spiritual Leadership

Gregory had a great love for liturgy and sought to enrich its celebration. He encouraged the proper use of music in liturgy and supported specifically written types of music for liturgical seasons. The Gregorian chant still heard in some churches today had its origins in the liturgical reforms of Gregory the Great. Although many chants preceded the era of Gregory, Gregory ordered them to be written down and thus saved for posterity.

Following the monastic habit of caring for those who were poor, Gregory gave an example of charity by using Church funds to aid those in need. He viewed the mission of the Church as one of caring for those who were poor and needy.

After the destruction of Monte Cassino, fleeing monks found refuge in Rome under the patronage of Gregory. Because he longed to live as a monk himself, Gregory established several monasteries following the Benedictine Rule. He also ordained more monks as presbyters and sent a number of them on missionary journeys throughout the world.

Political Leadership

When Gregory became pope, Rome was under the control of a Germanic group that supported Arianism and kept Rome continually at war. Gregory, drained by the atrocities of war, sought a pact which would at least guarantee some peace. His intent was to convert the Germanic group rather than battle them. The rulers of the eastern portion of the empire refused to accept any idea of a truce with the Germanic tribes.

When Gregory remained firm in his resolve to enter into a peace treaty, the ruler of the eastern portion of the empire threatened to invade Rome. Through his persuasive power of leadership, Gregory inspired the inhabitants of the city to form a powerful shield against the army of the eastern empire. Finally, in 599, Gregory signed a pact with the Germanic tribes, a feat no other leader in the empire had attained.

Augustine of Canterbury (died 605)

Among his many achievements, Gregory helped spread Christianity by sending monks as missionaries throughout the western portion of the empire to convert the Germanic invaders. At one point, a tribe of English invaded Britain, forcing the Christians in the land to flee. Some of the inhabitants on the western part of Britain managed to preserve their faith and civilization, but suspicion and occasional border wars frustrated any hope of converting the invaders.

Gregory the Great sent a monk named Augustine and forty specially chosen Benedictine monks to Britain. The forty monks, after hearing stories of the atrocities of the Anglo-Saxon tribes, stopped in Gaul and refused to move further. Augustine returned to the pope who then made him the abbot of the group. When he returned to the forty monks, they were given the choice of following him or facing rejection from the community. They chose to follow.

'Go therefore and make disciples of all nations, baptizing them in the name of the Father and of the Son and of the Holy Spirit, and teaching them to obey everything that I have commanded you. And remember, I am with you always, to the end of the age.'

Matthew 16:19–20

St. Augustine

Under the leadership of Augustine, the monks landed in southeast England in an area ruled by a king, who had gained some familiarity with Christianity when he married a Christian Frankish princess. Although the monks feared the worst, the Anglo Saxons received them with surprising kindness. At first, the king did not wish to accept baptism, but, within a few months of witnessing the holiness and dedication of the monks, he celebrated baptism with a number of his subjects.

Augustine built his cathedral in Canterbury and founded a monastery nearby. From his foundations in Canterbury, he continued to work for the conversion of the people of England. Although historians have an idea when he died, they have no record of his birth.

Gregory continued to send monks to England, and a number of them traveled to other parts of the country. They followed the procedure of first converting the kings and then their subjects to Christianity. As a result of Gregory's missionary vision, many of the inhabitants of England embraced Christianity.

Success of Monasteries

Although the purpose of monasticism was the salvation and devotional development of its own members, it contributed significantly to European civilization. For centuries, the only means of education were monastic schools, and the only educated people were the monks. The copying of manuscripts preserved practically all the records we now have of ancient Roman literature, sacred and secular. A few monks also kept journals of their own day for the benefit of future historians.

The monks provided social services not provided by the government, such as caring for the poor, the sick, travelers, or pilgrims. By their agricultural endeavors, they brought extensive areas of land into cultivation. They also provided a large number of courageous missionaries for the conversion of the non-Christian invaders. They provided qualified candidates to serve as bishops and as popes.

CLIPBOARD

1. List some similarities between Pope Leo the Great and Pope Gregory the Great and explain how they helped develop the image of the papacy as we have it today.

2. What personal qualities of Augustine of Canterbury make him such a good example for missionaries today?

3. How do the efforts of monastic life today compare with monastic life in the time of Gregory?

REVIEWING THE ERA

• 400

ST. PATRICK. Patrick was a saint who was responsible for the conversion of Ireland. He was an English monk who went to Ireland as a bishop and founded monasteries throughout Ireland as a means of converting the people of the country.

POPE LEO THE GREAT. Leo gave great prestige to the image of the papacy, bringing the pope respect as a spiritual and temporal leader. Unarmed, he faced Attila the Hun and the Vandals. Through his representatives, he presided over the Council of Chalcedon.

COUNCIL OF CHALCEDON. This was an ecumenical council which taught a doctrine already proposed by Pope Leo the Great, declaring that Jesus had a human and divine nature.

• 500

CLOVIS. As king of the Franks, Clovis gathered the many Frankish tribes into a unified group and conquered most of what we know today as France. He helped to overcome the power of Arianism in his kingdom.

ST. BRIGID OF IRELAND. Brigid is a patron saint of Ireland who founded a double monastery at Kildare in Ireland. She was recognized as a saintly person, and the inhabitants of the land developed many legends concerning her miraculous deeds.

ST. SCHOLASTICA. Scholastica was a sister of St. Benedict. She brought his Rule to monastic communities for women.

ST. BENEDICT. Benedict is noted for The Rule of St. Benedict, which was and is widely used by monastic communities. His rule was rigid, but balanced.

• 550

JUSTINIAN. This last great emperor in the East was followed by weaker emperors. He practiced caesero-papism and wanted to unite the empire under one Christian religion. He is noted for his attempt to rule the people through his Justinian Code.

• 600

POPE GREGORY THE GREAT. Gregory was an able ruler, both politically and religiously who continued to improve the image of the papacy by his decisive leadership. He sent many monks as missionaries to convert the Germanic tribes and Anglo-Saxons.

AUGUSTINE OF CANTERBURY. This monk was sent by Gregory to England to convert the Anglo-Saxons who were invading the territory and driving off the Christian inhabitants. His ministry was successful, and he became bishop of Canterbury.

KEY TERMS

Pope
Supreme Pontiff
Monophysitism
Caesero-Papism
Justinian Code
Double monastery
Motherhouse
The Rule of St. Benedict

A Voice from the Past

This week's editorial will be on monasticism. Using the key terms and key figures from the chapter, relay to your readers the history of monasticism. Show them how some of the early characteristics of monasticism still affect their lives today. Finally, write your own Rule for your readers to use as a guide in living their lives today. Use The Rule of St. Benedict as a guide. Your Rule should be designed to help your readers achieve balance and moderation in the demands and struggles of society.

Then and Now

From the period of Leo the Great to that of Gregory the Great, the image of the papacy continued to grow. Popes became recognized as political and spiritual leaders, and dedicated themselves to protecting and spreading the faith and protecting the people of the empire against the Germanic migrations.

The monastic movement spread and became the chief means of conversion. The monks converted whole tribes by establishing monasteries in their midst and inviting the members of the tribes to join in prayer and study with them. St. Benedict introduced moderation and balance to the monasteries with the Benedictine Rule.

Many of the monasteries helped to preserve the history of the era through their copying of manuscripts and their studies. They also brought some new approaches to the celebration of the sacraments. Led by the example of the Irish monks, people began to confess their sins and perform their penances privately rather than in public.

Many of the customs of the era continue today. Our present view of the office of the pope as central to the Church originated in this period. Some forms used in the celebration of our liturgy come from the practice of the era. In many parishes, monasteries, and convents, the community gathers to pray the Liturgy of the Hours, a practice begun in monasteries.

NEWS IN REVIEW

1. What was the situation in the eastern and western areas of the empire in the fifth century?
2. Who was Leo the Great, and what did he do for the papacy?
3. What important Church teaching did the Council of Chalcedon support in opposition to the Monophysites?
4. Why is Clovis important in Church history?
5. What are some accomplishments and failures of Justinian?
6. What are some characteristics of Irish monasticism?
7. What contribution did St. Benedict make to monasticism?
8. What made Gregory such a great pope?
9. Who was Augustine of Canterbury, and what did he achieve?
10. List some contributions to history made by monasticism.

chapter seven

The Changing Society

If we were living in the seventh century, we would have memories and stories of popes facing armies of Germanic tribes and negotiating with them. We would expect the pope to be a political leader as well as a spiritual leader.

If the Irish monks had evangelized our territory, we would be celebrating reconciliation in a new way. We would tell our sins to a presbyter and have our sins forgiven immediately with the presbyter's blessing. Before this, we would have confessed our serious sins to the bishop or the whole community and then performed a public penance before receiving forgiveness.

As society changes, the Church is challenged to adapt to the needs of the various cultures, while holding firm to the gospel message and tradition.

Muslim Invasions

The Christian Times

Seventh Century   Vol. 7   No. 2

Charles Martel Defeats Muslims

In a surprising victory, Charles Martel of France defeated the Muslims, the followers of Muhammad, on the borders of France.

As our readers know, a man named Muhammad, who claimed to be a prophet, founded Islam during the last century. Even after the death of Muhammad, the Muslims continued to spread his teachings by capturing lands and forcing the people to accept their faith in Allah (this is the name the Muslims use for God).

The Muslims successfully galloped through Egypt and into Spain. As they tried to force their way northward into France, a mayor of France, Charles Martel, met them in battle and defeated them.

Although he is not the king of France, Charles Martel is reportedly considered the true ruler by the people of France. At the pope's request, Charles offered protection to Boniface, who is known as the "Apostle of the Germans."

NOTEPAD
? ? ? ? ?

1. What did you learn about Muhammad? Charles Martel? Boniface?

2. What role did the military have in the spread of different faiths?

3. What information is revealed in this article about the Muslims?

The Rest of the Story

By the beginning of the seventh century, the Byzantine Empire was fighting enemies throughout the eastern part of the empire. The Byzantine armies were fighting a major war with the powerful armies of the Persians. Because of the great effort of this war, the Byzantine Empire and the Persians overlooked the buildup of still other armies which would soon gallop out of the deserts of Arabia to conquer a huge tract of land in the East and into Spain in the West.

KEY TERMS

Islam: a word meaning surrender or submission; religion, led by Muhammad, teaching that there was only one God.

Muhammad (570–632)

Most of the inhabitants of Arabia lived in the forbidding terrain of the desert, settling around any oasis which offered them the priceless gift of water. Christianity had touched only a portion of the desert inhabitants, while most of these nomads still worshiped many gods.

Around 600, a man named Muhammad began a movement which would change the face of the known world. Born in the region of what is now Saudi Arabia, Muhammad, in his youth, became a caravan trader. At the age of forty, he had a religious experience which greatly influenced the direction of world history. His extensive travel brought him into contact with Jewish and Christian writings. His own written revelations show the influence of these Scriptures on his thinking.

Muhammad became the leader of a new religion which would eventually receive the name **Islam**, which means "surrender" or "submission." The followers of Muhammad became known to the world as **Muslims**, or Moslems, which means "a believer in Islam." Muhammad rejected the belief in many gods, which was then common among his people, and he taught that there was only one God who was eternal, merciful, and all-powerful. The Muslim cry was "There is only one God, and his name is Allah."

Muhammad began to preach about this one God. This naturally caused problems for the merchants in his hometown of Mecca who were making profits on the people's worship of many gods. Because of the large number of people who followed Muhammad, the livelihood of these merchants was threatened. The merchants spread rumors throughout the area and caused a successful uprising against Muhammad, who had to flee from Mecca. The date of this flight from Mecca in 622 is the beginning date of the Muslim calendar.

When Muhammad fled from Mecca, approximately two hundred of his followers had already preceded him. He continued to spread his beliefs and found acceptance to the extent that he was able to return to Mecca in triumph. The number of his followers increased rapidly. The heart of his teaching was that an historical tension existed between the belief in the one God and the false allurement of belief in many gods.

Muhammad saw himself as the end of a long line of prophets found in Judaism and Christianity. He did not believe that Jesus was divine, but he did believe that he was a great prophet. Muhammad claimed that Allah spoke to him through the Angel Gabriel, and he passed these revelations on to his followers.

The Followers of Muhammad

At the time of Muhammad's death in 632, he had already proven himself to be a capable leader, by leading his followers to major triumphs. His followers, filled with his energy and zeal, contin-

ued his mission after his death. They gathered his revelations together into a sacred book, the **Qur'an**. Muslims grounded their faith on their belief in the one God, their dedication to prayer, fasting, and almsgiving, and their commitment to visit Mecca at least once in their lifetime. These obligations are sometimes referred to as the **Five Pillars of Islam**.

Like Judaism and Christianity, Islam began in a remote region of the world, but it rapidly swept across major portions of the Eastern empire. For Muslims, a just war was a religious war if it was authorized by the leaders of a Muslim nation. It was believed that a Muslim who died during a religious war would immediately enter paradise.

Muslims seized most of the area around the eastern and southern borders of the Mediterranean Sea and expanded their conquests across North Africa and eventually into Spain. In a single century, Islam spread across an area almost five-thousand miles long and a thousand miles wide.

The Byzantine Empire in the East experienced the major impact of the Islamic expansion as millions of people converted to Islam. In the West, however, the Muslims met greater resistance. While they had extended their conquests as far as Spain, they achieved little lasting effect in what is now called Europe.

Effects of the Muslim Invasion

The Muslim invasions had lasting effects on the world, as they brought with them a great deal of practical and philosophical knowledge.

The Muslims brought into common usage the numbering system now known as the *Arabic system,* and expanded the world of mathematics through their introduction of geometry, algebra, and trigonometry. They introduced forgotten philosophers of the past, such as Aristotle, to the scholars of

JOURNAL

Do you think there can ever truly be a religious war? Why or why not?

_____

_____

_____

_____

POINTS TO PONDER

An often positive result of war is that cultures collide, allowing cultures to share their strengths with each other, thus each culture becomes enriched.

The Church's relationship with the Muslims. 'The plan of salvation also includes those who acknowledge the Creator, in the first place amongst whom are the Muslims; these profess to hold the faith of Abraham, and together with us they adore the one, merciful God, ...'

Catechism of the Catholic Church, #841

St. Boniface

the day. The regained knowledge of the philosophy of Aristotle had an important influence on later Christian writers, especially on the great Christian theologian, Thomas Aquinas.

Charles Martel (690–741)

After their conquest of areas in Spain, the Muslims moved north toward southern Gaul where they met the army of a mayor of the Franks, Charles Martel. The name *Martel* means hammer, and the hammer crashed down heavily on the Muslim armies.

The descendants of Clovis still served as kings of the Frankish kingdom, but they were weak and unable to rally an army to defend the kingdom against the Muslims. The popular Charles Martel defeated the Muslim army at Tours in 732.

Although Charles was not a king, the people hailed him as their leader. They no longer held any hope for the leadership of the weak kings, and they wanted Charles to become their ruler. Charles, although making major decisions and leading the armies, declined the title of king.

St. Boniface (675–754)

After Charles Martel became powerful in France, missionaries again found a welcome resting place in Gaul as they journeyed to the western portion of the empire. When the pope asked Boniface, a learned and holy man, to convert the Germanic people, he also asked Charles Martel to provide protection for Boniface.

Boniface, the man chosen for the mission to the Germanic people, became a monk in England and followed the Benedictine rule. With the number of converts increasing in England, that country now became a great resource for missionary activity for the rest of the empire. Boniface wished to spread the faith, but he failed miserably in his first missionary endeavor. Undaunted, he went to Rome to seek permission from the pope to preach the good news to the Germanic tribes.

Boniface's next missionary attempt was very successful. The pope, recognizing Boniface's goodness and zeal, sent him as a missionary bishop to the Germanic groups. In time, Boniface was asked to reform the Frankish clergy. With the protection of the pope and the powerful Frankish leaders, Boniface was able to fulfill his mission. When other monks and nuns in England heard of Boniface's success, many came to join him in his missionary activity.

Boniface followed the practice of establishing monasteries throughout the area we know as Germany. Those who converted to Christ and wished to become monks or nuns had to undergo a thorough preparation for monastic life. Boniface met three times with the pope to ask advice on his missionary work.

As a result of his successful missionary work in Germany, St. Boniface received the title of *Apostle to the German people*. He continued his missionary activity until 754 when he and several new Germanic converts, who had just celebrated their baptism, were killed by a group of non-Christians.

CLIPBOARD

1. Do you think that a new religious leader like Muhammad could rise to power in our own day? Explain.

2. Give an example of a modern-day military leader, like Charles Martel, who became more popular and powerful than the ruler of a country?

3. If someone like Boniface were to become an apostle to the people in our society today, what would he or she teach us?

Crowning a New Emperor

The Christian Times

Ninth Century   Vol. 9 No. 1

Charlemagne Crowned Emperor

In a surprising move, Pope Leo III yesterday crowned Charlemagne (Charles the Great), the son of Pepin and the grandson of Charles Martel, as the new emperor of the West. Observers reported that Charlemagne was not altogether pleased with the move, since it seemed to give the power of choosing an emperor to the pope.

Charlemagne follows the spirit of his father, Pepin, who had become the new king of the Franks. Pepin rewarded the Church handsomely for its support, by giving it a tract of land known as the *Donation of Pepin,* or the *Papal States.* With this increase in land, the Church has become an even greater power in the world.

The pope's coronation of Charlemagne has vexed the emperor of the East, whose throne is too far from Rome for him to immediately intervene. Some claim that the motive behind the pope's choice of Charlemagne is the need for a protector of the Papal States.

NOTEPAD
? ? ? ? ?

1. What did you learn about Pope Leo? Charlemagne? Pepin?
2. Why was Charlemagne upset about being crowned emperor?
3. Why do you think the emperor of the East was upset with this coronation?

The Rest of the Story

With the defeat of the Muslims by Charles Martel, the Frankish kingdom became the central power in western Europe. The family of Charles Martel had a lasting influence on the Church. Pepin, the son of Charles, proved to be an able leader, and Charlemagne, Charles's grandson, made the Church even more influential in the world, due to his dedication to the spread of Christianity.

Pepin (714–768)

Pepin, the son of Charles Martel, was also known as *Pepin the Short.* He continued as a mayor of the Franks, but, unlike his father, he desired the title of king. His opportunity came when the Lombards threatened to invade Rome. Pope Zachary, in need of some powerful support against the threats of the Lombards, a Germanic group, supported a request from Pepin that he and his descendants be made king, in place of the current line of weak kings. Since the people already thought of Pepin as the king, the pope logically deduced that he should officially declare Pepin as king.

With the pope openly supporting Pepin for king, Pepin forced the reigning king to abdicate and enter a monastery. The pope commissioned Bishop Boniface to anoint Pepin as king. Several years later, the pope himself would anoint Pepin as king and anoint his son as the rightful heir of the kingdom.

After the death of Pope Zachary, the Lombards again threatened Rome. Pope Stephen II (752-757) first appealed to the Byzantine emperor for help, but the emperor lacked an army strong enough to fight the invaders. With the help of envoys from Pepin, Pope Stephen traveled across the Alps and met secretly with him. Pepin received the pope graciously and agreed to lead his army against the Lombards.

The Donation of Pepin

Pepin defeated the Lombards and compelled them to restore the Church's territory. He also added additional territory from central Italy to the Church's domain. The stretch of land became known as the *Donation of Pepin*, and, in time, as the *Patrimony of St. Peter*. This land also became known as the **Papal States**.

In the eyes of the people of the period, the more land a leader possessed, the more powerful the forces he could gather to protect that land. The amount of land also added to the prestige of the owner and allowed the lord of the land to act freely. The gift of this land gave greater power, freedom, and authority to the popes who would hold power over the Papal States until 1870.

Although the Donation of Pepin freed the papacy from the possibility of foreign control, it also brought with it political problems. Because of the wealth flowing from the Patrimony of Peter, some people saw the position of pope as an opportunity to gain personal wealth. The office of pope became vulnerable to bribery, treachery, and deception.

Within ten years, a powerful family in Rome wanted to control the wealth held by the pope, so they attempted to install a man of their choice as pope. Political intrigue and alliances drove this family from their powerful position in Rome, and a new pope, who took the name Stephen III, was elected by the people of Rome. Fortunately, this new pope clearly recognized the need for some protection against the power of wealthy families in papal elections.

A year after his election, Pope Stephen III convoked the **Lateran Synod** which introduced a decree that still affects papal elections to this day. A **synod** is a gathering of Church leaders with the task of resolving or advising on matters concerning the Church. The Lateran Synod decreed that only a cardinal could be elected pope, and that laypeople no longer had a vote in the elections. This proved to be a difficult rule to enforce.

Charlemagne (742–814)

After the death of Pepin, Pepin's son, Charles, succeeded him. Because of his great exploits and his effect on the history of the West, Charles became known to history as Charlemagne, a name which means "Charles the Great." He saw himself as a chosen agent of the Church, dedicated to the spread of

KEY TERMS

Papal States: the additional territory, in Italy, that Pepin gave to the Church; also referred to as the *Donation of Pepin*, and the *Patrimony of St. Peter.*

Synod: a gathering of Church leaders with the task of resolving or advising on matters concerning the Church.

Lateran Synod: decreed that only a cardinal could be elected pope, and that laypeople no longer had a vote in the elections.

In the Spotlight

St. Zachary, a native of Calabria and a Greek by descent, was the last of the Greek pontiffs. He became a deacon at Rome, and upon the death of Gregory III in 741, he was elected to succeed Gregory.

As pope, he was much concerned with foreign relations, particularly with the Lombards, the Byzantines, and the Franks. He ended the hostility of the Lombards with the papacy by persuading the Lombard, King Liutprand, to restore all the Roman territory that he had occupied for thirty years.

He was also able to convince Liutprand not to attack the exarchate of Ravenna, thereby acquiring the appreciation of the Byzantines under Emperor Constantine V (r. 741–755). He also took the politically acute step of granting the last Merovingian king, Childeric III, permission for the anointing of Pepin III the Short. He thus began the association of the Carolingians with the papacy.

Zacharay was also able to build up a strong relationship with the Franks, through Boniface. The correspondence between

Zachary and Boniface, which part of is still in existence, gives the impression of great vigour and deep sympathy. In the correspondence Zachary tells Boniface to suspend polygamous and murderous ordained priests, to abolish superstitious practices (even if these were practiced at Rome), and to recognize the baptisms of those whose Latin was extremely inaccurate.

While he was in office, he held two synods (743, 745) and translated the works of Gregory the Great into Greek.

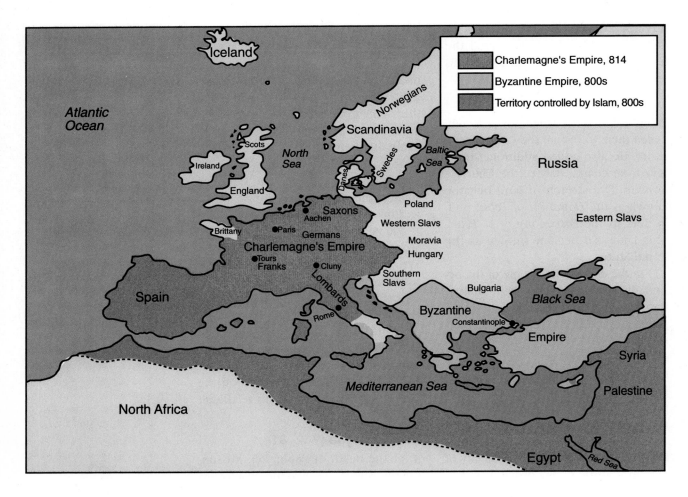

Map Search

Using the map find the following:

- Charlemagne's Empire
- Byzantine Empire
- Spain
- Constantinople
- England, Land of the Franks
- the Germans
- Britany, Land of the Lombards
- the Saxons

Christianity. His desire to convert the barbarians drove Charlemagne to his victories. His tactics, however, were often far from Christian.

Charlemagne spread the faith more by force, than by converting the minds and hearts of the people he conquered. His desire to bring people to Christianity was a political, as well as a spiritual quest. Following the lead of many great leaders before him, he recognized the value of having a huge empire united under a single religion.

The armies defeated by Charlemagne's forces had to accept Christian baptism or face death, and an astounding number of the conquered accepted death rather than convert. After such mass "conversions" took place, many of the newly converted rulers would lead their armies into battle against neighboring tribes and force them to convert to Christianity.

When the Lombards conquered areas in the northern half of Italy and threatened Rome itself, Charlemagne rushed to save the pope and the people of Rome and smashed the assault. However, Charlemagne began to act as though he controlled the pope and the Papal States.

As a result of Charlemagne's victory and his support of the Church, a grateful pope bowed to Charlemagne's judgments concerning some political and spiritual decisions for the Papal States.

Charlemagne Made Emperor

In the year 800, during the celebration of the Christmas liturgy at St. Peter's Basilica in Rome, Pope Leo III unexpectedly crowned Charlemagne as the new emperor of the Western Empire. The action on the part of the pope was not merely a generous act, but one that had political undertones. For more than three hundred years, the West did not have an emperor, nor a method for choosing one.

By taking the initiative in crowning Charlemagne, Pope Leo took for himself and the popes who followed him the right to crown emperors in the West. Although Charlemagne could do nothing when the pope made this move, he recognized its political significance and had no intentions of allowing the popes to seize this right for the future. He was already planning on a way to crown his own son, as the emperor of the West when the time came.

When the Byzantine Emperor in the East heard that Leo had crowned Charlemagne as emperor in the West, he and his supporters were furious. In his mind, the eastern empire still ruled the West, even if the eastern emperors were too weak to protect it from Germanic invasions. The emperors in the East continued to long for the day when they would again rule the entire Christian Empire. The action of Pope Leo III brazenly cut the West away from the authority of the Byzantine Empire, thus driving a deeper wedge between western and eastern Christendom.

Charlemagne as Emperor

Although Charlemagne did not agree with the pope taking the right to crown him, he took his role seriously and felt that his call as the new emperor of the West intensified his need to protect and spread Christianity. Like many rulers before him, he began to interfere in Church matters, thinking he was equal to a bishop or the pope. He ruled his people in religious, as well as civil, matters.

Charlemagne had a great concern for the Church and those who served the Church. In his decisions concerning the Church, Charlemagne demanded perfection in those he appointed and obedience to the rules he decreed for the Church. His approach differed from past rulers who rewarded friends and rich families, by appointing unsuitable choices for Church offices.

Charlemagne enriched the life of the Church, by appointing virtuous bishops to lead the people and ordering the monasteries to return to the strict observance of The Rule of St. Benedict. He established exacting standards for the clergy and for the celebration of the liturgy, affirming that Sunday be a day of worship and rest. He taxed the people to provide tithes for the support of the Churches.

Charlemagne's empire disintegrated quickly after his death. His son and grandsons lacked his skill of leadership, while facing a number of unfortunate civil wars and skirmishes within the empire. The Vikings (Norsemen) came in boats from the north, striking first at the northern coast of France, then moving more boldly inland. Between the civil wars and the invasions, the empire was again devastated.

Charlemagne's greatest gift to history and the Church was his support of learning. By recognizing the great thinkers of his age and placing them in positions where they could spread their teachings, he laid the foundation for future theological development in the Church. His efforts in the development of scholarship in the empire would continue long after his family lost their power.

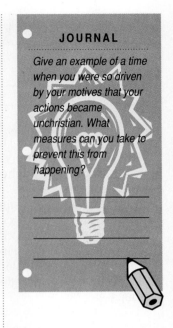

JOURNAL

Give an example of a time when you were so driven by your motives that your actions became unchristian. What measures can you take to prevent this from happening?

CLIPBOARD

1. List the pros and cons of making the pope the ruler of such a large country as the Papal States.

2. Today the cardinals, following the decree of the Lateran Synod, have the duty of electing a new pope when the previous pope dies. Do you think anyone else should share in this right to elect a new pope? Why? or why not?

3. Reflecting on Charlemagne's work and influence, would you agree that he earned the name of *Charlemagne*, which means Charles the Great? Why? or why not?

Feudalism

The Christian Times

Tenth Century   Vol. 10   No. 1

Invasions Causing Concern for the Church

Rumor has it that the Vikings are causing havoc on the western coast of the empire. In this age of invasions when missionaries are attempting to convert the Slavs, the Huns, and the inhabitants of Russia, an increase in these invasions challenges the Church to reach out to these new groups.

These new Christians with their new languages are causing problems for the Church.Cyril, a missionary monk from Constantinople, has already translated sections of the Bible into the Slavic language and celebrates the liturgy in that language. The German bishops sent from Rome protested to the pope that Cyril and his brother Methodius were not praying in Latin.

When the Vikings first invaded the borders of the Frankish kingdom, they ransacked the properties of rich land owners and the monasteries. A system of protection, called the feudal system, was thought to be sufficient protection against the invaders, but the growth of the wealthy land owners merely invites more invasions. The Church in the western portion of the empire has become helpless against the invaders.

In the meantime, many bishops have become rich from receiving wealthy parcels of land to administer. Some claim that the rewards of land, called benefices, given to a bishop with his appointment has led to the appointment of a number of bishops too weak to lead.

The serfs, or peasant farmers, live in poverty, while the lords and landowners grow wealthy. As usual, the serfs are often the first ones to die during an invasion.

NOTEPAD

? ? ? ? ?

1. List some of the challenges faced by the Church in this article.
2. What are some problems faced by the people along the western coast of the empire and by the missionaries?
3. What solutions were tried? With what success?

The Rest of the Story

Invading armies continued to cross the many borders of the empire and to pillage every village and farm in their path. At first, the invading armies seemed to threaten the faith, but many missionaries made these invaders the center of their missionary activities and converted them to Christianity. In turn, these invaders often became staunch defenders of the faith.

Due to the many wars and conquests, trade decreased. The dangers and losses involved in trading were counterproductive. Thus, land became the gauge of a person's power and wealth. The more land the people owned, the more powerful and wealthy they were. This attitude toward land led to a system known as feudalism, which flourished during the ninth and tenth centuries.

Cyril (826–869) and Methodius (815–885)

One group of invaders, known as the Slavs, occupied most of Eastern Europe. The Czechs, Slovaks, Croatians, Serbians, Bulgarians, Poles, and Russians can trace their origins back to the Slavs. Since the Slavs were actually a number of different tribes, leaders of the various tribes strongly desired to reach some type of political or religious unity.

Although the rulers of the Slav kingdoms sought to unify their kingdom under a common religion, they had learned from experience that conversions by western missionaries often paved the way for western conquest of an area. To avoid this outcome, the leaders of the Slavs invited missionaries from the eastern Church of Constantinople to bring Christianity into the area.

The Church at Constantinople responded by sending two outstanding and proven missionaries, the brothers, Cyril and Methodius. Having grown up in the Balkans among Slavs, they already had the advantage of knowing the Slav language and were well received by the inhabitants. The people of the kingdom overwhelmingly accepted their message.

Because no written Slavic language existed, Cyril constructed an alphabet which was named the **Cyrillic alphabet**. Using this alphabet, Cyril and Methodius translated parts of the Bible, the liturgy, and several other books into the Slavic language. The brothers encountered opposition from German missionaries from the West who maintained that Latin and Greek were the only proper liturgical languages. In desperation, Cyril and Methodius traveled to Rome to argue their case directly with the pope.

The pope agreed to the use of the Slavic language in the liturgy, but he also used the occasion to assert his leadership over the Church in the East. He placed Cyril and Methodius under his own jurisdiction, thus making them envoys of Rome rather than envoys of Constantinople. Cyril became seriously ill at Rome and remained there in a monastery until his death. After the pope ordained Methodius a bishop, Methodius returned to his mission among the Slavs.

The Hungarian Invasion

In the early tenth century (906), a group of invaders who resembled the Huns invaded the land and received the name Hungarians. Until a major defeat in the middle of the tenth century, they cast a shadow of fear across most of Germany and other areas they invaded. Missionaries, sent to Hungary from Germany and from the Byzantine Empire, eventually converted the king of the Hungarians. The next king, known as *St. Stephen of Hungary*, brought Christianity to its population peak when he forced his subjects to convert.

Russia

Toward the end of the tenth century, missionaries from Germany converted Queen Olga of Russia to Christianity. The Russians did not immediately follow the queen into Christianity, but she did influence the religious convictions of her family. Her grandson, Vladimer I, led his people into Christianity, but he sought missionaries from the Byzantine Empire and not from Rome.

Under Vladimer, the people of Russia converted to Christianity. There is some suspicion that they did not become Christians because of their own convictions, but because of the force used by Vladimer. Vladimer's son, Yaroslav, linked Russia even more closely with Constantinople and the East. For the next two centuries, Christianity would be the bonding force between Russia and the East.

Feudalism

Feudalism arose as a defense against the difficulties of living in regions where invading armies could attack and kill people in small villages. With travel

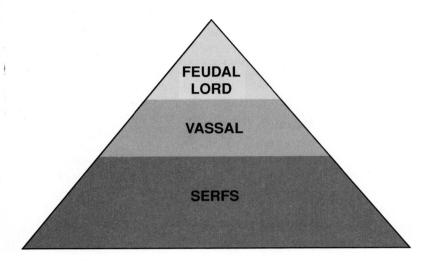

FEUDAL LORD

VASSAL

SERFS

KEY TERMS

Feudal lord: a tribal king or wealthy noble owning a large area of land.

Vassal: appointed by the feudal lord to administer to his land; this person paid taxes to the feudal lord, and provided a regiment of soldiers to protect the land; the serfs referred to this person as lord.

B *lessed are the meek, for they will inherit the earth. Blessed are those who hunger and thirst for righteousness, for they will be filled.*

Matthew 5: 5–6, NRSV

difficult and trade no longer a way of gaining wealth, land was wealth—the more land, the more wealth.

During the era of the feudal system, a large number of feudal lords were kings of a tribe. Countries and nations as we know them today did not exist. Large nations such as France or Italy had not yet developed. Instead, a number of tribes inhabited lands that would later become united to form a nation. During the period of the feudal system, these tribes often fought with each other.

The structure of the feudal system looked like a pyramid, with (1) the largest landowner at the top, (2) a group of nobles to act as landlords in the middle, and (3) the largest number of those who worked individual plots of land at the bottom.

1. The largest landowner. A tribal king or a wealthy noble often owned an extremely large area of land. The owner, called a **feudal lord**, divided this huge region into a number of large parcels of land to be administered by other members of the nobility who, in turn, paid taxes to the owner. The feudal lord referred to the noble administrating each parcel of his land as his **vassal**.

The feudal lord expected the vassal to pay extremely high taxes for the privilege of administrating the land. He also expected the vassal to provide a

regiment of soldiers to defend the land against attacks made by other feudal lords. Since most of the vassals came from noble families, they had received training in the use of weapons from the time of their youth and often relished the thought of going into battle. As a leader of a band of soldiers, the noble received the title of *knight*.

2. The administrator or vassal. Each vassal divided the large parcel of land he received into a number of small farms and appointed workers and their families to care for these plots. Those appointed by the vassals to work the land were called **serfs**. The serfs referred to the one who appointed them to the land as a *lord*. The lord's wife received the respectful title of *lady*.

3. The workers or serfs. Although the serfs were not slaves, their need for work and protection was so great that they had no choice but to live like slaves. From the produce of the land, the serfs paid excessive taxes to the vassals, who then kept a portion for themselves and paid the rest to the feudal lord. The more taxes the large landowner demanded of a vassal, the more the vassal demanded of the serfs. The large landowners and the vassals became very wealthy in the process, but the serfs were at their mercy.

The vassal also chose the more hearty men from among the serfs and trained them for battle. As a noble knight, he was required to lead an army of serfs into battle to defend the land of the feudal lord. Serfs chosen to serve in the military often lived better than those caring for the land.

Feudal villages were made up of farms. These farms circled the fortress or castle, in which the vassal, his family, and an array of soldiers lived. In case of invasion, the serfs fled to the safety of the enclosure and joined the army to fight off the enemy.

An honor system united the serfs. If a serf dishonored one of the lords, all the serfs felt shamed by the action and found it necessary to make amends. In their common need for survival and protection, they saw themselves as a community loyal to those above them. Serfs had little hope of ever escaping the system—once a serf, always a serf.

Despite their inability to escape the system the serfs found hope in their faith in God. Two such examples were St. Isadore and his wife St. Maria de la Cabeza. Together they spent their entire lives working on the farm of a wealthy landowner. They lived a simple, dedicated life caring for the land and the animals. Others working along with them witnessed their humility, their care for the poor, and their dedication to God and those who worked with them. In many ways, they reflected the simple, pious life of many serfs living throughout Europe. It was these kinds of people that kept the Christian faith alive amidst a time of such great corruption.

The Feudal Benefice

The tribal kings and rulers often made appointments of bishops. At times, the more powerful rulers appointed abbots and abbesses of monasteries within their region. They occasionally informed the pope of their choice, but sometimes they simply had other local bishops ordain the candidate they chose. Instead of choosing a suitable spiritual leader, rulers often chose a relative or friend who would be loyal.

The ruler often made the bishop a vassal with huge holdings. This gift of land came to be known as a **benefice**. The bishop who received an appointment to a large benefice could expect to reap a large amount of wealth from his appointment. This led some bishops to use their family influence and wealth to bribe a ruler to appoint them to a rich benefice.

Many monasteries also received gifts of land and became wealthy landowners. The monks in these rich monasteries, with vast holdings of land, had vassals to administer the land for

them. In some cases, this allowed them time for praying, learning, and teaching. In other cases, it led to a life of luxury and corruption. In the smaller and poorer monasteries, however, the monks still had to work hard to survive.

The wealth of the bishops and the monasteries led to a number of abuses. Since many of these bishops came from the noble class, they had grown up with military training and thrived on stories of military heroism. Some of them not only provided armies for the king at the time of war, but they themselves sometimes led these armies into battle. The Church forbade such activity by anyone in orders, but some bishops and abbots ignored this rule.

Many bishops invested their energies into temporal leadership, while ignoring their responsibility to provide spiritual leadership for the people. In light of the allurement of the power, luxury, and prestige attached to Church leadership, many nobles aspired to ordination as bishops, not for spiritual reasons, but for riches and power. Their positions allowed them to tax their subjects as they wished and to make important appointments within their region.

Despite the extravagant lifestyles of some bishops and abbots, the faith and dedication of pious Christians continued to thrive. At a time when many Church leaders were falling prey to the luxury and greed of the day, many others in the Church lived lives of holiness amid poverty. During this time dedicated Christian laypeople and clergy preserved the true spirit of the Church, despite the actions of many corrupt Church leaders.

Vikings

With the growth of the feudal system, many regions of the West became so rich that outsiders looked hungrily on the wealth and sought to loot the land. One major force came out of extreme northern Europe. The Scandinavians

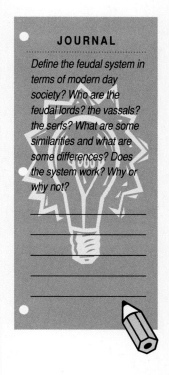

JOURNAL

Define the feudal system in terms of modern day society? Who are the feudal lords? the vassals? the serfs? What are some similarities and what are some differences? Does the system work? Why or why not?

Viking: name given to the scandinavian invaders from the north; the name means people who roam the sea.

from the north arrived in ships, propelled by sail and oar, which could carry close to a hundred men.

Because these invaders came from the sea, they received the name of **Viking**, which meant that they were people who roamed the seas. Because they came from the north, the inhabitants of the lands they ravaged referred to the Vikings as Norsemen.

As the empire of the West became too weak to defend itself, the Vikings met little resistance from the inhabitants. The invaders ransacked the monasteries and churches along the coast of northern France, but did not conquer the land. Instead, they fled back to their ships with slaves and booty.

Eventually, the lure of wealth drew the Vikings further inland, and they began to conquer and settle on the land. In lands such as current-day Scotland, Ireland, and England, the Vikings came into contact with Christianity. This contact with Christianity and intermarriage between the Norsemen and the occupants of the land led many of the Vikings to convert to Christianity.

While the Vikings were invading Europe, missionaries visited the lands of Denmark and Sweden where the king welcomed them. This led to the Christianizing of the Scandinavian countries.

CLIPBOARD

1. What, in your opinion, would motivate brilliant missionaries like Cyril and Methodius to dedicate their lives to converting people of other lands to Christianity?

2. Do you feel that the feudal system was a just system? Why or why not? How do you think that it could have been made more just?

3. By what standards are bishops appointed today? How do these standards differ from the standards that were used during the days of the feudal system?

REVIEWING THE ERA

- **600**

  MUHAMMAD. The founder of Islam was accepted as a prophet whose revelations are contained in the Qur'an. The Muslims conquered a large expanse of territory in the east and went as far west as Spain.

- **700**

  ST. BONIFACE. The Apostle of the Germans received permission from the pope to spread the message of Christ to the German population. Others followed in his steps.

  CHARLES MARTEL. This major of the Frankish kingdom stopped the Muslim invasion of southern Gaul. Although not a king, he actually ruled France in place of the weak kings of Clovis's line.

PEPIN. Pepin, the son of Charles Martel, was crowned king of France by the pope. He gave a portion of central Italy to the pope in an action known as the Donation of Pepin. The land forms the Papal States which were held by the pope until 1870.

- **800**

  CHARLEMAGNE. This son of Pepin was crowned emperor of the Western Empire by the pope, after the absence of an emperor for three hundred years. Charlemagne saw himself as the protector and administrator of political and religious decisions for the empire.

  CYRIL AND METHODIUS. These brothers served as missionaries to the Slavs. Cyril created a Slavic alphabet and prayed the liturgy in the Slavish language.

KEY TERMS

Islam

Muslims

Qur'an

Five Pillars of Islam

Papal States

Synod

Lateran Synod

Cyrillic alphabet

Feudalism

Feudal lord

Vassal

Serfs

Lord

Lady

Benefice

Viking

Then and Now

The many invasions during these centuries continually changed the map of Europe. The Muslim invasions captured large tracts of land in the East and resulted in the conversion of many to Islam. The invasions came to an abrupt halt at the boundaries of Gaul, where Charles Martel defeated the Muslim armies.

Pepin gave the Papal States to the pope, and this made the pope a strong temporal leader.

Charlemagne became emperor and helped the Church to spread, but his tactics were harsh. He also tended to interfere in Church matters.

With the weakness of the successors of Charlemagne, the inhabitants developed a new system of survival called the *feudal system*. This system, which lured many unfit candidates into the positions of bishops and abbots, led to a general decay of religious leadership in the Church.

In our day, we can still see the lasting effects of the Muslim invasion, as many countries in the East profess some form of the Islamic belief. The papacy no longer controls vast areas of land as it did after Pepin and Charlemagne. The pope no longer becomes a wealthy lord on the day of his election as pope, nor do bishops own a portion of the dioceses they lead.

A Voice from the Past

Your feature in this week's editorial is the feudal system. Relay to your readers, using ten of the sixteen key terms, what the feudal system was, the events that led to its development, and how it affected the Church. Discuss the pros and the cons of the feudal system, and show your readers how it is still present today. Give examples of modern day feudal lords, vassals, and serfs. Using Christ's message, point out problems in the system and suggest things that your readers can do to help turn the system around.

NEWS IN REVIEW

1. Who was Muhammad, and how did he affect the world?
2. What did the Muslim invasions add to scholarship in the empire?
3. Who was Charles Martel, and what was his greatest achievement?
4. Why is St. Boniface called the "Apostle to the German People"?
5. Who was Pepin, and how did he help the Church?
6. What were Charlemagne's contributions to and problems with the Church?
7. What was the significance of the pope crowning Charlemagne as the emperor of the West?
8. What contributions did Cyril and Methodius make to the Church?
9. How did the feudal system affect the Church?
10. Who were the Norsemen, and what led them to move their invasions further inland?

chapter eight

Decay and Reform

If we were living in the eleventh century, we would hear the stories and memories of the vast wealth of land belonging to the popes. We may even envy the popes for their wealth and easily forget that they were spiritual leaders. We might be working on farms as serfs, serving on some military force, or living a life of luxury as a landlord. Our relationship to the land would determine our status in society.

While land is still a symbol of wealth, it also reminds us of our call to stewardship.

Decay and Reform

The Christian Times

Twelfth Century   Vol. 12   No. 1

Abbot Bernard Visits Cistercian Monasteries

The abbot Bernard visited a nearby monastery this week to make sure that the monks are living a life of dedication and sacrifice. Bernard, who belongs to the rapidly growing Cistercian community, visits communities of Cistercians throughout the empire.

Over the past century, the Church has suffered major embarrassments over the extravagant lives of its popes, bishops, and abbots. Bernard has the duty of investigating the Cistercian's faithfulness to the rule of the Cistercian monks, a community founded by a monk named Robert.

Our reporter in France notes that the Cistercian monasteries are now taking the lead in reform. At one time, the monasteries, linked with the monastery at Cluny in France, led in the reform of monastic life. Since then, Cluny has fallen into corruption, and dedicated monks have seen the need for new centers of holiness and prayer.

In a recent interview, Bernard declared that the Church needs dedicated monks to offset the harm done to the Church by such corrupt popes as Pope John XII and other weak popes. Bernard also noted that Otto I, the newly crowned emperor of the West, attempted to control the Church, but the present pope rejected Otto's efforts.

Bernard believes that the day will come when kings and emperors will no longer choose Church leaders. He believes that not until the people of the Church choose their own candidates for bishop, will a true reform take place.

NOTEPAD

? ? ? ? ?

1. What did you learn about Bernard? Pope John XII? Otto I?

2. What are some issues expressed in this article?

3. What does Bernard state as being necessary for reform in the Church?

The Rest of the Story

Many factors contributed to a decay in Church leadership during the period of feudalism. Bishops, abbots, and monasteries suddenly became rich landlords. Kings, emperors, and nobles who owned a large region, chose and rewarded their own bishops. The system lent itself to corruption and decline for those holding high offices in the Church.

Lay Investiture

In the last chapter, we learned that wealthy feudal lords, and this included the king or the emperor, placed bishops over wealthy benefices. When a bishop died, the lord chose another person to serve as bishop and placed him over that same benefice. Because the benefice made its bishop immediately wealthy, it became a post sought after by those looking for a life of luxury and comfort.

When a king or emperor chose his bishops, he chose those whom he trusted and who had the capabilities of providing an army in case of war. When he chose his candidate, he invested him with the signs of the office—a cross and ring. This was called **lay investiture**. A bishop ordained the chosen candidate, often without receiving permission from the pope.

The lords often appointed relatives to Church offices, especially to the office of bishop, a practice known as **nepotism**. Sometimes a lord sold the office to one who was willing to pay a high price for it, a practice known as **simony**. As mentioned in chapter two, the practice of simony receives its name from the attempt of Simon the Magician to buy Peter's power of bestowing the Holy Spirit on people. It refers to buying spiritual powers or a spiritual office.

The office of pope was not exempt from the practice of simony. With the political control of the Papal States and titles of leadership over vast territories, the papacy became a highly desired position for those seeking power or wealth. Powerful noble families influenced the election of popes, sometimes choosing a relative to serve as pope and sometimes supporting another powerful family who paid a high price for support.

With rich families influencing the election of the pope, intrigue and murder became common during this period. When one family managed to install its chosen pope, another powerful family would begin to plot his murder.

Thirty-seven popes reigned within a hundred years. All-too-frequently, warring families strangled, poisoned, or beat the reigning pope to death and installed their own candidate. Some popes died in battle, while a small number died natural deaths.

As a result of these practices, the leadership of the Church was in the hands of a series of popes and bishops seeking political and financial power. These popes often hindered the efforts of those who worked for spiritual renewal.

The bishops, who bought their positions, commonly recovered their money by imposing heavy and unjust taxes on those who worked the land in their benefices. Many bishops never lived in their benefices, but rather spent their time hunting and traveling. Most people never knew the name of their bishop.

Miraculously, Christianity survived. During this time, a number of dedicated bishops and monastic communities worked for reform. The clergy, who worked among the common people, and many laypeople kept Christianity alive through their dedication and practices of devotion.

The struggle of the era became a struggle between those who sought to reform the Church by ending lay investiture and kings and emperors who wanted to retain the right to choose their own bishops. The reforming party saw that the only way to have worthy candidates for leadership in the Church was to take the right to choose bishops and abbots from temporal rulers. This struggle would continue for centuries.

Pope John XII (955–964)

Alberic II, head of an influential family in Rome, used his power to name at least five successive popes. When he was dying, he made his eighteen-year-old son his final choice. The young man, Octavian, was living a wild life of pleasure and luxury when he became pope.

*B*ishops, with [ordained] priests as co-workers, have as their first task 'to preach the Gospel of God ....,' in keeping with the Lord's command. They are 'heralds of faith, who draw new disciples to Christ; they are authentic teachers' of the apostolic faith 'endowed with the authority of Christ.'
Catechism of the Catholic Church, #888

And remember, I am with you always, to the end of the age.

Matthew 28:20, NRSV

Octavian chose the name of John XII, but being pope did not change his way of life. During his reign, the papacy reached its lowest level.

When John XII's enemies threatened his position, he sought help from Otto I of Germany, the most powerful European king since Charlemagne, to help him retain his position as pope. In early 962, John XII crowned Otto as the new emperor of the Holy Roman Empire (a position not filled since the fall of the empire of Charlemagne) in an attempt to win Otto's favor.

When he became emperor, Otto I accepted the pope's invitation to become the protector of Rome, but his view of his role as emperor differed from that of John XII. He began to see himself as the protector of the Church, as well as the protector of Rome. He decreed that no new pope could be consecrated without his consent or that of his successors. When faced with this unexpected seizure of power over the Church by Otto I, John XII began to plot his murder. Otto, however, learned of the pope's plot and planned to kill the pope.

As Otto neared Rome, resolved to kill the pope, John XII fled. In the absence of the pope, Otto, with some bishops, held a trial and deposed John as pope, declaring that someone who lived as shameful a life as John had no right to be pope. Otto and the bishops then chose their own pope. When Otto left Italy, John marched back to Rome and banished the new pope who had replaced him.

When Pope John XII died, reformers hoped for a restoration of spiritual leadership within the office of pope. The state of the papacy, however, did not change. For almost a hundred years more, dedicated Christians had to tolerate unworthy popes selected by the powerful families of the empire. Despite the bad popes, the community of disciples miraculously survived and remained united. Many historians believe that the Church should have failed during this time, but the promise from Christ, that he would be with the community until the end of the world proved true.

A Few Saintly Leaders

Despite the corruption in the papacy, there were a number of saintly leaders who were focusing on the mission of Christ, fighting to keep the faith alive. Three of special interest are St. Stephen of Hungary, a Holy Roman emperor named Henry II, and St. Kunegunda. These three leaders dedicated themselves to preserving the spiritual power of the Church during its time of crisis.

St. Stephen became the first King of Hungary in 997, and with the help of the German emperor and Pope Sylvester II, he united the people of his country and converted a number of them to Christianity. He also established centers for the development of the spiritual life of the people and supported missionary activity within and outside his kingdom. His work proved to be of great influence and strength for the people of his kingdom during a time of corruption in the Church and government. One such person was St. Margaret of Scotland, for it was in St. Stephen's kingdom that she was born and educated.

Henry II, a pious German king, became emperor in 1014. St. Henry directed his boundless energy toward Church reform and spreading the gospel through missionary activity throughout the empire. As emperors before and after him, he could have lived a comfortable life as emperor, but he chose to use his office to serve Christ.

The Church also honors Henry's wife, Kunegunda, as a saint who helped sustain the faith of the people. She became a Benedictine nun in 1024, after the death of Henry.

Cluny

While the papacy was enduring its period of decay, Duke William III of Aquitaine founded a small monastery at Cluny in France in 910. William chose a

In the Spotlight

St. Margaret of Scotland was born and raised in Hungary, but due to the hardship caused by the war in England she and her family were forced to flee from the country. As one of the last members of the Anglo-Saxon royal family, she was in danger after the Norman Conquest and took refuge at the court of Malcolm III, king of Scotland. Margaret and Malcolm fell in love and were married in 1069. Their marriage was exceptionally happy and fruitful. Together they had eight children.

As queen, Margaret helped Scotland acquire a higher level of civilization by promoting the arts of civilization and encouraging education and religion. She also made it her constant ambition to acquire good clergy and teachers for all parts of the country, and formed a kind of embroidery guild among the ladies of the court to provide vestments and Church furniture.

She was also a principal agent in the reform of the Church in Scotland. She exhorted Church leaders to convene local councils to eliminate the practice of simony and other abuses. Together, she and her husband, founded many churches and monasteries. One of the most notable churches is the Holy Trinity at Dunfermline.

Her personal life was one of extreme self-discipline and sacrifice and she was devoted to prayer and reading of the Scripture. She ate sparingly, and in order to to obtain time for her devotions she permitted herself very little sleep. Every year she kept two Lents, one at Easter and one at Christmas. At these times she always rose at midnight and went to the Church for Matins, the king often joining her in her

S. Margaret. Queen.

vigils. On her return she washed the feet of six poor persons and gave them alms. She and her husband both realized their need for God's help in running the country, and they became admired for their spirit of prayer and sacrifice.

Margaret died four days after her husband in 1093. Since her death, she has been revered as a saintly queen, mother, advisor to the king, reformer and spiritual counselor. She is the patron saint of Scotland and her feast day is November 16. She is usually represented by art as carrying a black cross as she goes about her charitable work caring for the sick.

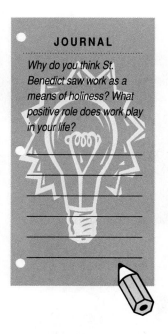

monk named Berno who was well known for his dedication to The Rule of Saint Benedict and who sought to reform the monastery in which he resided. Berno originally requested that William provide land for the new monastery.

William placed the deed for the land directly under the jurisdiction and protection of "Peter and Paul," naming the pope to act in the apostles' place. By doing this, he kept bishops or local lords from interfering with the daily life of the monastery. To protect against a weak pope, the deed explicitly forbade the pope from possessing that which belonged to Peter and Paul. This meant that the deed belonged to the Church, but the pope had no control over the land.

At the time, monasticism had deteriorated badly, due to pillage by invaders and the corruption of ambitious prelates and abbots. Those who sincerely wished to follow The Rule of St. Benedict encountered difficulty. Berno, chosen to begin the monastery at Cluny, sincerely worked for reform.

Berno reformed monastic life at Cluny and other monasteries leaving a legacy to his successors. Two centuries of faithful and dedicated abbots followed Berno, thus establishing Cluny as an example of the much needed revival in the Church. Following the example of Berno, the abbots at Cluny allowed other monasteries, dedicated to the strict monastic life, to join its reform.

Unlike the independent Benedictine monasteries, the Cluny monasteries all followed the same laws and procedures. The abbot at Cluny appointed the abbot of each monastery founded from Cluny, and the monks paid a small tax to Cluny.

Because of their relationship with Cluny, the new monasteries shared Cluny's privilege of freedom from control of a lay lord or a bishop. At a time when the control of a lay lord, bishop, or corrupt abbot often had disastrous influence on a monastery, the unity with Cluny provided an opportunity for interior control of the daily spiritual life of the monks.

The eleventh century saw the establishment of many monasteries of women which followed the same procedures of reform. By the twelfth century, over one thousand monasteries had joined Cluny, and the reforms of Cluny played a key role in the spiritual revival of Christianity.

Wealth and Decline

Although the monks at Cluny could own nothing, the monastery itself could accept gifts from those who endorsed the lifestyle of the monks or saw their donations as a means of salvation. Although the movement called for a simple life of poverty for its bishops and monks, Cluny became a powerful and wealthy monastic movement. According to the Rule, the monasteries had the obligation of sharing their wealth with the Church and the poor.

As a result of the growing wealth of the monasteries, many of the monks no longer needed to work for sustenance. They could spend most of their time in prayer. The community's main activity was the daily praying of the psalms and reading of the Scriptures during certain hours of the day. Their prayer life left little time for the Benedictine ideal of work, which Benedict saw as a means of holiness. Their work included the copying of sacred manuscripts.

In its first century of existence, Cluny had become so deeply involved in reform that it affected a reform of the entire Church, including the papacy. People found spiritual encouragement and religious example in the Cluny movement. Although most people did not become monks, many did adopt some of the spiritual practices found in the monastic life. Some of these people joined with the monks at Cluny to work for a reformed papacy.

Several reformers touched by Cluny eventually became pope. Inspired by Cluny, Pope Leo IX sought to make the papacy free from obligation to all civil authority, whether kings or nobles. Other popes eliminated the practices of simony and lay investiture of bishops. Following the monastic ideal, some popes demanded celibacy of their clergy, obedience to the pope, and a life of prayer.

As happened in so many other inspired movements within Christianity, the wealth of Cluny led to a decline in its monastic spirit. Simplicity of life disappeared, and a life saturated with ornate vessels for worship and more lavish living quarters replaced it. After two centuries of spiritual renewal, the movement floundered in its own wealth, lost the admiration of the people, and slowly disintegrated.

Cistercians

With the decline of the Cluny movement, many monks sought a return to the simple life. In 1098, St. Robert of Molesme, an abbot of a Benedictine monastery, left his monastery with twenty-one followers and established a monastery in Citeaux, a town in present-day France. At Citeaux, the monks developed a Rule based on simplicity of life and dedication to solitude, prayer, work, and community. The monks wore plain robes, prayed a simple form of daily prayer, and lived in huts.

Since the Latin name for the town Citeaux was Cistertium, the movement became known as **Cistercian**. The Cistercians could boast of many holy and dedicated monks, but the most notable is Bernard of Clairvaux. Around 1112, he came to the small and struggling community at Citeaux with a number of friends and relatives. Under him, the Cistercian movement grew rapidly.

When the community at Citeaux grew too large, Bernard received the call to found a new community. This new monastery grew rapidly and became the center of monastic and Church reform. Although Bernard longed for a life of solitude and prayer, he developed a reputation as a wise and learned preacher. He traveled extensively and played a leading role in settling civil and Church conflicts.

The Cistercians continued to grow and spread as they opened monasteries in other areas and provided a form of unity among these monasteries. Unlike Cluny, each independent monastery had its own leadership, and the Cistercian abbot would visit other Cistercian monasteries once each year. Although founded by the abbot Robert, it was the abbot Bernard who played the biggest role in the spread of the Cistercian movement.

KEY TERMS

Cistercian: a movement, started by St. Robert of Molesme in Citeaux, which worked to bring the Benedictine ideals back to monastic life; named after Cistertium, the Latin name for the town Citeaux.

CLIPBOARD

1. How does the Church's present practice of choosing bishops differ from the era of lay investiture?

2. How do the lives of the popes of the past fifty years differ from those of the popes who lived during the period of papal decay?

3. People expected monks such as those at Cluny and the Cistercians to practice a holier life than the ordinary person. What do you think constitutes a holy life? Do you think that ordained priests and nuns should be expected to live holier lives than the ordinary person today? Why or why not?

Problems Facing Reforming Popes

The Christian Times

Twelfth Century   Vol. 12   No. 2

Pope and Emperor End Lay Investiture

Late last week, Pope Callistus II signed an agreement with Emperor Henry V in an effort to end the emperor's role in appointing bishops. In the agreement, called the *Concordat of Worms*, the pope is given the sole authority to appoint bishops, likewise all bishops appointed must make an allegiance acceptable to the emperor.

This agreement brings to an end the controversy on lay investiture by rulers. This practice has dominated relations between the Church and rulers for centuries. Pope Leo IX brought reform to the Church, but he was not able to fully eliminate lay investiture.

According to Cardinal Humbert, the papal legate to the patriarch of the East, the refusal to reject lay investiture was one of the reasons why Patriarch Michael Cerularius broke with the Church in the West.

Most notable among the popes who fought with emperors over the issue of lay investiture was Pope Gregory VII, who actually brought the emperor to his knees at a place called Canossa.

NOTEPAD
? ? ? ? ?

1. What did you learn about Pope Callistus II? Emperor Henry V? Pope Leo IV? Cardinal Humbert? Patriarch Michael Cerularius? Pope Gregory VII?

2. What is the major issue mentioned in this article?

3. What do you think were the results of ending lay investiture?

The Rest of the Story

The close link between church and state continued to exist throughout the empire. Emperors were not only influential in appointing their own bishops, but they had a major influence in the choice of the pope. At times, the emperor was so powerful that no one would dare challenge his choice for a new pope.

Pope Leo IX (1049–1054)

In the year 1049, the western emperor, Henry III, chose a noted reformer bishop, Bruno, as pope. Bruno wanted to assure himself that the people of Rome agreed with the emperor's choice, so he declared that he would enter Rome as a pilgrim. As he walked barefoot across northern Italy on his pilgrimage to Rome, hoards of people came out to meet him and applaud him. With the people and clergy clearly favoring his appointment, Bruno took the name of Pope Leo IX.

When Pope Leo IX began his reforms, he surrounded himself with a number of like-minded reformers who would have an influence on Church policy for decades to come. Pope Leo traveled extensively and convoked a number of councils to reform abuses.

With the appointment of Leo as pope, reformers believed that a true reform of Christianity would take place. But Leo, despite his dedication to reform, was also a product of his age. Like any child coming from a wealthy family, he had received the usual training in the use of arms, and he was willing to bear arms when he felt the cause of God demanded it.

Leo led his troops into an unsuccessful battle with the Norsemen in Sicily and southern Italy. He was taken prisoner, and the pope who showed so much promise for reform died in prison after a mere five years as pope. Despite Leo's untimely death, however, the desire for reform had taken root, and many bishops were determined to keep it alive.

The Break between Constantinople and the Pope

The controversies involved in Leo's reign did not end with his death. The Church in the East and in the West had many differences throughout the centuries. Since the decline of the power of the emperor in the West, the popes became powerful political leaders as well as spiritual leaders. In the East, however, the emperors still had power, and they often interfered with Church matters. Some patriarchs of the Church in the East accepted this intervention, while others rejected it.

The Church in the West also differed from the Church in the East on some issues of importance. At the time of Pope Leo, an archbishop in the East accused the Church in the West of being in error concerning its call for ordained priests to abstain from marriage and its celebration of the Eucharist with unleavened bread.

Leo became embroiled in the controversy and sent Cardinal Humbert, an unfortunate choice, to meet with Patriarch Michael Cerularius. The Latin language and culture dominated the Church in the West, while the Greek culture and language dominated in the East. Humbert, unfortunately, had little knowledge of Greek culture and remained rigid in his stance against the Patriarch. Cardinal Humbert was a firm supporter of the Church in the West and staunchly supported its reform. He believed that reform could take place only with an unmarried clergy and a Church free from political domination.

Patriarch Michael Cerularius proved himself to be as unbending as Cardinal Humbert in his stances. He actually sought a break with Rome, which would make him head of the Church in the East. Humbert and Cerularius met in a bitter debate, insulted each other, and left the meeting seething in anger.

The day after Humbert and Cerularius met, Humbert stormed into the Church of St. Sophia and publicly excommunicated Cerularius in the name of Pope Leo IX. Unknown to Humbert, Pope Leo IX had already died. Patriarch Michael Cerularius reacted to the excommunication by declaring that he was the sole head of the Church of Constantinople and that the Church at Constantinople had some differences with the West which had not been resolved.

The extent of the break went unnoticed at first, since the East and the West had had their differences in the past. Besides, an excommunication on behalf of the dead pope had no power. Although the historical date given for the break between the Catholic Church in the West and the Orthodox Church in the East is 1054, the real events cementing the break did not take place until two centuries later, when a crusading army from the West pillaged Constantinople and humiliated the patriarch and the population.

Besides the Eastern Orthodox Church, there is also an Eastern Catholic Church, which uses its own language in liturgy and accepts the pope as the head of the Catholic Church. These Eastern Catholics bring the richness of the Eastern Church into their unity with Rome. In areas in the East, where a Greek Orthodox Church exists today, we can also find the Eastern Catholic Church.

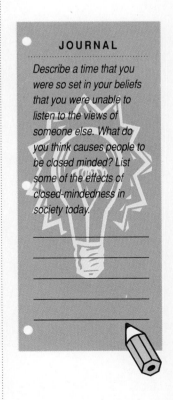

JOURNAL

Describe a time that you were so set in your beliefs that you were unable to listen to the views of someone else. What do you think causes people to be closed minded? List some of the effects of closed-mindedness in society today.

Protecting the Reform

At the death of Pope Leo, the bishops at first refused to allow the emperor or the people of Rome to select the pope. They feared that the powerful families in Italy would again seize control of the election and ruin their attempts at reform. In the end, the bishops allowed the Roman people to elect a pope, but they decreed that he had to be German, not Italian. This was to keep the powerful Roman factions in Italy from regaining the papacy.

The people elected a reforming pope, Victor II (1055-1057), who followed the example of Leo IX. When the emperor died, the new pope became the guardian of the emperor's seven-year-old son, Henry IV. Thus, the pope ruled both the Church and the empire for a short time.

Nicholas II (1059-1061) became pope two years after Victor's death, and he called a Lateran Synod in 1059 in an effort to reform the process of electing the pope. Three centuries earlier, a Lateran Synod stated that only cardinals may be elected pope and that the laity could not elect the pope. The honorary office of cardinals, however, included laypeople as well as bishops. Pope Nicholas decided to further clarify who could elect the pope.

The Lateran Synod, led by Pope Nicholas, decreed that only cardinals who were bishops could elect the pope. The other cardinals, along with the clergy and people of Rome, could only express their consent. The emperor received the right of confirmation, but the extent of the right was unclear and confusing.

By limiting the election of pope to the bishop cardinals, the council hoped to keep alive the movement to reform the Church. Since popes held reform in the Church as a priority, the bishop cardinals believed that the pope would appoint bishop cardinals who supported reform. These, in turn, would elect a pope who supported reform.

Gregory VII (1073–1085)

In 1073, the people of Rome clamored for the popular and pious monk, Hildebrand, to be chosen as pope. Hildebrand, as an advisor to a number of popes, had already served in many diplomatic positions for the Church. The people recognized his holiness and dedication, as well as his political abilities. Although Nicholas II had decreed that cardinals who were bishops would choose the pope, the situation changed slightly when the people chose Hildebrand and the cardinal bishops agreed with this decision.

Hildebrand took the name, Gregory VII, and continued to work for reform in the Church. Longing for the scriptural reality of having one shepherd and one flock, he dreamed of uniting the Muslims and the East with the papacy. However, his plans for unity under the papacy never reached fulfillment.

Gregory encountered problems from an unexpected source. When Henry IV became emperor, Gregory believed that the emperor would support the papacy, since two popes had had a hand in raising him as a child. Henry, however, believed that the bishops and other prelates were so powerful that he would have to control their appointment if he were to retain power. If the pope gave a powerful benefice to an enemy, the emperor would face the threat of rebellion within his own empire.

A confrontation between Gregory and Henry took place over the right of choosing a new bishop for Milan. Gregory appointed his own bishop, and Henry deposed him and appointed another in his place. Gregory ordered Henry to report to Rome by a specific date or face the loss of his soul. In response, Henry, with the support of a local council, decreed that Gregory was no longer the valid pope.

Henry did not arrive at Rome on the date specified by Gregory, so the pope decreed that Henry could no longer rule the kingdoms of Germany and Italy. He released Henry's subjects from all obedience and oaths of loyalty to Henry. Henry tried to resist, but his enemies used the pope's decree as an excuse for not obeying him. He realized that he had to seek the pope's pardon.

Henry asked Gregory for private forgiveness, but the pope ordered him to make public penance. The pope, still not sure whether Henry would come to repent or to murder him, set the meeting for Canossa, which was heavily fortified and offered protection to the pope.

When Henry arrived at Canossa, he had to beg for admission and was forced to do penance in the cold for three days before Gregory received him. Although Gregory suspected that Henry would not honor the terms of his repentance, he felt that he had to accept Henry's penitential gestures in the spirit of a forgiving Christian. He pardoned Henry and withdrew his sentence against him.

When Henry returned to Germany, he fought against his enemies who had used his difficulty with Gregory as a reason for rebellion. Gregory remained silent and refused to support Henry against the rebels when they elected their own emperor. When civil war broke out, Gregory, still not trusting Henry, supported the false emperor. Many of those who abandoned Henry in his first dispute with the pope, now supported him and elected a rival pope, who took the name, Clement III. The rebel emperor was killed in battle, and Henry again became the sole ruler of the empire.

In the spring of 1081, Henry marched on Gregory in Rome. Gregory's only possible allies were the Normans to the south, but Gregory had excommunicated them. The people of Rome first rallied to the support of Gregory, but when he refused to settle with Henry, they opened the gates of Rome for the emperor to enter. Gregory fled, and Henry established Clement III as pope.

The scene changed rapidly. The Normans took advantage of the situation and invaded Rome, forcing Henry to flee. They burned the city, murdered some of the inhabitants, and enslaved others. Gregory died before he could return to Rome, and Henry IV died in 1106 while preparing to wage war against his son, Henry V.

Concordat of Worms

In 1122, Pope Calixtus II (1119–1124) sought to end all disputes with the emperor through the **Concordat of Worms**. In this agreement, the emperor, Henry V, allowed the Church to choose its own bishops according to its own procedures. The emperor could attend these elections, but he was not allowed to exert any influence in the form of simony or military power.

The bishops chosen by Church authority were to pledge their allegiance to the emperor before receiving their feudal rights from him. After pledging their allegience to the emperor, they would receive their ring and crozier, the symbols of their office, from Church authority.

Although these solutions did not end the investiture controversy immediately, they did present a foundation for later developments in Church appointments. Calixtus convoked the first ecumenical council held in the West, known as the **First Lateran Council**, to ratify the decisions of the Concordat of Worms. The council met in Rome in 1123.

JOURNAL

What do you see as the cause for the invasion of Rome? How can you apply this to your personal life?

KEY TERMS

Concordat of Worms: an agreement, made in 1122 between Pope Calistus II and Emperor Henry V, that gave the pope the exclusive power of appointing bishops; the bishops chosen were required to pledge their allegience to the emperor.

First Lateran Council: first ecumenical council held in the West; called by Pope Calistus II to ratify the decisions of the Concordat of Worms.

CLIPBOARD

1. Would you expect a pope today to enter into battle? Explain.
2. Tell what you know about the Christian Church of the East today.
3. Compare the process of choosing bishops as agreed upon in the Concordat of Worms with the process that is used today?

The Age of the Crusades

The Christian Times

Twelfth Century   Vol. 12   No. 4

Uncontrolled Crusade Angers Pope

Pope Innocent III, yesterday, lashed out at the leaders of the Fourth Crusade when he received news that they invaded and captured the major city of Byzantium. The crusades, as we all know, began a little more than a century ago, when Pope Urban II called upon Christians to protect the Church in the East from the Turkish Muslims.

Since their beginning, the crusades have proven difficult to control. The well-known Peter the Hermit, for instance, performed wondrous tasks for the crusades, but he also wrought his degree of havoc. The children's crusades brought tears to many families in the empire.

The religious orders of the Knights Templars and the Knights Hospitallers were founded during this period to save the Holy Land from the non-Christian invaders. These orders were more sincere in their motivations than many of the armies, who used the crusades as a cover for their own desire to plunder other lands.

Reflecting on the past century, we must wonder whether the crusades had any lasting effect on the world. We discovered that the Muslim world was not only willing to fight, but, on a more positive note, we learned that they had preserved a great deal of learning from the past.

Perhaps the greatest profit of the crusades comes in learning, rather than in military conquests.

NOTEPAD
? ? ? ? ?

1. What did you learn about the crusades in this article?
2. Why was the pope so angry with the Fourth Crusade?
3. What was the reporter's opinion of religious orders of fighting men? How do you feel about them?

The Rest of the Story

Many popes of this time period came from the wealthy class, which trained its young men for battle with the expectation that they would someday lead some troops into war. These popes often attempted to solve religious problems through military force. Many believed that the way to spread Christianity was through conquest. Church and state had become so closely aligned that some popes felt helpless unless they could prove their military power. If they could not raise an army themselves, they looked to kings and lords to fight in the defense of the Church.

First Crusade (1095)
Despite the ill feelings the Byzantines held for the Church in the West, the Byzantine emperor felt that he had no choice but to call on Pope Urban II to protect his land and people against the Turkish Muslims. Urban saw the invitation not only as an opportunity to mend the fracture between the East and West, but also as an opportunity to liberate the Holy Land, which was then under Muslim control. After the split between the Orthodox Church in the East and the Church in the West in 1054, each new pope sought opportunities for reunion.

Pope Urban had to convince the people of the West to fight against the Muslims. Aware of the high esteem

Christians had for the Holy Land, Urban preached fiery sermons against the Muslims and their control of the Holy Land. With the Holy Land in the hands of the Turkish Muslims, Christians would never again be able to make their pilgrimages to the land of Jesus' birth and ministry.

Urban had aroused the people to such a degree that they willingly marched off to fight their first crusade against the Muslims in 1095. Pope Urban encouraged Christians to view the crusades as a holy war. He asked them to take up the cross (*crux* in Latin, thus the word *crusade*) against those who held the Holy Land. The battle cry became, "God wills it."

The response to the First Crusade was due to several factors. Some people found in the crusades an opportunity to escape their own poverty and diseased lands. Others, especially younger sons who could not hope to inherit property, found a career and prestige. Some simply desired adventure and travel. The pope introduced a new motive into the crusades by promising an indulgence to those who fought the crusade. With this somewhat ambiguous promise of salvation added to the usual motivations, the pope was able to rally a strong army, filled with the spirit of adventure and religious zeal.

The excitement of the crusading spirit spread across the West with the echoing ring of "God wills it." A crusader was signed with the cross, and the shields of the crusaders bore the emblem of the cross. Popular preachers inspired the people to join the crusades and sometimes led small armies to places where they knew they would link up with the crusaders.

Problems in the Crusading Spirit

The preacher, Peter the Hermit, rallied an army and led them toward Jerusalem to join the crusades. The trail these troops blazed to Jerusalem was one of shame for the crusades, since the army caused devastation and bloodshed in the lands along their journey.

Under-provisioned, they ravaged the lands to feed the army. They also slaughtered thousands of Jews, whom they perceived as heretics. Only a small number of this group were alive when they finally joined the real crusaders.

The Byzantine army and the crusaders fought valiantly against the Turkish Muslims. The two groups fought together against the common enemy, but they had to be kept in strict control by the Byzantine emperor to keep them from plundering the cities they conquered.

The battles became so intense and bloody that many of those who survived the battles finally abandoned the crusade before it reached the Holy Land. In 1099, a remnant of the crusaders reached Jerusalem. They found the fields around the city scorched and the water poisoned, and they met fierce resistance from the inhabitants defending the city.

As had happened in other areas of the empire, Muslim groups inside Jerusalem had weakened their own defense by squabbling among themselves. With the determination of soldiers fighting a religious war, the crusaders took advantage of this disunity within the Muslim ranks. They broke into Jerusalem and shamefully raped the women and killed most of the inhabitants—Jews, Muslims, and even a number of Christians. When many of the Jews took refuge in a synagogue, the crusaders burned the building with the Jews inside.

Crusading Monastic Groups

Some monastic groups in the East also felt the intense spirit of the crusades, especially in protecting the Holy Land from the Muslims. Many of them took the usual vows of poverty, chastity, and obedience, but they added the promise of protecting the Holy Land. These monks came from the rich class of nobles who were well trained for battle.

The **Knights Hospitallers**, the earliest foundation, originated before the crusades, about 1023, as a nursing group

'But I say to you that listen, love your enemies, do good to those who hate you, bless those who curse you, pray for those who abuse you. If anyone strikes you on the cheek, offer the other also; and from anyone who takes away your coat do not withhold even your shirt. Give to everyone who begs from you; and if anyone takes away your goods, do not ask for them again. Do to others as you would have them do to you.'

Luke 6:27–31, NRSV

KEY TERMS

Knights Hospitallers: a nursing group who cared for the pilgrims in Jerusalem; originated before the crusades as the earliest foundation in about 1023.

THOU SHALT NOT PERISH

Pope Innocent III

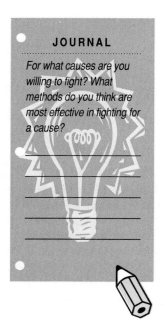

JOURNAL

*For what causes are you
willing to fight? What
methods do you think are
most effective in fighting for
a cause?*

for the care of pilgrims in Jerusalem. A century later (1120), they transformed themselves into the *Knights of the Hospital of St. John* in Jerusalem and became purely military. The **Templars**, another group, remained faithful to their medical work, and their red cross on a white field is a universally recognized symbol of mercy today.

The Remaining Crusades

The Second Crusade (1148-1149) was fought as a result of the renewed power of the Muslims, and their regaining of some of the land they had lost during the First Crusade. The Crusade failed when the Turkish Muslims dealt the crusaders a number of defeats.

The recapture of Jerusalem by the Muslims in 1187 became the occasion for the Third Crusade (1189-1192). Under the leadership of Emperor Frederick I, who died on the journey to the Holy Land, many internal problems among the crusaders began to surface. These problems and the power of the Muslim armies doomed this crusade.

The Fourth Crusade (1203-1204) began with the intention of freeing the Holy Land, but the crusades now were

more obviously motivated by the desire for material plunder. Although the original hope of Pope Urban II was to use the crusades to repair the disunity between the East and the West, the crusaders actually caused a major break between the two. The crusaders invaded and conquered Constantinople, and then established a patriarch from the Latin Church. They apparently believed that this would force the Church of Constantinople to unite with the West.

When Pope Innocent III heard about the conquest of Constantinople, he was furious. He had called the crusade to fight the Muslims in Egypt and had not prepared himself for the news of the invasion of Constantinople. His temper eventually calmed when he reasoned that this victory was perhaps God's way of uniting East and West. When the Byzantine army recaptured Constantinople, however, both sides realized that the breach between East and West had widened.

One crusading group of teenagers and children foolishly marched off to battle, believing that the power of God would help them defeat the powerful enemy forces. Some called this the *Children's Crusade*. The enemy killed most of the young people and forced the rest into slavery.

A number of small armies at times pursued their own personal crusade, with no official call from the Church. History does not count these small armies as legitimate crusades. When the crusades finally ended, they had covered a period of almost two hundred years.

Effects of the Crusades

The Muslims and Jews had a greater interest in learning than other groups of people within the empire, with the exception of the clergy. Muslims studied the ancient philosophers. Writings from philosophers such as Aristotle became known to the crusaders who now mixed with the people they had conquered. In the next centuries, this knowledge of philosophy would greatly influence the development of theology in Christianity.

The crusades facilitated the development of cities and of an economy where trade once again flourished. A new wealthy class emerged as trade became as important as land. Trade contributed to the growth of cities, where a new class, the **bourgeoisie**, began to emerge. The name means literally "those who live in the city." Merchants had become a new power in the world.

CLIPBOARD

1. What would be your reaction if Christians were prohibited from visiting the Holy Land today and the pope were to ask for a crusade against those in control?

2. If you had the power to control the lives of thousands of people and wanted to unite the world with Christ today, how would you go about it?

3. How have the crusades affected our lives today?

REVIEWING THE ERA

- **900**

WILLIAM OF AQUITAINE FOUNDS A MONASTERY AT CLUNY. The monastery was placed in the hands of Peter and Paul (the Church) to keep corrupt kings and popes from controlling it. Berno, its first abbot, reformed monastic life at Cluny and some other monasteries and left a legacy to his successors.

- **950**

POPE JOHN XII. This was the most depraved pope in history. He was also the first pope to change his name upon becoming pope.
KING OTTO I OF GERMANY CROWNED EMPEROR. Pope John XII crowned King Otto I of Germany emperor, in an attempt to gain a protector from his enemies. This renewed the Holy Roman Empire after three hundred years without an emperor.

- **1050**

POPE LEO IX. This pope sought to reform the Church by overcoming lay investiture.
THE EASTERN SCHISM. This term refers to the break between the Orthodox Church in the East and the Church in the West. Cardinal Humbert and Patriarch Michael Cerularius brought about the break.
POPE GREGORY VII. This popular and saintly pope believed that the pope had the right to rule the spiritual lives of the people and of kings. He made the emperor, Henry IV, humbly seek forgiveness for offenses against the Church.
BEGINNING OF THE CRUSADES. The crusades had as their original intent the recapture of the Holy Land from the Muslims. They lasted almost two centuries with many failures and a few successes.
ROBERT FOUNDS CISTERCIAN COMMUNITY. Robert, an abbot of a Benedictine monastery, left his monastery with twenty-one followers and established a monastery Citeaux in France. The name Citeaux is the root for *Cistercian*, which is the community's more popular name.

- **1100**

BERNARD OF CITEAUX. Bernard came to the small and struggling community at Citeaux with a number of friends and relatives. Under him, the Cistercian movement grew rapidly.
CONCORDAT OF WORMS. In 1122, Pope Calixtus II (1119–1124) received for the Church the right to choose its own bishops, as long as the bishops promised their allegiance to the emperor.

- **1200**

THE FOURTH CRUSADE. Crusaders captured Constantinople and later lost it. It made the rift between the East and the West wider.

KEY TERMS

Lay investiture

Nepotism

Simony

Cistercian

Concordat of Worms

First Lateran Council

Knights of Hospitallers

Templars

Bourgeoisie

 A Voice from the Past

As a concerned and dedicated editorialist you are going to educate your readers about an unpleasant period in our Church history. Using all of the key terms discuss the conflicts encountered with lay investiture and the abuses it brought to Church leadership. Explain how the schism in the Church occurred, and why the crusades were fought. End your column with a discussion of how the abuses that occurred in the Church and the crusades still affect us today.

Then and Now

The major conflict during this period was lay investiture. This was the practice of allowing kings, lords, and emperors to appoint bishops and give them the signs of their office. The practice led to many abuses in Church leadership, such as leaders favoring relatives with a Church office/position (nepotism) and the selling of offices (simony).

Reforming popes worked to revoke the practice of lay investiture. While doing this, the Orthodox Church in the East and the Church in the West split. With hopes of uniting the western Church with the Orthodox Church of the East,

Pope Urban II began the crusades. Almost two centuries later, when they ended, the split between the Churches was wider.

Today lay investiture no longer exists. The pope ordinarily chooses bishops for the Church throughout the world. The split between the Othodox Church of the East and the Catholic Church still exists, with the Orthodox Church refusing to recognize the leadership of the pope over the Church. The Church today seeks to reform the world through peaceful means, rather than by calling people to "holy war."

NEWS IN REVIEW

1. What were some issues the pope had to address in overcoming the practice of lay investiture?

2. Why is Pope John XII known as the most depraved pope in Church history? What custom did he establish that still exists today?

3. Why did William of Aquitaine feel a need to establish a new monastery, and how did he do it?

4. What did the Cistercians contribute to Church history?

5. What were some of the accomplishments and failures of Pope Leo IX?

6. Who was Pope Gregory VII, and what did he accomplish for the Church?

7. What did the Concordat of Worms achieve?

8. What was the purpose of the First Crusade, and who called for the crusade?

9. How did some monastic groups respond to the crusades?

10. What did the crusades do for the hopes for unity between the Church in the West and the Church at Constantinople?

chapter nine

Religious Revival and the Avignon Papacy

If we were living in the fourteenth century, we would expect the king to appoint bishops and may even resent the pope's intrusion in our country if he wanted to choose this right for himself. Since the pope himself was a ruler of a large country, we may suspect him of choosing bishops for political, rather than spiritual reasons. Our memories and stories would be of popes quarreling with lords and kings over the right to appoint bishops.

We would become accustomed to seeing bishops living in luxury and expect that a bishop would be either a relative of the king or one who paid well for his office. We could expect to have an increase in taxes whenever a new bishop had to raise money to replenish his funds after paying for his office.

As a minister of confirmation, the bishop expresses the apostolic unity of the Church.

Reaction to Church Wealth

The Christian Times

Fifteenth Century   Vol. 15   No. 1

Luxury of Church Leaders Draws Reaction

In a reaction to the luxurious lifestyle of some religious leaders, new ideas in monastic living are arising. For example, one new group of monks does not withdraw from the world. The monks live a life of poverty, beg for their food, and preach. Some people have used the expression *mendicant* for this new movement.

Two well-known founders of these mendicant groups are Dominic de Guzman and Francis of Assisi. Clare of Assisi has also established an order of women who are following a rule similar to that of Francis and his associates.

Word has reached us from France that the Church is begin-ning to show concern for a new heresy called *Albigensianism*, which is sweeping across southern France. The Albigensians teach that the body is evil and only the spirit is good. They claim that the elegance of the bishops shows that they are controlled by evil.

People have reacted to the scandalous lifestyle of some religious leaders differently. Peter Waldo and his followers have dedicated themselves to a life of poverty, but they have been publicly critical of the Catholic Church and, as a result, excommunicated by the pope.

NOTEPAD
? ? ? ? ?

1. What did you learn about Dominic de Guzman? Francis of Assisi? Clare of Assisi? Peter Waldo?

2. What did you learn from this article about the different movements taking place in the Church?

3. Who are some present-day followers of Dominic or Francis?

The Rest of the Story

As more bishops and popes became wealthy landowners, they began to live like wealthy nobles. Many Christians, resenting their example, began to live a life of extreme poverty and sacrifice. Some of the practices that they followed were so extreme that we would have a difficult time following them today.

KEY TERMS

Albigensians: a heretical group stemming out of Manichaeism; used two gods to explain the existence of good and evil.

Albigensians

One of the heretical groups that was fueled by the Church leaders' lifestyles was the **Albigensians**. A sect of neo-Manichaean, the group taught that creation had two gods, one good and one evil. The good God, the Christian God, created the angels and human souls, and the evil god, also known as Satan, created the material world. Because they saw Satan as the creator of the material world, they believed everything material to be evil. They believed that there was a constant raging battle between the two gods.

The Albigensian heresy prospered in southern France in the middle of the twelfth century, particularly in a town called Albi, from which the heresy received its name. It also prospered in northern Italy. Like other groups of people who rejected the elegant lifestyle of some religious leaders, the Albigensians went to the other extreme in their practice of austerity and poverty.

The Albigensians believed that a person had to live a life completely dedicated to the spiritual in order to reach salvation. Since the material world was evil, even ordinary acts, such as getting married or enjoying meals, were thought to be sinful. They believed that they were preparing themselves for an eternal reward through their austere practices to free themselves from material needs.

Albigensians caused problems for the political as well as the spiritual communities. Because everything material was evil, they felt that they could not bear arms. For political rulers, this meant that they could not depend on the Albigensians to defend them in battle. The Albigensian belief in a god of evil and a god of goodness contradicted the Christian Church's teaching. It also made the Albigensians highly critical of religious leaders who lived in luxury.

The Albigensians found themselves in the precarious position of alienating both the political and religious powers of the empire. In this situation, only God's protection could save them from destruction. Eventually they faced the onslaughts of ravaging armies.

St. Dominic de Guzman (1170–1221)

Dominc de Guzman, a young educated man dedicated to spreading the Word of God to those in need, accompanied Bishop Diego in 1203 to southern France, in an effort to convert the Albigensians. He respected certain qualities of the Albigensians, but rejected their severe solution to elegant living. Convinced that force was not the answer, Dominic attempted to convert them through preaching and example. In his teachings he followed a monastic order of the day, combining prayer and study. He aimed at showing the Albigensians the value of maintaining a

balance of education, prayer, and personal sacrifice. By meeting the Albigensians on their own ground he was able to win many of them over. With Bishop Diego he founded a house and school for women converts. The archbishop of the region, impressed with Dominic's success, furnished a church for his preaching and a house for his monastic community.

Upon receiving the Church and house for his monastic community, Dominic went to Pope Innocent III to ask for the pope's permission to establish a new order with its own rule. The pope refused, concerned about the proliferation of monastic rules, and urged Dominic to adopt an existing monastic rule while continuing his work. In 1215, Dominic and his followers adapted the Rule of the Canons of St. Augustine to their own needs, and the pope found this acceptable.

Dominic and his followers also adopted the rule of poverty. This enabled his group to refute the arguments of the Albigensians who claimed that orthodox Christianity was too worldly. Dominic traveled great distances on foot, establishing his order in France, Italy, and Spain. His enduring wish was to become a missionary to non-Christians, but his duties kept him from achieving his hope.

From the very beginning, the **Order of Preachers** (the official name of the Dominicans) stressed the need for learning, recognizing that preachers must be intellectually armed in order to refute heresy. The Dominicans lived in community, prayed and studied, and added a new dimension to religious life by allowing the community to elect its leadership.

Although the Dominicans recognized the necessity for personal sacrifice, they saw poverty as a means to an end. They gave top priority to learning, preaching, and teaching, even if it meant bending their rule of poverty. They lived poorly, but they recognized their need as

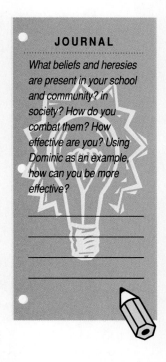

JOURNAL

What beliefs and heresies are present in your school and community? in society? How do you combat them? How effective are you? Using Dominic as an example, how can you be more effective?

_____

_____

_____

_____

KEY TERMS

Order of Preachers: the official name of the Dominicans, founded by Dominic; lived a communal life of prayer and study; introduced the practice of allowing the community to elect its leadership.

St. Dominic

a group to own property and to provide for their personal needs when their mission demanded it.

Because of the Domicans' interest in learning, they were soon recognized as respected teachers in the universities which were blossoming at the time. Paris and Oxford were the two main centers of theological studies, and the Dominicans had teachers in each of them. These Dominicans played leading roles in the development of theological learning and research in the Church.

Peter Waldo

Peter Waldo, a merchant from Lyons, sought to imitate the extreme poverty of some earlier monks. In 1273, he had a religious experience which touched him so deeply that he gave away his wealth, became a beggar, and dedicated himself to preaching a life of poverty and sacrifice. Unlike Dominic, however, Waldo did not value education, nor have the education necessary to preach. A number of men, aroused by Waldo's example of poverty and preaching, became his followers. They called themselves the **Poor Men of Lyons**.

As Waldo's group grew in numbers, the archbishop of Lyons became concerned when he realized that the group was attacking some central truths of the Church, such as prayers for the dead and the practice of confessing one's sins. He realized that the Poor Men of Lyons, although they practiced great poverty and sacrifice, did not have the knowledge necessary for preaching the message of the Church. The archbishop banned Waldo and his followers from preaching.

Waldo refused to accept this ban by the achbishop and appealed to the pope for support. The pope praised Waldo and his group for their edifying practice of poverty, but he supported the archbishop's ban against preaching. He ordered Waldo to remain obedient to his archbishop. Waldo refused to accept the pope's command, believing that only those who practiced poverty had a right to preach. The Poor Men of Lyons, despite their lack of learning, continued to preach, thus forcing the pope to excommunicate them.

Because of the pope's excommunication, Waldo and his followers retreated to villages in the Alps where they continued their mission. After Waldo's death, the group became more widely known as the Waldensians. They centered their belief and their preaching on the Bible alone, a practice which leads some commentators to view them as the forerunners of the Protestant Reformation. Three centuries after the death of Waldo in 1217, a group of Protestant reformers visited the Waldensians, and they joined the Protestant movement.

St. Francis of Assisi (1182–1226)

Young Francis of Assisi also had a deep religious experience which led him to leave his life of extravagance and comfort and live a life of service and poverty. Prior to his experience, he belonged to a wealthy merchant family and lived a life of extravagance and comfort. Like many young rich nobles of his time, he fought in a series of battles and was finally imprisoned. During his two years as a prisoner, he experienced a desire to change his luxurious lifestyle for one that would better serve God.

Upon his return home, Francis had a more profound religious experience which led him to embrace total poverty. When his father saw Francis distributing his wealth to poor people, he imprisoned him in the cellar, hoping to make him change his generous habits, or at least to prevent him from squandering his inheritance.

When Francis's father could not convince his son to abandon his desire to give away his fortune, he brought his case before the local authorities. Since bishops served as judges, Francis's father brought him before the bishop of Assisi. The bishop decided that Francis had to use his wealth wisely or renounce it completely. In response to the bishop's judgment, Francis opted to renounce all his worldly goods. He stripped himself of the clothes provided by his family, and left to work for lepers.

Francis continued to give away any gifts he received in order to help those who were poor. He praised the beauty of poverty and felt a harmony with nature. At one point, he rebuilt an abandoned chapel, believing that God was calling him to this task. In time, he realized that God was calling him to rebuild the entire Church, not just the little chapel building.

In 1209, Francis read in the Gospels that Jesus directed his disciples to leave all they had and to preach the good news. This inspired Francis to begin preaching. He ventured into the cities where he could preach to the people, while aiding those who were poor and those who were sick.

Although many of Francis's previous acquaintances mocked and ridiculed him when he returned to Assisi, he did encounter twelve men who wished to join him in his ministry and life of poverty. In time, Francis and his handful of followers traveled to Rome to seek permission from Pope Innocent III to found a new monastic order.

At Rome, Innocent showed no inclination to accept Francis's request. In 1209, however, after thinking that he had tested Francis enough, he granted permission. Within ten years, the Franciscans had grown to almost five thousand members. Francis's Rule was finally approved by Pope Honorius III in 1223.

The group founded by Francis received the title **Friars Minor**, which means "Lesser Brothers." They settled in Assisi, and from there, they spread out in small bands through central Italy, devoting themselves to prayer, work, and preaching. Francis also formed a group of laity known as *Brothers or Sisters of Penance*, later known as the *Third Order*.

With time the fame of his order grew rapidly, and Francis feared that the success of his movement would become its downfall. As the number of his followers increased, they began to receive gifts from those who witnessed their work and who wanted Francis and his followers to distribute these gifts. Tensions began to occur between those who supported the total poverty espoused by Francis, and those who felt it would be wise to have some security for the sake of the mission.

Shortly after Francis's death in 1226, two parties within his order sought two different ways of life for the group. One was a rigorist party, who wanted to remain faithful to Francis's strict way of poverty. The other was a more moderate group, who wanted to accept property if it helped the mission of the order.

In 1230, Pope Gregory IX declared that the will of Francis was not binding and that the order could ask Rome to alter the rule of poverty. As Francis feared, within fifteen years of receiving permission from the pope for a change, the order eventually came to have vast

St. Francis of Assisi

'*Sell all that you own and distribute the money to the poor, and you will have treasure in heaven; then come, follow me.*'

Luke 18:22, NRSV

KEY TERMS

Friars Minor: name, meaning "Lesser Brothers," given to the group founded by St. Francis.

JOURNAL

If you were able to found a religious order what would be your rules and principles? What would be your mission? In your journal write a hypothetical letter to the pope requesting permission to establish a religious order. In the letter outline your proposed principles, rules and mission. Also, give your reason for establishing a new order.

Poor Ladies: the name of the order founded by St. Clare, later known as Poor Clares.

holdings. The situation caused alarm for the rigorists and posed a challenge for the moderates.

In time, the missionary efforts of the Franciscans touched almost every area of the world. The work of the Franciscans in bringing an overwhelming number of people to Catholicism stands out as a miracle of history. The Franciscans continue to serve the Church throughout the world.

St. Clare of Assisi (1193–1253)

Clare of Assisi sought to join Francis in his life of complete poverty. As a young woman, she resisted a marriage arranged by her parents and sought advise from Francis concerning her dedication to God and poverty. Francis encouraged her in her ministry and offered support when she needed it. In 1212, she founded an order of women in Assisi modeled on Francis's Rule.

Clare, like Francis, realized that monasteries often became corrupt after they have accumulated wealth. Clare stated that individual sisters should not own any property, and she further stated that the order itself was not to own property. In time, however, the order had to own property for the sake of its own survival and for freedom from outside influences. At that time, all religious communities of women were required to be cloistered, that is, they lived secluded from the world and did not engage in outside ministries.

The name of the order founded by Clare was the **Poor Ladies**. After Clare's death, they became known as the Poor Clares. The Poor Clares, free from the cares brought by riches, spent their time in prayer, work, and meditation. They depended on the gifts from outside their convent walls for their sustenance. Like the Franciscans, they had a great effect on spirituality and today continue their ministry of community prayer, work, and meditation.

CLIPBOARD

1. What problems would Albigensianism cause for our society today?
2. Research and report on the work of the Dominicans in the Church today.
3. Name some people or groups who, like St. Francis, are dedicating themselves to lives of service and poverty.

Theological Activity

The Christian Times

Thirteenth Century   Vol. 13   No. 4

Bishop Wants Aquinas Condemned

Last week, the bishop of Paris condemned the writings of the Dominican theologian, Thomas Aquinas, for his use of the Greek philosopher, Aristotle, as a source in his writings.

Other theologians, like Albert the Great, have ventured into the use of pre-Christian philosophers in their use of reason. One can catch hints of Albert's influence as a teacher in Thomas's writings.

Since the theologian Anselm of Canterbury introduced the use of reason into the study of theology, many theologians have followed his method. Some, like Bernard and Bonaventure have safely followed Anselm.

The rapid spread of heresies such as Albigensianism came to an end with the crusades. The rapid growth of new theologies and individual heretics, however, calls for the Church to deal with heresy in a different approach. Church leaders have introduced a structure for weeding out heretics. This structure is called the *Inquisition*.

Church leaders are calling on the new mendicant orders to act as inquisitors. As inquisitors they must investigate and punish heretics throughout the empire.

NOTEPAD
? ? ? ? ?

1. What did you learn about St. Thomas? Albert the Great? Anselm of Canterbury? Bernard? Bonaventure?
2. What have you learned from this article about the issues facing the Church?
3. What did you learn from the article about the Inquistition?

The Rest of the Story

In addition to responding to heretical beliefs, Church leaders also felt a need to investigate the writings of a number of theologians who were taking new approaches in explaining the richness of the Christian faith.

St. Anselm (1033–1109)

Anselm changed the direction of theology by adding the use of reason to that of revelation in his search for truth. He taught that one could arrive at a knowledge of the existence of God by combining the intellect with Scripture.

The pope recognized Anselm's genius and his popularity with the crowds. Anselm was installed as archbishop of Canterbury, in England. Anselm, knowing that the position would put him in conflict with the king, who wanted to appoint his own archbishop, unsuccessfully tried to reject the appointment. Once he became archbishop, he had to flee into exile to avoid death. In exile, he spent his time studying and sharpening his theological skills. He continued his attempts at explaining theology not only through the use of Scripture and tradition, but also through the use of human reason.

I do not seek to understand that I may believe, but I believe in order to understand.

St. Anselm

KEY TERMS

Inquisition: forum established by the Fourth Lateran Council as an attempt to discover and punish heretics more effectively.

Inquisitors: Franciscans and Dominicans who formed a traveling tribunal with the mission of exposing and punishing heretics.

In exile, Anselm wrote a number of letters and treatises which served as foundations for later students of theology. He defined theology as "faith seeking understanding." In other words, Anselm believed that one could understand faith better through the use of reason. Many people welcomed this new approach to theology, but some rejected it as heretical. The Church eventually recognized St. Anselm as a great theologian who had a lasting influence on our understanding of the faith.

Pope Innocent III (1198–1216)

Under Pope Innocent III, the papacy reached the height of its power in Europe. The pope had become the moral leader of all of Europe and made important decisions for the empire. He chose his own candidate as emperor, forced the king of France to take back his wife, and made the king of England accept the papal appointment of an archbishop in England. Innocent III was highly educated and courageously confronted every challenge to Church authority at the onset of the 1200s.

As part of his reformation of the Church, Pope Innocent III dedicated himself to combating heresy. He sent representatives throughout the empire to communicate his rule to temporal leaders and to settle heresies. He also worked with the Dominicans and Franciscans during the early days of their foundations.

A dark mark on his papacy came in 1209, when he summoned a crusade against the Albigensians in southern France. Pope Innocent III tried to convert the Albigensians by sending representatives to meet with them, but they assassinated one of Innocent's representatives. The pope retaliated by calling for a bloody crusade against the Albigensians.

Wealthy nobles of northern France saw the crusade as an occasion to exploit the people and land of the southern portion of their country. They invaded the south under the guise of the crusade, killing the Albigensians along with many of their Catholic neighbors who came to their rescue.

The Inquisition

In 1215, at the Fourth Lateran Council, Pope Innocent III led the Church in establishing a forum for dealing with heretics. The name of this forum was the **Inquisition**, which had as its function the discovery and punishment of heretics. In introducing the Inquisition, the Fourth Lateran Council (1215) left the bishops with the responsibility of uncovering heresy in their diocese and destroying it.

At the time of the Inquisition, the Church could impose spiritual penalties, but it needed the state to impose most physical punishments, especially the imposition of the death penalty. The belief among many of the people of the day was that heretics would not reach eternal salvation, and anyone they influenced would also be deprived of eternal salvation. Some Church leaders believed that killing heretics kept these sinners from leading other people into sin.

In 1233, a later pope, Gregory IX, issued a decree which established procedures for identifying heretics. He placed this task under the direction of Franciscans and Dominicans who formed a traveling tribunal and became known as the **Inquisitors**. Punishment ranged from public penance to imprisonment or even death. The death penalty was carried out by civil authorities.

By the middle of the 1200s, Pope Innocent IV took the Inquisition a step further by allowing the inquisitors to torture the defendants, in an attempt to weaken and force them to admit their guilt. The Inquisitors would come to a town, call all those accused of heresy to appear before them, and urge people to denounce them secretly. Then the inquisitors would judge the heretics.

The accused had difficulty proving their innocence, although they could recant their heresy and accept the penance with no further harm. Those who did not recant often faced torture until they admitted their heresy. Admitting guilt did not necessarily free a supposed heretic from execution by civil authorities. Very often, a person accused of heresy, whether found guilty or not, was stripped of all his or her property and assets.

The use of the Roman Inquisition lessened in most places within a century. The Roman Inquisition condemned only a small number of people to death, but some local rulers took advantage of the Inquisition in their local regions. By falsely accusing their political enemies of heresy, they could have them executed. Other abuses were also common, such as: secret false witnessing against someone, in order to obtain a person's assets, as a means of revenge; the disregard for proof; the denial of appeal; persecution of Jews; Jewish converts; and the persecutions of Protestants as heretics. The worst abuse of the Inquisition took place in Spain and lasted far longer than in any other country.

Peter Lombard (1100–1160)

During the period of the Inquisition, theologians continued to prosper, despite the danger of being condemned as heretics by judges who did not understand them. Peter Lombard was a renowned scholar who was fortunate enough not to be condemned by the Inquisition. He contributed to theological development with his publication of a text called *Sentences*. In this work, he presented theology in an organized, brief, and timely manner.

Lombard's *Sentences* became a basic text used in all theological studies for centuries to come. All theology stu-dents had to read the Sentences and comment on a portion or all of the text. A number of later scholars published their reflections on Peter Lombard's *Sentences*. It took second place to the Bible in theological studies.

St. Bonaventure (1217–1274)

Many of the major religious orders not only provided preachers, but also scholars who worked at advancing the understanding of theology in the Church. Bonaventure, a Franciscan friar (brother), studied in Paris and helped the Franciscans put their Rule into an organized form, by ending the quarrels concerning the adherence to St. Francis's strict rule of poverty. His labors were so successful that he was given the title Second Founder. In 1263, he wrote a new life of St. Francis. This became the approved, official biography of the great saint and was declared in 1266 to replace all previous biographies.

Bonaventure's years of study and intelligence earned him a place of respect and honor in the Franciscan order and in the Church throughout the world. Popes sought his opinions, and he was eventually named a cardinal bishop by Pope Gregory X in 1273. Story has it that when Gregory's legates arrived with the red cardinal hat, Bonaventure was washing dishes. He told them to hang the hat on a nearby tree, since his hands were wet and dirty. The hat subsequently became his symbol.

In addition to his work with the Franciscans, Bonaventure also authored many books as a theologian and philosopher. Although he was a good friend of St. Thomas Aquinas, he rejected many of the Aristotelian elements of thought which played such a key role in Aquinas's writings. He believed that Aristotle was ill-suited for metaphysical study. Despite their philosophical conflicts, however, they were able to remain friends.

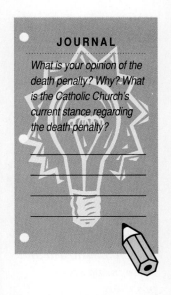

JOURNAL

What is your opinion of the death penalty? Why? What is the Catholic Church's current stance regarding the death penalty?

In the works of teaching and applying Christian morality, the Church needs the dedication of pastors, the knowledge of theologians, and the contribution of all Christians .... Faith and the practice of the Gospel provide each person with an experience of life "in Christ," ... Thus the Holy Spirit can use the humblest to enlighten the learned and those in the highest positions.

Catechism of the Catholic Church, #2038

JOURNAL

At school or home, whom do you call "the dumb ox"? Why? How can you be more appreciative of this person's talents and gifts?

_____

_____

_____

St. Albert the Great (1200–1280)

Albert the Great was a Dominican, a philosopher and a theologian, and is today the patron saint of the natural sciences. His early studies brought him to a familiarity with the Greek philosopher Aristotle. Intrigued by the philosopher and the possibility of adapting his method to theological thought, Albert deepened his study of Aristotle and passed his knowledge on to his students.

Albert had such an exceptional mind that he earned the title *Great* even during his lifetime. Like St. Anselm, he had the ability to find evidence of the Creator in all of creation-and not only in subjects immediately related to religion. He saw a connection between creation and truths revealed in the Scriptures. Later theologians would look to Albert as the one who opened up for them the riches of the philosophers in the study of theology.

Saint Thomas Aquinas (1225–1274)

Thomas Aquinas studied for a period under Albert the Great and reflected the influence of this great teacher in many of his writings. Thomas used Aristotle's philosophy as the foundation for many of his theological explanations. Some critics of Thomas's era forgot that other theologians, such as Augustine, also used ancient philosophers. Augustine developed many of his ideas from the writings of the philosopher Plato.

Thomas Aquinas, a Dominican like Albert, became the most famous theologian of the thirteenth century. When he was five years old, his aristocratic parents sent him to the abbey of Monte Cassino to begin his studies. At fourteen, he began his studies at the University of Naples, and there he first encountered Aristotle's philosophy.

When he announced that he was joining the Dominican Order, his mother and brothers (his father was deceased) tried to talk him out of it. When this failed, they locked him in the family castle for more than a year in an attempt to force him to change his mind. They threatened him and forced temptations on him, but he eventually escaped and joined the Dominicans. As a Dominican, he studied under Albert the Great.

After some years with Albert the Great, Thomas returned to Paris to continue his studies, to teach, and to write. He wrote extensively about many religious topics and laid a theological foundation used by many future theologians. The bishops of Paris and of Canterbury condemned his teachings and wanted him excommunicated.

Thomas was so big and quiet that during his school days his fellow students called him "the dumb ox." Before long, however, his true intelligence shone through his quiet exterior. He made use of Christian, Jewish, Muslim, and pagan authors to lead him to truth. He died in 1274 when he was scarcely fifty years old. His teacher, Albert the Great, outlived him and became his staunchest supporter. Forty six years later, the Church canonized Thomas Aquinas as a saint.

CLIPBOARD

1. Discuss some ways you use your "reason" in trying to understand your faith.

2. Do you think that teachers like Albert the Great can really have a great influence on their students? Explain.

3. Why do theologians like Thomas Aquinas sometimes have difficulty being understood by other theologians, like the bishop of Paris? Who are some modern day theologians? How are they misunderstood?

The Avignon Papacy

The Christian Times

Fourteenth Century   Vol. 14 No. 1

Catherine of Siena Leads Pope to Rome

Catherine, a young woman from Siena, has successfully helped the pope, Gregory XI, return the papacy from its exile in Avignon, France, to Rome.

Ever since the election of Clement V seventy years ago, only Gregory XI has returned from Avignon to reside at Rome. Six popes following Clement remained at Avignon, rather than return to the turbulent center of the empire.

Pope Clement V, the first pope elected at Avignon, was a French cardinal who claimed ill-health and his need to negotiate with the French king as his reasons for staying at Avignon. The next pope, John XXII, claimed that he needed to remain at Avignon to avoid sure death from the illegal emperor, Louis IV.

After the first two Avignon popes, the large number of French cardinals continued to elect one French pope after the other. It seemed that France had captured the papacy for good.

One of the saddest moments of Pope Clement's reign was his betrayal of the crusading order, the Knights Templars. King Philip of France wanted the wealth of the order and gave Pope Clement the choice of betraying the Knights Templars or the previous pope, the arrogant and ambitious Boniface VIII. Pope Clement felt he had no choice.

Now that the papacy has returned to Rome, the Roman population vows that they will never again permit the papacy to escape from that city.

NOTEPAD

? ? ? ? ?

1. What did you learn about Catherine of Siena? Gregory XI? Clement V? John XXII? Louis IV? King Philip of France?

2. What did you learn from this article about issues facing the Church at the time?

3. Why would a country want the pope to reside there?

The Rest of the Story

During the thirteenth century, the feudal system was disintegrating, due to the increase of trade and the development of a rich merchant class. With the number of independent feudal tribes taxing everyone who traveled over the land, wealthy merchants whose trade demanded travel found these taxes overwhelming.

The wealthy traders united with the kings to bring a number of feudal areas together to form a country. These loosely united parcels of land now became united under one king and one nationality. The map of the world changed as a new idea of nation and nationality came into being. In France, for instance, there were many parcels of land protected by independent lords. Now they united as one French nationality in a country recognized as France.

This new idea of having national boundaries affected the influence of the Church in the world. The Church no longer dealt with powerful rulers of a number of feudal lands, but with powerful rulers of nations.

Pope Boniface and the National Monarchies

Pope Boniface VIII came to office under strange circumstances. The saintly hermit pope who preceded him, Pope Celestine V, reigned only from July to December of 1294. The exhausted cardinals who met for the election squabbled and faced several interruptions before they elected the hermit as pope. The hermit took the name Celestine V. Pope Celestine soon realized that he lacked the necessary skills for his position. As a result, he resigned his position and returned to his hermitage.

When Boniface became pope, he feared that Celestine would have a change of heart and cause problems by demanding his rightful position as pope. To avoid any schism which would occur if the Church had two popes, Boniface had Celestine guarded, placing him under a form of house arrest. After the death of Celestine, Boniface's enemies spread rumors that Boniface had tricked Celestine into resigning, bribed the cardinals to elect Boniface, and then killed the gullible hermit.

When Boniface became pope in 1294, a new spirit of nationalism was on the rise. Both the king of England and the king of France wanted to rule the Church in their countries. They felt that the spiritual power of the pope placed some of the citizens of their countries under a foreign spiritual ruler. The ability of the pope to appoint bishops meant that the pope could choose bishops who were unfavorable to those ruling the country.

Pope Boniface VIII used all of his skills to keep the spiritual power of the papacy from being lost. He knew Church law well, had a wide experience with Church diplomacy, and came from a wealthy family. But his experience in Church law did not prepare him for the sensitive art of negotiation. Although he sought the good of the Church, he often earned the wrath of his opponents with his own ambitions, arrogance, temper, and inflexible nature.

Pope Boniface VIII and the King of France

Pope Boniface VIII protested to the kings of France and England when they taxed the clergy for wars they were waging. He reminded the kings that they did not have the right under Church law to impose such a tax. There were times, such as during the crusades, when the popes permitted rulers to tax the clergy, but each time the king received permission from the pope. Knowing beforehand that Boniface would protest taxes on war, the king threatened to block funds from going to Rome if he refused to tax. Boniface reluctantly agreed.

The king of France, the notorious Philip IV, further challenged Boniface by bringing a bishop to civil court. Boniface wrote an official letter to the king, stressing that he had no right to interfere with the Church and that he was still a subject of the pope. The French population reacted angrily to the pope's letter, but that only served to anger the pope further. He wrote a harsh letter to the king, declaring that the king's salvation depended on his subjection to the pope.

The king's supporters replied by attacking the personality of Boniface. They accused him of heresy, simony, witchcraft, murder, sacrilege, and idolatry. In light of these accusations, they called for a council to judge the pope.

In retaliation, Boniface prepared to excommunicate the king, but the king's supporters broke into Boniface's house near Rome and kept him prisoner. They accused him again of a number of crimes. Within two days, the pope's supporters freed Boniface and returned him to Rome. Three weeks later he died, overcome by the strain of the ordeal.

The Papacy at Avignon

Within a few years after the death of Boniface, the number of French cardinals had increased enough for them to choose a French archbishop as pope. At the time the cardinals gathered, they feared the power and wrath of Philip IV and decided that they would elect a candidate acceptable to Philip, yet dedicated to the Church. In 1305, the cardinals elected the archbishop of Bordeaux, in France, as the new pope. He took the name Pope Clement V.

After the election, Clement V remained in France due to his poor health and his need to continue negotiations on behalf of the Church with Philip IV of France. He moved to a town named Avignon where he remained as a guest of the Dominicans until his death. He intended to eventually return the papacy to Rome, but he had unwittingly become the first of a long line of popes who would remain at Avignon.

As pope, Clement had to deal with King Philip IV of France, who was still smarting over his conflicts with Pope Boniface VIII. One such dealing involved the Knights Templars who had become a rich order, and the king wanted their wealth. They had accumulated a great deal of wealth expecting to pay for their part in the crusades, but the crusades had ceased and the money still remained. The king, in his desire for the wealth of the Templars, circulated rumors accusing the templars of heresy, idolatry, and other crimes. These accusations gave him an excuse to arrest all the Templars in France.

Philip tortured and killed many of the Knights Templars. He not only had them falsely accused, but he also acted contrary to the law of clerical immunity from civil judgment. Philip took advantage of Clement's ill health by trying to force him to make a choice between an investigation of the Templars, or the condemnation of Boniface VIII. Clement felt that choosing the investigation of the Templars was the lesser of two evils.

A council met to determine the matter, and when they declared that the Templars could not be judged unless they could speak for themselves, Clement simply issued a decree dissolving the order without exonerating or condemning it. By law, the wealth was to go to another religious group, but Philip managed to take most of it for himself.

By the time of Clement's death in 1314, the number of French cardinals had grown considerably, giving them the advantage at the next election.

Pope John XXII (1316–1334)

The next pope was a compromise candidate of seventy-two who came from Avignon. The cardinals did not expect him to live long, but they believed that he would live long enough for them to find a suitable candidate. The new pope, who took the name John XXII, surprised the cardinals by living to the age of ninety and serving as the longest reigning pope of the Avignon period.

Pope John XXII engaged in a long and vicious controversy with the emperor, Louis IV, whom John had charged with being a usurper to the crown. The pope claimed that Louis was not actually emperor, since he did not have the papal approval as emperor. When Louis rejected the pope's right to approve him as emperor, the pope excommunicated him. The feud continued throughout the pope's reign.

The pope's dispute with the emperor persuaded him to remain in Avignon where he was safe. Wars within Italy made the journey to Rome far too dangerous. In 1348, after almost forty years at Avignon, Pope Clement VI purchased Avignon in an attempt to make it independent from France, and had a papal castle built there.

Although the popes remained at Avignon, all seven popes who resided in the city saw themselves as living in

Although popes had lived outside Rome for short periods of time in the past, the Avignon period became the first time in history that the pope had a permanent residence outside Rome. With the rise of nationalism, the rulers of other nations began to believe that the pope, by living in France, would naturally favor the French nation. The French spoke boastfully of the fact that the pope resided in France, and they honestly expected the pope to favor French interests. Both sides felt the pope was taking the side of France.

exile from Rome, and intended to return whenever they could safely do so. The problem of the role of papal approval in the choice of the emperor continued during the reign of the next two popes at Avignon, Pope Benedict XII and Pope Clement VI. The princes of Germany decreed that they alone had the power to elect an emperor and that they did not need papal approval. They declared that Pope John XXII was unjust in his actions against Louis IV. Louis caused his own downfall when he tried to set aside Church marriage laws for his own advantage.

In 1346, the electors chose a new emperor, Charles VI, who wisely secured papal approval by traveling to Avignon and promising whatever Pope Clement VI demanded. Despite his actions in seeking papal approval, he wrote a decree which spoke of the role of the electors while ignoring any role of the pope. The pope objected, but it was a feeble and ineffective gesture.

The Problems of Avignon

The Avignon popes were not bad popes for the era. They had among them reformers, two of whom became saints. Some showed great strength and courage in their leadership, while others were weak in their dealings with national rulers. Five were scholars who exhibited extraordinary administrative skills. Under the Avignon popes, the process of centralizing the government of the Church reached its peak.

Some of the popes of the Avignon period expected to live a life of luxury. Because the support coming from the empire was dwindling, however, the popes chose to tax the newly appointed bishops. When the pope appointed a bishop to an office, he was required to pay a tithe for a year. The bishops received funds for this tithe by taxing the people of their dioceses. The people objected to such heavy taxation, believing that their funds supported the French government as well as the pope in France.

An End to the Avignon Papacy

Catherine of Siena (1347–1380) was a Dominican sister who lived a life of prayer and sacrifice until God, in a vision, called her to an active ministry. She cared for the sick, visited prisons, accompanied prisoners to the gallows, and cared for the poor. She wrote critically of political and Church abuses and negotiated peace for the Church.

Saint Catherine of Siena played a major role in ending the Avignon papacy. In God's name, she went to Avignon to persuade Gregory XI to overcome all obstacles preventing his return to Rome. With Catherine's encouragement combined with his own desire to return to Rome, Gregory sent an army ahead to plan for his return. When he was confident that he could enter Rome safely, he began his journey back to the city of Rome.

In 1377, after more than seventy years of the pope living away from Rome, Pope Gregory XI arrived at the Vatican. All the people of Rome did not immediately support this return of the papacy. Armies, defending the pope, brutally checked revolts in the cities. Gregory died shortly after his return to Rome.

In the Spotlight

St. Catherine of Siena was born in Italy, the youngest of more than twenty children, to a Sienese dyer, Giacomo Benincasa. At an early age she led a life of prayer, penance, and solitude despite parental opposition. As a little girl, stories describe her as on the way upstairs kneeling on each step to repeat a Hail Mary. She is also known to have had a remarkable mystical experience at the age of six which sealed her vocation.

Refusing to marry she was finally allowed by her parents to enter the Dominican order. It was there that the Saviour is reported to have appeared to her, accompanied by His blessed Mother and a crowd of the heavenly host. Story has it that the blessed Mother held Catherine's hand up to her Son, who placed a

ring upon it and espoused Catherine to Himself, telling her to not to fear, for she was now armed with faith to overcome the assaults of the enemy. Although the ring was visible to her, it was not visible to anyone else. It was after this event that Catherine began her active ministry.

In her ministry Catherine dedicated her time to caring for the sick. Through her letters and travels she also acted as peacemaker. She is credited with playing a major role in convincing Pope Gregory XI to return the papacy to Rome.

At the young age of thirty-three, she died of a stroke. She was canonized in 1461, and declared a doctor of the Church in 1970. Her feast day is April 29.

CLIPBOARD

1. How does the manner of dealing with problems between the pope and national leaders differ today from that of the period of Pope Boniface VIII?

2. Using the Avignon papacy as a source for your discussion, give a number of reasons why it is a good idea for the Church today to have cardinals from as many countries as possible.

3. Looking at the role of St. Catherine of Siena at the end of the Avignon papacy, discuss how a person can live an active life like St. Catherine, and still become a saint.

REVIEWING THE ERA

- **1100**

ST. ANSELM. This theologian emphasized the use of reason in theological explanations. He taught that theology was "faith seeking understanding."

PETER LOMBARD. This theologian gathered together an organized body of theological thesis in a book called *Sentences*. This book later became second to the Bible in theological studies.

- **1150**

ALBIGENSIANS. This heretical group believed that there was a constant struggle going on between the good god of the spirit and the bad god of matter. This group saw an attaining of salvation only through a denial of the material world.

PETER WALDO BEGINS HIS NEW LIFE OF TOTAL POVERTY. Waldo and several followers practiced extreme poverty, but the Church did not allow them to preach due to their lack of education. Due to their disobedience, they were excommunicated. Despite this, however, they continued to preach and their numbers grew. Eventually, they became known as the Waldensians.

DOMINIC DE GUZMAN. Dominic founded the Order of Preachers, a mendicant order dedicated to prayer, study, and preaching.

FRANCIS OF ASSISI. Francis founded the Franciscans, a mendicant order dedicated to poverty and preaching.

CLARE OF ASSISI. Clare is the founder of an order of nuns, who lived the vow of poverty in the spirit of St. Francis.

- **1200**

ALBERT THE GREAT. This Dominican teacher used Aristotle's philosophy and believed that one could find an image of God in all of creation. He taught Thomas Aquinas.

POPE INNOCENT III. This most powerful pope of the era called a crusade against the Albigensians and called the Fourth Lateran Council for reform in the Church.

ST. BONAVENTURE. Bonaventure gathered together and put in order the rules of the Franciscans.

THOMAS AQUINAS. Thomas was one of the greatest theologians of Church history. He used Aristotle in his explanation of theological theses and influenced theology down to our age.

POPE BONIFACE AND THE NATIONAL MONARCHIES. Boniface ruled at a time when kings were gathering the separated groups of regions together to form countries. National pride became a new factor in the world.

- **1300**

THE AVIGNON PAPACY. The popes resided at the French town of Avignon for more than seventy years. This is the longest period of time popes have ever spent away from Rome.

POPE CLEMENT V. This first Avignon pope who remained in France after his election, due to illness and his need to negotiate with the French king.

POPE JOHN XXII. John was the second Avignon pope. He resided at Avignon because of his conflict with the king of Bavaria who had had himself elected emperor.

ST. CATHERINE OF SIENA AND AVIGNON. Catherine influenced Pope Gregory XI to bring the papacy back to Rome.

Then and Now

In the twelfth and thirteen centuries, theologians began to appear who, along with the Scriptures and tradition, were making use of human reason in the study of theology. Some of them, like St. Thomas Aquinas, had to face condemnations by some influential bishops because of their use of ancient philosophers, such as Aristotle, as resources for their understanding of theology.

Today, St. Thomas stands out as a major theologian who has influence on Church theology down to the present. Besides using Catholic tradition as a resource, theologians today make use of ancient philosophers and current secular philosophers as some of their resources for theological understanding. They also make use of every modern science in their attempt to explain our relationship to God.

The pope now resides at the Vatican in Rome. Since the Avignon papacy, the pope has not resided outside of Rome for any lengthy period.

KEY TERMS

Albigensians
Order of Preachers
Poor Men of Lyons
Friars Minor
Poor Ladies
Inquisition
Inquisitors

A Voice from the Past

In your column you are going to explain how reason was introduced to theology. In your explanation, be sure to include the key terms and the contributing theologians. Also discuss how the Church dealt with the heresies that resulted, as well as your opinions on the Church's methods for dealing with the heretics. End your column with a discussion of the heresies that are present today, and give your readers some suggestions for dealing with these heresies.

NEWS IN REVIEW

1. What do the Albigensians and Waldensians have in common, and how do they differ?

2. What differences do you find between the order founded by St. Dominic and that founded by St. Francis?

3. Why is Clare of Assisi important to Church history?

4. What was St. Anselm's contribution to theology?

5. What is important about the place of Pope Innocent III in history?

6. What was the purpose of the Inquisition, and what were some of its dangers?

7. Why did Albert merit the title of Great during his lifetime?

8. What contributions did Thomas Aquinas make to the Church?

9. What were some problems faced by Boniface VIII?

10. What problems did the Avignon papacy bring to the Church?

chapter ten

Reformation

If we were living at the beginning of the fourteenth century, we would have memories and stories of preachers traveling throughout our territory wearing different kinds of robes. We would find nuns not only living in monasteries, but serving outside the monastaries in the ministries of preaching the gospel and caring for the poor. If we were educated, we would be discussing the works of major theologians and studying the writings of non-Christian philosophers like Aristotle.

When we participated in the Eucharistic liturgy, we would find ourselves moved further away from the presider. He would have his back to us or be completely hidden behind a screen. We would not fully understand the language he was speaking. Our awe of the Eucharist would be so great that we would feel unworthy and would not share in Communion unless ordered to do so by law. In many churches, we would hear the choirs singing magnificent hymns during the celebration, and we would sit in silence, not joining in the singing.

Oftentimes, the window of the past provides us with an appreciative understanding of the present.

The Western Schism

The Christian Times

Fifteenth Century   Vol. 15   No. 1

Pope Nicholas V Renovates the Papal Residence

Pope Nicholas V has introduced some of the finest art of the period into the halls of the papal residence. Just a few decades ago, popes lived at Avignon and allowed the papal residence in Rome to deteriorate.

When Pope Urban VI became the first newly elected pope at Rome after the Avignon papacy, the world felt that the papal residence would improve. Pope Urban, however, had his problems when the cardinals who elected him declared his election invalid.

When the cardinals elected a false pope—Clement VII, who chose to reside at Avignon—Pope Urban and his successors became too busy to care for the papal residence. They were busy protecting their right to be known as the true pope.

The successors of Pope Urban VI and the false pope at Avignon met a new problem, some years after the split, when a group of cardinals elected a third pope named Alexander V. When Alexander V died shortly after his election, the cardinals elected a successor, who took the name John XXIII. The Church now had three men, each claiming that he was the true pope.

Pope Nicholas, the present pope, can look back to the day when the Council of Constance solved the problem by forcing all the popes to resign and elected Pope Martin V, who became the sole pope. Thus did the council end the Western Schism in the Church.

Between Pope Martin and Pope Nicholas, two other popes have lived and died without anyone challenging their authority. This indicates that the Church has accepted having one pope, who resides in Rome. In Pope Nicholas V, the Church has a pope who is truly a pope of our own age. His love for the arts will enable people for centuries to enjoy the elaborate works of art decorating his residence and the churches of Rome.

NOTEPAD

? ? ? ? ?

1. What did you learn about Pope Nicholas V? Pope Urban VI? Clement VII? Alexander V? John XXIII? Pope Martin V?

2. What problems regarding the papacy were mentioned in this article, and how were they solved?

3. If you had lived during the time when the Church had two or three popes, how do you think your religious beliefs and practices would have been affected?

The Rest of the Story

Although Pope Gregory XI had returned to Rome, there were still some pro-French cardinals who supported the papacy in Avignon. The people of Rome were aware of these sentiments, and they intended to keep the papacy in Rome.

Pope Urban VI (1378–1389)

In 1378, after the death of Pope Gregory XI, the cardinals met in Rome within ten days of his death to elect his successor. Among the sixteen cardinals who came to elect the pope, the French cardinals outnumbered those from other nations two to one.

The cardinals encountered a dark mood in Rome; angry crowds roamed the streets. The people of Rome wanted assurance that the next pope would remain in Rome, so they clamored for a Roman or an Italian pope. As the mobs grew more threatening, the cardinals could not decide on a candidate from their own ranks, so they elected an Italian archbishop from a nearby town. By that evening, when the newly elected pope had not yet arrived, the frightened cardinals decided to deceive the crowd to keep them from rioting. They had one of their colleagues, an elderly Italian cardinal, dress in the pope's garb and step out to greet the crowd as though he were the newly elected pope. When the crowd became calm, the cardinals secretly fled from Rome.

When the new pope arrived at Rome, the crowd willingly accepted him as pope. He took the name Urban VI. When the chaos surrounding the election waned, the cardinals returned to Rome and pledged obedience to Urban VI as the new pope. They treated him as the true pope, celebrating the Holy Week services with him, requesting favors from him, and accepting his gifts. They gave every indication that Urban was truly the pope.

Urban seemed to be the perfect choice. He had lived for ten years at Avignon, working as one of the officials of the Church alongside the pope. He had a good reputation with no signs that he ever bribed anyone for an office, nor did he profit from any office in the Church. He was well educated and had extensive experience in world and Church matters.

Within two weeks of his election, however, Pope Urban showed an unfortunate side of his character and soon infuriated the cardinals. He often acted spontaneously and imprudently, exploding with a quick temper and angry words. He publicly insulted some of the cardinals by calling them liars or men who bribed someone to make them a cardinal. He boasted of his great power and allowed no one to interfere with his judgments.

Urban's actions soon made the cardinals realize that they made a mistake in choosing him. Some hoped that he would reform the Church, but they did not expect him to be so arrogant and abusive. They knew that they did not have the authority to depose a pope, but they also realized that an election held under fear or force was invalid.

Election of a Second Pope

As the cardinals recalled their fear of the Roman crowds at the time of the election of Pope Urban VI, they found an opportunity to rid themselves of this annoying pope. They declared that their fear of the crowd forced them to elect Urban and that his election, therefore, was invalid.

St. Catherine of Siena and others told the cardinals that they had accepted Urban as pope by celebrating liturgy with him, accepting favors from him, and pledging themselves to him. These actions did not take place under fear, but willingly, with no pressure from any mob. These actions validated their choice of Urban as pope.

The cardinals used the heat at Rome to quietly leave the city and gather elsewhere. In this gathering, they issued a decree, declaring that Urban was not a true pope, since his election came as a result of their fear of the crowd. Even before they left Rome, they left notices asking Urban to resign. When Urban refused to resign, the cardinals elected a French cardinal as pope.

'The college or body of bishops has no authority unless united with the Roman Pontiff, Peter's successor, as its head.' As such, this college has 'supreme and full authority over the universal Church; but this power cannot be exercised without the agreement of the Roman Pontiff.'

Catechism of the Catholic Church, # 883

The newly elected "pope" took the name of Clement VII and established his office at Avignon.

Since all the cardinals except one left Urban and sided with the new Avignon pope, Urban retaliated by appointing new cardinals and excommunicating those who took part in the election of the Avignon pope, including Clement VII. Clement VII, believing he was the true pope, excommunicated Pope Urban VI. Now the Church had two popes with two sets of cardinals. A new era began, an era known as the **Western Schism**. It lasted thirty-eight years.

Historians tend to agree that Urban VI was the legitimate pope. Even if the election was held under fearful conditions, they believe with Catherine of Sienna, that the cardinals' actions in returning to Rome for the installation of the new pope and their recognition of Urban as the true pope showed that they believed their election was valid. It was only when Urban began to cause problems that they looked for reasons to declare that he was not the true pope.

The people were confused. Many made their decisions along political rather than religious lines. The French supported the pope who resided at Avignon in France, while their enemy, the English, chose to support the pope residing in Rome. Saints, theologians, members of the religious orders, and ordinary Catholics were divided over who was the true pope.

Attempts to End the Schism

When each of the popes died, their respective sides each elected a successor. Christians throughout the world longed to end the confusion arising from the presence of two popes. Leaders and scholars proposed different solutions. One solution called for both popes to resign in favor of a new election in which all the cardinals from both sides would vote. Although the popes from Avignon and Rome hinted at times that they would agree to re-sign if the other did, they never actually carried out this decision.

Another proposed solution to the problem was to call a council of the bishops and cardinals of both sides to resolve the matter. After thirty years of wrangling, the cardinals supporting each pope called the bishops of both sides together for a council to be held at the Italian city of Pisa. The bishops at the council deposed both the Avignon pope, Benedict XIII, and the Roman pope, Gregory XII, and chose another pope who took the name of Alexander V.

The council's choice, Alexander V, lived only a short time, so the cardinals chose as his successor a cardinal who took the name, John XXIII. Pope Benedict and Pope Gregory declared that, according to Church law, only a pope could call a legitimate general council. They both refused to accept the decision of the council at Pisa in electing a new pope. Now, instead of resolving the situation, the council made the situation worse by increasing the number of popes to three.

John XXIII lacked the strength of leadership necessary to serve as pope, and the emperor had no difficulty forcing him to convoke a new council to meet at Constance in 1414, five years after the council held at Pisa. The Council of Constance was a large council for its day. It lasted almost three and a half years and dealt with the issue of ending the Western Schism, among other decisions.

The Roman pope, Gregory XII, offered his voluntary resignation after first receiving the right to convoke the council. Benedict XIII, although he had only a few supporters left, stubbornly refused to resign. As a result, the council deposed him, accusing him of schism, lying, and heresy. John XXIII tried to flee, but the emperor's troops captured and imprisoned him. The council declared him deposed and forced John himself to approve the decision.

In November of that same year, 1417, the cardinals elected an Italian as the first acknowledged universal pope in forty years. He chose the name, Martin V. The former Roman pope, Gregory XII, died shortly before the election of Martin as pope. The Avignon pope, Benedict XIII, went into exile believing that he was still pope, and John XXIII became a bishop of an area in Italy. With the election of Martin, the Western Schism officially ended, and Rome became firmly established as the papal residence.

Questions of Belief

The representatives at the Council of Constance not only discussed solutions to the Western Schism, but they also considered questions of belief facing the church. They condemned as heretical the teaching of John Wycliff (1329 –1384) and John Hus (1369 –1415), two very popular preachers who proposed teachings similar to those championed a century later, during the Protestant Reformation.

John Wycliff, a teacher in England, berated the clergy in general for their luxurious lifestyle. Wycliff had a special dislike for unworthy clergy. He proposed the removal of all property from the Church, believing that much of the problem with the laxity of the clergy involved the enormous wealth of the Church. The Council of Constance found little difficulty with this call to a simple life, but it did have difficulty with Wycliff's teachings concerning the use of the Bible.

Wycliff, like some later Protestant reformers, believed that the Bible alone was the source for religious truth. If certain practices or teachings were not in the Bible, then they were not true. Catholics teach, however, that the Bible is part of a living Tradition. Although some practices of the Church life are not found in the Bible, they are found in the life of the early Christian community of disciples. These disciples lived

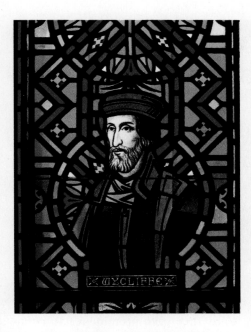

John Wycliff

around the time when the Bible was written, and they applied its message to their lives and worship. The writers of the Bible belonged to this community of disciples.

Although the Church authorities did not excommunicate Wycliff during his lifetime, the Council at Constance, held after his death, condemned his teachings as heretical. The council did not merely wish to condemn Wycliff, but it also wanted to send a warning to those who accepted his teachings, most notably a man named John Hus.

The bishops, aware that John Hus continued to spread Wycliff's teachings, invited Hus to the **Council of Constance** to defend his teachings, promising him protection against any physical attacks. When challenged at the council about his heretical views, Hus resisted any attempts made to force him to retract his heresy. Despite their promise of safety and protection given by those who invited him to the council, the council members shamefully ordered him to be burned at the stake as a heretic.

The Council of Constance also proposed the concept of **Conciliarism**. This heresy taught that councils were a

JOURNAL

Whom do you condemn? Why? Who does the media condemn? Why? How can we learn from the mistakes of the past?

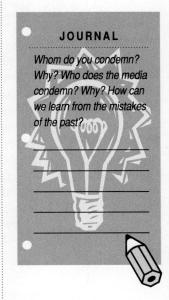

St. Peter's Basilica

based on a return to the ancient Latin and Greek artistic cultures. Nicholas recognized that the churches in Rome had deteriorated during the Avignon period and the Western Schism. He hired builders and artists to repair and restore these buildings.

The unity of religion and life at that time enabled some artists to draw the humanistic tendencies into their works of art, giving Rome and the Church treasures which have lasted to our present day. Nicholas had a great love for literature and founded the Vatican Library, to preserve not only religious writings, but even humanistic non-Christian writings of the past and of his own day.

Toward the end of Nicholas's life, the invention of the printing press was already having an impact on religion and the world. The first major work printed was the Bible, in Latin. This first book was the work of the German printer, Johann Gutenberg.

The presence of the Renaissance in the Church also brought with it some abuses. As the papacy became the center of study for the great writers and artists of the day, the pope hosted a number of meetings of artists. Luxury abounded within and without the Church as greed became a motivation for churchmen and others seeking power. Prominent families in Rome became more open in bribing cardinals at the time of papal elections. They often threatened the lives of those they could not bribe.

As a result, a series of unfit candidates became pope during this period. Although they were not married, some of them openly admitted to having children and even gave positions of honor to their children. The wealthy family of Pope Alexander VI bought him the papacy in 1492. He had several children and added immense disgrace to the papacy. The miracle of the era is that the sinfulness of its popes did not destroy the Church.

higher authority than the Pope. The end of the Great Schism by the Council of Constance gave prominence to councils and seem to support the idea that they had authority over the pope. Although the pope ratified other decrees from the council, he condemned conciliarism as heretical.

Renaissance

By the middle of the 1400s, a new pope, Nicholas V, brought to his role as pope a love for the humanist movement of his day. This was a movement

CLIPBOARD

1. What would happen today if we had three popes? How would you decide which one to follow? Why?

2. What would be missing from the Catholic Church today if every belief and practice were based on the Bible alone, as taught by Wycliff and Hus?

3. Because of the Renaissance popes, the churches in Rome have some magnificent works of art. Do you think Church leaders were right in sponsoring artists to create these priceless works of art? Why or why not?

The Reformation

The Christian Times

Sixteenth Century | Vol. 16 No. 1

Luther Faces Conflict and Gains Influence

Since presenting his ninety-five theses, Martin Luther, an Augustinian priest, has endured one conflict after another. He faced difficulty in his meeting with Cajetan, a representative of Pope Leo X, and in his debate with the scholar John Eck.

Luther sometimes muses over the indulgence controversy which brought him to reject Dominican John Tetzel's teaching that one can buy indulgences. (The widespread selling of indulgences has grown out of the financial woes of the Vatican.) Luther, frustrated with the corruption he saw in the Church, came to believe that the Bible alone teaches the truth.

Luther would not have survived this long if he had not found friends like Frederick of Saxony to protect him. After the Emperor Charles V condemned him at the Diet of Worms, Luther was fortunate to find a protector like Frederick.

On a related note, people throughout Europe are still lamenting the death of thousands of peasants in their rebellion last month. Luther is grieved by their plight. One of our older reporters tells us that he has not seen Luther so sorrowful since the days of his youth, when he had believed that God could never forgive him. Those were the days before he believed that Christ's faith brought him to salvation.

Despite the rumors and conflicts, Luther's reform seems to be spreading throughout the empire.

NOTEPAD
? ? ? ? ?

1. What did you learn about Luther? Frederick of Saxony? Cajetan? John Eck? John Tetzel?
2. What does this article say that Luther taught? What abuses was he addressing?
3. According to the article, how did the Church react to Luther's teachings?

The Rest of the Story

As the popes showed a more worldly interest in the arts during the Renaissance, they naturally needed more funds to support their interest. Michelangelo was working on the magnificent St. Peter's Basilica in Rome, and the papacy needed funds to support the artists involved in this work. Because of the corruption in the Church at this time, many of the funds went to churchmen and their families and friends rather than to the artists. Michelangelo himself was rarely paid for his work for the Church.

During this period, pious practices became identified with theology. In many cases, these practices were actually contrary to theology, but many had become more concerned with *experiencing* piety rather than learning sound theology. For a large number of people, the gap between God and human beings had grown so wide that they believed that their unworthiness made them incapable of approaching such an awesome God.

Martin Luther

G od sent Christ to be our sacrifice. Christ offered his life's blood, so that by faith in him we could come to God.

Romans 3:25, CEV

Indulgences

Many of the practices of the Church developed over its long history. During the period of the Renaissance, the common people had faith in the growing practice of performing certain deeds for the sake of gaining an indulgence. They feared suffering in purgatory after their death, the suffering needed to make up for one's sins during life.

At one time, indulgences included some type of good work done for the Church, often in place of a penance. The indulgence gained from doing this good work would reduce the time spent in purgatory. Among the good works meriting indulgences were works of charity, donations toward the building of churches, or fighting in religious wars, such as the crusades. In performing acts meriting these indulgences, people realized that they had to have a genuine sorrow for their sins. But over time, people forgot about the interior disposition and treated indulgences in a superstitious manner, as though, for example, they could buy their way into heaven by making donations for a particular project.

The preaching on indulgences at this time promoted this error. Since some Church leaders used the selling of indulgences as a means of supporting a costly lifestyle, they did not concern themselves with offering an accurate understanding on indulgences.

Martin Luther

In 1483 in Germany, Martin Luther was born. Although his father wanted him to become a lawyer, he was drawn to the monastic life. One summer, Luther had a harrowing experience during a thunderstorm when a lightening bolt barely missed him. Over the next months, he came to see this experience as a sign that God wanted him to dedicate his life to God. Martin was subject to religious scrupulosity and believed that life in the monastery would bring him a feeling of being saved. Despite an angry response from his father, Martin

remained firm in his desire to serve God as a faithful servant of the Church.

During his period of preparation as a monk, Luther continued to wrestle with thoughts of God's judgment and his unworthiness. His superiors, however, recognized his unique mental and spiritual abilities and decided to train him in advanced theology and to ordain him a presbyter.

But Martin's old fears began to haunt him again and assailed him throughout his early years as an ordained priest. Luther admitted that he never felt that he could please God, whom he saw as a strict judge. He sincerely wished to love God and to live as a dedicated and good monk. No matter how much he tried, however, he never felt that God could forgive him. He confessed his sins often, but after confessing, he experienced the weight of his guilt again.

Since Luther found no comfort in the Sacrament of Reconciliation, his confessor thought that he might find solace and joy in study, teaching, and being a pastor. Although he had attained some knowledge of the Scriptures from his life in the monastery, now, under orders from his superiors, he began to study the Bible with the intention of teaching it to others.

While Martin was preparing lectures on Paul's Letter to the Romans, he was struck by the passage which stated that a just person lives by faith. Martin, like many people of his day, often thought of justice in terms of punishment; thus he feared the justice of God. When he finally came to understand that the word *justice* as meaning "the righteousness of God" or "the harmony of a person with God," he felt his guilt slide away.

Luther reflected that it was not his good acts but God's goodness in Christ which brought salvation. Righteousness was God's gift through Jesus Christ to us. No one could merit or earn God's love, but God gives it freely as gift. Luther believed that we are justified through faith in Christ, rather than through good works. Luther did not deny the value of performing good works, but he believed that it was our God-given grace that gave meaning to those good works.

Luther's Ninety-five Theses

Luther lived in a university town in Germany and shared in the usual theological debates of the university. He had already begun sharing his new insights with some of his colleagues, and he wanted to use the opportunity of university debates to explain his insights more fully. He proposed his controversial subjects for debate, but found that his theses caused little excitement outside the university.

On October 31, 1517, he wrote a second series of proposals now known as Luther's *Ninety-five Theses*. The reaction to these ninety-five theses was unexpected. The points he raised were similar to those he had written earlier, and which had been received with little enthusiasm. It appears that the main challenge of his theses was not so much the theological content, but the consequences of what he had written. In his second set of theses, he included his negative reaction to the Church's teachings on indulgences. By so doing, he threatened the lavish lifestyles of some Church leaders.

Indulgence Controversy

In his Ninety-five Theses, Luther's attack on the sale of indulgences was an attack on the false teachings on and abuses of indulgences. In 1517, Pope Leo X, a corrupt pope, was generating funds for building St. Peter's Basilica in Rome by offering indulgences to those who contributed. Church leaders realized that Luther's attack on indulgences would seriously endanger that collection.

Albert, a bishop in Germany, wanted to add a very wealthy third diocese to his list of holdings. Since this was contrary to Church law, the bishop bribed the pope for permission to take on this third diocese. Albert promised to

Martin Luther posting his ninety-five theses

pay the pope an excessive amount of money for the dispensation. The pope agreed and allowed Albert to recover his expenses by "selling" indulgences.

A Dominican friar, John Tetzel, was one of the presbyters chosen to preach on indulgences for Albert. Instead of presenting an accurate teaching about indulgences, Tetzel made indulgences sound suspiciously like spiritual coins in a slot machine. He did not mention the necessity of living a good life, but led people to believe that at the moment the donation sounded in God's ears, a soul awaiting entrance into heaven flew off to paradise.

Luther was not the only one who viewed such preaching about indulgences as a sign of corruption in the Church. Others also joined in the criticism of Tetzel and his band of preachers. Luther declared that the pope, if he had the power to free souls for paradise, should dispense this gift freely and expansively. Obviously, he did not believe the pope had such powers.

Luther's attack on indulgences threatened to destroy the fiscal interests of the papacy, as well as Albert's ability to pay his debts. Albert dispatched Luther's ninety-five theses to the pope, asking him to intercede in the problem. The emperor also became involved when he requested that the pope silence Luther. It was in the interests of the emperor to promote a unified Church, so that he could more easily keep together the empire, which was being threatened by growing national interests.

Luther's Struggle with Rome

Since Luther belonged to a community of friars known as the Augustinians, the pope asked the superiors of the Augustinian order to settle the matter. However, a number of his fellow friars enthusiastically endorsed Luther's teachings. Luther returned home heartened by this support.

In 1518, Pope Leo X arranged a meeting between the unyielding Cardinal Cajetan and Luther at Augsburg in Germany. At the meeting, Cajetan expected Luther to retract his teachings without debate. When Luther realized that Cajetan had authority from the pope to arrest him, he asked for time to reflect and secretly fled from Augsburg during the night.

Luther found safe refuge with the ruler, Frederick of Saxony, who offered to protect him for the sake of justice, not because he agreed with his teachings. When Luther returned to the safe grounds of the university, he challenged the authority of the pope by requesting that a council review his case. Some people saw Luther's call for a council to review his case as a sign that he believed councils held more authority than the pope (conciliarism).

The pope was embroiled in political squabbles and badly misjudged the extent of the impact of Luther on the Church. In his need to protect his political holdings, the pope gave little attention to his problem with Luther. During this time of distraction, Luther's supporters were growing in number and influence in Germany.

Luther and Eck

In 1519, Luther agreed to a debate with John Eck, a university professor. Eck was a shrewd opponent who cleverly steered Luther into stating that the Council of Constance had erred in condemning Hus. This meant that Luther was declaring that an ecumenical council could err; Eck then declared that this statement was contrary to Christian faith. When Luther openly admitted that a council can make mistakes, the charge of heresy against Luther was cemented. In the end, Luther denied papal authority and declared that the Bible is superior to all councils and to the pope.

When he heard the results of the debate, Pope Leo X gave Luther sixty days to seek forgiveness or face excommunication. When Luther refused to repent, the pope ordered copies of his books to be burned. Word did not travel swiftly from Rome to other parts of the world in Luther's day, so the pope's decree took some time to reach Luther. When Luther finally received the pope's decree, he defiantly burned the letter.

Diet of Worms

Martin Luther became even more embroiled in his struggle with the pope. In his study of Scripture, Luther found support for only two of the Church's seven sacraments. He accepted baptism, based on the Gospel accounts of baptism, and he accepted the Eucharist, based on the Last Supper. Luther rejected the other sacraments. He denied the need for a sacramental priesthood and taught instead the "priesthood of all believers."

In 1521, the emperor, Charles I of Spain, called Luther to appear before him and a number of lords, German princes, and armed guards. At this meeting, called the **Diet of Worms**, this group laid Luther's books out before him and ordered him to recant. Luther first noted that many of his teachings in his writings were basic doctrines that even his opponents within the Church believed. He stated that his conscience would not allow him to retract the teachings in the books.

Luther won the support of many people at Worms. Since no one proved from the Bible that he was in error, he felt that he could not recant his beliefs. When the emperor again asked Luther if he would recant what he had written, Luther stated that he must follow his conscience.

At a time when nationalism was on the rise, Luther wisely made his last statement in German, "Hier, Ich stehe . . . Here, I stand . . . . I can do no other." Since a large number of the people in the hall were German, this statement in their language gained him their support and protection as he left the hall. Luther's apparent appeal to nationalism was viewed favorably by German princes who wished to separate from the Holy Roman Empire and the burdensome taxation the empire enforced. Such nationalism was growing in many areas of the empire, aided by the use of vernacular languages via the printing press and in speech.

Although Luther continued to think of himself as a Catholic, Church officials in Rome clearly saw him as a heretic. The people and princes began to take sides. The emperor placed a ban on Luther, which meant that anyone in the empire could hand him over to the emperor's soldiers.

Frederick continued to offer protection to Luther after the Diet of Worms by hiding him, lest someone find him and kill him. During his time in hiding, Luther translated the Bible into German, thus helping to shape the German language. He later wrote a catechism in German to help spread the Christian message as he understood it.

The Peasants' Revolt

In 1524, Luther faced an unforeseen predicament. The peasants of Germany rebelled against the ruling class; feudalism had run its course. The peasants

Diet of Worms

first made economic demands of the princes, and Luther supported their cause. When the peasants took their revolt a step further, however, and threatened war, Luther first pleaded with the peasants not to use force. Because the peasants refused, he then called upon the princes to restrain the rebellion. The princes reacted savagely against the peasants. To Luther's pain and embarrassment, the princes slaughtered over 100,000 peasants.

Luther was blamed for the rebellion and its outcome. Catholic princes denounced Luther for beginning the rebellion, while many peasants shunned Luther for abandoning them.

Luther and Protestantism

In 1525, Luther, no longer an active presbyter, married a former nun. During their marriage, they had several children. Martin died in 1546. By that time, **Lutheranism** had spread. Unlike Catholicism, which had a single visible head in the pope, Lutheranism did not

KEY TERMS

Lutheranism: the religious movement which evolved as a result of Martin Luther's teachings.

possess a hierarchical structure. In place of a hierarchical structure, Lutheranism relied on the Bible and Luther's writings for its unity. Luther and his followers saw their religious expression as a needed and authentic reform of the Church.

By 1529, one could easily distinguish the princes who supported Luther from those who did not. Those who supported Luther protested against the decision of the emperor and the Catholic princes to implement the condemnation of Luther in their region. This protest gave the movement its name, *Protestantism.*

Saints Reforming the Church

While Luther was seeking to reform the Church by challenging Church teachings, holy men and women were reforming the Church by calling others to lives of dedication and working for the poor and the sick. During the time of the Reformation, remnants of the plague continued to take the lives of many people. Saintly men and women took the risk of exposing themseles to the plague while ministering to the needs of the sick. Among this group were holy people such as St. Cajetan, St. Jerome Emiliani, and St. Angela Merici.

St. Cajetan of Thiene (1480–1547) lived at the same time as the Dominican named Cajetan who bore his name and who confronted Luther on behalf of Pope Leo X. St. Cajetan began his career as a highly educated layman who studied law, served as a senator in his country, and later received an appointment to the papal curia. He eventually became an ordained priest and dedicated himself to serving the poor and sick.

St. Cajetan and three other presbyters joined together to form the Theatine order, an order dedicated to living in community while continuing to serve the poor, the sick, and the elderly. They became poor in order to live and preach among the poor. They sought reform by challenging the clergy to live dedicated lives and through preaching. Because of their dedication, religious and civil rulers professed great admiration for the Theatine monks.

St. Jerome Emiliani (1483–1587) began his career as a soldier, but reformed his life after spending some time in prison. After escaping from prison, he spent a short time in politics before becoming a presbyter. Since the plague had left so many children homeless, he worked among the orphans and eventually founded a religious institute to care for them. He dedicated himself to working for the poor and the numberless people from the plague.

St. Angela Merici (1476–1540) gathered together a group of twenty-five women who consecrated themselves to God under the protection of St. Ursula. Although she did not have her group take vows, they dedicated themselves to virginity, poverty, and obedience. Like many others of their day, they served the poor and sick. They especially dedicated themselves to the educating of the poor, young girls who ordinarily would not have the opportunity to learn. Through the education of these young girls, they hoped to bring Christian practices back into families. After Angela died, her group took vows and became known as the congregation of St. Ursula.

JOURNAL

Why would men and women who served the poor and sick be called reformers of the Church?

CLIPBOARD

1. What were the strengths and weaknesses in Luther's arguments against the Church?
2. Do you think that Luther was forced into rejecting Church teachings?
3. Did Luther intend to establish a new religion? Explain.

The Reformation Spreads

The Christian Times

Sixteenth Century   Vol. 16   No. 2

John Calvin Mourned

The people of Geneva are mourning the loss of their leader, John Calvin. As Calvin's followers passed his simple casket, they prayed that God would predestine them for eternal glory, as God had clearly done for Calvin.

Calvin is rightly credited with organizing the doctrinal system of the Protestant Reformation. He also believed that some people are predestined for heaven, while God allows some other people to be damned in order to manifest God's justice.

With Calvin's influence, the laws of Geneva became strict, and the city grew to become a model of the best in Protestant thought. Critics of Calvin have compared the punishments inflicted upon lawbreakers to the cruel punishments inflicted by Ferdinand and Isabella in Spain.

Ferdinand and Isabella, you may recall, were the rulers who supported Christopher Columbus's voyage to the New World. They also led a bloody inquisition in Spain and reportedly did the same in the New World. The pope, Alexander VI (not a saintly man by any means), gave Ferdinand and Isabella the right to make religious decisions in Spain and in the New World. This permission gave the Spanish rulers immunity, as they launched their inquisition against the Jews and Muslims.

Many followers of Ulrich Zwingli have come to Geneva to pay their respects to Calvin. Although Zwingli and Calvin brought Protestantism to Switzerland, their approaches differed in many ways. Some people see Calvin as the midpoint between Luther and Zwingli.

NOTEPAD

1. What did you learn about John Calvin? Ferdinand and Isabella of Spain? Pope Alexander VI? Ulrich Zwingli?

2. What did the article reveal about Calvin's teachings?

3. How does the article tie Ferdinand and Isabella in with the Protestant reform?

The Rest of the Story

Switzerland belonged in name to the Holy Roman Empire, but it actually consisted of a number of regions with separate governments. The inhabitants resisted Church authority and placed a great deal of trust in government. In addition to the changes brought about by the followers of Luther, other significant elements of the Reformation took root in Switzerland and spread throughout the empire.

The Church in Spain

In 1474, when Isabella became queen of Spain, she too found a Church in need of reform, although she went about her reform in ways very different from those of Martin Luther and later leaders of the Protestant Reformation. A number of bishops in Spain preferred to fight wars or to live a life of luxury, rather than serve the Church as spiritual leaders. The regular clergy were not even well trained. Isabella began her reform of the Church when she received from the pope the right to name her own bishops.

It doesn't matter if they are Jews or Gentiles. But all who do right will be rewarded with glory, honor, and peace, whether they are Jews or Gentiles. God doesn't have any favorites.

Romans 1:9–11, CEV

With the help of her confessor, a dedicated Franciscan presbyter whom she made archbishop of a large diocese, Isabella visited and reformed monasteries and dioceses in Spain. The pope refused to listen to any complaints against her from the bishops under her charge, and these bishops realized that they must either help with the reform, or suffer the loss of their positions.

Isabella had an excellent education and supported the education of others. With the support of Ferdinand, her husband, she furthered the establishment and use of the printing press to spread learning. Her confessor began a university which would eventually become the center of learning for people like Ignatius of Loyola, the founder of the Society of Jesus.

During the time of Ferdinand and Isabella, an Italian explorer, Columbus, persuaded them to support his voyage in search of a westward passage to India in order to take better advantage of its profitable trade. Columbus discovered the Americas in 1492, the year that Alexander VI became pope. Since church and state were inseparable in Spain, Columbus brought missionaries with him to the New World in order to convert the native people. It was commonly believed that they would not be saved unless they were baptized.

Ferdinand and Isabella received from the pope the right to name their own bishops in their territories in the New World. Their reason for looking toward the newly discovered lands across the ocean was financial, and secondarily religious. Ferdinand and Isabella wanted to use the newly discovered land and its native population to increase the wealth of Spain.

The Spanish Inquisition

Although Isabella supported learning, she also punished anyone who departed from accepted Church teaching. She became such a strong defender of the faith that she received from the pope the right to have the Inquisition in Spain placed under her power. She appointed a Dominican presbyter who was a staunch and tireless supporter of the Church to head the Inquisition in Spain. Thus began one of the most tragic chapters in the history of Christianity.

The Inquisitor, driven by a zeal for true teaching, became the most feared person in the country. His attacks first centered on Jews who had converted to Christianity under force and were not practicing the Christian faith. Hundreds of thousands of these Jews were forced into exile, where many faced certain death. In their travels, they were easy prey for looters and killers who roamed the roads of Europe. All their property and possessions were confiscated—giving the inquisitors a motive to prosecute unmercifully.

Muslims were numerous in Spain, due to the migration of the Moors in earlier centuries. They also became targets of the Inquisition. Those who refused to accept baptism faced punishment and sometimes death for their stand. As with the Jews, the property and possessions of Muslims were confiscated. The unworthy popes of the time did not really care how the rulers of Spain carried out the Inquisition. The number of people put to death by the Spanish Inquisition was so widely known that the term *Spanish Inquisition* became synonymous with terror and death.

Ulrich Zwingli

Ulrich Zwingli (1484–1531), while serving as chaplain at a shrine in Switzerland, began to doubt the spiritual profit of pilgrimages to such shrines. He left his charge as shrine chaplain and moved to Zurich, the largest city in Switzerland. There, Zwingli became a popular preacher.

Some wealthy merchants in Zurich wanted to introduce Lutheran teachings into their reformed Church. Because these wealthy leaders governed the city

In the Spotlight

St. Ignatius of Loyola was born the youngest of thirteen children in the family castle in the Basque province of Guipúzoca (modern-day Spain). As a youth he spent some time in the court of King Ferdinand. He then entered the military but found his career cut short when he was shot in the leg. While recovering from the wound, he read about Christ's life as well as the lives of the saints, and converted to Christianity.

After recovering, Ignatius pilgrimmed to Monserrat, where he symbolically dedicated his life to Christ by hanging his sword over the altar. He remained there for a year while he ministered to the needs of the poor and sick at the hospital. His selflessness attracted so much attention that he chose to withdraw from society into a life of solitude and austerity. During his retreat, he wrote his famous Spiritual Exercises, which were later published in 1548.

Still unclear about the direction his life should take, Ignatius returned to Spain and studied Latin and philosophy. He eventually graduated from the universtiy in Paris with a Master of Arts.

In Paris Ignatius attracted a group of students who practiced his Spiritual Exercises and pledged themselves to the work of the Gospel. Their plan seemed to receive divine guidance when a vision of Christ appeared to Ignatius, as he travelled to Rome with the rule of his new order and the terms of their vows to lay before Pope Paul III. In the vision Christ promised that all would go well. They received official approval from the pope in 1540 and called themselves the Society of Jesus. The hall-mark of the Jesuits was total commitment, obedience, and spiritual discipline.

The Jesuits, dedicated to evangelization, tirelessly evangelized the Far East. They reached England in 1542, and became an influential force in the Catholic resistance to Reformation. The order also proved a potent force in the Catholic Counter-Reformation, as they provided high-quality Catholic education in their schools and colleges throughout Europe and argued effectively against the creeds of Luther and Calvin. Ignatius insisted that this counter-attack be pursued in a spirit of charity and prayerfulness. He believed in the power of teaching by example.

His feast day is July 31 and he is the patron saintt of retreats and spiritual exercises.

and trusted Zwingli as their religious leader, they made many laws which were influenced by Zwingli's thought. Zwingli convinced the leaders to forbid any preaching of beliefs not found in Scripture.

Zwingli denied a number of teachings of the Catholic Church, as well as some of Luther's teachings. While Luther still believed in Christ's bodily presence in the Eucharist, Zwingli did not. He saw Christ as spiritually present in the Eucharist, but not as a real presence.

Since the Scriptures do not mention celibacy, Zwingli also maintained that presbyters and nuns received no benefits in practicing celibacy. Following Zwingli's direction, many people left the monasteries to marry. Zwingli also rejected the authority of the pope and believed that many Catholic practices were unscriptural and should be discontinued.

Catholics in Switzerland waged war against Zwingli and his followers. In 1531, Zwingli died in battle. Despite Zwingli's death, his reformed Church continued to thrive in many areas of Switzerland and beyond.

John Calvin

John Calvin (1509-1564) grew up in France in a family that owned enough property to allow him to live comfortably and to receive a good education. Since his father wanted him to study law, he left his chosen course of study to follow his father's wishes. When his father died, Calvin returned to the study of humanism and religious reformers, such as Luther. His study of law gave him an ability which later proved useful in his contributions to Protestantism.

While in France, Calvin dedicated himself to the reformed Church, which was Protestant. When he was twenty-five, however, the French government began a persecution of Protestants, and he had to flee the country. He fled to Switzerland where he continued his study of Scripture.

Two years after arriving in Switzerland, Calvin published a major and extremely popular theological work, entitled *The Institutes of the Christian Religion*. This influential book explained the teachings of the Reformation in an orderly fashion and is Calvin's great contribution to Protestantism. Luther introduced the Reformation; Calvin organized it.

Calvin settled in Geneva, a town in Switzerland which had already embraced Protestantism. The Protestant leaders there gave him the opportunity to shape the city according to the ideals of Protestantism as he viewed them. Calvin taught that the Church had the duty to preach the word of God and to celebrate the sacraments. The duty of the government was to defend the Church and punish those who were guilty of heresy or who lived immoral lives.

Calvin's Teachings

Calvin introduced a stern and disciplined form of religion in Geneva. He established penalties—from beatings to death—for moral wrongs. A person could face death for adultery or for disagreeing with Calvin's teachings, which formed the basis for the laws of the city. One extreme punishment was a severe beating for a frivolous motion during worship.

Calvin introduced the work ethic, which he based on spiritual principles. Since God gave time to human beings as a special gift, human beings were to use this gift in productive toil. God calls us to use the wealth gained through this hard work for charity and reinvestment. Economic success was a sign of God's blessings. This work ethic has had a powerful influence on the United States.

The basic theme of Calvin's writings is God's majesty. He concluded that, since everything in creation depends on God, God had freely chosen or predestined some for salvation. He believed that those who are not chosen receive the condemnation they deserve because they are sinners. Christians had to remain obedient to God with the hope that they were among the elect. This teaching was known as **predestination**.

Calvin's Protestant tradition came to be known as the Reformed Tradition, or **Presbyterianism**. It influenced Protestants in countries such as Poland, the Low Countries, France, Scotland, England, and the newly discovered Americas.

CLIPBOARD

1. When you look at the teachings of Luther, Zwingli, and Calvin, what differences do you see? What similarities? What is the "common thread"?

2. How does the idea of predestination differ from the belief that God already knows that we will enter heaven? Are you comfortable or uncomfortable with the assumption that some will not?

3. How does the faith lived by your Protestant friends compare with that found in the lives and teachings of Luther, Calvin, and Zwingli?

- **1375**

POPE URBAN VI. Urban was the first Italian pope elected in Rome after the Avignon papacy. His aggressive and harsh manner caused the cardinals to claim that his election was invalid.

POPE CLEMENT VII. This pope was chosen by the cardinals while Pope Urban VI still reigned in Rome. He was the first pope elected to the Avignon line during the Western Schism.

- **1400**

COUNCIL OF PISA. This council was called to solve the problem of the Western Schism. The participants elected a third pope. The popes at Rome and Avignon refused to resign.

POPE JOHN XXIII. John was the false pope elected to succeed Alexander V, who was elected at the attempted council at Pisa. John was eventually forced to resign by the Council of Constance.

POPE GREGORY VII. Gregory was the last reigning Roman pope during the period of the schism. He resigned when he was allowed to call the Council of Constance in his name. He died before the council elected another pope.

POPE BENEDICT VIII. Benedict was the last of the Avignon popes during the Western Schism. He was forced to flee, but still believed he was pope until his death.

POPE MARTIN V. Martin was elected pope at the Council of Constance, which now gave the Church a single pope.

JOHN WYCLIFF. Wycliff lived during the 1300s. An early reformer, he taught that Scripture alone was the source of truth. For this, he was posthumously condemned by the Church hierarchy at the Council of Constance in 1414.

JOHN HUS. Hus followed the teachings of John Wycliff and was offered protection to the Council of Constance. However, the Church regarded him as a heretic, and he was burned at the stake.

POPE NICHOLAS V. Nicholas is an example of the Renaissance popes who brought art and literature to the Vatican, along with the works of learned humanistic thinkers.

- **1475**

ISABELLA BECOMES QUEEN OF SPAIN. Queen Isabella became queen and attempted to reform the Church in Spain. She received permission to appoint bishops, and introduced the infamous Spanish Inquisition.

CHRISTOPHER COLUMBUS DISCOVERS AMERICA. This Italian explorer was sponsored by Isabella to look for a water route to the West Indies.

- **1500**

MARTIN LUTHER. In 1517, Luther proposed ninety-five theses concerning teachings of the Church, which he presented for debate. The indulgence controversy became a central issue. Luther taught that Scripture alone held all truth and that we reach salvation through faith alone. His ideas stimulated the Reformation and laid the foundation for Lutheranism.

POPE LEO X. This Renaissance pope allowed the buying and selling of indulgences in order to raise money to build St. Peter's Basilica in Rome and to support the lifestyle of the Church hierarchy. He excommunicated Luther.

JOHN TETZEL. This Dominican presbyter preached indulgences as a means of helping people out of purgatory.His misguided teachings regarding indulgences made the buying and selling of indulgences common.

CAJETAN. This theologian represented the pope in a meeting with Luther, but had no interest in discussion. He intended to arrest Luther if Luther did not repent. Luther escaped during the night.

FREDERICK OF SAXONY. This protector wanted to treat Luther justly. Pope Leo X could do nothing against Luther as long as the papacy needed Frederick's help.

JOHN ECK. This scholar debated Luther and forced him to publicly state that the Bible was superior to the pope and the council and that councils could make errors.

EMPEROR CHARLES V. This Spanish king was chosen to be the emperor. He was the one to pass judgment on Luther after the Diet of Worms.

DIET OF WORMS. This was a meeting of Luther, the emperor, and a number of world leaders at Worms in Germany. Luther refused to recant.

PEASANTS' REVOLT. German peasants revolted because of the conditions under which they were forced to live. Many were slaughtered by German princes incited in turn by Luther, who had changed his mind about supporting the peasants when they turned to violence.

- **1525**

ULRICH ZWINGLI. This reformer introduced a form of Protestantism in Switzerland which based its teachings on the Bible alone. He established a town ruled by biblical, religious teachings.

JOHN CALVIN. Calvin organized the Reformation and established the roots of Puritanism and Presbyterianism. He taught predestination and established his rule in the city of Geneva in Switzerland.

Western Schism

Council of Constance

Conciliarism

Diet of Worms

Lutheranism

Predestination

Presbyterianism

A Voice from the Past

Your goal this week is to relay to your readers the story of the Reformation. Be sure to include the events that led up to the Reformation as well as the people who played the key roles. As usual use your key terms as a guide. End your article with a discussion of how the Reformation still affects us today, as well as some insights on what needs to occurr before the Christian Church can once again be reunited.

Then and Now

The Protestant Revolution began with Martin Luther in 1517. He based his teachings on the Bible as the only source of truth and on faith alone as the source of salvation. The reform spread to Switzerland through the ministries of Ulrich Zwingli and John Calvin. John Calvin organized the reform, but ruled sternly in Geneva.

The major theological difference between the teachings of the reformers and Catholic teaching was that Catholics based their teaching on the Bible and Traditon, and the reformers on the Bible alone.

The Reformation eroded the centrality of the Catholic Church. Its teachings affirmed the priesthood of all believers, the freedom of the individual Christian, and the sanctity of the life of laypeople.

Today the Lutheran, Presbyterian, and other Protestant denominations have thriving congregations. The rigidity found in Calvin has generally disappeared, due to the influence of later leaders who followed a less stern and more compassionate approach. The word of God rather than the Eucharist plays the central role in most Protestant services.

NEWS IN REVIEW

1. What caused the Western Schism, and how was it solved?

2. What did the Council of Constance achieve?

3. What is the Renaissance, and why is it important to Church history?

4. What was the indulgence controversy?

5. What issues led Luther to reject some of the teachings of the Catholic Church?

6. What role did John Eck have during his meeting with Luther?

7. Where did the name Protestantism originate, and what did Calvin do to organize Protestantism?

8. Why do some people view Queen Isabella as a saint, while others view her as a cruel despot?

9. Who is Zwingli, and what did he teach?

10. What is predestination, as taught by Calvin?

chapter eleven

Counter Reformation

During and after the Reformation, people faced a new type of conflict. If we were living then, we would find ourselves discussing our faith with neighbors who practiced a different form of Christianity. This would seem strange. We would have a difficult time understanding how people could feel that the celebration of the Eucharist was not as important as the preaching of the Word of God.

As we gathered for the celebration of the Eucharistic liturgy, we would find some practices different from those of our present day. Depending on the mood of the presider, the readings could go on and on, or end after a few verses. With no common book to determine the readings during liturgy and few common rituals, we would find customs differing from region to region. Most of the celebrations would resemble the liturgy held in Rome, but there would be many differences, some of them significant.

A greater variety in worship services would be apparent in the Protestant Churches. While some continued the celebration of the Lord's Supper every Sunday, other groups would do so only once a month. Still other Churches would not include the Eucharist in their worship, focusing on the Word alone.

Today, we have a common book which contains the readings and rituals used during Liturgy.

The Reformation in England

The Christian Times

Sixteenth Century   Vol. 16   No. 3

Elizabeth Supports the Policy of Henry VIII

Last week Queen Elizabeth introduced laws which follow the direction established by her father, Henry VIII. Henry broke with the authority of the pope over Henry's desire for a divorce from his first wife, Catherine, the mother of Mary Tudor.

After his break with the pope, Henry had himself declared head of the Church in England and required the clergy to take an oath supporting his position. Bishop John Fisher and Henry's former chancellor, Thomas More, refused to take the Oath of Supremacy, and the king had them both beheaded.

Anne Boleyn, Henry's second wife and the mother of Elizabeth, was also beheaded. Elizabeth has succeeded in driving most Catholic bishops out of the country and has firmly established the Anglican Church as the national Church. Her persecution against the papists is as violent as that of her half-sister, Queen "Bloody" Mary Tudor, the previous queen who persecuted the Anglicans.

Besides keeping out the papists, Elizabeth has tried to keep Lutheranism from gaining a stronghold in the country. Since the teachings of the Lutheran Reformation were so clearly listed in the Augsburg Confession by the Lutheran theologian, Philip Melanchthon, Lutheranism has spread rapidly throughout parts of Germany, Denmark, and Sweden.

As Anne Boleyn's daughter, Elizabeth I is predisposed to Protestantism, although she refuses to align herself with any Protestant movements. Lutheranism is spreading rapidly, and the teachings of John Calvin are also making inroads across the world. John Knox, following some of Calvin's ideas, has established the Reformed Church of Scotland.

NOTEPAD

? ? ? ? ?

1. What did you learn about Queen Elizabeth? Henry VIII? John Fisher? Thomas More? Anne Boleyn? Philip Melanchthon? John Knox?

2. What important historical events were mentioned in this article?

3. Did the article change any of your previous ideas regarding Protestant religions? Explain.

The Rest of the Story

The Reformation initiated changes which have affected our lives to this day. Luther may never have realized the impact that his challenge to the Catholic Church would have on the Christian Church.

KEY TERMS

Augsburg Confession: the teachings of Luther as presented in Augsburg by Philip Melanchthon.

The Augsburg Confession

At a meeting in Augsburg, Germany, a Lutheran theologian, Philip Melanchthon, discussed a list of declarations of Lutheran teachings before Emperor Charles V. Melanchthon presented these teachings, now known as the **Augsburg Confession**, in order to defend Lutheranism against accusations of heresy. He stressed issues of agreement between Catholics and Protestants with the intention of minimizing the differences.

The differences named by Melanchthon were Communion under the forms of bread and wine, permission for the clergy to marry, and the reform of various rituals in the celebration of the

Eucharist. Melanchthon prudently avoided more sensitive issues such as the leadership of the pope, the number of sacraments, and the effects of ordination. The emperor at first supported the Confession as presented by Melanchthon.

John Eck, who had caused problems for Luther in the past, refuted the Confession by offering a written paper approving nine articles outright and six with qualifications, and condemning thirteen. He also joined with others in convincing Charles not to trust the Lutherans to abide by the Confession. As a result, Charles agreed to suppress Lutheranism by force if other countries would support him. When Charles did not receive the support he sought, he did not carry through on his threat to lead an army against the Lutherans.

In 1531, Melanchthon wrote an *Apology*, which means an "explanation," and which is accepted as the authentic commentary on the Confession to this day. Although Melanchthon had a genius for organizing the theological thought of Lutheranism, he lacked the skills and diplomacy necessary for leadership. After the death of Luther in 1546, Melanchthon was the natural choice to lead Lutheranism, but he made a series of mistakes which led other followers of Luther to look elsewhere for leadership.

The Spread of Lutheranism

Wars in Germany between Catholic and Protestant princes were dividing the country so badly that the princes came together at Augsburg in 1555 to adopt a compromise. Each ruler was free to choose either Catholicism or Protestantism as the established religion for the region. The religion of the ruler would determine the religion of the people.

For example, when the newly elected king of Denmark gained control of the country, he established a national Church and allowed the nobles to seize Catholic Church property.

The king brought in Lutheran preachers to spread Lutheranism throughout Denmark and appointed his own bishops without recourse to the pope. By the middle of the 1500s, Lutheranism was firmly established in Denmark.

Finding himself in financial need, the king of Sweden seized the wealth of the Catholic Church. He supported the spread of Lutheranism and ignored the pope completely. By the end of the 1500s, the Swedish Church turned fully toward Lutheranism by officially adopting the Augsburg Confession. Luther's catechism became the foundation for religious instruction.

The Augsburg Confession

Henry VIII

Royal families often established alliances by arranging for a son of a royal family in one country to marry the daughter of another royal family in another country. The countries thus became allies through marriage. The daughter of Ferdinand and Isabella of Spain, Catherine of Aragon, was fifteen years old when the king of England arranged a marriage between her and his son Arthur. This fusion of England and Spain was an important defensive move on the part of England because of the continual feud between England and France.

Arthur, who was in line to be the king of England, died after four months of marriage. The King of England wanted the alliance with Spain to continue, so he negotiated with Ferdinand and Isabella to permit Catherine to marry the king's next son, Henry. In those days, Church law forbade a marriage between a brother-in-law and a sister-in-law. Catherine and Henry received a dispensation from the Church law and were permitted to marry.

After Henry VIII became king, he championed the cause of the Catholic Church against Lutheranism and defended the Catholic teaching of seven sacraments against Luther's rejection of some of the sacraments. He refused to allow Protestantism to gain a hold in England. Because of his defense against Luther, Pope Leo X honored Henry with the title, *Defender of the Faith*. For the Catholic Church in England, all looked well.

Henry Breaks with the Catholic Church

But Henry soon grew tired of his wife Catherine and began to create reasons for the pope to declare his marriage to Catherine invalid. Of the children born of Catherine, only one, a daughter named Mary, survived. In the meantime, Anne Boleyn had captured the king's heart, but she insisted that she would not be his mistress, only his wife. Between his desire for Anne and his longing for a son to rule England, Henry needed a way out of his marriage. He declared invalid the dispensation received from the pope to allow his marriage to Catherine.

Pope Clement VII did not respond immediately to Henry's request for an annulment. Since Catherine was the daughter of the rulers of Spain and an aunt of Emperor Charles V, the pope had political, as well as spiritual, reasons for delaying any decision in the case. The emperor had invaded Rome in 1527 and captured the pope. The pope hesitated in responding to Henry, so as not to alienate the powerful emperor.

Henry asked Thomas Cranmer, the archbishop of Canterbury, to meet with leading scholars in England. They were to explore reasons why his marriage to Catherine was not valid. With the support of a number of these scholars, Henry then petitioned the pope, stating that the pope did not have the right to grant a dispensation from his marriage to Catherine. The scholars reasoned that the pope could not set aside a Church law.

In 1529, the pope decided to have the issue judged in Rome rather than through a delegate in England. At a time in history when nationalism was on the rise, many people who supported the pope now turned against him, resenting his apparent snubbing of the English courts.

Henry Seizes Control

Henry began to work within England to have the Catholic Church there declare his marriage to Catherine invalid. In 1533, Thomas Cranmer decreed that Henry's marriage to Catherine was invalid. Henry then married Anne Boleyn. Parliament gave the king a number of rights which laid the foundation for a schism between the Church in England and the Catholic Church in Rome.

Among these rights, parliament gave the king the right to nominate bishops, make the clergy subject to civil law, and declared that it was not a heresy to state that the pope was not the head of the Church.

A year later, parliament passed the **Act of Supremacy**, which declared that the king was the only earthly head of the Church in England. A second act (law) required all officials and clergy to take an oath supporting the succession of Anne Boleyn's children to the throne. A third act declared anyone refusing to support the new title of the king, as head of the Church, guilty of treason. Most bishops and people supported these acts and took the **Oath of Supremacy**.

One bishop, John Fisher, refused to take the Oath of Supremacy, so the king had him imprisoned in the infamous Tower of London. This was an ancient castle where political prisoners were held until they repented of their crimes or until their death. John Fisher was beheaded in 1535, a year after the oath of supremacy became law.

A second person, Thomas More, a layman, was a friend of King Henry and served as the chancellor of England. Because he could not in conscience support the king's actions, More resigned his position, but refused to publicly condemn the king. He spent a long and difficult year in the Tower of London awaiting his execution, while his family desperately tried to talk him into taking the oath. To the end, he refused to turn against the Catholic Church. He was beheaded a few weeks after John Fisher. Four hundred years later, John Fisher and Thomas More each received the title of saint from the Catholic Church.

Heirs to the Throne

Anne Boleyn, like Catherine before her, produced only one heir to the throne, a

St. Thomas More

daughter named Elizabeth. Three years after this marriage, Henry, still seeking a male heir to the throne, had Anne beheaded for adultery. Finally, Jane Seymour, who followed Anne Boleyn as Henry's wife, died twelve days after giving birth to a son, Edward. Henry married three more times. One of these wives received a divorce and left England because she was unhappy there. Henry had his fifth wife beheaded on the charge of adultery, and his last wife was awaiting execution when Henry himself died.

After Henry's death, nine-year-old Edward came to the throne, but died six years later at the age of fifteen. Those who raised young Edward took advantage of their position to further the cause of Protestantism in the country. They followed the simple teachings of Zwingli.

Henry himself had rejected many of the Protestant teachings and still considered himself a Catholic. He believed that he was simply rejecting the role of the pope as the head of the Church.

KEY TERMS

Act of Supremacy: declared the king the only earthly head of the Church in England.

Oath of Supremacy: an oath supporting the act of supremacy which declared anyone refusing to support the new title of the king, as head of the Church, guilty of treason.

JOURNAL

If Henry were ruling today, how would his actions differ? Why?

In the Spotlight

John Fisher was a son of a textile merchant in Beverly. He was educated at the Minister School until the age of 14, when he then entered Cambridge University. In 1491 he was ordained, and in 1501 he was appointed Vice-Chancellor of the University. After a short time, in 1502, he resigned in order to become the chaplain to Lady Margaret Beaumont, the mother of Henry VIII.

Together, Fisher and Lady Margaret worked to reform the university, as they founded St. John and Christ Colleges. Their main focus was on improving the standard of scholarship.

In 1504, he was appointed Bishop of Rochester. While performing the responsibilities of this office, Fisher also managed to devote a lot of time to his writing. He writings were widely read, and he was especially famous throughout the continent. He received much acclaim for his work against Luther and his defense of orthodox Catholic doctrine on the sacraments.

Because of his renowned holiness and learning, he was appointed confessor to Catherine of Aragon, the first wife of Henry VIII, in 1527. When Henry began his proceedings of divorce from Catherine, Fisher, despite Henry's wishes, defended the validity of the marriage. Henry, angered by Fisher's defense of the marriage, sent Fisher to the Tower along with Thomas More.

Fisher aggravated Henry further when he refused to take the Oath of Supremacy, and he was sentenced to death.

His body was buried without rites and his head was displayed for two weeks on London bridge, after which it was cast into the river.

His feast day is June 22.

KEY TERMS

Anglicanism: the Reformation in England.

Anglican Church: the Church in England.

Puritans: group in England who championed the Calvinist movement in its purist form.

Henry's Daughters

Mary Tudor, the daughter of Catherine, ruled from 1553 to 1558. She restored relations between England and Rome, but she was unable to undo the progress of the Reformation in the country. Resorting to force, she became known as *Bloody Mary* because of the many executions of Protestants which took place while she reigned.

Elizabeth I (1558–1603), the daughter of Anne Boleyn, became queen and firmly established the English Reformation in the country. Although she never received the title *Bloody* for her executions, they matched those of Mary Tudor. Her victims, however, were Catholic. Elizabeth's reasons for supporting the Church of England were not theological, but political—she could use the Church to help keep England united. Like her father, Elizabeth made heresy an act of treason. She solidified the Church of England during her forty-five years as queen.

The Reformation in England became known as **Anglicanism** and the Church in England as the **Anglican Church**. In the United States, it is known as the Episcopalian Church. During the reign of Elizabeth, some people in England championed the Calvinist movement in its purist form. This group, who became known as **Puritans**, followed many of the rigorous tendencies of Calvinism. Since the Puritans were a minority and not supportive of the religion of the land, they faced terrible persecution.

The Reformed Movement in Scotland

Lutheranism and Calvinism became the models for later movements in Protestantism. In Scotland, the Protestants had captured a castle belonging to the Catholic Church and killed the archbishop. John Knox (1513–1572), the best known of the Scottish reformers, became the central preacher and agent of Protestantism in the country. When the French recaptured the castle for Scotland, they forced Knox to labor under brutal conditions for almost two years.

After his release, Knox went to England for a brief time, but had to leave the country when the persecutions of Protestants began. He went to Switzerland where he met and stayed with Calvin. Knox later became acquainted with the successor of Zwingli, from whom he learned more about Protestantism. He eventually received word from the nobles of Scotland that they wanted him to return as the leader of Protestantism in the country.

Shortly after Knox's return to Scotland, he was able to establish the Reformed Church of Scotland, which was similar to later Presbyterianism. When the government was too weak to defend itself against the Protestant nobles, the nobles began to seize Catholic Church property. They expected to use the property to enrich themselves, but Knox and some of his followers wanted to use it for support of the poor and the Church of Scotland. Tensions developed between Knox and some of the leading Protestants of Scotland.

By the time of his death, Knox had successfully turned Scotland toward the beliefs of the Reformed Church. Calvin's form of Protestantism led not only to the Reformed Church of Scotland, but also to the Reformed Churches in France, England, and the Netherlands. In the newly discovered Americas, many groups adapted Protestantism to fit their needs; Knox's views were respected and followed to some extent by some of these groups.

CLIPBOARD

1. Discuss what you know about the Lutheran Church today. Compare and contrast the information you have acquired from personal experience, social studies classes, and this text.

2. Discuss the Episcopal Church today. Compare and contrast the information you have acquired from personal experience, social studies classes, and this text.

3. Discuss what Bishop John Fisher or Thomas More would do today if they lived in a country where religious sentiments were not permitted to be expressed in public schools, buildings, or meetings.

The Council of Trent

The Christian Times

Sixteenth Century   Vol. 16   No. 5

Council of Trent Ends

Early this week, the Catholic Church ended its nineteenth ecumenical council. The council took place at Trent, a compromise location in northern Italy where the inhabitants are German-speaking.

Although the council took almost eighteen years to complete, the bishops met in only three sessions with little more than a year set aside for each session. The council resolved many topics related to the teaching and discipline of the Catholic Church. The bishops who attended the council are confident that there will no longer be any problems identifying the differences between Catholics and Protestants.

At a time when the popes feared that councils would take control of the Church, it took courage for Popes Paul III (in 1545), Julian II (in 1551), and Pius IV (in 1562), in turn, to gather the council together.

There seems to be an emphasis lately on Gothic architecture, in which a building rests on a firm foundation and soars toward the heavens. Perhaps this new trend in architecture is symbolic of the changes that seem to be taking place in the Catholic Church.

NOTEPAD

? ? ? ? ?

1. Who was named responsible for arranging the Council of Trent? Why did this take courage?

2. What historical events do you find mentioned in this article?

3. How did the new architecture reflect new attitudes surfacing in the Catholic Church?

The Rest of the Story

Twenty-eight years after Luther posted his ninety-five theses, the Catholic Church finally held its long-needed council of reform at Trent, a city in northern Italy. Unfortunately, the men who served as popes during this period were often more concerned with protecting the Papal States and the wealth of the Catholic Church, than they were with working to avoid the tragic rupture taking place in the Church. Many of the popes miscalculated the impact the Protestants would have on the Catholic Church.

Planning the Council

Pope Paul III, who convened the Council of Trent, appeared to be a poor choice for the role of a reforming pope. Once he became pope, he did not hesitate to give positions of honor to his illegitimate children. As a cardinal, he witnessed the sack of Rome by the Emperor Charles V. At this point, he became concerned about preserving the Catholic Church. Despite his personal weaknesses as pope, he began his reform by appointing reform-minded cardinals who presented him with a blueprint for action.

The notion of a council to help reform the Catholic Church was not a new idea, but most popes shied away from such an undertaking. Many popes still feared conciliarism and the possibility that a council could get out of control and set itself above the authority of the pope. Some popes feared that a council would incite a further invasion of Rome or the city where the council took place. Still others feared that a council would favor the needs of one country over another.

First Phase (1545–1547)

Even before the sessions began, the pope and the emperor quarreled about the purpose of the council. Although many Christians in the empire were turning toward Protestantism, most Christians did not believe that they were leaving the Catholic Church when they did so. They considered themselves Catholics with different attitudes toward faith and certain practices ordered by the Catholic Church, such as the requirement of celibacy for the clergy.

The emperor sought a council which would bring about unity between Protestants and Catholics, while the pope thought the central purpose of the council should be to clarify Catholic teaching. He thought that the Protestants' attacks on Catholics were about Catholic Church teachings and that, in clarifying these, Catholics would be better equipped to support themselves against any attacks made on their beliefs.

Paul III dispatched representatives to Germany to discuss topics of reform with Lutheran representatives. He also invited Lutherans to be represented at the council. The meeting between Pope Paul's delegates and the Lutheran representatives unfortunately ended in total disagreement, and the council met without the Lutherans. Thus, the Council of Trent had significance only for the Catholic Church.

Without the Lutherans attending, the bishops decided that they would deal with Catholic Church discipline as well as doctrine. They recognized that the Reformation not only attacked Catholic Church teachings, but it also voiced a needed call for reform in the lives of Catholic Church leaders. Although learned theologians assisted the bishops at the council and generally

wrote the decrees, the bishops alone had the right to vote on each decree of the council.

Because of disease, wars, and political intrigue, the council which began in 1545 did not end until 1563. It really met only three times in those years, 1545-1547, 1551-1552, and 1562-1563. By the time the council ended, the bishops had drawn a clear line between Catholic teachings and the teachings of the Protestant reformers. After the council, Protestants generally no longer considered themselves to be Catholics.

The first period of the Council of Trent, meeting between 1545 and 1547, dealt with the place of tradition in the Christian faith. Protestants based their faith on Scripture alone, whereas the bishops at the council declared that Catholics depend on Scripture and tradition. The council declared that the emphasis on Scripture alone was heretical. However, they also said that "Scripture and tradition" does not mean that God's revelation is found partly in Scripture and partly in tradition. Rather, Scripture and tradition together are one source of God's revelation.

During this first period, the bishops also addressed the issue of the depravity of human nature due to original sin. In essence, Luther felt that humanity cannot earn salvation, but that God's love and omnipotence were enough. Following on his interpretation of Paul's letters, especially Romans, Luther saw Christ as covering our sin. The bishops, on the other hand, supported the value of "good works" along with faith. Over the years, as the gap between the two groups widened, the Catholic Church began to emphasize the concept that creation was good and even sin cannot destroy this goodness. Some Protestant groups rejected this line of thinking to the extent of using the term *depraved* to characterize the human race.

The bishops defined and explained the sacraments, with special emphasis on the Sacraments of Baptism and Confirmation. They reiterated that there

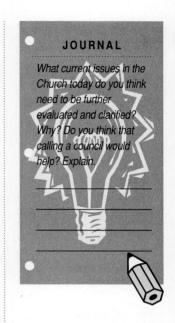

JOURNAL

What current issues in the Church today do you think need to be further evaluated and clarified? Why? Do you think that calling a council would help? Explain.

_____

_____

_____

_____

S acred Tradition and Sacred Scripture, then, are bound closely together and communicate one with the other. For both of them, flowing out from the same divine well-spring, come together in some fashion to form one thing and move towards the same goal.' Each of them makes present and fruitful in the Church the mystery of Christ, who promised to remain with his own 'always, to the close of the age.'

Catechism of the Catholic
Church, #80

While they were eating, Jesus took a loaf of bread, and after blessing it he broke it, gave it to the disciples, and said, 'Take, eat; this is my body.' Then he took a cup, and after giving thanks he gave it to them, saying, 'Drink from it, all of you; for this is my blood of the covenant, which is poured out for many for the forgiveness of sins.'

Matthew 26:26–28

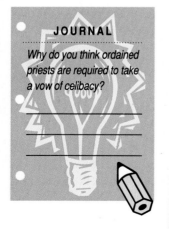

are seven sacraments, thus rejecting the Protestants' acceptance of only two sacraments.

At this point, sickness and military threats interrupted the council, and the pope became distracted by political matters.

Second Phase (1551–1552)

The new pope, Julius II, reopened the Council of Trent in 1551. The bishops debated the meaning of the Eucharist and defined the Catholic Church's belief in the real presence of Christ in the Eucharist. They clarified the Catholic Church's teaching about the Sacrament of Reconciliation-the rite of absolution, the requirement to confess to a presbyter, and the need to make amends.

During this period, a group of Protestants, persuaded to attend the council by Emperor Charles V, arrived to take part in the council. Charles V believed that the Catholic Church could still achieve unity with Protestantism. The Protestants, however, brought with them a list of demands which essentially rejected the past decisions of the council.

The Protestants demanded that the bishops make no further decisions on matters of faith until the Protestant theologians arrived, and that all previous decrees of the council be revoked. They also demanded that the pope not participate in the council, that bishops be freed of any allegiance to the pope, and that the council be considered superior to the pope. Needless to say, the bishops rejected these proposals, and the pope forbade any further negotiations with the Protestants.

The second period of the council ended when the German princes revolted against their rulers.

Third Phase (1562–1563)

Pope Paul IV refused to reconvene the Council of Trent, because he believed he could bring about reform more effectively and quickly on his own initiative. Although he worked for reform, his

methods were often ruthless. He had no time for clarification of teaching, since he felt that the real problem was the corruption of Catholic Church officials and the "heretical tendencies" of the Protestants.

He ordered bishops to live in their own dioceses and had them cast into prison if they remained in Rome. He reintroduced the use of the Inquisition, causing pain and death for many people. He introduced the *Index of Forbidden Books* and placed a number of seemingly harmless books on the list. He also restricted Roman Jews to a ghetto, imagining that they were in some way assisting Protestants.

By the time Pope Paul IV died, the people had become so enraged with him that they raced through the streets of Rome, attacking every remnant of his papacy. They freed prisoners, destroyed his statues, and tore apart the halls of the Inquisition.

The following pope, Pius IV, reconvened the council in 1562. The religious and political problems in France led the pope to call the bishops into the third period of the Council of Trent. The bishops clarified the Catholic Church's teachings concerning the Eucharistic celebration as a sacrifice of Jesus Christ. They clarified Catholic teaching about the Sacraments of Holy Orders and Marriage and made rules concerning proper procedures for a Catholic marriage.

In January of 1564, Pope Pius IV approved all of the decrees of the Council of Trent. The council had come to an end, but the responsibility of implementing the council belonged to the future. The bishops were now required to live in their dioceses and to establish seminaries to train candidates for the ordained priesthood. Ordained priests were to remain unmarried, the Eucharistic liturgy was to be celebrated in Latin, and the rituals of the Eucharistic celebration were firmly established.

Signs of Change

Art very often expresses the experiences of an age. One of the major changes taking place throughout Europe during the Renaissance was the form of architecture being used for churches. These forms of architecture tell their own story.

Shortly before the year 1000, a heavy, stone style of architecture, called **Romanesque architecture**, dominated the style of church buildings. The churches were built with thick walls which held thick stone arches. In turn, these arches held up the roof. Immense pillars rose to the arches to hold the heavy stone in place. Because of these massive structures, the buildings had room for only small windows. Without large windows, the inside of the churches were often dark. The message given by these solid structures was a message of sturdy but unyielding and somber power.

By the twelfth century, a new style of architect, **Gothic**, became dominant. This architectural style had a soaring quality and made for higher and thinner-appearing churches. These churches did not depend on the walls of the church for total support, but rather on its framework of arches and columns. An architect had come up with the daring idea of having the walls of the Gothic churches supported by buttresses which reached out from the top to the lower roofs of the structure. They called these buttresses **flying buttresses**, a name derived from the image of flight through air.

The Gothic style allowed for huge windows and high peaked arches that speared the sky. Light flooded into these churches through huge windows. Where the Romanesque churches emphasized firm, unchanging footing, the Gothic style emphasized a thrusting toward the heavens, a solid foundation reaching out to new discoveries. The style reflected the new ranges in study, art, and styles of leadership dominant in the changing world of the Renaissance.

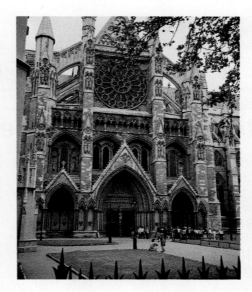

Westminster Abbey

By the end of the fifteenth century, the Catholic Church had entered a new Counter-Reformation era. At this time, the Gothic style of architecture became even more popular and could aptly be seen as a compliment to the new directions of the Christian Churches. Through the Council of Trent, the Catholic Church set forth its doctrine, providing for its followers a firm foundation to soar into the centuries ahead. Catholic teachings were clearer now than they had ever been. Similarly, Protestant teachings were more organized and well disbursed throughout most of Europe.

KEY TERMS

Romanesque architecture: a heavy, stone style of architecture which dominated the style of church buildings before the year 1000.

Gothic architecture: a form of architecture which depended on a framework of arches and columns for support; had a soaring quality that made for higher and thinner-appearing churches.

Flying buttresses: provided support by reaching out from the top to the lower roofs of the structure; derived from the image of flight through air.

CLIPBOARD

1. What do you see as most significant about the Council of Trent? Why?

2. The Council of Trent had to clarify a lot of its teachings because of the controversies occurring during that time. Discuss some important Church issues a council would have to face if it met today.

3. From what you have heard and learned, how do you think the Second Vatican Council impacted the daily life of the Catholic Church in the twentieth century?

Spiritual Reform

The Christian Times

Sixteenth Century   **Vol. 16   No. 6**

Council Reform Continues

At a meeting held yesterday morning, Pope Pius V introduced the modern Latin ritual for the celebration of the Eucharist. This ritual can be found in the *Roman Missal*. The pope continues to implement the direction of the Council of Trent by bringing the Catholic Church into the modern world.

Two important names among those working for reform are Teresa of Avila, who reformed the Carmelite nuns, and John of the Cross, who reformed the Carmelite monasteries of men. A major reformer, Ignatius of Loyola, a former soldier, founded an order called the *Company of Jesus*, later referred to as the *Society of Jesus*. He brought together some courageous men who are already having an effect on preaching the Word of God.

Other Catholic Church reformers have already made their mark. Charles Borromeo, who was a major influence in the election of Pope Pius V, worked in an office of the pope and had great concern for the poor. Philip Neri, an ordained priest, gathered a group of clergy into a community called the *Oratory*. Francis de Sales and Jane Frances de Chantal, who founded the Visitation Sisters, provided practical approaches to a life dedicated to God.

The Council of Trent still brings a new breath of air into the Catholic Church, and the saintly men and women of our era are keeping alive that breath of fresh air.

NOTEPAD
? ? ? ? ?

1. What did you learn about Pope Pius V? Teresa of Avila? John of the Cross? Ignatius of Loyola? Charles Borromeo? Philip Neri? Francis de Sales? Jane Frances de Chantal?

2. How has the Council of Trent started to affect the Church, according this article?

3. What religious communities does this article mention and how are they working for reform? Which of them are you familiar with?

The Rest of the Story

As we evaluate the Council of Trent and its effects on the Catholic Church, we must keep in mind its relationship to the period in which it takes place. There is often a period of some turmoil and adjustment following a council. On a more positive note, there is usually joy and hope as people dedicate themselves to new ideals.

Teresa of Avila (1515–1582)

Throughout history, corruption in the Catholic Church was often balanced by the many heroic men and women who lived dedicated and holy lives. The great saints of history often rose up during the periods of greatest corruption among leaders of the Catholic Church. Two notable saints of the sixteenth century who reformed the monastic life of the Carmelites were Teresa of Avila and John of the Cross.

The roots of the Carmelite order go back to the twelfth century. The order receives its name from the original place where a group of hermits gathered and established a community. They began their community on Mount

Carmel in the Holy Land, and it quickly spread to other areas. The community combined strict rules with community living. By the time Teresa of Avila joined a house of Carmelite nuns in Spain, that particular community had become less rigid and sometimes lax. It was in need of a reform.

Teresa of Avila was the granddaughter of a converted Jew who had relocated to Avila because of the Inquisition. As a young child, she felt drawn to the monastic life, but she also feared such a dedication. She enjoyed the company of people, and her wit and good humor easily drew people into her company. When she decided to join the Carmelite monastery, she surprised many of her friends who had difficulty picturing her in a convent. Despite her father's unhappiness with her choice, she entered a monastery for women.

Life in the monastery did not deprive Teresa of visitors. Her humor and her insights in the area of spirituality made her the center of attraction for many people of the area who loved to come and talk with her. She had a high degree of intelligence and loved to read books on spiritual and theological topics.

Unfortunately, Teresa had to abandon some of her books when the Spanish Inquisition put them on the list of forbidden books. In time, despite her popularity and her many visitors, Teresa longed for a more dedicated life of prayer and solitude. Feeling an emptiness in her half-hearted convent life, she became very unhappy.

Discalced Carmelites

Without warning, Teresa began to experience visions. At first, she did not understand them and sought help from her confessors in trying to understand the visions. After many disappointing visits to various confessors, she eventually found help from some learned friars who convinced her that her visions

were indeed authentic. Later, when she was superior of the other nuns at her convent, she insisted on educated confessors, and not confessors noted only for their piety or spirituality.

In a vision, Teresa received a call to establish her own convent where she could follow a more strict monastic life. Despite an overwhelming amount of antagonism and ridicule from religious leaders and the nearby elite who enjoyed her company, she founded a small convent in which the nuns lived the original rules of the Carmelites.

Soon her visions increased, and Teresa felt called to establish more convents. Although some people continued to ridicule her, she received support from some bishops and other influential people who recognized the importance of her convents in the needed reform of the Catholic Church. Her order flourished and spread throughout Spain and beyond its borders.

Since Teresa's nuns wore sandals instead of shoes, they added the word *discalced*, which means "barefoot," thus becoming the **Discalced Carmelites**. Even in this strict form of life, Teresa kept her sense of humor and her desire for learning.

Teresa had many mystical experiences of God's presence and wrote extensively about them. Her writings became classics on the subject of mysticism. She encouraged and inspired a saintly man, John of the Cross, to work for the reform of Carmelite men. Both John and Teresa wrote of their deep spiritual experiences. In the twentieth century, Pope Paul VI bestowed the title of *Doctor of the Church* on Teresa for her learned contributions to spirituality. She and St. Catherine of Siena are the only two women who bear this title.

Ignatius of Loyola (1491–1556)

Ignatius was a young Spanish soldier who dreamed of a life of glory in the military. While in battle, his leg was wounded; this wound caused him to limp for the rest of his life. During his painful and long recovery, he used his time to read, immersing himself in books on piety and the lives of the saints. He eventually experienced a vision which turned his dreams away from the military toward God. He began to fight a peaceful battle, as a spiritual soldier in God's service.

After his recovery, he continued his long hours in reflection and prayer. After a lengthy, tormenting struggle with an awareness of his sinfulness, he experienced God's grace and release from his guilt. Unlike those who sought to find God in the monasteries, Ignatius chose to spread the gospel message through traveling and preaching.

During his time of reflection, Ignatius wrote a course of meditations called *The Spiritual Exercises*. These meditations are still in wide use today. Ignatius intended these meditations and directives as aids for people with the strong desire to stay in touch with God's presence in their lives. The exercises reflect Ignatius's deep understanding of human nature and the means of directing one's nature toward serving God.

The Jesuits

Recognizing his need to learn theology, Ignatius attended a number of universities. At the university in Paris, a group of fellow students, inspired by his dedication and faith, joined him in his mission. In 1534, he and his small band of followers vowed to live a life of poverty, chastity, and obedience. His military training was reflected in the regimental rules he established for himself and his followers.

At first Ignatius intended to minister to the Turks in the Holy Land, but the rapid increase in the number of his followers brought with it new directions. His group, the Company of Jesus or the Society of Jesus, eventually came to be known popularly as the

Jesuits. The Jesuits were soon ministering throughout the known world. Wherever explorers went, the Jesuits were not far behind. The community also took a strong stance against Protestantism.

Because Ignatius used the military form in organizing his community, he and his followers were able to react swiftly when a need arose. The men dedicated themselves to the service of the pope and became the pope's staunch defenders throughout the world. In addition to the vows of poverty, chastity, and obedience, they added a fourth vow of service to the pope.

Ignatius required the Jesuits to pray the daily prayer of the Church, the Divine Office, but instead of praying it in common as the monks in monasteries do, they were to pray privately. This form of prayer better suited the diverse ministries of the Jesuits.

In 1540, Pope Paul III gave Ignatius permission to form his religious society, which received the name The Company of Jesus, and he allowed the group to begin accepting up to sixty new members. Four years later, the pope allowed them to accept all men who wished to join them. The missionary zeal of the Jesuits became visible at the Council of Trent and in countries such as Italy, Spain, Portugal, Poland, and parts of Germany.

Later in the century, a learned and energetic man, Peter Canisius, joined the Jesuits and brought the Catholic faith back to several Protestant strongholds in Germany. His tactic was to attract back to the Catholic Church the most influential people of the area, including the princes, and then to reach out to the ordinary people through them. His piety and overwhelming energy earned him the title of the *Second Apostle of Germany*. He organized a Jesuit province in Germany and established Jesuit colleges to provide a foundation for the revival of Catholic spirituality and training.

Charles Borromeo

The Council of Trent not only drew the line between Protestantism and Catholicism, it also challenged leaders in the Catholic Church to reform their lives. Charles Borromeo (1538–1584) is a good example of the effects of the council on many Catholic Church leaders of the day.

Charles came from a rich and influential family in northern Italy. Although he was not ordained a presbyter until he was twenty-five years old, his family's influence in the Catholic Church enabled him to begin his Church career at the age of twelve. Before his ordination, he received from his uncle, Pope Pius IV, the title of archbishop of Milan at the age of twenty-one and the title of cardinal at the age of twenty-two. At that time, these titles did not require ordination to the priesthood.

Borromeo was a good example of the abuses in the Catholic Church before the council. Pope Pius IV called his brilliant nephew to Rome to serve as his secretary of state. Placing relatives in high positions was a common abuse in the Catholic Church at that time, but as Charles matured, he proved himself a skilled secretary of state. During his time in Rome, he had a religious experience which led him to reform his own way of life and dedicate himself to reforming the Catholic Church.

Charles worked hard to introduce the reforms of the council. He wrote a catechism which would reflect the decrees of the Council of Trent, and he revised the book of daily prayer used in monasteries and convents and by pastors and missionaries. When his uncle, Pope Pius IV died, Charles returned to Milan, where he was still archbishop, and dedicated himself to reforming his diocese. During the remainder of his life, he reformed the clergy, established seminaries, visited parishes, taught catechism, cared for those who were poor and sick, and preached.

Pope Pius V (1566–1572)

Two years after the end of the council, Charles Borromeo, recognizing Pope Pius V as someone well suited to the office of pope, used his influence to successfully get Pius elected. Pius V was a saintly man with a passion for reform in the Catholic Church. Since, the Council of Trent shaped the direction of his time as pope, he viewed himself as a servant to the council. He immediately established congregations to implement the council's decrees.

Pius began his reform by appointing dedicated and holy cardinals who wanted to work for the reform of the Catholic Church. He introduced the **Roman Catechism**, which offered a summary of the teachings of the Council of Trent, and revised the **Breviary**, the prayerbook used by presbyters and monks in their daily prayer.

Before Pope Pius V became pope, the Eucharistic liturgy was not celebrated in the same manner throughout the world. To bring about unity in the manner of worshiping, Pope Pius V had the Roman Missal published. The **Roman Missal** (revised since the Second Vatican Council) is the book used in all Catholic churches throughout the world. It assures that all Catholics follow a common ritual, no matter where the Eucharistic liturgy is celebrated. The Missal published by Pius V established Latin as the language of the liturgy worldwide. This changed only after the Second Vatican Council in the late-twentieth century.

Despite his good intentions and good work, Pope Pius V caused problems for Catholics in England when he excommunicated Queen Elizabeth in 1570. His actions seemed unnecessary, since the queen no longer considered herself subject to the pope. As a result of the excommunication, Catholics in England had to face a more intense persecution.

KEY TERMS

Roman Catechism: introduced by Pope Pius V as a summary of the teachings of the Council of Trent.

Breviary: the prayerbook used by presbyters and monks; revised by Pope Pius V.

Roman Missal: first published by Pope Pius V in Latin; book used in all Catholic churches throughout the world.

Spiritual Reformers

Although the Council of Trent took place during the sixteenth century, its effects, both positive and negative, reached down through the centuries. Many great reformers brought the Catholic Church into a new era of dedication and spiritual development still felt in the world today.

St. Philip Neri (1515-1595) was an Italian presbyter who became well-known for his holiness. He inspired a number of presbyters to join him in the Congregation of the Oratory, a group of ordained priests who lived together in community to offer each other spiritual support and to nurture competent preaching. Their spiritual ideals, humility, joy, and charity, reflected those of their founder, Philip Neri.

St. Francis de Sales (1567-1622) was a bishop who became a dedicated and well-known spiritual director and a spiritual writer. He had a capacity for linking the daily lives of people with a practical form of spirituality. Many people today still read and reflect on his famous work, *Introduction to the Devout Life.*

St. Jane Frances de Chantal (1572-1641) became a widow while still young and thereafter dedicated her life to God. She developed a spiritual friendship with Francis de Sales and with him founded the Visitation order for women. She based her spirituality on contemplation which would lead to a sincere and deep love of God and neighbor.

CLIPBOARD

1. Although religious orders such as the Carmelites or the Jesuits did not make any laws for the people, they had a great impact on the Catholic Church. Discuss the impact of religious orders today, and indicate whether or not they are having the impact they should.

2. Pope St. Pius V brought about a unity in Catholic worship throughout the world. Discuss your feelings about having the same ritual in all Catholic churches. How does the ritual differ from Protestant worship services?

3. Many founders of religious orders helped in the spiritual reformation of the Catholic Church. Discuss the importance of these founders and their effect on the Catholic Church today.

REVIEWING THE ERA

- **1475**

HENRY VIII. As King of England, Henry refuted Luther and gained from the pope the title Defender of the Faith. He later founded the Church of England and was excommunicated by the pope.

THOMAS MORE AND JOHN FISHER. Both men were beheaded because they refused to sign the Oath of Supremacy which declared Henry VIII head of the Church of England. The are both martyrs of the Catholic Church.

PHILIP MELANCHTHON. This Lutheran theologian was a close friend of Luther and a reformer who produced the Augsburg Confession, an orderly presentation of Lutheran doctrine.

THE COUNCIL OF TRENT. This major counter-reformation council defined Catholic teaching clearly and called for reform in every area of Catholic life. It forged a clear distinction between Catholic and Protestant beliefs.

- **1550**

MARY TUDOR. Mary was the daughter of Catherine and Henry VIII. She became queen of England and led a persecution of members of the Church of England in an attempt to bring the country back to the pope. She received the name Bloody Mary because of the persecutions led by her.

ELIZABETH I. This daughter of Anne Boleyn became queen of England after Mary Tudor, restored the Church of England, and led a persecution of Catholics, after she was excommunicated by Pope Pius V. She refused to accept Puritan trends of Protestantism and kept a number of Catholic customs.

JOHN KNOX. Knox established the Reformed Church of Scotland by adapting some of Calvin's teachings to the situation in Scotland.

TERESA OF AVILA. Teresa reformed the Carmelite order of nuns and founded the Discalced Carmelites. She supported John of the Cross, who reformed the Carmelite monasteries of men.

IGNATIUS OF LOYOLA. The influence of the founder of the Jesuit Order spread throughout the world. He wrote a series of meditations called the Spiritual Exercises, which are still used today.

CHARLES BORROMEO. This reformer, caretaker of the poor, and founder of seminaries was influential in the election of Pope Pius V.

POPE PIUS V. This Dominican pope implemented the directives and ideals of the Council of Trent. He unified Catholic teaching by publishing a Catechism of Trent and unified liturgical worship by publishing a Roman Missal.

KEY TERMS

Augsburg Confession

Act of Supremacy

Oath of Supremacy

Anglicanism

Anglican Church

Puritans

Romanesque architecture

Gothic architecture

Flying buttresses

Discalced Carmelites

Jesuits

Roman Catechism

Breviary

Roman Missal

A Voice from the Past

Use your key terms to highlight for your readers the events which led up to the Council of Trent, what happened at the Council of Trent, and how that council still affects us today. End your article with a discussion of what reform needs to take place in the Catholic Church today, and how that reform could best be accomplished.

Then and Now

When Protestantism began to spread, many Protestant reformers did not see themselves as breaking away from the Catholic Church, but rather as reforming it.

The Church of England sought to become a national Church free of papal authority. It intended to remain Catholic with no desire to become Protestant, although some Protestant tendencies infiltrated the practice and teachings of the Church of England.

A number of new religious orders flourished and many previously existing ones were reformed. The Jesuits, Carmelites, and other orders founded during the sixteenth century are still in existence and have contributed greatly to the Catholic Church. Pope Pius V made a major contribution in restoring the spiritual image of the office of the pope.

The Catholic Church began a long process of reform with the Council of Trent. The council was called in response to the challenges set forth by Luther and Calvin. Through the

Council of Trent, the bishops drew a clear line between Catholic teachings and Protestant teachings. The council brought about a reformation in the lives of the people and the clergy by unifying teaching and liturgical worship, and insisting on the proper training of the clergy.

Today the Council of Trent stands out as a major council in the history of the Catholic Church. The need for reform is obvious from this vantage point many centuries later. Many older Catholics still recall the Latin liturgy, as well as teachings and practices of the Catholic Church which came about as a result of that council.

Later councils and current developments in theology and Church practice were and are not intended to contradict the Council of Trent, but rather to shed a clearer light on the earliest traditions and practices of the Catholic Church and to assist Catholics in their efforts to faithfully live the gospel in a technological and interconnected world.

NEWS IN REVIEW

1. What is the Augsburg Confession, and why is it important?

2. What caused England to reject the authority of the pope?

3. What differences were there in England between the rule of Queen Mary and Queen Elizabeth?

4. How did Zwingli, Calvin, and John Knox help to spread Protestantism in their own way?

5. What issues made the Council of Trent a counter-reformation council?

6. What caused Pope Paul IV to become an unpopular pope?

7. How did the reform of the Carmelites take place?

8. Who is Ignatius of Loyola, and what effect did he have on the Catholic Church?

9. Why is Pope Pius V so important in Catholic Church history?

10. Who had an important role in implementing the council, and how did they do it?

chapter twelve

The Missionary Church

If we were living toward the end of the sixteenth century, we may find ourselves abandoning our homeland with the hope that we would find religious freedom in the new world. Although we would have heard of missionaries traveling throughout the world, the only land that would attract us would be the new land across the seas. In the new world, we would meet some French and Spanish missionaries who left their Catholic homeland to spread the faith among the natives. We would also meet people who fled from their homeland because of the persecutions of Catholics.

In time, we would witness the same religious problems existing in Europe coming to the shores of America. The Church of England and a group of Puritans would continue to make life difficult for Catholics, even in the new world. Despite our hardships we would be thankful that the French or Spanish rule would at least allow us, as Catholics, to practice our faith. In practicing our faith, however, we would sometimes make life unpleasant for Protestants.

A variety of different cultures comprise the Catholic Church.

Spreading the Faith to New Lands

The Christian Times

Sixteenth Century   Vol. 16   No. 7

Missionaries Facing New Challenges

Reports are slowly arriving about the work of the missionaries in the Philippines, Africa, India, Japan, and China. The problems faced by the missionaries range from the explorers' abuse of the natives to the challenge of adapting Christianity to the culture and customs of the various countries.

The Spanish missionaries in the Philippines are strongly objecting to the abuses imposed by the Spanish settlers on the native population. Likewise, the Portugese missionaries in Africa are enraged at the slave trade imposed on the friendly African people.

The reports that we have received inform us of a courageous Jesuit, Francis Xavier, who directed successful missions in both India and Japan, but did not live long enough to see his ministry in Japan destroyed when the Japanese rejected the Western culture brought to the country by Christianity.

The necessity of adapting Christianity to the various cultures seems to be posing a challenge for all of the missionaries. Following Xavier much later in India is another Jesuit, Robert de Nobili, who introduced the strange practice of dressing like the upper-caste people of India in order to gain converts. A later Jesuit, Matteo Ricci, has also caused a stir in China by adapting Christianity to the Chinese culture. The Chinese ruler has condemned a large number of Christians to death. His motives were not religious, but cultural.

He suspects that Christians are attempting to introduce the barbaric western culture into China.

NOTEPAD
? ? ? ?

1. What did you learn about Francis Xavier? Robert de Nobili? Matteo Ricci?

2. What challenges did the missionaries encounter as they attempted to spread Christianity?

3. What difficulties did the missionaries encounter as they adapted Christianity to the different cultures?

The Rest of the Story

POINTS TO PONDER

Most people who learned the Catholic faith in Europe often lacked the ability to distinguish between Catholic practice and European culture. This led to confusion and misunderstanding between some missionaries and the Church leaders in Rome.

In the 1500s the missionaries began to spread the word of Christ virtually everywhere. In spreading the word of Christ, the missionaries discovered that different regions had different cultures. Thus the missionaries found themselves faced with the challenge of adapting Christianity to the different cultures.

Spain in the Philippines

In 1521, Spain claimed the island of the Philippines, and the Spanish missionaries had great success there. In addition to spreading the Word of God, however, the missionaries found themselves having to protect the native people from the Spanish settlers.

As the settlers took possession of the land, the Spanish military forces protected them from the native people who were forced off the land. The military also enabled the settlers to use the native inhabitants as slaves. Although the missionaries often did not object to the conquest of the native population and the establishment of farms on the land taken from the native people, they strongly objected to the killing, ravaging, and enslavement of the native people.

In converting the Philippine people to Christianity the missionaries also introduced Spanish feast days and religious customs. The religious practices of the Philippines reflected that of the Spanish.

The Spanish king rejected the need for a native clergy, so he issued a decree against ordaining native men. This effectively kept the Filipino converts from positions of leadership in the Catholic Church. It would take the Philipines two more centuries to gain independence from Spain, and establish a stable native clergy.

Missionary Activity in India

At the beginning of the sixteenth century, a small group of missionaries arrived in India along with Portugese explorers. These original missionaries had little time for converting the inhabitants, since they were busy working among the Portugese sailors. Later missionaries moving into India, however, were able to explore new ways of sharing Christ's message with the people there.

The Spanish Jesuit, St. Francis Xavier (1506–1552), was one of the original small band who joined St. Ignatius Loyola in the early days of the Jesuit order. Because of his ministry in India and Japan, he later received the titles, Apostle of the Indies and Apostle of Japan.

Xavier worked along the coast of India among the Portugese settlers. When he saw the weak faith of these Portugese settlers, he tried to preach to them, but they simply ignored him. He then introduced a new tactic for spreading the gospel message. He walked among the settlements ringing a bell and inviting the children to come with him to learn the catechism.

When Xavier sent the children home, he told them to share what they learned with their parents. The Portugese adults came to appreciate Xavier and eventually flocked to listen to him preach. As a result they changed their manner of living. As Xavier moved into the interior of India and later into Japan, he continued to use this method of gathering the people to listen to him.

After spending almost half a year with the Portugese settlers, Xavier moved inland. Some of the people of the area had already converted to Christianity because of their belief that the Christian God of the powerful Portugese must be stronger than their gods. Xavier expanded and clarified their notion of the Christian God, thus giving them a fuller understanding of the Christian faith. In turn, he sent these new converts to preach to others in India.

Through his missionary work, Xavier learned that India had a kind of hierarchical order which separated one group or caste from another. While he was able to convert and baptize thousands from the lower caste, he was not as successful with those of the upper caste. Because of the power of the upper caste, a number of Christian converts suffered martyrdom.

De Nobili in India

In 1605, more than fifty years after Xavier left India, an Italian Jesuit named Robert de Nobili began a new approach to missionary activity in India. He attempted to reach those of the high caste of India, by wearing their clothing and practicing many of their customs. When questioned about his clothing, he simply told the people of the upper caste that he belonged to the upper caste in his society, and therefore had the right to dress in that fashion in their society. He even referred to himself with the title of teacher.

Robert de Nobili allowed his converts to retain the customs of their caste as long as they were not contrary to Christianity. He adopted the vegetarian

...Let the little children come to me, and do not stop them; for it is to such as these that the kingdom of God belongs. Truly I tell you, whoever does not receive the kingdom of God as a little child will never enter it.

Luke 18:16–17, NRSV

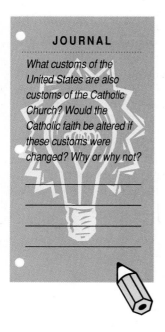

diet of the Hindus and learned to speak the Sanskrit language. Following the customs of India, he would not allow the Christians of the lower caste to mix with the upper caste. He avoided a few ritual Christian practices which the Indian population found repugnant.

Robert de Nobili's approach caused some missionaries to condemn him before the Pope. Robert, being able to separate cultural custom from religious custom, defended his actions by stating that the caste system was not a religious system, but rather cultural. He believed that if he could convert the upper caste, the lower caste would follow. In the end, the Pope rejected many of Robert de Nobili's arguments.

Other missionaries followed in de Nobili's footsteps. They also found it necessary to adopt the life-style of other castes in India, in order to share Christ's message with them.

Missionary Activity in Japan

In 1545, Francis Xavier left India, and four years later, he and his band of missionaries entered Japan. He traveled from town to town, gathering the people together and preaching to them about Christ. Within the next fifty years, Jesuits, Dominicans, and Franciscans would be ministering in Japan. In many areas, they would erect churches as centers of worship. Hundreds of thousands of Japanese embraced Christianity.

Xavier did not think of separating Western culture from his preaching of Christianity. When he baptized new converts, he gave them Portugese Christian names and clothed them in western style clothing. The more educated and powerful leaders of the country resented this intrusion of Western culture into their land.

After the death of Xavier, some traders from Protestant countries warned the Japanese against these Catholic missionaries. These traders painted the missionaries as having ambitions of colonizing Japan.

In reaction to the rumors of the traders and the mounting anger over the western customs practiced by Christian converts, the leader of the Japanese people banished the missionaries and closed his ports to all foreigners. Many missionaries went into hiding. Those that were found, were forced to choose between either retracting their beliefs or being put to death. A number opted to die for their faith. In addition to the missionaries, thousands of Japanese Christians also gave their lives rather than deny their faith.

Despite the massive persecutions and two centuries of isolation from the world, Japan never fully stamped out Christianity. When missionaries returned to Japan in the nineteenth century, they found that Christianity had remained alive as families quietly passed on their faith to their children.

Christianity in China

Missionaries were not able to make inroads into China until the Italian Jesuit, Matteo Ricci (1552–1610), moved into the interior of China. He recognized that the Chinese saw themselves as a highly civilized culture and the rest of the world as barbarian. Like Robert de Nobili, he chose to dress and act in the same manner of the leaders of the community. He also spent some time at the edge of China, learning the language and customs of the country. Finally, when the Chinese had enough respect for him, he was allowed to further enter into the country.

Matteo Ricci, a man of many talents, was an astronomer, a mathematician, a writer, and a clockmaker. Because of his many writings, the Chinese saw him as a wise man, and the intellectuals among the Chinese came to speak with and learn from him.

Ricci mingled the practices of the Chinese people with Christian belief to make Christianity more acceptable to the Chinese people. He converted a small number of followers, so as not to draw too much attention to his missionary activity. He believed that these small numbers of mostly educated Chinese would spread the faith to others, which is what occurred.

The Pope approved the translation of the Bible and liturgical texts into the Chinese language and permitted certain customs to be adapted to Christianity. Many Jesuit missionaries followed Ricci's example and were readily accepted in China. By the middle of the 1600s, the number of Chinese Catholics exceeded 150,000.

Some missionaries, however, did not approve of Ricci's use of Chinese words in worship and in reference to God. In 1704, Pope Clement XI disapproved of the adaptation of Christianity to the Chinese culture and tragically decreed that people in missionary lands should adopt western custom along with Christian faith. The emperor of China considered the pope to be a barbarian, and he became enraged when he learned that the pope, who was ignorant of the Chinese, was going to instruct the Chinese people. Upon hearing of the decree, he immediately outlawed all Christian missionary work, banished the missionaries, and initiated a horrible execution of a large number of Chinese Catholics.

Spreading the Word in Africa

Portugese explorers sailed down the western coast of Africa in the 1400s, searching for a sea route to India. As usual, missionaries traveled with these explorers and traders with the intention of converting pagans. On their journey, down the coast, to the Congo River they met the king of Congo, who not only aided the sailors and missionaries while they resided in his palace, but also accepted baptism.

The Portugese found in the Congo an opportunity for wealth in the capture and sale of slaves. Some of the slaves believed that the Portugese sailors would make them household slaves, which meant that they would receive good treatment. When they reached their final destinations, however, they discovered that they had lost their right to protest or object to their poor treatment. They were sold as laborers for field work.

Some of the missionaries, falling under the influence of the sailors, succumbed to the wealth of the slave trade. The missionaries who remained true to their profession themselves arguing vehemently with the traders, thus making themselves unwelcomed guests on future voyages.

The new king of the Congo was a convert who had taken the Portugese name of Alfonso I. He had agreed to the slave trade at first, but when he became aware of the abuses that were taking place he tried to end it. He even tried, in vain, to get his message to the pope.

Missionary endeavor requires patience. It begins with the proclamation of the Gospel to peoples and groups who do not yet believe in Christ, continues with the establishment of Christian communities that are 'a sign of God's presence in the world,' and leads to the foundation of local churches. It must involve a process of inculturation if the Gospel is to take flesh in each people's culture.

Catechism of the Catholic Church, # 854

CLIPBOARD

1. Francis Xavier taught the adults by first teaching the children. What do you think about this method of teaching the faith to adults? Would it work today? Why or why not?

2. Do you agree with Robert de Nobili's acceptance of India's class distinctions in order to convert the people of India? Why or why not?

3. Do you think Matteo Ricci and his followers were correct in adapting Christianity to the language and customs of the people of China? Why or why not?

The South and Central American Missions

The Christian Times

Sixteenth Century   Vol. 16   No. 7

Missionaries Support Natives

Today, the Catholic Church ordained Bartolome de las Casas as the first bishop of the new world in Mexico. Bartolome de las Casas, a former landowner himself, has gained the love of many of the natives of the new world and, likewise, the hatred of many of the settlers.

To the settlers' dismay, Bartolome continually fights for the rights of the native people. He has made the long and difficult voyage across the ocean on several occasions in an attempt to convince Spain to pass laws against using the natives as slaves. Currently, the ministry of the Franciscans, Dominicans, Augustinians, and Jesuits is the only hope the native people have for justice.

The Jesuits in Brazil and Paraguay are gathering local native people into small villages to protect them against the settlers and to teach them. This new innovation seems to hold some hope for the future.

In addition to the missionaries efforts, the peasants have also received a sign of God's blessings in the form of a vision. A peasant, named Juan Diego, claims he had a vision of Mary, the mother of Jesus, and that she has miraculously imprinted her image on his cloak. This vision seems to fit with other peasant stories about the miraculous action of the Blessed Mother, known as Our Lady of Guadalupe. If the vision is authentic, it is certainly a sign of God's blessings on the peasant population.

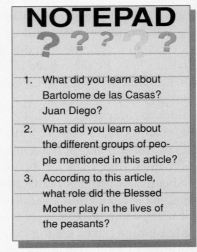

NOTEPAD

1. What did you learn about Bartolome de las Casas? Juan Diego?

2. What did you learn about the different groups of people mentioned in this article?

3. According to this article, what role did the Blessed Mother play in the lives of the peasants?

The Rest of the Story

JOURNAL

Who do Americans exploit today, in an attempt to gain wealth and status? What does this say about our values as a country?

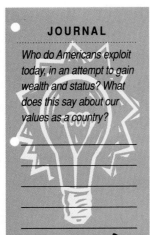

While Luther was busy defending his Lutheran teachings and Protestantism was spreading throughout Europe, Catholicism was taking its message to the new world. Ferdinand and Isabella of Spain had opened the door to the new world by supporting the Italian explorer, Christopher Columbus. In 1492, he discovered the new world across the great ocean to the west, twenty-five years before Luther posted his ninety-five theses and began the reformation in Germany.

Bartolome de las Casas (1474–1566)

In 1502, Bartolome de las Casas ventured into the new world and found an appalling situation among the native people. He soon discovered the reason for the daring explorations of the Spanish and Portugese adventurers. Their motive was to find wealth and status in this new land, and they had little concern for the plight of the native population.

Las Casas expected to find missionaries among these early explorers of the new world. The Church was so closely aligned with the government that one could hardly expect Isabella to send out explorers without missionaries to convert the native people to Christianity. Most of the explorers considered themselves devout men, but many of them envisioned the native people as being less than human. The conquerors from Spain treated them like animals.

The earliest missionaries in the Spanish colonies in South America were the Franciscans, who were later joined by the Dominicans, Augustinians, and Jesuits. Although las Casas mourned the ill treatment of some of the native people by his countrymen, he had no problem with the society established by the settlers. The settlers offered protection and provisions to the natives, who in turn repaid them with work. The problem was that once the natives allowed themselves to accept this arrangement, they inadvertently became slaves of the settlers.

Las Casas owned a large parcel of land and had inherited a number of Native Americans who worked on his land. In 1512, las Casas was ordained and continued to have natives working as slaves on his land. Unlike some other settlers, he treated them kindly and gave little thought to the indignity of their situation. One day, he heard a Dominican missionary preaching against the practice of making slaves of the natives, and he looked with horror on his own approval of the practice.

Las Casas freed his slaves, gave up his land, became a Dominican, and returned to Spain to plead the cause of the natives. He lashed out against the practice of compelling people to convert to Catholicism by force. He believed that conversions should result from a loving and peaceful concern for the natives of the area.

Because of las Casas's negotiations with Spain and the papacy on behalf of the native population, Pope Paul III confirmed that the native people should enjoy freedom and that no one should compel them to convert. Las Casas also influenced the Spanish rulers to outlaw the practice of forcing the native people into slavery, but because the colonies were too far away for Spain to enforce its laws, the settlers easily ignored them.

Las Casas as Bishop

In 1543, las Casas became bishop, but his support for the native people antagonized the landowners who united against him. He urged his clergy to protest the settlers' treatment of the native people as slaves. Although the king had banned enslaving the native people, he could not support las Casas because of his need for the income from the settlers in this new land. The strain from the protests and threats of the settlers became so great that Las Casas resigned his post eight years after becoming bishop.

In addition to making slaves of the native population, the Spanish and Portugese settlers began importing slaves from Africa. Unfortunately, las Casas's concern for the native people in the new world led him to implore the colonists to use Africans as slaves. He argued to the settlers that the blacks worked better under these rugged conditions and survived longer. He later repented, realizing that he had made a grave error in his reasoning.

After he resigned his post as bishop, las Casas returned to Spain where he continued his fight for the native people of the New World. Although he had alienated many of the settlers in the colony, he continued to protest the injustices of the system. He wrote a number of books against the practice of enslaving the native people and was responsible for the enactment and enforcement of several laws aimed at ending the abusive treatment of the native people. He died in 1566 and his books were later put on the *Index of Forbidden Books* by the Spanish Inquisition.

Missionaries in South America

Not all missionaries shared the ideals of people like Bartolome de las Casas. In fact, some, like the settlers, believed that the native people were less than human. Although they did not condone treating them as slaves, they hesitated to allow them to share in the sacraments. They would baptize and witness marriages for the native people, but they rejected the idea that natives were human enough to celebrate such a sacred act as sharing in communion. In addition, decrees from authorities in the homeland forbade the missionaries from ordaining native men as presbyters.

In some areas, the missionaries became the only authority over the native people and ruled them in the name of the conquering Spanish government. They collected taxes from them on behalf of Spain, recorded births, deaths, and marriages, and administered the land given to the Catholic Church. Some missionaries were becoming quite wealthy and enjoying the prestige of their position of authority. These few began to court their own luxury and comfort and abandoned their original mission of converting the natives. To make matters even worse some missionaries believed that they were bringing civilization to a backward people. They thought they were helping the natives by forcing on them rules, customs, and languages from the homeland.

The majority of the missionaries, however, respected the the culture and customs of the native population. Many of the missionaries who traveled with the settlers into Latin America attempted to learn the language of the people for teaching them about Christ. They prepared alphabets and wrote catechisms in the language of the people. They often put themselves at risk, facing disease or death.

Signs of God's Blessing

Despite the number of saintly men and women among the missionaries, the one chosen for a special visitation from heaven was a Mexican boy, Juan Diego. According to legend, Mary, the Mother of Jesus, appeared to Juan and told him to tell the bishop to build a Church on the spot where she stood. When Juan could not convince his bishop about the vision, he asked Mary for a sign to convince the bishop. The sign given had a major effect on the religious history of Mexico.

Our Lady of Guadalupe

In response to Juan's request, Mary told him to gather flowers from the spot where she was. Although it was not the season for these flowers, Juan found them, gathered them in his cloak, and ran off to the bishop. When he poured the array of flowers out of his cloak for the bishop, the miracle that appeared was not just the flowers, but a perfect replica of Mary's image on Juan's cloak.

Today, hundreds of thousands of people of Latin America still venerate this image on Juan's cloak. The name given to the image is **Our Lady of Guadalupe**. The people of the area see in this vision a sign of God's special blessings on the people. In choosing Juan as the subject of the vision, God was choosing the native population and showing a sign of approval and protection. Devotion to Our Lady of Guadalupe is an important devotion of the people of Latin America and Mexico, as well as the native people who migrated into North America.

Jesuit Missionary Sanctuaries

The newly founded order of the Jesuits, who came to Paraguay and Brazil, introduced a new tactic into their missionary endeavors. They collected the native people into small towns and areas which resemble our modern day Indian reservations and taught the natives to read, weave, and farm. These small communities offered the native people the ability to defend and rule themselves.

The success of these self-ruling areas caused irritation for many of the settlers. The more successful the native people became in their small sanctuaries, the more the settlers began to harass the Jesuits. In the end, the settlers forced the Jesuits to abandon their work with the native people.

As Spanish and Portugese power waned, they no longer controlled the seas. They lost their ties with Latin America, thus opening the way for the

Our Lady of Guadalupe festival

ordination of native clergy. With the native people free from foreign domination, they were able to take advantage of the educational opportunities brought into the country by the missionaries. In time, large numbers of churches, monasteries, and convents sprouted up and the Catholic faith became dominant.

KEY TERMS

Our Lady of Guadalupe: the name given to image of Mary which appeared on Juan Diego's cloak.

CLIPBOARD

1. Bartolome de las Casas worked for the people, but sometimes, because of the atrocities of the settlers, the people distrusted him and the missionaries. How does a lack of trust cause negative generalizations still today?

2. Members of missionary orders dedicated their lives to working for the conversion and justice of people of far away lands. How would your relatives and friends react if you announced that you were going to a foreign land to dedicate your life to serving the poor?

3. How did the small villages established by the Jesuits in Brazil and Paraguay differ from the reservations set aside for native Americans today?

Settlements in North America

The Christian Times

Seventeenth Century   Vol. 17   No. 1

England Colonizes the New Land

Great Britain has now established thirteen colonies in North America with most of them outlawing the practice of Catholicism. Some Catholics, who were welcomed in Maryland before laws were passed against them, have migrated to Pennsylvania where the Quaker, William Penn, has established a law tolerating all religious groups.

The colonization by the English hopes to block an extended period of colonization of North America by the French and Spanish traders and settlers.

The French have settled in the north around Quebec and continue to explore the land west of the Mississippi as far south as the Gulf of Mexico and New Orleans. The English have taken the land around Montreal for their own colonization.

The Spanish have established a colony in Florida, but most of its North American colonies are in the southwest, along the Pacific Coast and just above Mexico.

An English spokesman reports that the English have established colonies in the east for the sake of trade and to stop the Spanish from gaining too much land north of Florida.

The missionaries are still protesting the abuses of the traders and settlers on the native population.

NOTEPAD
? ? ? ? ?

1. What does the article reveal about English colonization? French colonization? Spanish colonization?

2. According to the article, why are Catholics migrating to Pennsylvania?

3. How are the missionaries responding to the colonization?

The Rest of the Story

While Europe was struggling with the Reformation and Counter-reformation, the new world was struggling with exploration, martyrdom, hardship, and cruelty to the native population.

Discovering Canada

As the French explorers were making maps and new discoveries in the northern portion of North America in the land which now forms Quebec and other areas of Canada, they made a discovery which would guarantee future exploration of the land by their country. Not only did they discover a new land, but they also encountered native people in this new land who traded for gold, furs, and precious metals. These items were guaranteed to reap a healthy profit back in France.

The French explorers first stopped at a place they named Quebec. It would take more than fifty years of trading before they would establish a trading post there. In 1608, an adventurer named Samuel de Champlain founded Quebec with plans of establishing a Catholic territory in the area. In time, Catholic settlers came into Quebec and from there they spread out to other areas along the northern parts of North America.

The trading post at Quebec opened the territory known to the French as the *New France*. The natives called it

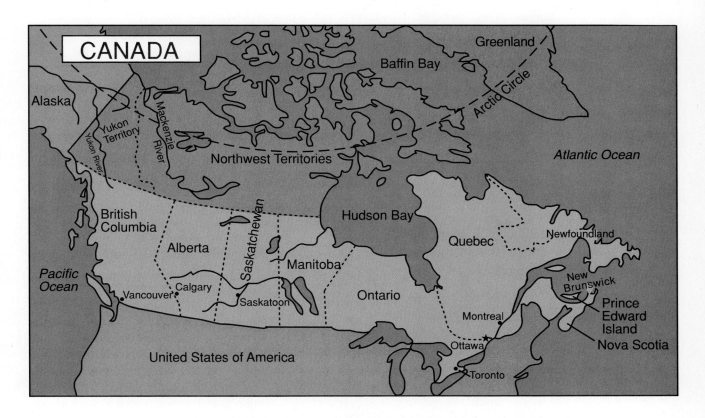

Canada, which means village or community. The French established friendly bonds with the native people in order to gain their trust and to keep alive the lucrative trading market. The French became friendly with the Huron tribe, which in turn made them enemies of the Huron's enemies, the Iroquois.

In 1632, French Jesuits sailed into the waters off Canada, now known as Nova Scotia. A year later, a courageous Jesuit missionary, Jean de Brebeuf, arrived intending to convert the native population. He soon impressed the native people with his extraordinary strength and obvious love for them and the God he served. Later, when a rebel group tortured and killed him, the natives that he had converted cut out his heart and ate it in hopes that eating his heart would nourish them with his courage.

Expanding the Mission

The Jesuits' hopes of converting the native people led them to travel throughout Canada and to move southwest. In their search for people to convert they also helped the French to expand their settlements. As the native people, who were nomads, moved from place to place, the Jesuits moved with them. They helped to open up the whole of North America by charting rivers, lakes, mountains and valleys.

Although the Huron nation supported the French and the Catholic missionaries, they also viewed Christianity as a threat to their own beliefs. Very few Hurons accepted baptism. Besides their suspicion of the Christian God, they were always on the move, never stopping long enough to receive instructions. Unlike some early Spanish missionaries and traders, the French rejected the use of force to convert the native people.

In time, the French traders and missionaries traveled the Mississippi River, setting up trading posts along the way. Although the missionaries converted very few natives on these trips, they were able to spread the faith by providing religious support for the traders and trappers.

Map Search

Using the map, which shows Canada as we know it today, find the following:

Quebec

Nova Scotia

Montreal

The Great Lakes

United States

Toronto

The French traveled as far south as the Gulf of Mexico and established a settlement in a place familiar to us today as New Orleans. New Orleans still has many remnants of its French origins. Since the name of the king of France at the time of the exploration was King Louis XIV, the French named a large western portion of the current United States Louisiana.

In the end, the missionaries did not gain many converts from among the native population. The large number of French (and later Irish) Catholics settling in Canada accounted for the large Catholic population. The French farmers, merchants, artisans, and laborers who came to Canada made Catholicism the dominant religion. The Church of New France welcomed its first Bishop in 1659. His diocese included all of French America, as far away as Louisiana.

Other Missionary Endeavors

Although France did not support its overseas ventures with the interest shown by Spain to its colonies, some French kings did take special notice of the colonies of New France. **The Company of the Blessed Sacrament** known also as the Recollects, a reformed branch of the Franciscans began in France in the middle of the 1500s. They were one of the first groups of missionaries to serve the rapidly growing Catholic population in Canada.

Various communities of nuns also appeared in Canada to help in the missions. In 1639, the Ursulines and the Sisters of Charity arrived. The best known among the Ursulines was a mystical writer known as Marie of the Incarnation who founded the first Canadian school for girls in 1672. The Congregation of Notre Dame and others sent nuns to care for the people who were poor and sick and to develop a sense of spirituality among the French-born people living in Canada.

The Jesuits in Canada

The best known and most successful missionaries in Canada were the Jesuits who established schools, places of refuge, training centers and seminaries. Most Americans are most familiar with the North American Martyrs, who endured inhuman torture and death during their efforts of bringing the gospel to the Native Americans in modern upstate New York and southeastern Canada. The Church declared them saints in 1930.

One of the famous missionaries, Jesuit Isaac Jogues, lived among the Hurons for a period of time. In 1642, a party of Mohawks captured him, forced him into slavery, and tortured him. He eventually escaped and returned to France with the help of some strongly anti-Catholic colonizers who recoiled in horror at the torture Jogues endured.

After a lengthy period of recuperation, Isaac Jogues returned to work among the Hurons. In 1645, while on a mission negotiating for peace, the Mohawk Indians recaptured and killed him. Since his death took place near Auresville in upstate New York, the area currently stands as a memorial to his work among the natives and his martyrdom.

Within thirty years of the founding of the colony at Quebec, there were three thousand Catholics, and by 1670, there were sixty-seven hundred. Two centuries later, by 1870, there were more than eighty thousand, and by the middle of the twentieth century, there were more than three million French Catholics in Canada.

English Colonies

The situation in Europe threatened Canada. In a treaty signed at Paris to end the seven years war which involved England and France, independent French Canada fell under the control of Protestant England. The Catholics living under the control of Anglican England found themselves in a difficult situation for a short period of time.

The Quebec Act of 1764 guaranteed Catholics the right to participate in the

In the Spotlight

Blessed Kateri Tekakwitha (1656–1680), also known as "the lily of the Mohawks," was a famous convert from the Mohawk tribe. She was born among the Mohawks to a Mohawk warrior and an Algonquin Christian mother, but was orphaned as a small child when an epidemic of small pox hit the Mohawk tribe. Although Tekakwitha survived the epidemic, she was left with facial scars, a weakened body, and damaged eyesight.

Tekakwitha, the daughter of a Mohawk chief, was considered a highly desirable woman to marry, but Tekakwitha, more interested in the missionaries, refused. Thus, she alienated herself from the Mohawk tribe.

Her desire to become Christian was brought to the attention of the Father Jacques de Lamberville, who gave her formal instruc-

tion. At the age of twenty, on Easter Sunday, in 1676, she celebrated her baptism and took the name Kateri, which means Catherine.

Since her baptism caused further hostilities with the Mohawk tribe, Tekakwitha fled with the help of her Christian warriors and sought refuge in the Salt Mission on the Richelieu River. While she was there she dedicated herself to prayer, and caring for the sick, the aged, and the dying. She served as an inspiration to many of the Jesuits at the mission.

In April of 1680, she fell ill and died. Those who attended her funeral noted that the scars that had been with her since childhood had disappeared. Soon after her death, miracles were reported through her intercession. She was declared Venerable by Pope Pius XII in April of 1943, and she was beatified by Pope John Paul II in June of 1980. Her feast day is June 14.

---

daily life of the country and to practice their faith, on the condition that they pledged their allegiance to the rulers of England. Since that time, Quebec has retained many of its French traditions and language, while Montreal and the surrounding territory have become predominately English.

Early Beginnings of the United States

The first settlers from Europe were Spanish explorers who moved into the southwestern portion of the United States. Traveling west in the mid 1500s, in quest of gold, they encountered nations of Native Americans living in villages, or **pueblos** (the Spanish name for villages). Because of this, the settlers called them the **Pueblo Indians**.

The Spanish explorers ravaged the Pueblo people as savagely as they had the other native people in other areas. They enslaved, mutilated, and killed them. Once again, the missionaries found their work undermined by the viciousness of the settlers.

Despite these setbacks, the Franciscans founded the town of Santa Fe, which is now in New Mexico, in 1609. By 1630, the Christian population in the New Mexico region had grown to almost thirty-five thousand Christian Native Americans.

The presence of the missionaries, however, was not enough to make up for the abusive actions of the settlers toward the native people. When the Spanish traders continued their raids on the native population, in search of slaves, the native people rebelled. The Pueblo people, fed up with being abused by the settlers, turned their backs on the Christian teachings. They

KEY TERMS

Pueblos: the Spanish name for village; where the Native Americans, living in the southwestern portion of the United States, lived.

Pueblo Indians: the Native Americans encountered by the Spanish explorers, in the southwestern portion of the United States.

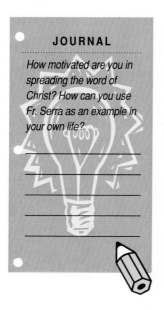

JOURNAL

How motivated are you in spreading the word of Christ? How can you use Fr. Serra as an example in your own life?

slaughtered a third of the Spaniards, burned Christian churches and reverted to their original religious practices. The Spanish, however, with their superior weapons, soon recaptured the territory.

When missionaries arrived again to work for the conversion of the natives, they discovered that a large number of them had already abandoned the territory in an effort to elude the Spanish settlers.

Expanding to California

In the second half of the 1700s, a presbyter by the name of Father Junipero Serra led the Franciscan missionary activity in California. After teaching in the seminary for a number of years in Spain, he decided to dedicate his life to service in the Mexican missions. When the Spanish settlers received Serra's request to come to the colonies, they immediately accepted his application, hoping to have him teach in their schools. Father Serra, however, did not plan on spending his time teaching. Instead, he dedicated himself to spreading the faith to the southwestern part of the current United States.

Serra's voyage to the new world became a nightmare. Those who managed to survive the voyage were gasping for water when they finally arrived. Strongly driven to begin his missionary activity, Serra rested for a short time, and then treked two hundred and fifty miles to Mexico City. On this trip, some type of poisonous insect bit him, leaving his leg so critically infected that he developed a limp which lasted the rest of his life.

During his journeys, Fr. Serra taught and baptized thousands of Native Americans, despite the unbearable pain in his leg. At times, however, those traveling with him found it necessary to carry him. There were several occasions where he nearly died on these journeys, but quickly rallied after a short period of recuperation.

Serra established nine missions on the Pacific coast, among them San Diego, Santa Clara, and San Francisco. Along with his talent as a theologian, Serra also had a genius for administration.

He organized the activities of the missionaries along with the administration of the government of the settlements by the Spanish leaders. Whenever leaders exploited or abused the native people, they knew that Serra would come storming into their presence, berating them for their inhumanity. The leaders often responded in anger and inflicted abuse on him.

Serra lived to the age of seventy and used every moment of his life in an energetic effort to spread Christ's message in the new world. At an age when people today are enjoying their retirement, Serra was marching across dry desert lands with a sense of urgency to convert as many to Christ as possible. When he was finally near death, he had himself measured for a casket and planned his own burial.

In time, the Spanish missionaries established twenty-one missions in California. They taught farming and helped the people cultivate their vast orchards and vineyards. Unable to distinguish their own Christianity from their Spanish culture, they not only taught the Christianity, but introduced Spanish customs into the region which are still visible today. These customs stand as a reminder of the Spanish Catholic presence in the early history of North America.

English Colonization Continues

In 1565, Spanish settlers made a second expedition into Florida and established the first parish in the southeast known as Saint Augustine. An unsuccessful attempt made by Spanish explorers almost forty years earlier had ended in failure. The new presence of the Spanish army and settlements in Florida gave the English government incentive to establish colonies along the east coast of the present United States.

In 1607, a group of English settlers established the first successful and long-lasting English colony in the New World in Virginia. Hoping to establish the Church of England in this new land, the settlers brought an Anglican chaplain with them. By settling in Virginia, the English intended to block the northerly expansion of the Spanish. They not only feared the growing military power of the Spanish, but also the spread of the Catholic Church in the New World.

The English settlers real motive for coming to Virginia did not differ greatly from the first purpose of the Spanish settlers. They were looking for opportunities to become wealthy through trading with the natives and through cultivation of the rich lands of this new world. The major sponsors of these settlements were the rich merchants of England.

Some of those merchants in England were also interested in introducing the Puritan principles into the colonies. They felt that the rigidity of the Puritan religion would provide the colony with religious laws which would also guide the lives of the people. The laws included worship, as well as stern penalties for disobedience to parents and civic leaders.

King James of England, who was fighting against the Puritan influence in England, totally rejected the introduction of strict Puritan rules into the colonies. Because of his efforts, the power of Puritanism in the colony of Virginia dwindled. Virginia continued to thrive economically, producing and selling tobacco and importing slaves from Africa to work in the fields.

The settlers did not try to convert the slaves, as there was an old prohibition which forbade Christians from having Christian believers as slaves. Because of this law, the settlers had greater concern for economic profits than for the conversion and baptism of the slaves. The settlers did strive to keep the slaves in ignorance, however, in an attempt to keep them submissive.

The English colonies eventually moved south into the Carolinas, again for economic purposes. They then moved even further south into Georgia, seeking a place of refuge for their prisoners and outcasts. The settlement in Georgia was also a strategic move as it assured the English that the Spanish settlements in Florida would not move northward.

The lower class, and a small number of rich landowners, in these colonies began to embrace the Quaker belief. The new mode of Anglicanism later known as Methodism was becoming apparent.

Catholics in the Colonies

In 1632, Charles I granted Cecil Calvert, known as Lord Baltimore, a portion of the territory of northern Virginia. Charles gave the territory to Calvert, because Calvert was a Catholic and Charles needed some support from the Catholics in England. The king, however, did not intend to establish a Catholic colony. Instead he allowed the colony religious freedom. This new territory gave Catholics undergoing hardship in Anglican England an opportunity to find acceptance and practice their faith in the New World.

Some rich Catholic settlers came to Maryland with a large number of Protestant servants. These Catholics of the richer class ruled Maryland, although they were greatly outnumbered by the Protestant population.

Jesuits, moving to Maryland with the English Catholic colonizers, supported themselves with the land granted them by the Catholic governor. They used the land for farming, herding, milling grain, and overseeing other operations of their plantations. They hired workers to care for their land so they themselves could be free to preach the gospel. They rode a circuit of plantations, covering three to four hundred miles a week, celebrating the sacraments and teaching religion.

In 1704, when Protestant settlers far outnumbered Catholics in the colony, and Puritans had gained a firm hand, laws were passed against Catholics, depriving them of churches as well as the right to hold political office. These laws caused many of the Catholics to seek freedom elsewhere in the United States.

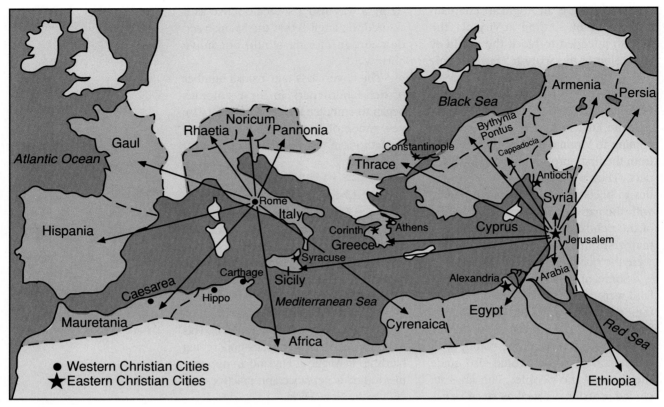

● Western Christian Cities
★ Eastern Christian Cities

Map Search

In reviewing the centuries, it would be helpful to get an overall picture of the countries involved in sending settlers and missionaries.

Follow the lines of the following:

Rome to Africa
Rome to Hispania
Rome to Gaul

Jerusalem to Cappadocia
Jerusalem to Greece
Jerusalem to Thrace and
        Constantinople
Jerusalem to Egypt

Religious Freedom in Pennsylvania

Being forced from the colonies in Maryland, large numbers of Catholics found religious freedom in the Pennsylvania colony, established by William Penn, a member of the tolerant Quakers, or the Society of Friends. Pennsylvania law insisted on toleration of religion for all people. Catholics eventually built the only Catholic church permitted in the British colonies; it was given the name St. Joseph.

British colonization established thirteen colonies in the new world, reaching from the Massachusetts Bay Colony in the north to Georgia in the south. With the exception of Pennsylvania, Catholics faced some form of rejection in these colonies. By the time these thirteen colonies rebelled and declared their independence from Great Britain in 1776, ten percent of the total population of the colonies was Catholic.

CLIPBOARD

1. What early French Catholic influences are still present in Quebec or New Orleans today?

2. What would you do if our country suddenly outlawed Catholicism and told us we could either move to South America or try to survive

here with no rights to work or to own property?

3. How are our roots of Catholic history tied in with the roots of United States history? How does the fact that these roots are tied together affect us today?

REVIEWING THE ERA

•**1500**

BARTOLOME DE LAS CASAS. A Spanish presbyter who defended the native people of Central America against the atrocities of the settlers. Eventually as bishop, he was influential in having Spain write and pass laws protecting the native people of the colonies.

OUR LADY OF GUADALUPE. A peasant, Juan Diego, had a vision from the mother of Jesus in which she asked him to tell the bishop to build a church for her at the site of her appearance. As a miraculous sign, she imprinted her image on Juan's cloak.

SAINT FRANCIS XAVIER. He is known as the Apostle of India and the Apostle of Japan for his missionary successes in both places.

•**1575**

ROBERT DE NOBILI. He was a Jesuit missionary in India who adapted his lifestyle to the culture of the upper caste. Because of the culture's laws and traditions he forbade the lower caste from worshiping with the upper caste. His ideas were later rejected by the pope.

MATTEO RICCI. As a Jesuit missionary in China, he adapted himself to the culture of the Chinese and used Chinese names for God. The few followers which he converted continued his work, until the Chinese ruler rejected Christianity because of its connection with the western culture.

CONGREGATION FOR THE PROPAGATION OF THE FAITH. The congregation was established to help missionaries, to make decisions concerning the works of the missions, and to provide for missionaries to mission countries.

SAMUEL DE CHAMPLAIN. He began a French colony in Quebec with the intention of establishing a Catholic colony.

JEAN DE BREBEUF. He was a Jesuit martyr who worked among the native people in the northern sector of North America.

ISAAC JOQUES. He was a Jesuit martyr who worked among the native people as far as the northern section of what is now New York State.

•**1650**

KATERI TEKAKWITHA. She was a Native American woman who converted to Christianity and devoted her life to prayer and caring for the needy.

LORD BALTIMORE, CECIL CALVERT. He was a Catholic who was charged with colonizing Maryland as a land of toleration for all religions. He was only partially successful .

•**1750**

JUNIPERO SERRA. This missionary was responsible for taking the Catholic religion into Sante Fe and other areas of the southwest.

A Voice from the Past

This week features the struggles of the missionaries in the New World. Explain to your readers the challenges these missionaries faced as well as the creative approaches they devised in spreading Christianity to the native populations. Discuss your opinions of these approaches and show your readers how some of these approaches still affect us today.

End your article with a discussion of religion and culture. Explain to your readers how the two commonly affect each other. Use some examples from the past and present to discuss the pros and cons of combining the two. Discuss the possibility of keeping religion and culture separate.

Then and Now

The reason for the exploration of North America was primarily economic, although conversion of the native people also became an important part of their exploration. Missionaries endured hardship and death in spreading the faith, sometimes fighting the atrocities of their own people. Some people fled to America to escape religious persecution in their own land.

Today, Canada still has a mixture of two cultures, one which is French and centered around Quebec, and another which is English, surrounding Montreal.

The Spanish, English, and French settlements are now part of the United States, with some Spanish settlements outside the United States in South and Central America.

Many of the people still honor Mary, under the title of *Our Lady of Guadalupe*. Kateri Tekakwitha and the Jesuit Martyrs are venerated as saintly people. Catholicism still dominates in many Spanish speaking areas, and is especially strong in the northeastern areas of the United States, and in the California area.

NEWS IN REVIEW

1. Why is St. Francis Xavier called the Apostle of both India and Japan?

2. Why did the pope disagree with de Nobili's approach to converting the people of India?

3. What was Matteo Ricci's approach to converting China and why did it fail?

4. What did Bartolome de las Casas do for the native population in the missionary countries?

5. What led to the large number of Catholics in Canada in the seventeenth and eighteenth centuries?

6. Who are two of the North American martyrs and why are they important in the history of the Church?

7. What made Junipero Serra such a heroic person?

8. Why did the English want to establish colonies in the new world?

9. What problems did Catholics face in the early years of the colonization of the British colonies in North America?

10. Who are Juan Diego and Kateri Tekakwitha, and why are they important in the history of the new world?

chapter thirteen
The Church and Revolution

In the early 1600s, Galileo correctly taught that the sun was the center of our universe and that the earth revolved around the sun as other planets did. Some Church leaders, believing the Bible to also be a book of scientific fact, saw Galileo's teaching as contradictory with an Old Testament passage that spoke of the sun standing still. The judges from the Inquisition believed Galileo was teaching heresy and placed him under house arrest, where he remained until his death.

In 1992, Pope John Paul II, on behalf of the Church, apologized for the manner in which Galileo was treated by the Inquisition. He stated that no contradiction exists between a *correct* understanding of revelation and science.

If we were living in the 1700s, we would be part of an exciting world of new scientific discoveries. We would be beginning to understand for the first time that many tragedies in the natural world, such as highly destructive storms, were not the result of God's wrath, but rather the result of natural conditions in the atmosphere. We would begin to suspect that perhaps Galileo was correct and that the Church was not correct in all their answers, especially those pertaining to science.

The majority of theologians did not recognize the formal distinction between Sacred Scripture and its interpretation, and this led them unduly to transpose into the realm of the doctrine of the faith a question that in fact pertained to scientific investigation.

Pope John Paul, II,
Lessons of the Galileo
Case, 1992

Today, Scripture and Science are not perceived as being in conflict with each other. Instead, they work together to enhance our understanding of God and the world around us.

The Age of Enlightenment

The Christian Times

Eighteenth Century   Vol. 18   No. 1

Pope Suppresses Jesuits

Pope Clement XIV published a declaration this week which formally suppressed the Jesuits. As far back as the middle of the last century, King Louis XIV, who wanted full control of the Catholic Church in France, attacked the Jesuits as heretics. Since that time, the Jesuits have come under attack in other countries as well.

Many problems faced by the Jesuits in France came from their resistance to four demands, called the *Gallican Articles,* made by the French General Assembly. In these articles, the assembly asserted the government's rights over the pope. The Jesuits objected.

With the dawn of the Age of the Enlightenment movement in France, the Jesuits became even more unpopular as they rejected scholars who denied a personal

God. The Enlightenment stressed the use of reason over faith. These scholars felt that the Jesuits were confusing the masses with superstitious Catholic beliefs.

Just fifteen years ago, Portugal joined the fight against the Jesuits by putting hundreds of them into prison. Six years ago, Spain exiled them to the Papal States.

Other countries have joined in the move to suppress the Jesuit order which numbers almost 20,000 members and has missions in every land. Under pressure from influential people all over Europe, Pope Clement XIV finally suppressed the Jesuit order. Observers noted that the pope appeared pained as he signed the decree.

Rumor has it that Russia and countries around it have refused to accept the pope's decree suppressing the Jesuits.

NOTEPAD

? ? ? ? ?

1. What did you learn about Pope Clement XIV? King Louis XIV?

2. What did you learn about the *Gallican Articles?*

3. According to the article, how did the Age of the Enlightenment contribute to the unpopularity of the Jesuits?

The Rest of the Story

Attitudes were changing rapidly throughout Europe as a number of scholars began to explain the universe scientifically. In France, important thinkers who would have an influence on the thinking of Europe and the New World contested the role of the Catholic Church and its teachings. Spiritual reform and the need to harmonize scientific discoveries with religious beliefs became the major challenges.

Spiritual Reform in France

After the Protestant Reformation in Europe, some saintly men and women of the Catholic faith, gifted the people of France with new orders (religious communities) to assist in the spiritual renewal of the country and of the world. These men and women dramatically changed the clerical lifestyle by caring for those who were poor and sick, and by helping to educate the minds of school-age children.

Jean-Jacques Olier (1608–1657) was a French presbyter who founded the Society of St. Sulpice (Sulpicians) to provide teachers for seminaries. Members of his society founded seminaries in many other places. He also established the Seminary of St. Sulpice in Paris.

The French presbyter, St. John Eudes (1601–1680), after preaching extensively for many years, eventually founded the Congregation of Jesus and Mary to train seminarians. Today, this congregation works in secondary education.

St. John-Baptist de la Salle (1651–1719) organized a religious order, later known as the Brothers of the Christian Schools. Today, they are also known as the de la Salle Christian Brothers. La Salle provided educational opportunities for children who were poor. His genius in teaching led him to develop new procedures in education and to establish schools for training and educating teachers. His order greatly influenced religious and educational development in France. Pope Pius XII named St. Jean-Baptist de la Salle the patron of schools.

St. Vincent de Paul

St. Vincent de Paul (1580–1660) is another excellent example of the spirit of the reform movement which took place in France. Five years after his ordination, Vincent de Paul set out on a voyage which changed his life. During his voyage his ship was seized by pirates. He and the other passengers were forced to work as slaves. It was two years before he was able to escape and return to Paris.

In Paris, as an energetic preacher, Vincent de Paul came face to face with the plight of the poor. He was so moved by their circumstances that he began to establish associations to aid those who were needy. Together with these associations, he worked with people who were convicts, slaves, poor, sick, and outcast.

In 1625, Vincent founded the Congregation of Priests of the Missions in Paris at a priory known as St. Lazare. People of the time referred to his new congregation as the Lazarists; today the congregation established by Vincent is usually known as the Vincentians.

A few years after Vincent founded the Lazarists, the members of the congregation began teaching in seminaries. In an attempt to improve the spiritual life of the Catholic clergy, Vincent began giving retreats for those who were about to be ordained. News of Vincent's work in reforming the clergy reached other bishops who began sending their clergy to his retreats. As an extension of his work for the clergy, Vincent established a seminary; within a few years, other seminaries were given over to the direction of his congregation.

Vincent also worked with Louise de Marillac, to establish The Sisters of Charity, a group of nuns who dedicated themselves to working with the poor in hospitals and schools. This group received its approval as a religious order in 1668. The Sisters of Charity, living without any written rules, differed from any of the other religous women communities of the day. Because they worked in the world instead of living in a convent, they considered themselves **secular**.

Louis XIV of France

King Louis XIV of France came to power in 1643 and immediately began to unite France by establishing himself as the undisputed king and fortifying his power over the state and the

KEY TERMS

Secular: a group that is not bound by rules or vows.

'A secular institute is an institute of consecrated life in which the Christian faithful living in the world strive for the perfection of charity and work for the sanctification of the world especially from within.'

Cathechism of the Catholic Church, 928

church. He believed that his power to rule both the state and the Catholic Church in France came to him from God. He rejected anyone who insisted that the pope had religious power in France.

King Louis XIV strongly believed that the Catholic Church should be under the direction of the nation, rather than the pope. This idea was given the name **Gallicanism**, and it took two forms. One form allowed the bishops of the country to make decisions for the Catholic Church in the country, while the second form allowed the king alone to make decisions for the national Church. King Louis XIV rejected the power of the bishops and the pope over the Catholic Church in France and stated that the king alone had authority over the national Church.

The king originally had the right to receive taxes from certain lands when the position of bishop, who ordinarily received the taxes, was vacant. The king also had the right to appoint someone temporarily to serve as bishop of that area. King Louis XIV incited a conflict with the pope when he extended his power to all lands awaiting the appointment of a new bishop. When the pope refused to accept this extension of the king's power to further land holdings, a general assembly of the clergy who sided with the king met to discuss the situation.

The general assembly agreed to a list of judgments called **The Four Gallican Articles of 1682**. These articles stated the following:

1. Neither the pope, nor the Catholic Church has any power over temporal rulers, and so they cannot depose a ruler or free subjects from allegiance to the ruler.

2. The pope's power is limited by the power of general councils.

3. The pope's power is limited by the customs and privileges of the national Church.

4. The pope's decisions, in matters of faith, may be altered unless they receive the consent of the Church.

Pope Innocent XI refused to accept these articles. When the king insisted and required these articles to be taught throughout France, including in the seminaries, the pope refused to give his approval to any appointments to bishops in France who had participated in the assembly. The king, on the other hand, wanted to appoint only those who had taken part in the assembly.

When more than thirty positions for bishop were vacant and the need for bishops became alarming, Louis XIV promised to cancel the articles, if the pope would approve his appointments of bishops. The pope agreed to appoint the men chosen by the king, but he insisted that they take an oath renouncing the assembly of 1682 and its articles. After getting what he wanted, Louis XIV did not cancel his order concerning the spread of his articles.

When a Jesuit writer defended the authority of the pope, Louis called his writing a new heresy of the Jesuits. The forceful Jesuits, numerous in the country, strongly supported the pope. French leaders, concerned about the growth and opposition of the Jesuits, found in the Jesuits' support of the pope an even greater reason to suppress the religious order.

The Enlightenment

Toward the end of the reign of Louis XIV, a new movement which placed reason above faith, began to dominate the thinking of many scholars. This movement, which would influence the attitudes of the western world down to the present, received the name **The Enlightenment**.

The term Enlightenment is commonly used to refer to the way of thinking which was prevalent from the early 1700s to the French Revolution in 1789. The enlightened thinkers believed only those things which could be explained by the use of reason. This approach began in England, took root in France, spread throughout Europe, and even reached North America.

The proponents of the enlightened thought were given even more fuel when Isaac Newton discovered the law of gravity and scientists delved into other laws of nature. Scienctists found answers in nature which religious leaders in the past attributed to God. In fact, science offered answers that appeared to have nothing to do with God. Many scholars, driven by these new understandings of the laws of nature, suspected religion of teaching superstition.

The enlightened refused to accept anything more than a natural religion. They tried to create a religion based on the truths that human beings could attain through the use of reason alone. Some of the scholars of this age believed in a God who created the world, since this seemed to be the only logical explanation of creation. However, they believed that God does not speak to the world through revelation, miracles, or in answer to prayers. The enlightened thinkers, who believed in an unconcerned and distant God, were called **Deists**.

Some enlightened thinkers rejected the authority of the Church, believing that the clergy were confusing the peasants with false and superstitious teachings. They suspected the clergy of using their superstitious messages to keep the people loyal to the king, who they believed was exploiting them. They felt an equal hatred for the clergy and the ruling class and its power.

Jesuit preachers gained even more enemies in their staunch defense of Catholic beliefs against Enlightenment thinkers.

Suppression of the Jesuits

By the middle of the 1700s, the Jesuits numbered more than 20,000 and served in almost three hundred missions worldwide, including the Americas. At a time when there were many weak popes and a general decay of religious practices on the part of kings and nobles, the Jesuits stood as a major force for Christianity in society. For those leaders who wanted to control the Catholic Church, the Jesuits were a major obstacle to their success.

In addition to encountering enemies outside the Catholic Church, the Jesuits were also finding enemies within the Church. The bishops who supported the articles of King Louis XIV had to confront the Jesuit preachers who rejected the articles. These bishops also found support from the members of monastic orders living a life of severity who thought the Jesuits should be living in monasteries, instead of working in the world. Enemies of the Jesuits among these groups joined with civil rulers in their desire to suppress the order.

Portugal also moved against the Jesuits in 1757, by falsely accusing them of illegally profiting from the work of the native people of South America. The Portugal government confiscated all Jesuit property, arrested more than two hundred of their leaders, and sent the rest to the papal states. Whenever countries suppressed the Jesuit order, the Jesuits lost their property and faced prison or exile.

In 1764, the French Parliament suppressed the Jesuits, after falsely accusing them of criminal financial dealings. In 1767, some areas of Spain also suppressed the Jesuits. Spain was where St. Ignatius Loyola founded the Society of Jesus and where the Jesuits had their largest foundation. Other countries followed until Pope Clement XIV, in 1773, reluctantly and under great pressure, suppressed the order in the name of the Catholic Church.

Whenever any country suppressed the Jesuits, the Jesuits serving the missions for that country joined the local clergy or other missionary groups, or returned to safety in Rome. People of the Americas felt the impact of the loss of the Jesuits, just as the rest of the world did.

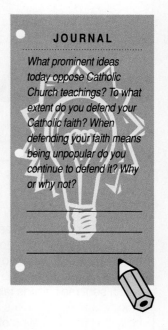

JOURNAL

What prominent ideas today oppose Catholic Church teachings? To what extent do you defend your Catholic faith? When defending your faith means being unpopular do you continue to defend it? Why or why not?

_____

_____

_____

CLIPBOARD

1. How does the Catholic Church continue to serve the poor and needy today, as St. Vincent de Paul did in his day? Why should the Church be involved in this ministry?

2. What differences would take place in our country, if the government suddenly introduced the Four Gallican Articles?

3. What influences of the Enlightenment are still present today? How do these influences affect the Catholic Church today?

Orthodox Russia and surrounding territories did not enforce the pope's suppression of the Jesuits. Some Jesuits found refuge in Russia where the Russian ruler, Catherine the Great, asked them to establish schools. The pope knew of these arrangements and quietly supported the Jesuits there. In 1801, the reigning pope established the society in Russia, and in 1814, a later pope reestablished the society for the whole world.

A Revolution in France

The Christian Times

Eighteenth Century   **Vol. 18   No. 3**

Reign of Terror Continues

Reporters stood watching in disgust yesterday as frightened but brave men and women took their turns laying their heads on the block for the stroke of the guillotine, which sent their heads falling into a bloody basket. When the governing body first began cutting off the heads of those who rejected the revolution, the people stood around cheering as each head rolled into the basket. Now crowds gather to shout, "No more."

One reporter, who has followed the current Reign of Terror for the last two years, estimates that somewhere between two thousand to five thousand clergy have lost their heads to the guillotine. This count does not include the many men and women who were beheaded simply because a powerful enemy falsely accused them.

One anonymous spokesman for the National Assembly, originally

known as the Estates General, claimed that the assembly simply wanted to reform France. When they first met in 1789, they wanted to weaken the control of the pope in France and grant everyone freedom and equality.

As the spokesman stood watching some clergy being publicly beheaded, he wept openly, stuttering through his tears, "This reign of terror is not what we intended when we voted to pass The Civil Constitution of the Clergy. We just wanted the clergy to take an oath to support the revolution."

As the revolution spreads throughout Europe, some religious communities such as the Passionists, who were founded by Paul of the Cross, and the Redemptorists, who were founded by Alphonsus Ligouri, still thrive. These orders, founded before the French Revolution, have had a

great influence on helping the people remain faithful to the Catholic Church in the midst of so much terror and bloodshed.

NOTEPAD

? ? ? ? ?

1. According to this article, what was the original motive behind The Civil Constitution of the Clergy?

2. What affect did the Revolution have on the religious communities?

3. Why did some of the attitudes of the supporters of the Revolution change after it was in full force?

The Rest of the Story

In 1776, the War of Independence ended in the American colonies, with the thirteen colonies declaring that they were now a free and independent nation. In 1789, representatives met in a Constitutional Assembly to draft and sign a new constitution. As the United States celebrated their newly achieved freedom and independence, France, in 1789, held an assembly which was to have a major impact on life in Europe for decades to come.

The Passionist Order

Despite the difficulty experienced by the Jesuits, other religious communities came into existence and were able to perform some of the duties previously undertaken by the Jesuits. These orders, the Passionists and Redemptorists, spread the Word of God across Europe through their preaching.

Paul of the Cross (1694–1775) founded a community dedicated to the Passion of the Lord in 1720, because of a vision that he received. In his vision Mary appeared to him in a black habit with the name of Jesus written on her chest below a white cross. She directed him to establish a religious order committed to proclaiming the passion of Christ. Paul himself became a powerful and popular preacher.

The Passionists received papal approval in 1741. Paul of the Cross founded the order for his preachers to work for their own personal salvation and for the salvation of others. The members of the community served in many areas of the world, fulfilling their mission of preaching the passion of Christ. Today, this order is known as the Passionists.

The Redemptorist Order

Alphonsus Liguori (1696–1787) founded the Redemptorists, which is also known as the Congregation of the Most Holy Redeemer. In his young adulthood, Alphonsus was a brilliant lawyer with an abundance of energy. When he dedicated himself to God's service, he took a vow never to waste a minute of time.

St. Paul of the Cross

He used his great energy to preach about God's love, and he taught that God willed the salvation of all.

When the pope asked Alphonsus to accept an appointment as bishop, he reluctantly accepted. He worked tirelessly to educate the people, to reform the clergy, and to develop a strong devotional life throughout his diocese. During a devastating famine in his diocese, he completely emptied the bishop's residence of food and finances to help those in need.

Alphonsus wrote an astounding number of devotional books as well as a major theological book on moral theology. This book spoke of living in harmony with God as a Christian in the world. In his moral theology, Alphonsus fought the harsh Jansenist heresy which presented God as stern, domineering, demanding, and condemning. He called Christians to a life that was neither too rigid, nor too lax. He chose the middle road between the two.

Alphonsus envisioned the ministry of the Redemptorist Congregation as one of working with Catholics who were poor and virtually abandoned in the remote districts of Italy. He demanded that his preachers use a simple style of preaching, rather than the flowery style frequently heard from the pulpits of his day. The Redemptorists preached retreats and parish missions, and ministered in the foreign missions. Alphonsus called his congregation to a life of prayer, community living, and the apostolic life.

Alphonsus founded the Redemptorists in 1732 and received papal approval for the community in 1749. In 1750, he cofounded the Redemptoristine nuns, a contemplative order of religious women.

The Revolution of 1789 in France

In France in 1789, a number of representatives converged in a meeting hall, intending to hold a National Assembly. On the surface, it appeared that the assembly would bring about some needed changes, but those entering the assembly had no idea that they were about to propel the nation and all of Europe into years of bloodshed and terror.

Three groups, known as the *Three Estates,* came to the meeting. The First Estate represented the clergy. About a third of the group were wealthy and powerful bishops and abbots, while two thirds of the estate were members of the lower clergy ranks who served in parishes and received just enough support for survival. The Second Estate were the rich nobles, and the Third Estate consisted of common people.

The Assembly opened with a bitter dispute concerning the manner of voting. The nobles and wealthy clergy wanted each of the estates to have equal voting power, while the lower clergy and the common people wanted to allow each person involved to have a vote. Under pressure, the king and the wealthy clergy and nobles agreed to allow each person represented to cast a vote. The lower clergy originally cast their votes with the common population, giving them greater influence in making changes.

Effects of the National Assembly

At the time of the National Assembly, France, despite its great wealth, had not managed its wealth properly and had fallen into financial difficulties. To increase its wealth, the government increased the taxes on the lower class. The poor people knowing that they were paying for the magnificent comforts of the rich, naturally resented this injustice.

As the members of the Assembly continued to meet, they attempted to balance the injustices in the country. However, their national pride led them to solutions which not only hurt the rich, but also the Catholic Church. The Assembly voted to eliminate the taxes. With no right to collect taxes, the wealthy clergy, along with the lower clergy, now had to depend on the government to support them. This effectively gave the state power over the Church.

The members of the Assembly also realized that they had to find income to replace the lost taxes. They solved their problem by allowing the government to seize and sell Church property. This tactic had a twofold effect. The money raised provided the government with strong allies who were against the Church. These allies had bought Church property and fought any attempt by the Church to reclaim Church possessions.

Anticlericals used the seizure of Church wealth as an opportunity to weaken and destroy the Catholic Church. They convinced the Assembly to pay a sum of money to nuns and monks who left their monasteries and renounced their religious vows. The Assembly then closed a number of religious houses and gathered those who refused to abandon their religious commitment into a handful of government controlled convents and monasteries.

Civil Constitution of the Clergy

A year after their first meeting, the Assembly met and passed a document known as **The Civil Constitution of the Clergy**. The local clergy now collected their pay from the government, but they had to obey the directives of the government to receive their income. The people, Catholic and Protestant alike, had the right to select Catholic bishops and other clergy for their area. The government notified the pope of the outcome. The pope had no role in the appointment and the clergy had to sever all ties with Rome.

After the Civil Constitution of the Clergy became law, most of the clergy ignored it and performed their duties as they had in the past. When the Assembly discovered this, they forced the clergy to take an oath of loyalty to their diocese, parish, nation, and king. The oath also demanded that they accept everything ordered or to be ordered by the Assembly in the future. This gave the Assembly total control over the role of the clergy in France.

About half of the lower clergy took the oath, in addition to four bishops. Most of the bishops fled the country. The lower clergy who took the oath were apparently not well-educated and so were unaware of the full implications of the oath. The bishops who refused to take the oath lost their right to their dioceses. The Assembly banned the lower clergy who refused to take the oath from their churches, forcing them to celebrate liturgy wherever they could assemble the people.

A large number of people in the lower classes supported the clergy who refused to take the oath. The government imposed severe penalties on these clergy. The Church of France became divided in its religious allegiance. While some people supported the constitutional Church, the majority of the common people supported the Church of Rome. The government reacted by imprisoning or sending into exile those who refused to take the oath.

The Reign of Terror

As the revolution progressed, the mood became darker. Many people, who once supported the clergy who refused to take the oath, turned against them. They came to resent the power of an outsider like the pope having spiritual power in their country. In 1793, an uncontrollable mob stormed through the streets of Paris, dragged hundreds of priests out of the jails and butchered them. Once the persecution began, it spread rapidly throughout France, leading to the deaths of thousands of the clergy.

As a result of the massacre, a number of the clergy fled to other countries in Europe and to asylum in the United States. A large group refused to leave. They went underground, and, risking their lives, secretly celebrated the liturgy for, and ministered to, the people of the countryside.

The Assembly instituted a new religion called the Religion of Reason, later it was known as the *Cult of the Supreme Being*. They changed the calendar from seven days to ten with the intention of abolishing Sundays and all holy days. Civil celebrations replaced religious festivities, and clergy faithful to the Assembly had to swear allegiance to the state before the altar of freedom.

KEY TERMS

The Civil Constitution of the Clergy: put the clergy under the rule of the government, and gave the people the right to select Catholic bishops and other clergy for their area.

---

*B*rother will betray brother to death, and a father his child, and children will rise against parents and have them put to death; and you will be hated by all because of my name. But the one who endures to the end will be saved.

Matthew 10:21–22, NRSV

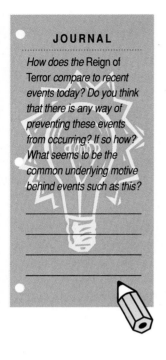

The Assembly transformed the Cathedral of Notre Dame into the Temple of the Goddess of Reason and placed a dancing girl on the high altar to impersonate the new goddess.

In addition to attacking the Church, the members of the National Assembly turned their wrath against the king. In 1793, they had revoked the monarchy in France and declared that the country was not a republic. They put the king on trial for treason, convicted him, and finally executed him.

When the peasants grew tired of waiting for the new government to solve their problems, they revolted against the government. The Assembly, fearing that other nations would use the time of internal strife as an opportunity to invade, responded savagely against the revolt. Those who dared to express a doubt or a complaint against the government found themselves condemned to die at the guillotines.

The remaining clergy again became likely candidates for the *Reign of Terror*. If they did not swear allegiance to the government before the altar of freedom, they faced charges of being against the new government. The people were growing accustomed to the wagons carrying the clergy to their death at the guillotines. Despite this renewed persecution, many of the clergy courageously continued to lead the peasants and secretly held liturgies and ministered to them.

The common people lost the security of believing they would escape the guillotines. They watched as innocent neighbors, relatives, and friends rode the wagons to the guillotines. An influential enemy could accuse someone of complaining against the government and could have that person executed. Some faced the guillotines without knowing what crime they had committed.

In 1794, the frightened and angry crowds rebelled and this time overthrew the extreme revolutionary government, replacing it with a new revolutionary government. The *Reign of Terror* ended and a surprising number of clergy who had refused to take the oath came out of hiding. A bitter dispute erupted, dividing the clergy between those faithful to the government and those faithful to Rome.

French armies waged successful military campaigns throughout parts of Europe. They imposed the principles of the revolution on conquered countries, paying special attention to destroying the power of the Catholic Church. The French armies suppressed religious orders, seized Church property, closed monasteries and convents, and imprisoned or killed the clergy who resisted these changes.

In 1797, a new government was about to take control of France.

CLIPBOARD

1. What would happen in our country today if the government tried to impose the Civil Constitution of the Clergy?
2. How important are the pastors of our parishes today?
3. Why do some governments attempt to kill the clergy when they want total control of a country?

A World Struggling for Freedom

The Christian Times

Eighteenth Century   Vol. 18   No. 2

Pope Reinstates Jesuits

Pope Pius VII yesterday reinstated the Jesuit Order. The Jesuits had touched every part of the world in their early missionary days, until leaders of several countries no longer wanted these defenders of the popes in their countries.

To realize how far the influence of the Jesuits extend, one need only look to the United States. The pope's newly appointed bishop of the country, Bishop John Carroll of Baltimore, was a former Jesuit who returned to his hometown of Maryland to serve in the colonies after the suppression of the Jesuits.

Word has reached us from the United States that Bishop Carroll has called upon the saintly Elizabeth Ann Seton to care for children of the poor and open schools for them. She has established an order of nuns known as the Sisters of Charity.

Besides reinstating the Jesuits, Pope Pius VII is currently offering help to the family of the defeated Napoleon.

Napoleon's problems did not center around the Jesuits, but around his dispute with the stubborn Pope Pius VII. The pope never forgave Napoleon for insulting him when the pope traveled to France to crown Napoleon as emperor.

In the Concordat of 1801 between Napoleon and the pope, Napoleon agreed to work together with the pope in Church matters. Shortly after this, however, he attempted to gain control of the Catholic Church by secretly publishing laws against the Church. These laws are known as the Organic Articles.

Leaders throughout the world are applauding the courage of Pope Pius VII for his stand against Napoleon, his restoration of the Jesuit Order, and his support of the Catholic Church in the United States.

NOTEPAD

? ? ? ? ?

1. What did you learn about Pope Pius VII? Napoleon? Bishop Carroll? Elizabeth Ann Seton?

2. What conflicts arose between Napoleon and Pope Pius VII?

3. What does this article applaud Pope Pius VII for doing?

The Rest of the Story

In 1797, a new revolutionary group took control in France. Once again the government imposed an oath on the clergy and persecuted them if they refused to take the oath. This time, however, the oath no longer contained a clause promoting allegiance to the king; this oath was against the monarchy. Into this new revolutionary government came a successful general, Napoleon Bonaparte, who had a great effect on the Catholic Church in Europe.

Napoleon Bonaparte

The new revolutionary government in France had little respect for the spiritual leadership of the pope. Because he was head of the Papal States, they considered him a ruler of a country, the same as any other temporal ruler. Under the leadership of the brilliant young military general, Napoleon Bonaparte, the French sent the army against the pope. Napoleon captured a large portion of the Papal States and installed a ruler over the states to rule on behalf of the French government.

A year later, after Napoleon's victory, a French general seized Rome and declared that it was now under French rule. The French government realized that the presence of the pope in Rome would always be a threat to their leadership, so they forced Pope Pius VI to abandon Rome. In 1799, the pope died in exile.

Although some Catholic Church leaders feared that the military situation would hinder the election of a new pope and possibly end the long line of popes, a papal conclave did meet and elected the courageous Pope Pius VII. The new pope was anxious to return to Rome, knowing that he could easily be used as a pawn by any country offering him refuge.

When Napoleon seized full power in France in 1799, he aligned himself with the Catholic Church. Although he had few religious convictions, he realized the importance of religion in the lives of the people and decided that he could win the people to his side, if he gained favor with the Catholic Church. He strongly desired a united France and realized that unity hinged on religion.

Concordat of 1801

With Napoleon heading the new government in France, Pope Pius VII returned to Rome and began to negotiate with Napoleon. In 1801, they both agreed on a concordat which granted religious peace in France and its conquered territories. In the concordat, the pope agreed to abandon the Church's rights to any Church property that had been seized in France. In return, Napoleon received the right to nominate bishops, but the pope retained the right to name and install them.

Besides helping restore the relations between French government and the pope, and reestablishing a process for choosing bishops, the concordat also aided in revitalizing other areas of Catholic life in France. Many communities of nuns and clergy, who had disbanded during the revolution, found under the concordat a new freedom and began to reunite.

Mother St. John Fontbonne is an example of a woman religious who took advantage of the concordat. She entered the Sisters of St. Joseph in 1778, became a superior in 1785, and witnessed the disbanding of her order in the revolution of 1789. She then spent time with her family, but later was sent to prison. With the signing of the concordat, she was able to gather the sisters together and restore the Sisters of St. Joseph in 1808. As the number of Sisters of St. Joseph grew, they expanded their missions throughout Europe and into the United States.

The concordat freed the clergy from the obligation of taking a civil oath, and the government agreed to finance the clergy. To all appearances, the difficulties imposed by the French Revolution had ceased. Unknown to the pope, however, Napoleon secretly enacted laws regulating religion in France.

Napoleon introduced the **Organic Articles**, which decreed that all representatives of the pope coming into France must receive permission from the government, and all decrees of Catholic Church councils must receive government approval before being accepted by the Church in France. The Organic Articles also called for reintroducing the Gallican Articles in all French seminaries.

JOURNAL

Why do you think so many powerful leaders relied on religion to obtain unity? Why do you think that the United States is able to maintain unity despite its differences in religious practice?

KEY TERMS

Organic Articles: introduced by Napoleon; decreed that all representatives of the pope must receive permission from government before entering France; reintroduced the Gallican Articles into all French seminaries.

Napoleon Becomes Emperor

In 1804, the pope agreed to go to Paris to crown Napoleon emperor. He had learned of the Organic Articles and hoped to use the occasion to have Napoleon revoke them. Napoleon considered Pope Pius VII to be a weak pope, and he snubbed him when he arrived in the country. He showed his disrespect for the pope by not offering him a formal reception.

During the crowning ceremony, Napoleon arrogantly seized the crown from the pope's hands and placed it on his own head. The pope, humiliated at Napoleon's arrogance, returned to Rome, determined to treat Napoleon with greater harshness and stubbornness in the future.

As Emperor Napoleon defeated country after country, he commanded that each country refuse to trade with the English. He did not intend to confront England in battle, but he resolved to weaken this enemy by cutting off all its trade with Europe. When Napoleon bade the humiliated pope not to trade with the English, the pope stubbornly declined. An angry Napoleon again captured the Papal States, annexed them to France, and went on to capture Rome.

Napoleon and the Pope

When Napoleon annexed the Papal States to France in 1808, Pope Pius VII fought back by excommunicating Napoleon and all who took part in the attack on Rome. Napoleon forced the pope out of Rome and compelled him to endure a strenuous trip to France. Napoleon wanted to control the Church by having the pope live in France as a servant to the government.

The pope used the same tactics in France that a previous pope had used against King Louis XIV, when he wanted to impose the Galican Articles on the Church. He refused to approve any bishops nominated by Napoleon. The embarrassed emperor soon had many dioceses in France without a bishop.

Napoleon sent envoys to the pope to have him change his mind. When these envoys failed in their negotiations with the pope, Napoleon had the pope moved closer to Paris, so that he could more easily meet the pope and intimidate him into action.

When the pope finally entered into negotiations, he was physically weak and apparently near death. He reluctantly agreed to surrender the Catholic Church's right to the Papal States. He further agreed that a specially designated bishop could install other bishops when the pope took more than six months to act. A day later, after further reflection, the pope changed his mind and revoked the agreement. Napoleon refused to publish the pope's retraction of the agreement.

In 1814, as Napoleon faced a number of defeats, he returned the Pope to Rome. He also attempted to appease some of his enemies by offering to return the Papal States to the pope. Pope Pius VII again surprised Napoleon by refusing to accept the Papal States from him. The pope claimed that Napoleon never had a true title to the Papal States, but had taken them illegally. Thus, they still rightly belonged to the pope and the Catholic Church.

On the pope's journey back to Rome, French and Italian citizens thronged the streets, cheering him on his journey. Shortly after, when Napoleon met his final defeat and went into exile, the feeble and infirm pope stood out as the one who finally prevailed.

The saintly Pope Pius VII did not glory in Napoleon's humiliation. He spoke with deep compassion of the sufferings of Napoleon in exile. He recalled for the people the honorable goals of the young Napoleon before he became so overwhelmed by power. The pope gave shelter and protection to Napoleon's family who lived in exile in the Papal States.

It was Pope Pius VII who restored the Society of Jesus in 1814. With the

*B*ut I say to you that listen, love your enemies, do good to those who hate you, bless those who curse you, pray for those who abuse you.

Luke 6:27–29, NRSV

In the Spotlight

St. Elizabeth Ann Seton (1774–1821) is the first canonized saint born in the United States. Her mother, Catherine, passed away when she was three years old, and her father, Richard Bayley, a professor of anatomy at Columbia College, chose to educate her and her sisters. As a child Elizabeth showed great sympathy and concern for the poor. She was often called "the Protestant Sister of Charity" and her youthful writings are known for their deep spirituality.

In 1794, Elizabeth married William Magee Seton, a successful merchant. Together, they had five children. Throughout her marriage Elizabeth continued her works of charity, founding the Society for the Relief of Poor Widows with Small Children. Ironically, she became a poor widow herself when her husband passed away in 1803. It was at that time, when she stayed with her Catholic friends, that she began to consider the Catholic faith.

When she returned to New York she became Catholic despite great opposition and ostracism from her family and friends. In 1808, Elizabeth accepted an invitation to move to Baltimore and open a school, from the rector of St. Mary's Seminary in Baltimore. She was soon joined by other women, and in 1809 the small community was transferred to Emmitsburg to take over a house that had been established to care for poor children. In Emmitsburg the community of women trained teachers, wrote textbooks, translated religious books from the French, wrote spiritual treatises, and counseled the

other sisters. They also visited the poor and the sick of the community. This community marks the beginnings of the Catholic parochial school system in the United States.

The community followed a modified version of the rule of St. Vincent de Paul's Sisters of Charity, which was approved by Bishop John Carroll in 1812. They were the first religious community formed by Americans for Americans. Elizabeth, elected superior, lived to see the community grow to some twenty communities spread across the various states. Her community has now grown to thousands throughout the states.

Elizabeth was canonized by Pope Paul VI in 1975. Her feast day is January 4.

downfall of Napoleon, the pope cultivated closer relationships between the Catholic Church and the European community and began a spiritual and intellectual revival in the Church.

Independence in America

While Europe dealt with the French Revolution and, later Napoleon, the thirteen British colonies in America were busy rebelling against Britain, and in 1776, they declared their independence. At that time, there were approximately two and a half million people in the colonies, about twenty-five thousand of them Catholics. Catholics supported the revolutionary war and rejoiced in the country's religious toleration and separation between church and state.

During the revolutionary war, Catholics played a large role. Despite the problems developing in France just before the French Revolution, Catholics were able to coax France into supporting the colonies in their struggle against England. On July 4, 1776, Charles Carroll, a Catholic landowner in Maryland, added his name to the Declaration of Independence. He was a delegate from Maryland to the Continental Congress.

In 1789, when the leaders of the French Revolution were attempting to control the Church in France, the Continental Congress of the United States signed the U.S. Constitution and established a new form of government with a complete separation of church and state. The writers of the United States Constitution rejected the use of religion as a means of unifying the country. In the United States, many religions now exist side by side. This is known as **religious pluralism**.

The First Bishop of the United States

In 1789, the year of the revolution in France, the United States elected George Washington as its first president. The same year, twenty-six members of the Catholic clergy in the United States elected Father John Carroll as the country's first Catholic bishop. The pope had appointed him earlier as the spiritual leader of the Catholic Church's mission in the colonies.

Before he became a bishop, Father John Carroll spent twenty years as a Jesuit. When the pope suppressed the Jesuit order in 1773, Carroll returned to Maryland (where he had been born) to work as a missionary. When the clergy elected Carroll as their bishop, they selected Baltimore as the center of the first diocese in the United States. Bishop John Carroll became first Catholic bishop of Baltimore in 1790.

At the time of Bishop Carroll's appointment to the diocese of Baltimore, the diocese included all thirteen colonies. With the Louisiana Purchase, Bishop Carroll's diocese immediately doubled in size.

Bishop Carroll soon proved that the pope and the U.S. clergy had made a wise choice. He had the task of bringing order to the Catholic Church in the United States, and he performed his task well. By 1791, he had established the first seminary in the New World.

Bishop Carroll helped with the foundation of Georgetown College in Washington, organized four large dioceses to the west, and found clergy to care for the people who spoke many different languages when they came into the country. In the twenty-five years between 1790 and 1815, the number of Catholics in the United States grew from 25,000 to 200,000. The majority of the increase came from immigration of Catholics from other countries.

CLIPBOARD

1. Can you think of any situations in recent times when the leader of a country and the pope have openly disagreed?

2. How does the freedom of the Church in the United States differ from the image of the Church held by Napoleon?

3. What ministries are women religious performing in the United States today?

• **1625**

ST. VINCENT DE PAUL. Vincent and his followers performed an outstanding number of charitable works for the poor and outcasts of the community. He founded the Congregation of Priests of the Missions (Lazarists), now called the Vincentians.

• **1650**

LOUISE DE MARILLAC. With St. Vincent de Paul, Louise founded the Sisters of Charity, a group of women who originally did not take vows and who worked with those who were poor and outcast.

JEAN-JACQUES OLIER. Olier founded the Society of St. Sulpice (Sulpicians), who dedicated themselves to teaching in seminaries.

ST. JOHN EUDES. John Eudes founded the Congregation of Jesus and Mary to provide seminaries for teachers. Today members of the community teach in secondary schools.

ST. JEAN-BAPTIST DE LA SALLE. This Frenchman organized a religious order known as the Brothers of the Christian Schools (or the de la Salle Christian Brothers) to provide a good education for children of the poor. He established schools for the training of teachers and reorganized and improved the manner of teaching.

FOUR GALLICAN ARTICLES. These articles were an attempt to weaken the power of the pope in France and to make the king the ruler of the national Church.

• **1700**

THE ENLIGHTENMENT. This movement, during the 1700s, glorified reason over religion and looked suspiciously on any religious beliefs which could not be proven by reason.

ST. PAUL OF THE CROSS. Paul founded the Passionist Order to preach the passion of Christ. The Passionists continue to play a major role in the spiritual renewal of the Church.

ST. ALPHONSUS LIGOURI. Alphonsus founded the Redemptorist Congregation to preach and to care for the poor. He wrote a major work on moral theology, served as a dedicated bishop, and wrote more than a hundred devotional books. His congregation continues to flourish today, preaching missions, retreats, teaching, and serving in parish ministry.

JESUIT ORDER SUPPRESSED. Pope Clement XIV suppressed the Jesuit order and its thousands of members, after the order had spread throughout the world. Remote areas of the world were able to preserve the community, and Pope Pius VII reinstated the order in 1817.

• **1785**

FRENCH REVOLUTION. This famous revolution in France did away with the monarchy and attempted to bring the Church under the control of the government. Many members of the clergy died during the reign of terror that accompanied the revolution.

JOHN CARROLL. John Carroll of Baltimore was the first bishop in the United States. He established schools, helped to establish dioceses, opened a seminary, and helped to organize the Catholic Church in America.

ST. ELIZABETH ANN SETON. This mother of five children became a Catholic after her husband's death. She established the Sisters of Charity in the United States to work for the poor and in schools. She is the first American-born saint.

NAPOLEON. This ruler of France and emperor tried to control the Catholic Church in France and attempted to make a puppet of the pope. He signed the concordat of 1801 making Catholicism the religion of France and giving the right to name bishops to the ruler of France, with the pope's approval and appointment.

Secular

Gallicanism

The Four Gallican
Articles of 1682

The Enlightenment

Deists

The Civil Constitution of
the Clergy

Organic Articles

Religious pluralism

A Voice from the Past

This week's column features the French Revolution. Explain how it affected the Catholic Church. Be sure to mention the ramifications that it held for the religious life, especially the Jesuits. Also, make note of how the various religious orders helped to keep the Catholic Church alive during the Age of Enlightenment and the Reign of Terror. End your column with a discussion of the Reign of Terror. Explain its similarities to other events that have happened and are still happening in the world today. Get at the possible motives behind such events, as well as possible ways of preventing them in the future.

Then and Now

The eighteenth century boasts saints and sinners, spiritual triumphs and spiritual disasters. While the revolution of 1789 brought an attempt to destroy the Catholic Church in France, the Constitution of the United States, signed in 1789, strove to give all people the right to worship as they wished.

Saints founded religious communities to bring God's word into a world where leaders were denying anything that could not be explained by reason. At a time when Napoleon wanted to control the Catholic Church and rid himself of powerful Church leaders, the United States paved the way for religious freedom.

Today, a number of congregations of men and women who had their birth in the seventeenth and eighteenth centuries are ministering throughout the world. The Passionists, Redemptorists, Sisters of Charity, Vincentians, Jesuits, Visitations, Sisters of St. Joseph, and many other congregations are spreading the word of God through a variety of ministries.

In the United States, religious leaders can preach on any topic without experiencing censure from the government. There are many Dioceses, but the Catholic still honors the diocese of Baltimore as the first diocese in the United States.

NEWS IN REVIEW

1. Name four founders of orders, and explain how their lives affected the spiritual reformation of the Catholic Church.
2. What was the purpose of the Galican Articles, and how successful were they?
3. Why was the Enlightenment successful in France?
4. Explain why so many countries wanted to suppress the Jesuits.
5. Explain why the French Revolution which began in 1789 was so successful.
6. What was the purpose of the Constitution of the Clergy?
7. What problems did Napoleon Bonaparte face in attempting to control the Church?
8. How did the conditions in the United States in 1789 compare with conditions in France?
9. How did the organization of the Catholic Church in the United States develop in the early days?
10. Why is Elizabeth Ann Seton important to Catholic history?

chapter fourteen
A New Era

If we were living in the United States at the beginning of the nineteenth century, we would be experiencing a new relationship between the Church and the government. Prior to this era, we would have presumed that as Catholics we had to belong to the dominant religion of the area, in order to find acceptance. Once in control, we might find ourselves discriminating against people of other religions. Sometimes we, as Catholics, would also face persecution if we were living in a strongly Protestant area. The Constitution of the United States sought to end all religious prejudice.

Although we have made headway in our fight against prejudice, we still have a long way to go.

The Church and the United States

The Christian Times

Nineteenth Century   **Vol. 19   No. 1**

Immigrant Catholics Flood the Country

Some Protestant leaders yesterday expressed concern over the large number of Irish, German, Italian, French, and Mexican Catholics coming into the United States. They fear that the Catholic Church is trying to take over the country.

At the time of the Revolutionary War, only twenty-five thousand Catholics lived in the colonies. Charles Carroll of Maryland, a Catholic, signed the Declaration of Independence of the United States in 1776, but few other Catholics took part in politics at the time.

Some Protestant leaders fear that the pope plans on being the spiritual ruler of the United States. They believe that he took the first step in this direction in 1790 when he made Father John Carroll, a former Jesuit, the first Catholic bishop of the United States.

Bishop Carroll, a cousin of Charles Carroll, is proving himself to be fully American and supports the separation of church and state.

Under Carroll's leadership, five new dioceses have been formed in the United States. Lay leadership is strong in most parishes. To staff these parishes, the bishop continues to invite clergy from Europe to work in the United States. However, he insists that they learn the new ways of the young country.

Carroll is having a special problem with the French clergy who are seeking freedom from the difficulties of the French revolution. Bishop Flaget of the Bardstown, Kentucky Diocese has invited clergy from France into the United States. Because of their difficulties with the rulers in France, the French clergy tend to distrust any government, including that in the United States.

Bishop Carroll has invited an American-born widow with five children to begin a school for girls in the country. Elizabeth Ann Seton is the founder of the Sisters of Charity of St. Joseph, and her nuns teach in these Catholic schools. Other religious communities of women and men have begun Catholic schools throughout the country.

Some Protestant leaders do not fear the growing Catholic population. They believe that the immigrants will have the same spirit of acceptance of the Constitution as shown by Bishop Carroll.

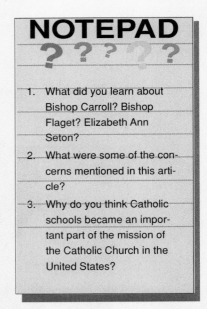

NOTEPAD
? ? ? ? ?

1. What did you learn about Bishop Carroll? Bishop Flaget? Elizabeth Ann Seton?

2. What were some of the concerns mentioned in this article?

3. Why do you think Catholic schools became an important part of the mission of the Catholic Church in the United States?

The Rest of the Story

With the colonies becoming discontent with paying taxes to Britain for little in return, the people began to speak of revolt. They had many grievances against their mother country and felt that the problems between England and the colonies had become unsolvable. It was time for the successful American Revolution during this period. The Catholic Church in the United States had the good fortune of being represented by capable leaders.

Bishop John Carroll

John Carroll was born in Maryland in 1735 and went to Europe at the age of thirteen to study. While in Europe, he joined the Jesuit order, eventually taught for a number of years, and finally became a tutor of the son of a wealthy Englishman who was making a tour of Europe. This tour gave Carroll an opportunity to learn about the political life of Europe. He would most likely have spent his life teaching, if the pope had not been forced to suppress the Jesuit order in 1773.

Disillusioned by the role of Pope Clement XIV in the suppression of the Jesuits, Carroll returned to Maryland, his homeland, to work with Catholics in the colonies. Carroll met other former Jesuits in the colonies, who had banded together under the leadership of Father John Lewis. In time, Carroll became known and respected by the twenty-six priests who ministered in the colonies.

Delegation to Canada

Two years after Carroll returned to Maryland, he was sent by the Continental Congress with a delegation to seek Canada's support for the colonies' war against Britain. The members of the congress chose Carroll because of his learning and because he was a Catholic presbyter. They felt the presence of an ordained priest would help them in their negotiations with the largely Catholic Canada. Another member of the small delegation, who became a close friend of Father John Carroll, was Benjamin Franklin.

Another Catholic, Charles Carroll, joined the small delegation to Canada. He was a layman and a cousin of Father John Carroll, who was an able diplomat and a popular leader in the colonies' struggle for independence. When the First Continental Congress met in Philadelphia two years earlier in 1774, Charles Carroll was present. At the time of his trip to Canada, he was Maryland's representative to the Continental

Bishop John Carroll

Congress. He became one of the signers of the Declaration of Independence.

After a short time in Canada, Benjamin Franklin became ill, and Carroll escorted him home while the other two members of the delegation remained in Canada. Although the people of French Canada were already antagonistic toward Britain, they were also unhappy with the discrimination against Catholics in the colonies. The rest of the delegation returned home later, after failing to convince Canada to join them in the Revolutionary War.

Between the support the colonies received from Catholic France and the role of Catholics in the politics of independence, Catholics began to find themselves more easily accepted by some Protestant groups. Bigotry against Catholics did not disappear, but it softened, enabling Catholics to find some acceptance in this New World. A small number of Catholics, like Charles Carroll, helped the country politically.

Separation of Church and State

On July 4, 1776, as a representative of Maryland, Charles Carroll signed the Declaration of Independence. The population of the colonies had reached almost twenty-five thousand by this time, with fifteen thousand Catholics in Maryland and seven thousand in Pennsylvania.

Three thousand more were scattered throughout the remaining eleven colonies.

The Constitution of the United States was signed in 1789. It promoted the separation of Church and the government, commonly called the State. The Constitution prevented the government from establishing a national religion and from prohibiting the freely chosen practice of any religion.

Father John Carroll recognized that the separation of church and state was a new notion for many people, including the pope. The leaders of European countries used religion to promote unity. These countries favored one religious expression and made life difficult for those who refused to accept that religion. Catholic and Protestant leaders alike resisted the favoring of any religious belief which they themselves did not accept.

Father Carroll feared that a bishop for the United States who came from Europe would not understand this new country. The idea of the government not supporting or imposing a particular belief on a nation was unknown to Europeans. After centuries of fighting for the support of kings for Catholicism, the pope and religious leaders in Rome had a difficult time understanding this new concept of freedom of religion.

United States Church

In 1789, the year that George Washington became the first president of the newly formed United States, the twenty-six clergy in that same country elected Father John Carroll as their first bishop. Six years before he became bishop, Carroll recognized that many of the former Jesuits, who made up the bulk of the ordained priests in the colonies, were growing old and needed a strong leadership for the changing times. Father John Lewis, their chosen superior, had no authority over the clergy in the country, because he lacked the necessary approval from Rome.

Father Carroll organized the twenty-one Jesuits and wrote a letter to the pope in their name. The letter asked the pope to make Father Lewis the superior and leader of the Church's mission in the colonies, and to grant him the authority and privileges necessary to lead the Catholic Church in the United States. The former Jesuits, fearing that the pope would appoint a bishop or leader from another country, begged the pope not to appoint a bishop, but rather a superior for the clergy in the United States.

The former Jesuits had two reasons for not wanting a bishop. They feared that the naming of a bishop by the pope would ignite the lingering fear of the Protestants that the Catholic Church was plotting to take over the country. The Jesuits also feared that a bishop or leader from another country would not understand the mentality of this newly formed nation.

To the surprise of the group, especially to Father Carroll, the pope agreed to choose a leader, but he chose Carroll instead of Lewis as superior of the mission. Before making this decision, the pope had conferred with French and United States diplomats, among them Benjamin Franklin, who greatly admired John Carroll.

Carroll Appointed Bishop

In time, the clergy in the United States, under the leadership of Father John Carroll, became concerned about their place in the Church. They found themselves directly under the control of an office in Rome, and they sought independence from that office. Carroll and his fellow presbyters believed that the American situation of freedom was so unique that foreign spiritual leaders would not understand it.

Since other denominations in the United States had begun to appoint bishops, the clergy no longer feared that Protestants would see the appointment of a Catholic bishop as an effort of the

Catholics to control the new government. Feeling misunderstood by the authorities in Rome, the clergy now began to petition for a bishop from the United States, who would be answerable to the pope and not to a lesser office in Rome.

The clergy in the United States, filled with the new democratic spirit of the land, petitioned the pope to allow them to elect their own bishop. The pope agreed, and the clergy voted for Father John Carroll. Baltimore became the first center of the new diocese, and in 1790, John Carroll became the first Catholic bishop of Baltimore.

When Bishop John Carroll accepted this office in 1790, his diocese at the time included the whole of the United States. Thirteen years later, in 1803, President Thomas Jefferson purchased the Louisiana Territory from France and Carroll's diocese doubled in size. Carroll helped to organize the newly purchased western portion of the United States into four dioceses.

American Mentality

Bishop Carroll had developed an American mentality which he wanted to share with newly ordained priests in the United States. He believed strongly that this mentality differed from that of Europe, and he wanted to ordain as many presbyters from the United States as possible. He also wanted to establish schools for the education of Catholic laymen who would have an influence on the development of the United States.

Bishop Carroll established the first seminary at St. Mary's in Baltimore in 1791. Besides providing for this training of clergy from the United States, he wanted clergy from Europe to learn English and to adopt the mentality of the people of the United States. With the influx of Catholics from other countries, he felt a need to recruit presbyters from Europe who could speak the native language of the immigrants. He found himself torn between his desire to help his priests understand this new

government and his need to provide clergy to minister to the daily needs of the large number of immigrants coming into the country.

St. Elizabeth Ann Seton

Bishop Carroll invited religious communities of women to come into the country to educate Catholic students. Within a year after Carroll became bishop, a small group of Carmelite nuns opened a contemplative monastery. A handful of Poor Clare nuns opened a school for girls in Georgetown and were soon replaced at the school by a group of Visitation sisters, allowing the Poor Clares to return to the contemplative life. Bishop Carroll also welcomed into Baltimore a group of nuns from the community founded by Elizabeth Ann Seton (1774–1821).

Elizabeth's father was a devout Anglican doctor who taught anatomy to college students and who remained faithful to Britain during the Revolutionary War. Her mother was an equally devout Anglican. Elizabeth was raised in the Anglican faith.

After Elizabeth married, she devoted her spare time to working with people who were poor, forming the Society for the Poor Widows with Children. She herself became a widow with five young children when she was

The Good Shepherd ought to be the model and 'form' of the bishop's pastoral office. Conscious of his own weaknesses, 'the bishop . . . can have compassion for those who are ignorant and erring. He should not refuse to listen to his subjects whose welfare he promotes as of his very own cildren. . . The faithful . . . should be closely attached to the bishop as the Church is to Jesus Christ, and as Jesus Christ is to the Father'. . .

Catechism of the Catholic Church, # 896

St. Elizabeth Seton

MOTHER SETON EDUCATOR

thirty. At the time of her husband's death, Elizabeth became acquainted with a Catholic Italian family who inspired her so much that she decided to become Catholic. Her family and friends became extremely unhappy with her decision to become a Catholic, but she dedicated herself to her new religion with the same intensity she brought to all her endeavors.

Elizabeth worked with Irish immigrants in a parish in New York until she received an invitation from Bishop Carroll and the rector of St. Mary's Seminary to open a school for girls in Baltimore. During this time, while struggling to care for her children, she also found herself drawn to caring for the poor. In 1809, she and a group of women who worked with her formed the Sisters of Charity of St. Joseph. The community established their center in Emmetsburg, Maryland, where they staffed a school and an orphanage. This was the first community of women religious founded in the United States.

Elizabeth based the rule for her group on that of St. Vincent de Paul and followed his spirit in her care and education of the people who were poor. The work of the Sisters of Charity in teaching in Catholic schools set a pattern for and laid the foundation of the Catholic school system in the United States.

The United States Church and the Pope

Bishop John Carroll recognized that the attitudes toward religious freedom in the United States differed from the attitudes in most countries of Europe. Before he became bishop, he championed those laws which promoted toleration of religion while avoiding the support of any particular denomination. Catholics fought the idea of taxing the people to support religion, because they feared that it would eventually lead to one religious denomination being favored over others.

Carroll's support for the separation of church and state caused some concern in Rome. At the time, the belief in the Vatican was that governments had the obligation to favor the Catholic Church as the one true Church and to tolerate other religions. Carroll recognized that the number of different religious denominations in the United States could not allow such favoritism to exist. This was such a new idea that many officials in the Vatican did not understand it.

Since the clergy had elected him as bishop, Bishop Carroll continued to seek their input when he suggested names for bishops in the United States. He had suggested the formation of four dioceses in the western portion of the United States. Although there would be no election for the bishop of these dioceses, he sent Rome a list of names suggested by the clergy. The pope appointed those Carroll suggested for bishops.

When the Vatican formed the Diocese of New York, the pope did not ask Bishop Carroll to submit the name of a candidate for bishop of this new diocese, but instead named a bishop who had never lived in the United States. Bishop Carroll, at first, was disturbed by this. He felt that bishops from Europe did not understand the mood and mentality of the United States. In time, however, he offered his support to those appointed as bishops by the pope, even when it was done without consultation from the United States.

Congregational Parishes

Because of the limited number of ordained priests in the colonies, Carroll urged a strong role for the laity in the formation of parishes. He encouraged the preparation of laypeople as teachers of religion and as administrators of parishes. The number of parishes multiplied and thrived under the direction of a lay board called **trustees**. This form of parish run by the laity became known as a **congregational parish**.

Although Bishop Carroll never abandoned his support of the congregational parish, he did encounter difficulties. Laypeople often ran these parishes well, teaching religion and caring for the day-to-day needs of the parish. Some parishes, however, became a problem when a board of trustees felt they had a right to refuse a pastor appointed by the bishop, or insisted on choosing the pastor.

The problems with the trustee system became so widespread that every diocese was affected. Along with his fellow bishops, Carroll attempted to end this abuse, but it was destined to plague the Catholic Church in the United States throughout the nineteenth century.

Extending the Frontiers

As the new settlers moved westward, many Catholics were among them. Within a short period of time after Carroll became bishop, almost ten thousand Catholics moved into the area which would become the Diocese of Bardstown, Kentucky. Today, it is the Diocese of Louisville.

Many members of the clergy and religious orders in the western portion of the country spent a large part of their time riding on horseback over dangerous and difficult trails. They were courageous and dedicated men and women who risked their lives and lived in uncomfortable circumstances to spread the faith and minister to Catholic Church members.

The first bishop of Bardstown was Father Benedict Flaget, a dedicated cleric who had already worked in the area before being appointed bishop. Flaget had come from France during the French Revolution. Like other French missionaries, he distrusted the emphasis on freedom in the United States. In his homeland, the revolutionaries were persecuting the Catholic Church in the name of freedom.

Flaget's diocese covered the immense area west of the Alleghenies and east of the Mississippi. Needing more ordained priests to care for his large territory, Bishop Flaget recruited presbyters from France to minister in the United States. Understandably, some of these missionaries had difficulty with the new ideas of government found there.

JOURNAL

As a layperson in the Catholic Church, how do you fulfill your responsibilities? How can you improve?

CLIPBOARD

1. What do you see as the strong and weak points concerning the separation of church and state in our country?

2. What obstacles would someone like Elizabeth Ann Seton encounter today, if she decided to establish a community of women religious in the United States?

3. What are the pros and cons of having the Church elect the bishop? How would this affect the Church today?

S ince, like all the faithful, lay Christians are entrusted by God with the apostolate by virtue of their Baptism and Confirmation, they have the right and duty, individually or grouped in associations, to work so that the divine message of salvation be known and accepted by all men [and women] throughout the earth. This duty is the more pressing when it is only through them that men [and women] can hear the Gospel and know Christ. Their activity in ecclesial communities is so necessary that, for the most part, the apostolate of the pastors cannot be fully effective without it.

Catechism of the Catholic Church, # 900

Pope Pius IX and the Papal States

The Christian Times

Nineteenth Century   **Vol. 19   No. 2**

Vatican Council Ends First Phase

A North American bishop yesterday expressed doubt that another session of the Vatican Council would take place. After the first session of the council, King Victor Emmanuel of Italy seized control of the Papal States. The Pope now lives as a self-proclaimed prisoner of the Vatican.

The situation in Rome is no longer secure enough for a council meeting to be held safely. Although King Victor Emmanuel has published the *Law of Guarantees* to support the pope and to allow him to act freely in Catholic Church matters, the pope refuses to accept this protection from an illegal ruler.

In the first and only session of the Vatican Council, the bishops declared that the pope was infallible in matters of faith and morals. Fifteen years earlier, the pope, acting infallibly, proclaimed that Mary, the mother of Jesus, was free from all the effects of sin from the first moment of her conception. This doctrine is known as the *Immaculate Conception*.

Pope Pius IX has had a stormy reign as pope. Aside from his political problems, the pope is still causing an uproar in the Church after publishing The Syllabus of Errors which seems to condemn everything modern. In the United States, the bishops are not as enthusiastic about

infallibility, as they are about the pope's efforts on behalf of the education of youth.

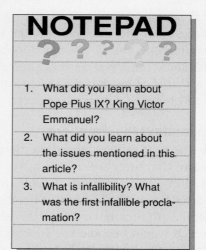

NOTEPAD

? ? ? ? ?

1. What did you learn about Pope Pius IX? King Victor Emmanuel?
2. What did you learn about the issues mentioned in this article?
3. What is infallibility? What was the first infallible proclamation?

The Rest of the Story

As a result of the Enlightenment and French Revolution, many leaders in France also rejected the idea of the separation of church and state as found in the United States. Instead of a separation, they wanted a state without a church. Napoleon, however, was wise enough to realize the importance of supporting the Church in areas where he did not wish to alienate the Catholic population.

Napoleon and the Papal States

During the time Napoleon controlled the Papal States, the people experienced greater peace within the country. Church leaders often lacked the experience to govern the Papal States as they should, when they served in government positions. Mobs roamed the streets at will, harassing and robbing the inhabitants. Church leaders lacked the organizational abilities necessary to patrol the Papal States or to guarantee safety.

Under the French, the conquered people of the Papal States experienced a new sense of pride in their country. The French army easily controlled the roving mobs, and the people experienced a period of peace. After the French returned the Papal States to the Catholic Church, many inhabitants again became unhappy with Church leadership and began to grumble against the Catholic Church. They wanted a new, united and independent Italy, free from the control of Church leaders.

Pope Pius IX (1846–1878)

In 1846, the cardinals elected Pope Pius IX, a pope considered liberal at the time of his election. The new pope immediately attempted to improve the situation in the Papal States. He involved laypeople in governing the Papal States, planned to build a railroad system, and intended to clean and light the streets of Rome.

The people of Italy had already experienced the rewards of having a strong government. At a time when nationalism was becoming dominant throughout Europe, the people of Italy wanted their own united nation. They petitioned the pope to allow them to form a united Italy, but the pope refused to accept their demands. Some of the Italian leaders seized Rome and declared a revolutionary government.

Pope Pius IX felt betrayed by the people he intended to help. When the revolutionaries murdered the pope's prime minister, Pope Pius IX had to flee from Rome in disguise. A short time later, the French armies responded to the pope's plea for help and recaptured Rome from the revolutionaries. A greatly changed and angry Pope Pius IX returned to Rome.

Pope Pius IX realized that the threat to the Papal States still remained. As long as he had the protection of France, he could retain control of the territory. He knew, however, that the French conquest of the Papal States did not dampen the desire for a united Italy. King Victor Emmanuel, the king of Italy, still longed to add the Papal States to his realm.

Loss of the Papal States

When France waged war with Prussia in 1870, it had to pull its soldiers out of the Papal States to protect its own borders. King Emmanuel took advantage of the French withdrawal and marched into Rome, declaring that it and the Papal States now belonged to a united Italy. The pope refused to surrender his claim to Rome and withdrew to the Vatican, declaring that he was now a "Prisoner of the Vatican."

For the next sixty years, until 1929, the popes would consider themselves prisoners of the Vatican. Believing that they were the proper rulers of Rome, they refused to live in the city of Rome as common citizens, subject to Italian law. In 1870, the Italian government passed the Law of Guarantees which gave the pope protection equivalent to that of a king. He was given the position of a ruler and freed from any possibility of arrest.

In the Law of Guarantees, the Italian government kept control of the Vatican, but it allowed the pope to use the papal buildings. The government also granted the pope a stipend of $600,000 a year for Church personnel in the Vatican, a personal military guard, and free communication with foreign bishops and governments. The pope received his own post office and telegraph service. Despite the generous appearance of the offer, Pope Pius IX reminded the Italian leaders that they were not the true rulers of Rome. He believed that he, as a leader of Rome, should have part in the negotiations and not simply accept them from those who had stolen the Papal States from the Catholic Church.

Syllabus of Errors

Because of his perceived mistreatment by those favoring modern thinking, Pope Pius IX distrusted modern thought and developments. He spoke out against several concepts prominent in modern thought, and he issued a document known as the Syllabus of Errors. In this

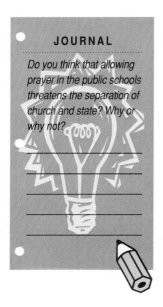

JOURNAL

Do you think that allowing prayer in the public schools threatens the separation of church and state? Why or why not?

L et the message about Christ completely fill your lives, while you use all your wisdom to teach and instruct each other.

Colossians 3:16, CEV

letter, he rejected many modern attitudes and scientific developments.

The Syllabus of Errors rejected attitudes which hurt the family, and it also rejected the separation of church and state and the notion that a pope should seek harmony with modern civilization. The document shocked many Catholics in its stance against progress and modern civilization. The document even listed as errors several concepts that were fully explored in previous documents of popes. A brilliant French bishop, Felix Dupanloup, helped to clarify the intent of the Syllabus of Errors by publishing a commentary on each error and thereby placed the errors in their correct context.

First Vatican Council

Despite political problems, Pope Pius IX continued to act as a spiritual ruler for the Catholic Church. In 1869, Pope Pius IX convened the First Vatican Council. The Catholic Church had not held an ecumenical council since the Council of Trent which began in 1545. Before the council members gathered, bishops and theologians met to discuss the agenda for the council. Due to fighting taking place in Europe, the council lasted less than a year and addressed only a small part of its agenda.

Despite its brevity, the council did define the **infallibility of the pope**. With the approval of the pope, the council decreed that the pope is infallible when he speaks officially as pope on matters of faith and morals. This means that the pope, when he officially declares that he is speaking in his official capacity as pope, cannot teach error in matters of faith and morals.

The teaching on the infallibility of the pope at this time was especially important because of an earlier decision made by Pope Pius IX concerning the **Immaculate Conception of Mary**. In 1854, the pope declared that Mary was conceived with the fullness of grace granted to those who share in the gift of salvation which comes from Christ.

This statement teaches that Mary was free from original sin from the time of her conception. Because she was destined to be the Mother of Jesus Christ, she shared in this great privilege given to her by God. When the pope proclaimed this mystery, he defined it as coming from his position as pope and not as a personal opinion of a theologian. Since it concerned Catholic belief, the Catholic Church accepted it as the first infallible statement of the pope.

Encouragement for the United States

Pope Pius IX encouraged Catholic education of youth at a time when the bishops of the United States were discussing the place of Catholic schools in that country. The bishops recognized that many of the public schools tended to emphasize a Protestant agenda of prayer and Bible reading. The bishops had moved from their support of public education to a strong desire to establish Catholic schools in as many parishes as possible. While the pope condemned the separation of church and state in the United States, he saw the need for a separate school system in a country where the public schools did not really reflect the separation of church and state.

The Catholic school system became a major vehicle for supporting the faith of the immigrants. At first, many of the bishops had doubts about establishing Catholic schools, fearing that such schools would deprive the family of the right to offer religious education to their own children. With the Protestant influence being felt in the public schools, however, the bishops ordered pastors to establish Catholic schools and obliged parents to send their children to these schools where they were available.

Many Catholic schools served the needs of people who were poor, especially among new immigrants. A number of religious communities of women served in these schools. Some of these religious communities had deep roots in Europe, while others were new manifestations of ministry and service in the New World. The dedication of the nuns throughout the nineteenth and twentieth centuries had a major impact on Catholic life in the United States.

JOURNAL

What is your opinion of the bishops obliging Catholic parents to send their children to Catholic schools? Support your opinion.

CLIPBOARD

1. Why is it necessary for the Catholic Church to adapt itself to the modern world? In adapting itself what does it gain? What does it lose?
2. What is your understanding of the teaching about the infallibility of the pope, and do you think it helps or hinders the Church's relationship with other denominations? Explain.
3. How have Catholic schools helped to develop a strong Catholic laity?

A New Image of the Pope

The Christian Times

Nineteenth Century Vol. 19 No. 2

Pope Lifts Ban on Knights of Labor

Pope Leo XIII, at the request of Cardinal Gibbons of New York, has lifted the ban on the Knights of Labor, a union which he condemned a little more than a year ago.

In a recent interview, Gibbons said he felt confident that the pope, who had written a letter on the rights of laborers, would support Gibbon's request. With the immigration of the Irish, German, Italian, French, Mexican, and other laborers into the United States, Gibbons believes that labor needs the support of the Catholic Church.

Rumor has it that the pope is planning a letter to Gibbons concerning the heresy of Americanism. The letter implies that Americans are attempting to establish their own national Church, a charge Gibbons denies. He says that he has no knowledge of any heresy called Americanism in America.

America has generally approved the decisions of Pope Leo XIII. He has written letters supporting the study of Scripture and of the theology of St. Thomas Aquinas and has opened the Vatican archives to historians. Unlike his predecessor, Pope Pius IX, Pope Leo XIII seems to be more open to the modern world.

NOTEPAD

1. What did you learn about Pope Leo XIII? Cardinal Gibbons?
2. What did you learn about the issues mentioned in this article?
3. According to this article, how did the Catholic Church become involved in the labor movement?

The Rest of the Story

With the loss of authority over Rome and the trappings of a temporal ruler, Pope Pius IX feared that he would also lose spiritual prestige in the world. In reality, the opposite was true. Freed from the need to be a political ruler, the pope could now dedicate himself to serving the spiritual needs of the people and could challenge governments to fulfill their leadership roles.

Pope Leo XIII (1878–1903)

When Pope Pius IX died, the cardinals elected a sixty-seven year old cardinal who took the name, Pope Leo XIII. Despite his fragile appearance, Pope Leo XIII served twenty-five years as pope and changed the attitude of the world toward the papacy. When he died, Catholics and members of many other faiths paused to pay their respects to this great man.

Pope Leo XIII had a long diplomatic career. He had been governor of the Papal States, proved his skills as an administrator, went as a papal delegate on delicate missions, and served as a bishop of a large diocese. His experience as a delegate of the pope enabled him to recognize that the Catholic Church must adapt itself to the developing society.

Like previous popes, Pope Leo thought that separation of church and state was a sign of a godless nation. Christianity, he believed, needed support from the state to fulfill its call to bring Christ into the world. He believed that the Catholic Church was the spiritual hope for the world.

Germany and Pope Leo XIII

In 1871, the German leader, Bismarck, began his battle for cultural control in Germany by attempting to weaken the control of the Catholic Church in the country. He began by placing the Church and the clergy under strict government control. The clergy had to attend government schools and were forced to serve in the military. Members of religious orders were exiled, and a number of the clergy faced imprisonment and exile.

By 1878, Bismarck realized that the Catholic population had not weakened under the government's many laws against its leaders. The general population had grown tired of Bismarck's laws, and he badly needed the support of the people against a socialist group gaining power in Germany. He looked for an opportunity to gracefully end his battle for culture, and the election of Pope Leo XIII provided him with that opportunity.

Shortly after his election as pope, Leo sent a letter to Bismarck encouraging an end to the religious persecution in Germany. Bismarck entered into negotiations with the pope's delegate. While Bismarck conceded on many points, the pope refused to compromise the role of the Catholic Church in Germany. Finally, in 1887, Bismarck officially ended the battle for the culture in Germany and praised the pope. Pope Leo gracefully avoided any act which would humiliate Bismarck.

Italy and Leo XIII

In his dealings with Italy, Leo adopted a more stubborn attitude than he did with Germany. Like his predecessor, Pope Pius IX, Leo saw the capture of the Papal States by Italy as a form of robbery, and he refused to condone it. He rejected the Act of Guarantees offered by the Italian government, and retaliated by condemning the government. He directed Italian Catholics to boycott national elections, which he viewed as invalid.

Officials of the Italian government attacked the new pope almost from the beginning. They hurled insults at him, kept Catholics from celebrating his election, sponsored anti-Catholic rallies and mobs, and harassed the pope to such a degree that he actually began to make plans to flee from the Vatican to Austria. The government seized Church property, forbade religious teachings in the schools, blocked appointments of bishops, and forced the clergy to serve in the military.

Both Pope Leo and the officials of the Italian government believed that the pope's spiritual power hinged on his temporal power. Since the time of Constantine, the Church had been accepted as a political power with a spiritual message. Pope Leo XIII believed that he had to fight for temporal power in order to maintain his spiritual influence in the world.

Only in time would the world recognize that the Catholic Church would have a greater influence in the world when it shed itself of political power. In the meanwhile, Pope Leo continued to view himself as a prisoner of the Vatican and to send out his messages to the world through his delegates.

Rejection of Communism

When Pope Leo XIII became pope, several modern movements were influencing people throughout the world. The Industrial Revolution, which drew people from the farms into cities and factories, set the working class against the factory owners. Although Leo supported the needs of the working class, he rejected communism as a solution.

Karl Marx presented the basic concepts of communism when he stressed that the class distinctions between laborers and capitalists would eventually cause a revolution. Such a revolution on the part of the working class would lead to all property being held in common. This in turn would lead to a classless and cooperative society with mate-

rial prosperity for all. Marx denied the existence of God and accused the Churches of using superstition to control the minds of people and make them submissive.

Pope Leo rejected Marxist atheism and materialism and refused to accept violence as a means of solving the problems between labor and management. He believed that communism deprived human beings of their basic rights.

Scholarship

Besides communism, other scientific theories arose to challenge Church teachings. Darwin's theory of evolution seemed to oppose the Genesis Creation Story. Pope Leo wisely approached these new ideas with an educated clergy and Catholic leadership.

Pope Leo wrote that Christians could find truth in religion and in nature, and he urged Scripture scholars to continue their research of the Scriptures. He recognized the need to establish in the Catholic Church a more scholarly understanding of Scripture and nature. He established the **Biblical Commission for the Catholic Church** to study the Scriptures and to address these new scientific discoveries.

The Pope also called for a renewed investigation of the writings of St. Thomas Aquinas. He stated that he found in St. Thomas the best systematic treatment of theology and ordered that seminarians and clergy study his works. Pope Leo helped to establish the special graduate school of Thomistic philosophy at the University of Louvain in Belgium.

Leo XIII also saw the value of the study of history. Before Leo XIII, historians had difficulty getting permission to go through the many documents found in the Vatican Archives. Leo opened the Vatican Archives to students of history. The Vatican Archives contain the valuable documents of popes from the early Middle Ages to modern times. Leo urged students not to fear approaching

KEY TERMS

Biblical Commission for the Catholic Church: established by Pope Leo XIII in an attempt to give the Catholic Church a better understanding of the relationship between Scripture and science.

their studies with truth and balance. He knew that the history of the Church could open up important insights into its saints and sinners.

The Industrial Revolution

By the middle of the 1800s, Pope Leo XIII recognized that a new and bloodless kind of revolution dominated the scene throughout Europe. The revolution was the Industrial Revolution. Large factories had appeared and changed the way of life for a multitude of people who now worked in factories instead of on farms. They no longer sold goods, food, or homemade items, but they now sold their time and labor. Leo addressed the social problems accompanying this new revolution.

Wherever Leo looked, he found people who were oppressed and living in poverty. Despite the wealth of many factory owners, the neighborhoods surrounding the factories were rat-infested slums. Since there were no controls on the wealthy factory owners, women and children joined the men in working the entire week, under horrible conditions and for long hours. Leo realized that workers often received very little pay for their labor, and he sought ways to remedy these injustices.

Leo realized that socialism was gaining too much attention in some areas and rejected this proposal as a false and godless solution to the workers' plight. Socialism proposed a society deprived of personal ownership, in which everyone works for the state. The *Communist Manifesto*, written by Karl Marx, was already beginning to influence the thoughts of strong leaders. Leo recognized the potential for misuse and for a loss of human dignity in such a movement.

Leo's response to the plight of the working people has become the best known work of his time as pope. He brought the power of the Catholic Church to the support of the working class when he wrote his famous encyclical letter, "On the Condition of Labor." He supported the rights of workers to a just wage, the duty of the state in protecting the right of the worker to just treatment, and the value of labor unions.

Many leaders denied that a problem even existed. Catholic laborers greeted the encyclical with joy, but there were reports of wealthy factory owners walking out of churches when the encyclical was read from the pulpit. The letter became the foundation for a number of social justice letters written by later popes.

Americanism

During the time of Pope Leo XIII, a movement in the United States was proposing creative ideas for the Catholic Church in that country. The Americanists wanted to fashion a Catholic Church which incorporated American ideals into its daily life. These ideals included the separation of church and state, the acceptance of a country in which a number of religious beliefs thrived, and a desire for some democratic ideals in Catholic Church appointments and activities.

Despite the Constitution of the United States, there were still some people in the United States, several bishops among them, who rejected the separation of church and state. They believed that a country had an obligation to favor the truth, under which they included the true Catholic faith. A country in which many religious denominations flourished side by side was a new concept for the churches in Europe.

Americanist bishops, such as Bishop Gibbons and Bishop Ireland declared their loyalty to the pope, but they also defended individual conscience. They were not rejecting unity with the pope or the Catholic Church throughout the world, but they wanted a Catholic Church in America which would support and promote freedom and justice as seen in the Constitution.

At this time, a biography of Isaac Thomas Hecker, founder of the Paulist Fathers, came off the press. The book caused no great stir in America, but when a French author translated it into French and wrote an introduction to it, the book caused a furor in France. Some French theologians misunderstood the book and thought the Americanists were proposing American ideals for all of Europe. They called the "heresy" **Americanism**.

These French theologians accused the Americanists of denying the importance of prayer, having little regard for the spiritual life, and proposing a change in the structures of the Catholic Church. They urged Pope Leo XIII to condemn the United States bishops for these views, but the pope chose to write a letter to the bishops of the United States in which he discussed true and false Americanism. When the bishops received the letter, they assured the pope that Americanism as he saw it did not exist in the United States.

Many historians consider Americanism a phantom heresy and believe that it never really existed. Unfortunately, because of a false interpretation of the book about Isaac Hecker translated in French, the pope and others believed that it did exist. Some Americanist ideas were close to those pointed out by the French theologians, but the Americanists insisted that they believed strongly in the need for prayer, spirituality, and unity with the pope.

Although Americanism did not exist in the United States as described by Pope Leo, the letter to the American bishops led them to be more cautious in their statements concerning the adaptation of Catholicism to the United States. In their desire to be loyal to the pope, bishops and other clergy shied away from discussing new ideas arising from the American experience.

The Immigrant Church

Among immigrants, the Irish stand out as the earliest and largest group of immigrants to come to the United States. By the time of the Revolutionary War, there was already a considerable number of Irish settlers in the country. Many more emigrated to the United States when the potato famine hit in Ireland in the late 1840s. Those who came before the potato famine were predominantly Protestant.

The potato famine brought almost a million Irish immigrants to the shores of the United States within a six year period. Within a hundred years, over four million Irish had migrated to America. The Irish immigration at the time of the potato famine and the years following it was largely Catholic.

The increased immigration of Catholics from other nations in Europe rapidly swelled the number of Catholics in the United States. The major immigration of Germans into the United States began shortly after the middle of the 1800s. By the end of the century, out of the approximately five and a half million Germans who had migrated to the United States, more than a million and a half were Catholic.

During the last two decades of the nineteenth century, almost a million Italians, most of them Catholic, migrated to the United States. Polish immigrants did not come into the United States in large numbers until the last quarter of the nineteenth century. However, by the early part of the twentieth century, over a million Polish immigrants had come to the United States.

French Canadians accounted for an immigration of approximately a million people at about the same time as the Polish immigration. In the Southwest, a large number of immigrants came into the United States from Mexico. With the conquest of New Mexico by the United

JOURNAL

To what extent do you think that the Catholic Church should be involved in social issues? Support your answer.

KEY TERMS

Americanism: a phantom heresy resulting from the false interpretation of the French translation of the biography of Isaac Hecker.

In the Spotlight

Isaac Thomas Hecker (1819–1888), an American Catholic evangelist and founder of the Paulist Fathers, was born in New York City to John Hecker and Caroline Friend.

In the summer of 1842 Hecker became troubled by a private mystical experience and under the direction of Orestes Brownson, a frequent houseguest, he joined the Brook Farm Community in West Roxbury, Massachussetts. It was there where he fell under the influence of George Ripley and Ralph Waldo Emmerson.

Initially attracted to the Episcopal Church, Hecker was baptized a Roman Catholic in August of 1844 by Bishop John McCloskey. His conversion to the Catholic faith ended his spiritual disorientation and marked the beginning of his lifelong goal of converting the Protestants of America.

Shortly after his conversion, Hecker joined the Redemptorist Order, from which he was sent to Belgium for studies. In October of 1849 he was ordained a priest by Cardinal Nicholas Wiseman in London, England. After becoming ordained he returned to the states and joined some fellow Redemptorists in forming an English language mission band. With this band, Hecker preached in Catholic churches throughout the east coast of the United States. A growing dispute over the nature of their missionary work, however, led them to eventually disband.

In July of 1858, Hecker received permission from Pope Pius IX and Archbishop Hughes to found the Paulist Fathers in New York City. As a leader of a new religious community, he was now free to develop an evangelical outreach to non-Catholic America, which he touched upon in his works, *Questions of the Soul* (1855) and *Aspirations of Nature* (1857).

Hecker believed that if he could present the case for Roman Catholicism in a nondefensive manner and in an open forum of public inquiry, those not of the Catholic faith would seriously consider his arguments and join him as a Catholic. In April of 1865, he began *The Catholic World*, a monthly journal that sought to demonstrate the compatibility of Catholic thought with American culture. In 1866, he founded the Catholic Publication Society that would eventually become the Paulist Press. Hecker was also able to raise funds in 1872 to purchase a New York newspaper, which he transformed into a national Catholic daily. Increasing health problems, however, prevented him from completing the project.

Despite his poor health, he was able to continue editing the *The Catholic World*, and in his latter years he enthusiastically supported the idea of a national Catholic university. The Catholic University opened a year after his death.

States during the Mexican-American war, a large number of resident Mexicans became part of the United States.

As a result of this dramatic increase in the Catholic population, the Catholic Church moved from a minority religion at the time of the Revolutionary War to the dominant religion in the United States. Despite the increase in the numbers, Catholics still experienced discrimination in many parts of the country. Some prejudice came from an unfounded fear that the Catholic Church intended to control the country. Bigotry against Catholics continued until the middle of the twentieth century.

Labor in America

When Pope Leo XIII wrote his letter "On the Condition of Workers," most leaders of the Catholic Church in the United States received it with delight.

Since most of the immigrants were laborers who were easily exploited, strong labor unions became a necessity. Without them, most laborers were powerless against rich owners who made them work long hours under inhuman conditions for a small wage.

One union, the Knights of Labor, welcomed every labor group into its union. At first, a religious oath was part of their initiation, but they did away with the oath to make the union more acceptable to the Catholic clergy who sometimes preached against it. Some clergy were uncomfortable with the secrecy of the union, and disturbed by union wars.

It were these concerns that led a bishop in Quebec to convince the pope to forbid Catholics from belonging to the Knights of Labor. Cardinal Gibbons of the United States then begged the pope to reconsider his ban. Gibbons warned that the ban would turn labor and public opinion against the Catholic Church. Gibbons firmly believed that working people had a right to join unions.

More than a year later, Gibbons received word from the Vatican that the ban against the Knights of Labor had been lifted. Catholics could now join the union. The only condition was that the union remove from its constitution any hint of support for socialism or communism. Laborers in the United States saw the lifting of the ban as a victory for labor.

CLIPBOARD

1. Do you think that the Catholic Church should have gotten involved in the Labor Union issues? Support your answer.

2. What are some characteristics of the Catholic Church in the United States today? How does the Catholic Church in the United States differ from what you know of the Catholic Church elsewhere in the world?

3. Do you think that Catholics should take adult or college courses on Scripture or theology, as Pope Leo XIII wanted? Explain.

REVIEWING THE ERA

• **1776**

CHARLES CARROLL. This Catholic was one of the signers of the Declaration of Independence, in 1776.

BISHOP JOHN CARROLL. This former Jesuit served as superior of the clergy for several years, before becoming the first bishop in the United States in 1790.

ST. ELIZABETH ANN SETON. This widow with five children founded the Sisters of Charity to serve the poor and to teach. She helped to establish the first Catholic schools in the United States.

BISHOP BENEDICT FLAGET. Flaget was the first bishop of the Diocese of Bardstown, Kentucky, which later became the Diocese of Louisville. He recruited French clergymen for the missions in the western part of the United States.

• **1845**

POPE PIUS IX. Pius IX was pope when Italy seized the Papal States. By his own choice, he became a prisoner of the Vatican. He wrote the Syllabus of Errors, supported Catholic education, and convened the First Vatican Council.

• **1875**

POPE LEO XIII. Leo wrote encyclicals on labor, Scripture studies, and the theology of St. Thomas. He spoke out against communism and the "phantom heresy" of Americanism.

CARDINAL GIBBONS. Bishop Gibbons of Baltimore persuaded the pope to lift his ban on the Knights of Labor.

KEY TERMS

Trustees

Congregational parish

Infallibility of the pope

Immaculate Conception of Mary

Biblical Commission for the Catholic Church

Americanism

 A Voice from the Past

This week you are going to tell your readers what effect the separation of church and state had upon the Catholic Church. Discuss how the Catholic Church in the United States was viewed by the rest of the world. Use your key terms to explain the various struggles and challenges that the Catholic Church in the United States faced. Be sure to show your readers how such issues as the labor conditions and unions were addressed by the Catholic Church. Close your article with a discussion of the role of the Catholic Church in social issues. Explore the responsibilities of the Church concerning social issues, as well as the extent to which these responsibilities should be taken.

Then and Now

The separation of church and state as found in the United States Constitution was new in a world where religion and government were closely linked. Pope Pius IX condemned many modern innovations in his Syllabus of Errors. He also convened the First Vatican Council which defined the infallibility of the pope. Pope Leo XIII helped labor by asserting that laborers had a right to join a union. He condemned communism.

Today, the separation of church and state is a part of Catholic Church teaching. The Catholic Church continues to adapt itself to the modern world while remaining true to its traditions, and it continues to reject communism and to defend the rights of individuals.

NEWS IN REVIEW

1. Why did some Catholic Church leaders in Rome have a problem with the separation of church and state as found in the Constitution of the United States?

2. Why was Father John Carroll a good choice as the first bishop of the United States?

3. What problems did Bishop John Carroll face in his ministry in the United States?

4. What is trusteeism, and why was it a problem?

5. How did Pope Pius IX lose the Papal States?

6. What were some accomplishments of Pope Pius IX?

7. What were the accomplishments of Pope Leo XIII?

8. What was the problem with Americanism, from the point of view of Catholic Church leaders in Rome?

9. How did Elizabeth Ann Seton help shape the history of Catholic education?

10. Why do we call the Catholic Church in the United States an immigrant Church?

chapter fifteen

The Church in the Modern Age

If we were laborers at the end of the nineteenth century, we would find ourselves challenged to join unions. The encyclical of Pope Leo XIII on unions would tell us that we could belong to a union and still remain faithful to our call as Catholics. For many of us, this would be a welcomed and new idea.

As Catholics, we would take pride in our popes whom we believed to be spiritual leaders. Most of us would have forgotten that the popes were once temporal leaders who ruled the Papal States.

The wars of the past are a constant reminder of the Church's responsibility to work for peace.

The Modern Era

The Christian Times

Twentieth Century   Vol. 20 No. 1

Bishops Publish Letter on the Social Order

Early this week, the Catholic bishops of the United States published *The Bishops' Program of Social Reconstruction*. In it, the United States Catholic bishops support the rights of workers and a number of other rights.

An unidentified spokesman for the bishops informs us that the document on social reconstruction is largely the work of Father John Ryan, who is already well known for his support of the working class.

Father Ryan seems to have no fear of new ideas in this age when many scholars have been condemned as modernists. Modernism had been defined as the misuse of modern develop-

ments in the field of theology. Since the previous pope, Pius X, has condemned Modernism, many groups within the Catholic Church have used the condemnation to silence every modern theologian, even those faithful to the Catholic Church and its teachings.

Father Ryan has commented that the present pope, Benedict XV, and Pope Pius X have not written any social justice encyclicals. Ryan noted that Pope Pius X emphasized several spiritual aspects of the Church, such as frequent reception of communion and reception of communion by children. Benedict XV, he said, is

attempting to bring greater peace to the world after the First World War.

NOTEPAD
? ? ? ? ?

1. What did you learn about Benedict XV? Father John Ryan? Pius X?

2. What did you learn about some of the issues mentioned in this article?

3. According to this article, what is so controversial about Modernism?

The Rest of the Story

With the support given to research in theology and Scripture by Leo XIII, a new age dawned in Catholic studies. Theologians began to adapt the discover-

ies of the modern age to theology. This adaptation, however, created tensions in the Catholic Church which exist to our present day.

Pope Pius X and Modernism

When the cardinals met to elect the successor of Pope Leo XIII, they cast their votes for a pastoral, saintly, and well-loved cardinal who chose the name, Pope Pius X. He chose as the motto of his pontificate, "To restore all things in Christ."

In his office, Pope Pius X felt compelled to confront the influence of the

modern world on the Catholic Church. Some scholars departed from the tradition of the Catholic Church and presented new messages which conflicted with Catholic Church teaching. To combat the rejection of prior Catholic Church doctrine in the name of modern developments, the pope issued an encyclical which attacked Modernism.

Effects of the Condemnation of Modernism

In his encyclical, the pope condemned modern errors in such general terms that it was difficult to separate people who were not Modernists from those who were. Since they were not a single, organized group, modernist theologians did not always agree with each other. Pope Pius X's condemnation provided the perfect weapon for those who opposed modern research. These critics applied the pope's condemnation to every modern theologian, even those who remained faithful to Catholic Church doctrine.

Catholics in the United States deeply felt the impact of Pope Pius X's condemnation against Modernism. Many Catholic leaders, among them bishops, felt it was important to adapt Catholicism to the culture of this growing country. Their opponents immediately branded them as Modernists and accused them of heresy. Although a number of theologians and Catholic leaders were presenting teachings which would eventually be accepted by the Catholic Church leaders, they ceased speaking of adapting Catholicism to the United States scene and retreated into a safe silence.

Seminaries in the United States lost some of their best teachers. Very few theologians dared to propose any new applications of the Christian message. Between the "phantom heresy" of Americanism and the condemnation of Modernism, the intellectual life of the Catholic Church in the United States eroded. The shadow cast by the pope's condemnation affected the Catholic Church for decades to come.

The Pope of the Eucharist

Pope Pius X became known as the "Pope of the Eucharist." When he became pope, many Catholics held the Eucharist in such high esteem that they felt more comfortable with worshipping the Eucharist than than they did with receiving it in Communion. Pope Pius X sought to correct the thinking which kept Catholics from sharing in Communion on a regular basis.

The pope changed the age of when children were first allowed to receive the Eucharist from eleven to the **age of discretion**. He taught that the age of discretion exists when a child knows the difference between ordinary bread and the Eucharist. Most interpret the age of discretion to be seven years of age. The pope also urged all Catholics to share in Communion frequently, not just once a year, as was the custom.

Institutional Reform

Pope Pius X brought about many changes in the organization of the Catholic Church. He reorganized the offices which assist the pope, known as the **Curia**. He ordered the cardinals to keep secret the proceedings of the election of a new pope. At the election of Pope Pius X, the largest number of cardinals were Italians. After his election, the pope added cardinals from other countries, balancing the number of cardinals outside of Italy with the number of Italian cardinals.

Pope Pius X also recognized the need to revise the code of law for the Church. Over the centuries, popes made a number of decrees which Catholics could learn about only by searching the letters of the popes. Previous popes, unaware of some earlier decrees, sometimes repeated a decree or even contradicted it.

Pope Pius X established a commission to perform the overwhelming task of researching and finding all previous decrees and listing them together in a code of law. When Pope Pius X died in 1914, the commission was still working on the code. Under the direction of the next pope, the commission continued its work, and Pope Benedict XV finally promulgated the **Code of Canon Law** in 1917.

Pope Benedict XV

Pope Benedict, elected shortly after the First World War began, dedicated a major portion of his time as pope to

JOURNAL

How did the Catholic Church's involvement in World War I compare to that of the Persian Gulf War? What do you think the Catholic Church's involvement should be in the event of war? Support your answer.

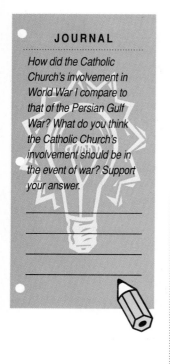

solving the problems brought on by the war. Since Catholics fought on both sides of the war, the pope refused to favor one side over the other. The fact that both sides accused him of supporting their enemies shows that he offered help to both sides.

Instead of accepting the neutrality of Pope Benedict XV, many people believed his unwillingness to take sides was a sign of weakness. At the end of the war, however, the people reevaluated the pope's stance and recognized the value of his neutrality during the war.

Pope Benedict established an office in the Vatican to arrange for the exchange of prisoners and innocent victims of war. He depleted the Vatican's treasury in order to provide food and medical supplies to suffering men and women on both sides of the conflict. He organized a system for discovering the names of prisoners and informing their relatives that they were alive.

Benedict XV continually worked for peace in this conflict which took millions of lives. In 1917, he offered a proposal for peace, but none of the countries involved in the fighting responded. In 1917, the United States entered the war, and in 1918, the war ended. At the end of the war, the pope pleaded for countries to work for justice. He feared that a country such as Germany would face such humiliation that the situation would eventually lead to another war. This fear proved to be prophetic.

The pope was not invited to participate in the negotiations which led to the end of the war. This rejection apparently originated with the leaders in Italy who feared that the pope would demand the return of the Papal States during the peace negotiations. The pope asked Catholics to pray for a stable and lasting peace, recognizing that the peace treaty would not easily erase the hatred generated by the war.

The United States Church and Reconstruction

During the war, the United States bishops banded together in 1917 to form the National Catholic War Council. Through this council, the bishops dedicated themselves to the American principles of peace by supporting the war effort and the President, as well as, Catholics at home and abroad touched by the war.

After the war ended, several groups suggested plans for a post-war reconstruction of life in the United States. In the early part of 1919, the United States bishops published a document, written primarily by Father John Ryan, a brilliant spokesperson on justice issues. Catholics and Protestants alike praised the document as one of the most forward-looking documents of the era on social justice.

Father John Ryan was well-suited to expound on the social message of his day. He wrote his first book on the religious obligation to pay a living, minimum wage to workers, and soon became famous for his stand on important social issues in the United States. He supported the rights of people who were poor and challenged Church leaders to become involved in social issues. The bishops' document on social reconstruction originated as a speech Ryan intended to deliver at an important conference.

In publishing this speech as a letter of the bishops' National War Council, the United States bishops were asserting their support for the sentiments contained in Ryan's speech. Among their numerous social directives, the bishops proposed a minimum working age with minimum wage limits, laws protecting the rights of laborers to unionize, provision for public housing, insurance for the protection of people who were elderly, sick, and unemployed, and the right for labor to gain some ownership in the companies in which they worked.

Anti-Catholic Mood in America

Despite the support the United States bishops offered in the areas of reconstruction and social issues, many people were still openly hostile to Catholics. The overwhelming immigration of Catholics was a concern to those who feared that the Catholic Church intended to take control of the country. Many Catholic leaders, including the bishops, took every opportunity they could to prove their patriotism and support of the United States Constitution.

The Ku Klux Klan movement sought to protect the country from Catholics, Jews, and Blacks. The Klan was powerful in the southern and midwestern portions of the United States. Klan members burned crosses, tarred and feathered some of the targets of their bigotry, and on some occasions murdered their victims. They kept their identity hidden by wearing white hoods over their heads.

In 1928, the Democratic party nominated a Catholic, Alfred E. Smith, as their candidate for president of the United States. Although some people objected to his political views, most of the attacks he endured during his campaign were due to his Catholicism.

The Ku Klux Klan, which had grown to approximately four million members, strongly denounced this or any Catholic candidate for President. Fundamentalist Protestant groups often joined in the attack against Smith, claiming that a Catholic president would turn the country over to the pope. Smith defended himself against the anti-Catholic bigotry, but he lost his bid for the presidency to Herbert Hoover.

Such discrimination against Catholics must be balanced, however, with the support from a number of Protestant groups for Catholics as rightful citizens of the country. Catholics were gradually becoming part of the mainstream in the United States. When the Great Depression struck in 1929, Catholics suffered along with the rest of the nation. Twenty-five percent of the work force had no work and no income, and they had to depend on each other for survival. Religious differences seemed to be a petty reason for divisions.

Let peace and justice rule every mountain and every hill. Let the king defend the poor, rescue the homeless, and crush everyone who hurts them.

Psalms 72:3–4, NRSV

JOURNAL

Why do you think the members of the Ku Klux Klan wanted to keep their identity hidden? How is bigotry hidden today? What do you think is the motivating factor behind prejudice and bigotry? How can this motivating factor best be addressed?

_____

_____

_____

CLIPBOARD

1. Do you think that the Catholic Church today is too modern or not modern enough? What could be done to help Catholics face the modern world while remaining faithful to the teaching of Christ?

2. How important do you think it is for the Catholic Church to speak out on and be involved in social issues?

3. Do you think that there is any discrimination against Catholics today in the U.S.? Do you think that Catholics discriminate against any others groups? If so, which groups?

The Shadow of War

The Christian Times

Twentieth Century   Vol. 20   No. 2

Pope Pius XII Appears Weary

An ailing Pope Pius XII looked weary as he blessed the faithful yesterday afternoon. One of his aides reminded us that the pope had long been agonizing over the Second World War. Now, with the war over, he has a great concern for the people facing the further misfortunes of the post-war period.

One correspondent felt that Pope Pius XII must envy Pope Pius XI who served between the two World Wars. Free from the concerns of war, Pope Pius XI was able to negotiate with the government of Italy. In exchange for giving up the Church's right to the Papal States, he received the right to have the Vatican recog-

nized as an independent state.

Pope Pius XII has not had the occasion to publish a new social justice encyclical as Pope Leo XIII and Pope Pius XI did. Pope Pius XI celebrated the fortieth anniversary of Pope Leo XIII's letter on the condition of labor by writing another letter in support of labor. Pope Pius XI's letter on workers received enthusiastic support from the U.S. social activist, Father John Ryan.

Pope Pius XI wrote letters condemning Mussolini, Hitler, and communism. He is better known, however, as the "Pope of Catholic Action" for his encyclical on the role of the laity in the apostolate of the hierarchy. In his efforts to build

up the Catholic Church after the war, Pope Pius XII published encyclicals on the spirituality of the Church, the liturgy, and Scripture.

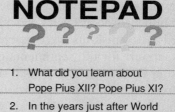

NOTEPAD
? ? ? ? ?

1. What did you learn about Pope Pius XII? Pope Pius XI?

2. In the years just after World War II, what seem to be the major issues facing the Catholic Church?

3. How did Pope Pius XII try to build up the Catholic Church after the war?

The Rest of the Story

The popes continued to live as prisoners of the Vatican, although they no longer stressed this fact. As time passed, the popes were growing to ap-

preciate this freedom from temporal concerns. Ironically, the lack of temporal power gave the popes a more influential moral voice in time of war.

Pope Pius XI and the Papal States

In 1922, under the leadership of Bonito Mussolini who became prime minister, Italy became a **totalitarian state**. A totalitarian state is a state in which only one political party exists. This type of state maintains its position by force. The citizens of the totalitarian state exist only for the state. When Mussolini began his bid to take control of Italy, the Catholic bishops of Italy initially sup-

ported him because of his promises concerning Church welfare, but they turned against him when he began to pass laws interfering with Catholic Church matters.

In 1929, after years of intense negotiation, Pope Pius XI signed a treaty with Mussolini. In the treaty, known as the Lateran Treaty, the Italian government recognized Vatican City as a completely independent state with the pope as its ruler or head of government. Italy also paid the Catholic Church the funds owed since the passage of the Laws of Guarantees (a document the Church had not accepted prior to this agreement). Italy also paid the Catholic Church for Church property seized illegally.

In the treaty, the pope agreed not to call upon any powerful countries to help regain lost land. In a concordat attached to the treaty, the Italian government agreed to give the Catholic Church a privileged position in Italy. The settling of the question of the Papal States stands out as a major work of the pontificate of Pope Pius XI. In 1929, the pope ceased being a prisoner of the Vatican.

The Pope and National Movements

In 1933, another totalitarian government arose in Germany under Hitler and the Nazis. Hitler fanatically believed that the German race was superior to all others and should rule the world. His leadership policies, and aggression led to the Second World War, the loss of millions of lives, the systematic extermination of six million Jews in concentration camps, and a devastated Europe.

Related to his rejection of totalitarianism, Pope Pius XI denounced atheistic communism in a letter to the world. In 1917, Russia had become a communist country in which the communist party ruled in the name of the workers, but usually for its own ends. Pope Pius XI condemned communism for its denial of God, its acceptance of materialism, and its advocacy of class struggle. He accused communists of denying the rights, dignity, and freedom of the human person.

Yet another form of totalitarianism became dominant in Spain, but the Pope did not speak out against it. In 1937, the forces of General Francisco Franco successfully overpowered and brutally punished a revolutionary force which had controlled the nation. The anticlerical revolutionary force had controlled the nation for six years, seized Church property, killed a number of the clergy and nuns,

and attempted to purge Catholicism from the nation. After his victory, in contrast, Franco offered a privileged status to the Catholic Church. Thus, it was difficult for the pope to take a stand against Franco, despite his totalitarian methods.

Social Teaching

Pope Pius XI has received the title of "Pope of Catholic Action" because he emphasized the need for lay involvement in the mission of the Catholic Church. He did not see Catholic action as a call which came directly to the laity through their baptism (as we do today), but rather as a share in the ministry of the hierarchy. Catholic action groups are not pious societies, but groups which bring the gospel into daily life. These groups remain under the authority of the bishop.

On the fortieth anniversary of the encyclical of Leo XIII on the condition of the working class, Pius XI published an encyclical on social justice. Like the letter of Pope Leo XIII, this encyclical became well-known throughout the world. In his encyclical, Pius XI spoke of the right and duty of the Catholic Church to address social issues. He also addressed the fallacies he found in Communism. The pope also warned of the dangers to be found in too great an emphasis on individual achievements which ignore the community.

According to the encyclical, the right of individuals to own property is protected but the point is made that even private property cannot be used in a manner contrary to the common good. Those who hire workers have rights and obligations, but the workers also have rights and obligations.

Care For the Poor in the United States

In the United States, Father John Ryan, who had written the bishops' letter on social reconstruction, greeted the encyclical of Pope Pius XI on social issues with excitement. He saw in it a much needed support for labor at a time

Social action can assume various concrete forms. It should always have the common good in view and be in conformity with the message of the Gospel and the teaching of the Church. It is the role of the Laity 'to animate temporal realities with Christian commitment, by which they show that they are witnesses and agents of peace and justice.'

Catechism of the Catholic Church, # 2442

In the Spotlight

Catherine de Hueck Doherty was born into a wealthy family in Russia, on the Feast of the Assumption, in 1900. Her father was a Polish Catholic who passed his faith on to Catherine. At the age of fifteen, she married Baron Boris de Hueck. Two years later, after the October revolution of Russia in 1917, Catherine and her husband had lost everything to the revolution. They had to learn to endure the horrors of the Communist persecution, living with the frightening conditions of civil war and the lack of food.

Catherine and her husband later managed to escape from Russia with only the clothes on their back. They lived in povery as they first traveled to England and then, with a baby son, on to Canada. Since the war in Russia had ruined her husband's health, Catherine had to find work wherever she could. Her work as a maid, a laundress, a waitress, and a salesclerk which brought her into contact with the suffering poor. She and her husband moved several times between Canada and New York.

Catherine used her boundless energy and gift for speaking to find work with a speaking bureau, where she quickly moved up to the position of company executive. Her new position brought her out of poverty to the refreshing experience of amassing wealth. While in this position her husband died, and she had to hire someone to care for her son.

In time, Catherine experienced a new restlessness. She questioned why God had saved her from her poverty and suffering in Russia in order to bring her to her place of luxury and wealth in America. Christ's message kept gnawing at her, "Sell all you possess, give it to the poor, and come follow me." The desire to dedicate herself to the needs of the poor haunted her. She spoke to a number of confessors about her obsession, but they reminded her God's will for her was to raise her son.

At one point, she went to the Archbishop of Toronto who heard her story, believed it, and directed her to pray over her vocation for another year. The archbishop felt that this would give her son another year to mature and also allow her to test her call. A year later, she set aside a sum of money for her son's education, sold all she had, and went with her son to live in the slums of Toronto. The pain of the depression was being felt by the people at this time and Catherine wanted to aid them by joining in their plight.

Over a period of time, her energy and dedication drew a number of people who joined in her ministry to the poor. She exuded such a strong concern for the poor, that others were easily touched by it. Some others, however, found her obsession and dedication strange. They misunderstood her and eventually forced her to leave Toronto. Her first *Friendship House* in Toronto was a dismal failure.

Catherine eventually established a house in Harlem and lived in strict poverty. Her energy and spirit of poverty again drew others to join her in her ministry. Her apostolate for the poor and outcast spread from Harlem to other cities such as Chicago, Washington, and Portland. She also encountered people who found her strange. They did not understand her selfless dedication to the poor, and she again found herself and her foundations being rejected.

In 1943, she married Eddie Doherty, a journalist, and together they opened a *Friendship House* in Toronto. The beginnings were difficult and seemingly hopeless. Despite the discouragements of their early beginnings in Toronto, they continued their apostolate, trusting in God's help. Others, including presbyters, came to join in her ministry, and they stayed.

Catherine's apostolate, now called *Madonna House*, developed gradually to the point where almost thirty years later there were one hundred twenty-five full time members which included fourteen ordained priests. *Madonna House* had twelve missions, each serving the communities in a number of ways.

The *Madonna House* is now a spiritual center in which those who dedicate themselves to serving various human needs live as a community. The community at *Madonna House* dedicate themselves to prayer, silence, and love for all who come to them for help.

when most laborers in America were without work and suffering the effects of the Depression. The letter supported the government's right and obligation to help workers, something Ryan felt was badly needed in the U.S.

In 1933, Dorothy Day, a new member of the Catholic Church, and Peter Maurin, started the Catholic Worker Movement and published a newspaper entitled *The Catholic Worker*. The newspaper and work of Dorothy Day and Peter Maurin spread the social gospel in very practical ways, as it fostered religious ideals in action. The group offered community and hospitality to people who were poor as well as to those who cared for the needy and worked for peace.

Within a decade, the Catholic Worker Movement established more than thirty houses and farms of direct assistance, and hospitality. Dorothy Day's work was joined by Catherine de Hueck, a Russian immigrant to Canada. Hueck established Friendship House in Toronto to promote racial justice. Like the Catholic Worker Houses, Friendship Houses also spread throughout the United States, providing refuge and service to people in need. Workers in these houses were taught the social gospels and trained to lobby the government for the needs of people who were poor and oppressed.

Pope Pius XII

When Pius XII became pope in 1939, he directed his energies to the impossible and unsuccessful task of preventing a new world war. When Germany invaded Poland, a new and terrible war began its sweep across Europe, causing a massive loss of life and overwhelming destruction. Italy and Germany battled against France, Great Britain, and the United States.

During the war, Pope Pius XII strove continuously to bring an end to the conflict. Even when battles raged in Italy, he refused to leave the Vatican for safe refuge. He supported efforts to aid the victims of war, especially relief for the people who lost everything in the bombings. The pope established soup kitchens in the Vatican and opened the Vatican lands for refugees from war-torn areas.

Pope Pius XII was concerned not only for the suffering people of the world, but also for the dedicated Catholics who suffered so greatly in totalitarian countries. Where the leaders of totalitarian countries sought to stamp out the power of religion, Catholics and other Christians had to worship in secret. Many religious people faced torture and death for their faith, while those who escaped lived in fear.

In some countries, clergy and ministers were drafted into the military and placed in the front lines to engage the enemy in battle. A number of clergy chose death rather than kill others. Where countries exempted the clergy from military service, many volunteered to serve as chaplains. Thousands of clergy died during the Second World War.

When the war came close to Rome, the pope, as bishop of Rome, pleaded with the warring nations not to bring the war into the city-to no avail. After the bombing raids in Rome, the pope went out into the streets to minister to the wounded, frightened, and dying people. He experienced firsthand the suffering, fear, and loneliness which came with war. Throughout the war, he relentlessly worked for peace, sending delegates to every place possible in an effort to end the war.

Pope Pius XII and the Holocaust

Pope Pius XII willingly accepted criticism for remaining silent during the Holocaust. The Catholic Church in Europe saved approximately 800,000 Jews from death; with a little more than 30,000 who were saved in Rome. But the Pope feared that many more Jews would face death, if he spoke out openly against this great evil.

Rabbis in Rome feared that the Nazi reign of terror against the Jews would become worse if Pius XII spoke against it publicly. They urged the pope to remain silent. When the pope spoke out earlier on Nazi atrocities, the Nazi army reacted by sending more people to the concentration camps. Jewish leaders who knew of the pope's agonizing concern for the Jewish people wrote to him after the war, thanking him for not speaking out, despite the criticism he faced.

United States Catholicism and World War II

The Second World War brought Catholics fully into the mainstream of American life. Catholics joined the military in large numbers, lived and fought closely with Protestants, Jews, and atheists, and gradually found acceptance

JOURNAL

Pope Pius XII chose to remain silent despite criticism and pressure. Describe a time when you were required to make a tough choice that was controversial. How did you handle the criticism and opposition? Would you still make the same choice? Why or why not?

_____

_____

_____

_____

with people who had never before met Catholics. Catholics returning from the war took advantage of educational opportunities open to veterans, and attended college in large numbers.

Following the war, there was a boom in religious vocations. Large numbers of men were ordained, other men became religious brothers, and many women became nuns. Parish schools flourished, with women religious and men religious teaching in every classroom. Many Catholic children were educated in Catholic schools. The Catholic Schools not only provided the children with a sound education which prepared them well for higher education, but they also educated them about their faith.

Post-War Church

After the war, theologians throughout Europe began to investigate the early traditions of the Church more thoroughly. They called for reforms in the liturgy and in Scripture study. Pope Pius XII wrote encyclical letters on the spiritual unity of the Catholic Church and he called people to active participation in the liturgy. He also wrote an encyclical on Scripture study and permitted Scripture scholars to use new methods in their research.

Unknown to most members of the Catholic Church, the work of theologians after the war and the letters of Pope Pius XII were laying the foundation for the Second Vatican Council, a major ecumenical council of the Catholic Church.

CLIPBOARD

1. How has the loss of the Papal States affected the Church today?

2. Do you think Pope Pius XII was right in not speaking out against the killing of millions of Jews by the Nazis?

3. How do Catholics fulfill their social, political, and spiritual roles in the United States today?

The Winds of Change

The Christian Times

Twentieth Century   Vol. 20   No. 3

Pope John Paul II Visits New York

Thousands of people lined the sidewalks of New York as Pope John Paul II rode through the streets waving from a bulletproof "popemobile." Since Pope John XXIII called the bishops of the world together in the Second Vatican Council more than thirty years ago, the popes have traveled extensively. John Paul II has traveled more than any other pope in history.

Pope John XXIII brought a glow to the papacy with his warm smile and gentle nature. In addition to calling for and opening the Second Vatican Council, he also wrote significant encyclicals about social justice issues. Pope Paul VI convoked later sessions of the Second Vatican Council. He too spoke out about his concern for the dignity of all people.

When Pope John Paul II first traveled to the United States, he marveled at the success of the separation of church and state in the country. A Jesuit, Father John Courtney Murray, has had a great influence on a document of the Second Vatican Council which deals with this issue.

NOTEPAD
? ? ? ? ?

1. What did you learn about Pope John XXIII? Pope Paul VI? Pope John Paul II?

2. What did you learn about the issues mentioned in this article?

3. According to the article, how has the papacy responded to social justice issues?

The Rest of the Story

Rapid changes took place in the 1960s, not only in the world, but also in the Catholic Church. During that decade, the Catholic Church went through a dramatic change which is still being felt today.

Pope John XXIII

When Pope Pius XII died in 1958, respect for the role of the pope had risen to new heights among Catholics. Many people wondered whether anyone could replace so holy and skillful a leader. To the surprise of many, the cardinals elected a seventy-seven-year-old cardinal who took the name of John XXIII. Many people suspected that the cardinals were merely electing someone to serve as pope for a few years until they could decide on a better candidate.

Pope John XXIII surprised the world. He served as pope for only five years, but in that short time, he set in motion a chain of events which would change the image and direction of the Catholic Church in the modern world. He set aside much of the pomp surrounding the office of the pope, greeted people simply and with a broad smile, visited prisoners in a Roman jail, and began to address Protestants as "our separated brethren." It is no accident that since his time as pope, Christian Churches are moving closer together rather than farther apart.

John XXIII had many personal and diplomatic skills. He had served as an ambassador of the Catholic Church to many countries during times of crises. Unlike

Pope Pius IX who had a suspicion of anything modern, Pope John XXIII recognized the need to weave the Christian message into the modern world. He believed the message of Christ could speak to every generation. The role of the Church was to apply Jesus' message to changing world conditions.

John XXIII was very concerned about human dignity in every area in the world. He had witnessed a great deal of suffering in his years as a papal ambassador and supported the rights of workers, the dignity of women, the importance of the family, and the rights of nations to live in peace. He spoke out strongly for peace in his encyclical letter, *Peace on Earth*. He condemned racial discrimination and other forms of prejudice and called all people on earth to work for peace.

The Second Vatican Council

After only three months as pope, John XXIII shocked Catholics throughout the world when he announced his intention to convene an ecumenical council. Some critics saw it as a foolish and dangerous venture, too huge in light of the number and differences among bishops throughout the world. Other people greeted the council with joy, viewing it as a chance to draw upon the experiences and learning of the many saintly and learned bishops and theologians throughout the world.

The Second Vatican Council opened on October 11, 1962, in Saint Peter's Basilica in Rome. In his opening address, the pope deplored those "prophets of doom" who saw only darkness in the modern world. He expressed his faith that the modern world would continue to open new avenues of ministry for the Catholic Church. The pope called for a new breath of fresh air in the Catholic Church and unity among all Christian denominations.

The largest council before the Second Vatican Council was the First Vatican Council, with a little more than 730 representatives and few native representatives from mission countries. More than 2,600 bishops participated in the Second Vatican Council. Native representatives from all over the world attended. The council set forth a highly impressive image of the Catholic Church as a true world Church, and it pooled together the attitudes and concerns of people in developed countries with those of less developed countries.

Three years later, in December, 1965, the council came to an end after four sessions and the publication of many significant documents. The theme of Church was central to every document of the council, often with a broader definition of Church, that included more than the Catholic Church. The documents of the council emphasized the Church's place in the modern world and brought many changes into the daily life and worship of Catholics.

Pope Paul VI

Pope John XXIII died in 1963, after the first session of the Second Vatican Council. The cardinals elected Pope Paul VI, who quickly announced that the council would continue. Paul VI was a brilliant pope who had taken a leading role in establishing the direction of the council. During his time as pope, he showed a great concern for poor people worldwide and expressed this concern most forcefully in his encyclical, The *Progress of People*. He expressed special concern for the suffering of people in less developed nations.

Following the example of Pope John XXIII, Paul VI brought many innovations to the office of the pope. He continued to simplify the ceremonies surrounding papal visits. He broke through the imaginary wall surrounding the papacy by occasionally leaving Vatican City on official trips to several countries. He was the first pope to address an assembly of the United Nations.

Pope John Paul II

When Pope Paul VI died in 1978, the cardinals elected Pope John Paul I, who served a mere thirty-three days before his sudden death. This pope had chosen his title, John Paul I, to show that he was supporting the direction of the two previous popes and the direction taken with the Second Vatican Council. With the death of John Paul I, the cardinals gathered for the second time in two months to elect his successor.

In October of 1978, the Catholic cardinals surprised the world by electing a Polish cardinal to take the place of Pope John Paul I. The new pope chose the name John Paul II to show his agreement with the direction taken by the Second Vatican Council and the three popes who preceded him. This was the first non-Italian pope elected since 1522.

Pope John Paul II proved to be an energetic, zealous, and visible pope. He visited many countries where hundreds of thousands of people came out to meet him. During his pontificate, he wrote a number of encyclicals on moral, spiritual, and social themes. In theological matters, Pope John Paul II chose a moderate interpretation of the documents of the Second Vatican Council.

Many world leaders credit the fall of Communism to the influence of Pope John Paul II. He inspired the people of Communist countries to reject Communism and seek freedom. His presence alone had a liberating effect on the minds of thousands of people. During his time as pope, Communism collapsed as a major threat in many countries of Eastern Europe and some parts of Asia.

In 1984, Pope John Paul II introduced an updated version of the Code of Canon Law which includes the innovations found in the Second Vatican Council. He also established a commission to work on a new catechism for the Catholic Church based upon the teachings of Christ and the documents

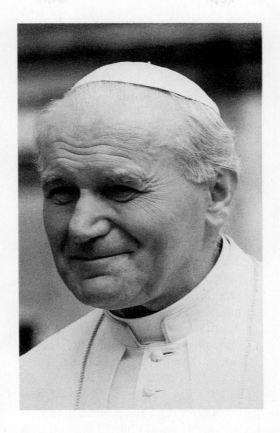

Pope John Paul II

of the Second Vatican Council. In 1992, he promulgated the *Catechism of the Catholic Church*.

The World Church

When Pope John XXIII opened the council, he directed the bishops of the world to throw open the windows of the Church and to adapt Christ's message to the modern world. The bishops responded by developing an understanding of the Church which would enable it to fulfill its mission of bringing Christ's message to all people of all ages.

The central theme of the Second Vatican Council was the Church. As stressed earlier, the Church is not a building, but a community of disciples, a People of God. The Church is the Body of Christ, a pilgrim Church, and a Church of saints and sinners. The image of the Church as a rock gave way to the image of the Church as a boat, the bark of Peter from which Jesus preached during his lifetime.

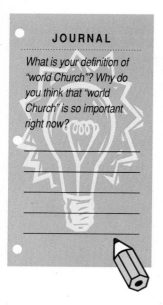

The council stressed that the voice of Jesus is still heard through the Church. Jesus' mission was to preach and share the gifts of the reign of God. His life, death, and resurrection attest to this reign. The Church fulfills its mission by offering Christ's gifts of healing, teaching, and sanctifying. Like Peter's boat on the Sea of Galilee, the Church must move through calm and stormy seas in fulfilling its mission. Under the guidance of the Holy Spirit, the Church can and does fulfill its mission in the world.

During the Second Vatican Council, the bishops witnessed a new experience of Church. Bishops came from Europe, Africa, Asia, North and South America, Australia, and from every corner of the earth. For the first time in its history, a council met with bishops matching almost every nation on the face of the earth. As the bishops glanced around at the array of nationalities and races taking part in the council, they recognized that the Church had truly become a "world Church." Bishops from prosperous countries joined together with bishops from poverty stricken countries to discuss the role of the Church in the world.

Since the end of the council, the image of the Church as a world Church has continued to develop. At the beginning of the twentieth century, the college of cardinals was predominantly Italian. By the end of the twentieth century, cardinals hailed from a variety of nations. Many Church offices in Rome were previously headed by Italian cardinals or bishops, but after the council, successive popes chose cardinals and bishops from around the world to head these offices. From its leadership to its newest member, the Church had become a true world Church.

Cultural Changes

With so many nationalities from every country of the world making up the Church, the bishops at the Second Vatican Council taught that the Church in each area of the world should choose, from the culture of that area adaptations in worship and Christian life appropriate to the area, adaptations which fit well in the life and worship of the Church. As we saw in our study of history, the Church had become identified with western culture. Missionaries who attempted to bring the culture or its language into the worship or daily life of the Church were often suspected of acting contrary to the mission of the Church. The Second Vatican Council opened the Church's heart to the rich cultures of the many people of the world, learning and teaching at the same time.

In the United States, adaptations to cultural changes offer a new challenge. The rapid influx of Spanish-speaking Catholics into the country means that nearly one-third of the Catholics in the United States now speak Spanish. Besides the desire on the part of the Spanish-speaking Catholics for liturgies in their own language, they also desire liturgies which reflect their cultural backgrounds. The Catholic Church in the United States is attempting to meet this challenge.

Many Black Catholics have also incorporated their own cultural spirit into liturgical worship. The Church in the United States has encouraged this spirit within the Black community and has sought out leaders who share this common cultural experience.

Although the charismatic movement is not a strictly cultural movement, it has brought a new experience into the lives of many Catholics. Some Catholics desire a more involved and dynamic form of worship which allows them to experience the power of the Spirit in a more expressive manner in their worship. The Church's openness to cultural adaptation has also allowed it to open itself to a number of expressions which are not cultural, but which are different from the more conventional liturgy experience in the United States.

Liturgical Life

The bishops at the council declared that the liturgy is the center of Catholic life. For that reason, they proposed some immediate changes and offered directions for future changes. Older adults recall days when the presider at the Eucharistic liturgy faced an altar set against the back wall of the sanctuary. He prayed with his back to the people, in the Latin language, with boys serving and answering the prayers in Latin.

Since the council, the presider faces the assembly which prays and sings in their language. Men and women both read the Scriptures, present the gifts, distribute the Eucharist, and are servers or song leaders at the liturgy. Many modern worship areas are built in a manner that allows the assembly to face each other during worship. The newer structures are less prone to have statues and candles lining the walls, thus emphasizing the centrality of the Eucharistic Liturgy and the importance of the role of the assembly of worshipers over an assembly of statues.

Laity

Since the Second Vatican Council, the Church identified the lay state as a vocation in the Church which comes through the Sacraments of Initiation. The council recognized the rights and obligations of the laity in bringing the message of Christ into the working place and to other areas not inhabited by the clergy. At the parish level, the pastor and lay teachers provide opportunities for adults to learn more about the faith, and the laity incorporate this message into their daily lives and work.

In parishes throughout the world, laypeople have become more active in liturgical celebrations. The daily operations of the parish are also open to lay involvement. Today more laity than ever take part in parish activities by teaching in Catholic schools, serving as catechists in religious education programs, serving on parish councils,

preparing couples for marriage, and performing many pastoral services previously done by the clergy. Pastors realize that the laity often have experiences and talents which the parish needs, but which the pastor does not have. Bishops, recognizing their call to listen to the voice of the laity, often invite the laity to serve on special diocesan committees or councils. Today, more than ever, the role of the laity has become prominent in the Church.

Ecumenism

Ecumenism refers to the sharing taking place between Christians of different traditions. Among the many surprises of Pope John XXIII in calling the council, was his invitation to Protestants and Orthodox leaders to join in the council as observers. Although they had no vote on final decisions, leaders of other denominations attended and came into close contact with the bishops making the decisions at the council. One journalist reported that a number of important discussions between the bishops took place "in the coffee shops," where bishops and clergy of other denominations met on an informal basis and discussed some of the concerns of the council.

Before the council, Catholics frequently shunned people of other faiths, and they, in turn, often shunned Catholics. Some staunch Catholics shuddered in horror if a Catholic attended a Protestant service, and a number of Protestants openly expressed bigotry against Catholics. When Catholic and Protestant leaders met together, they often expressed their differences rather than discussing the many points on which we agree, especially those concerning the humanity and divinity of Christ.

Since the Council, Catholics take part in services and dialogue with people of other denominations and other faiths. Catholic and Protestant scholars meet to discuss points of agreement as well as their differences, Catholics join

JOURNAL

How are you sharing your talents and gifts with the community?

with people of other denominations and faiths to minister together on social issues, and to share in prayer services. A number of the faithful are learning that Christian Churches share many common beliefs, whether they are Catholic, Protestant, or Orthodox.

A dramatic meeting between Pope Paul VI and Patriarch Athanegoras of Constantinople took place in Jerusalem in early January of 1964. The world watched as these two leaders embraced each other and prayed that their meeting would be a sign and prelude of the future in which both Churches would work together for the greater glory of God and the illumination of the faithful. A little more than a year later, in 1965, the pope and the patriarch mutually lifted the excommunications exchanged between Patriarch Michael Cerularius and Cardinal Humbert in 1054.

Pope John Paul II continued to meet with members of different faiths. In 1979, on a visit to Turkey, he met with the Patriarch of Constantinople and they attended each others liturgies, but without sharing in Communion. By this time in history, the people of the world had grown accustomed to such meetings between the pope and leaders of other denominations and other faiths. The spirit of the times had broken down many walls between Catholics and other believers, but tensions and differences still exist in some areas.

Justice and Peace

Although popes, bishops, clergy, and laity became involved in social issues before the council, the council placed greater stress on such activity. Six years after the council ended, in 1971, a group of bishops representing the Catholic bishops of the world met in a Synod at Rome to discuss the issues of justice and peace. They declared that work for justice touched the very foundation of the Church. Since Christ called the Church to love God, one's neighbor, and one's self, then the Church would not be fulfilling its mission unless it reached out in love to those in need.

Catholics in the United States saw their clergy and women and men religious marching along with other white and black men and women in civil rights marches. Many Catholics were unfortunately bigoted against blacks and became angry with their religious leaders for taking part in these marches. Other Catholics recognized that their religious beliefs allowed no room for prejudice, and they supported the role taken by the marching clergy and men and women religious, sometimes joining in the marches themselves.

Many Catholics also joined peace movements during the 1960s and early 70s. Catholics not only watched clergy and women and men religious marching for peace, but they also witnessed situations where some were imprisoned for destroying public property in their protests against war and the super-weapons of war. At the beginning of the Vietnam War, most Catholics supported the war. In time, however, many of them reevaluated that support and changed their views. A large number of Catholics joined in the peace marches protesting the war.

Civil rights in the United States had become a major issue during the 1960s.

Black Americans were angry with the treatment they received at the hands of political and community leaders, and they joined together to assert their rights as citizens of the United States. They staged marches to draw attention to their plight and courageously faced insult and sometimes death in their quest for their rightful place in American society.

The United States bishops have continued to speak out on issues of peace and justice. Over the decades since the Second Vatican Council, the United States Catholic bishops have written pastoral letters calling for racial justice in the United States, urging peace in the world, rejecting the free use of nuclear weapons, speaking out against abortion and capital punishment, demanding economic justice and assistance for the poor, and supporting a number of other justice issues.

Religious Liberty and the Church in the United States

A Jesuit theologian in the United States, Father John Courtney Murray, became a famous advocate for the ideal of separation of church and state as expressed in the United States Constitution. He believed that a government had no right to force a person to accept a particular religion. In the United States, the government had no right to favor or prohibit the practice of any particular religion.

Murray encountered opposition from some theologians and bishops at home and in the Vatican. Murray's Jesuit superiors finally received orders from an office of the Vatican, forbidding him to teach about the separation of church and state. Murray quietly obeyed.

During the Second Vatican Council, Murray had a leading role in the development of the document on religious freedom. The document supported Murray's view that everyone has a right to religious freedom. The government should not force a person to accept a particular religion, nor should it pro-

hibit a person from practicing his or her religion. People of all religions have an equal right to practice their faith.

Murray's views were helped by the changing situation in the United States in the early 1960s. The people of the country had elected John Kennedy, a Catholic, as president. Many people in the United States who were not Catholic began to realize that having a Catholic president would not mean that the pope was going to rule the United States. Kennedy convinced the people of the country that he had to follow the Constitution and that he believed it was not contrary in any way to the teachings of the Church.

Option for the Poor

Issues dealing with human dignity and the right to life, such as abortion, euthanasia, family abuse, captial punishment, world-wide poverty, and nuclear war became central issues for the Church after the council. In the United States and throughout the world, bishops' conferences challenged the leaders of their countries to pass laws protecting the rights and dignity of all people.

In 1968, a large number of bishops of South America met at Medillin, Columbia, and proclaimed that the Catholic Church had a preferential option for the poor. In many areas of South

America (which has a large number of
Catholics), most of the people live in
poverty and are exploited by those who
are rich and who often have the support of military regimes to keep people
who are poor in their place. In light of
this situation, the bishops opted to support and stand for the rights of people
who are poor.

Since the exploitation of the poor
by the government and rich landowners was the major problem in many
areas of the world, a new theological
movement developed. This movement
centered on concern for those who
were poor and oppressed. The new
theology received the name **liberation theology**. Because it made use of
some language similiar to Marxist communist language, some suspected it as
a leaning towards Marxism. In actual-
ity, the language of liberation theology
is more gospel-based than Marxist. The
accusation and misunderstanding,
however, have caused some Church
leaders to speak out against this theological perspective.

Liberation theology is an attempt to
apply Christian principles to the needs
of people who are poor and oppressed
by strong national leaders. The movement has grown rapidly in South and
Central America. Many members of the
clergy, men and women religious, and
laity have faced death because of their
concern for the poor. These modern-day
martyrs who saw the face of God in people who were poor became threats to
the rich who profited greatly from the
plight of the poor.

One such martyr was Archbishop
Oscar Romero of El Salvador. When
Romero first became archbishop, he believed that the rich were sincerely concerned for the plight of people who
were poor and that the poor were causing some of their own problems. As he
learned more about the oppression of
the poor by the rich landowners, he had
a change of heart and became a staunch
defender of the poor.

Romero spoke out courageously
and fearlessly against the oppressive
injustices of the government. Although
he knew he was living in constant
danger of death, he refused to sur-
round himself with bodyguards. One
day in 1980, while celebrating the
Eucharistic liturgy, he was killed by a
gunman who entered the church and
machine-gunned him.

Later in 1980, on a dark and lonely
road in El Salvador, a group of men
raped and killed three nuns (Sisters Ita
Ford, Maura Clark, Dorothy Kazel) and a
laywoman (Jean Donovan). By their dedicated work for those who were poor
and oppressed, the four had become targets of some people in the government.
Although the women knew the dangers
of their work, they dedicated themselves to their ministry and faced death
with courage.

The death of the many such martyrs
in parts of South and Central America
brought worldwide attention to the
plight of the suffering people in these
countries. The deaths of the nuns and a
laywoman from the United States
brought the problems of El Salvador to
the attention of many people. As a result
of the dedication of such martyrs and
the work of others in fighting for the
rights of the poor and the oppressed,
some countries have been forced to
change their policies and show more
consideration for all the people.

Role of Women in the Church

Although many of the contributions of
women in the Church have not found
their way into history textbooks, the role
of women has always had a great influence in Church history. In the Gospels,
we read of women who were disciples
of Jesus. In the letters of the New
Testament, we read of their services as
widows and deaconesses in the Church.

In our study of Catholic history,
we have mentioned only a few of the
struggles of courageous and holy
women who have influenced Catholic

history. Women who have served in hospitals, schools, prisons, orphanages, serving the needs of the indigent and elderly, and a number of other important areas of service have had an immeasurable impact on the development of Catholicism and Christian service throughout history.

After the Second Vatican Council, a new emphasis on the role of women in the Church has emerged. In 1963, Pope John XXIII spoke of the growing consciousness among women of their human dignity and of their rights in domestic and public life. The synod of 1971, which dealt with the theme *Justice in the World*, called for a recognition that women have a right and an obligation to participate in society and the Church.

People in the parish witness women serving as readers, ministers of the Eucharist, altar servers, and song leaders. In addition, women serve as administrators in parishes and in central diocesan offices and in a number of other significant positions in the Church. Many women, following in the spirit of St. Teresa of Avila and St. Catherine of Siena, are proving themselves to be able and insightful theologians and Scripture scholars. They have made extraordinary contributions to theology, which was controlled by men in the past, and have brought a new feminist persepctive to our understanding of the Scriptures.

CLIPBOARD

1. Pope John Paul I and Pope John Paul II both chose the names of John and Paul to show their support for the two popes of the Second Vatican Council. In what ways have the writings and actions of Pope John Paul II reflected the two popes whose names he took (Pope John and Pope Paul)?

2. How did the election of a Catholic president affect the acceptance of Catholics in the United States?

3. What effect does the Second Vatican Council have on your life today?

REVIEWING THE ERA

• 1900

POPE PIUS X. This pope condemned Modernism. He became known as the "Pope of the Eucharist" because he lowered the age for children to share in Communion and he urged frequent Communion.

POPE BENEDICT XV. Benedict became pope during the First World War and spent most of his time as pope working for peace and assisting the victims of the war.

FATHER JOHN RYAN. The writings of this ordained priest in the United States were used by the bishops of the United States in their suggestions for the reconstruction of the social structure in 1919.

• 1920

POPE PIUS XI. This pope served between the two World Wars. He settled the dispute over the Papal States, giving them to Italy and accepting a plot of land in Rome as the independent Vatican City. He supported labor and became known as the "Pope of Catholic Action" because of his emphasis on the role of the laity in the ministry of the Catholic Church.

DOROTHY DAY. Dorothy Day joined Peter Maurin in his work for peace and justice. They began the Catholic Worker Movement, which is still in existence today.

POPE PIUS XII. Pius XII was pope during the Second World War. This saintly pope personally helped victims of the war and refrained from making any comments about the Nazi treatment of Jews in order to protect the Catholic Church and the Jewish people from further reprisals. He wrote important encyclicals on the spiritual aspects of the Church, the liturgy, and the study of Scripture.

• 1955

POPE JOHN XXIII. This pope convened the Second Vatican Council, a major council of the Church. He changed the image of the pope by presenting a more human, friendly, and pastoral image to the people.

FATHER JOHN COURTNEY MURRAY. This Jesuit worked for the Catholic Church's acceptance of the notion of the separation of church and state as found in the United States Constitution. He believed that no country could force a person in conscience to accept a new belief or deny one's belief.

POPE PAUL VI. This pope continued the council after the death of John XXIII. He wrote an encyclical on the progress of people throughout the world, with special concern for underdeveloped countries.

POPE JOHN PAUL I. This pope died thirty-three days after his election. He took the names of John and Paul to show that he intended to continue the spirit of the Second Vatican Council.

POPE JOHN PAUL II. This first Polish pope took a more conservative stance in interpreting the Second Vatican Council. He traveled extensively to all parts of the globe and promulgated the new Code of Canon Law and the Catechism of the Catholic Church.

Then and Now

The twentieth century began with attacks on some modern theories in theology. During the period of the popes who followed, some Church authorities ordered major modern theologians to cease teaching their theories. In the 1960s, most of these major theologians had a great influence on the documents of the Second Vatican Council.

Throughout the century, Catholics moved from a struggling, immigrant Church unwelcome in many groups and Churches, to a Church whose members eventually became a major part of the middle class in the United States. After the Second World War, many Catholics took advantage of educational opportunities in the United States.

Today, the effects of the Second Vatican Council are seen in the dedication of Catholics who work for social justice, for ecumenical endeavors, and for the continued involvement of the laity in the ministry of the Church during worship, teaching, and in their daily lives.

A Voice from the Past

This is your final editorial. Your readers are anxiously waiting to hear how the past ties into today. Give them a brief synopsis of the Catholic Church's work during the world wars. Be sure to make note of the Holocaust. Unfold for them what led up to Vatican II and as well as the significant changes which resulted from it. Show them how Vatican II still affects the Church today. Discuss the concept of a "world Church," and challenge your readers to use their gifts and talents in striving for peace and justice.

NEWS IN REVIEW

1. What were some positive and negative effects of Pope Pius X's condemnation of Modernism?

2. Why is Pope Pius X known as the "Pope of the Eucharist"?

3. What agreements were contained in the Lateran Treaty?

4. Why is Pope Pius XI called the "Pope of Catholic Action"?

5. What was the bishops' Document on Reconstruction of 1919?

6. Why is Pope Pius XII called the "Pope of Peace"?

7. What are some achievements of Pope John XXIII?

8. What are some achievements of Pope Paul VI?

9. What are some important themes of the Second Vatican Council?

10. What are some achievements of Pope John Paul II?

A Final Note

The Hope and the Glory of Catholic History

Once upon a time there was a beautiful princess. A witch cast a spell on the princess which put her into a deep sleep. In order to awaken her from this deep sleep, a handsome prince would have to make a long and dangerous journey to capture a magic apple and touch it to her lips. If he does this, she will awaken and fall in love with him.

When the handsome prince sees the princess sleeping, he falls in love with her. He sets off on the journey to capture the apple with hopes of marrying her. For the next three years, he must travel through storms and shipwrecks, fight off dragons, climb dangerous mountains, swim a lake filled with snakes, fight a three-headed monster, and climb a tree completely covered with thorns to get to the apple.

On his way home with the apple, the prince endures one of his most difficult challenges. He passes through a land where he hears beautiful music and

meets enchanted people. He stops his journey and remains in this enchanted and peaceful land for a year. One morning, he remembers the princess, grabs the magic apple which is still fresh, covers his ears with his hands, and runs until he can no longer hear the music of the enchanted land.

Seven years after he began his journey, the prince arrives back at the bedside of the princess, touches the apple to her lips, and smiles as she opens her eyes. She sees him and falls instantly in love with him. The father of the princess orders a royal marriage for his daughter and the prince who certainly has earned his daughter's love. The prince and the princess live happily ever after.

If the prince in this story had merely to go out in the backyard, pick an apple from a tree, and touch it to the lips of the princess, we would not find this story very interesting. It would prove very little. In fairy tales, we expect the prince to face overwhelming difficulties in proving his love for the princess. It is his hope that she will love and marry him that drives him. It is his endurance and dedication to his quest that assures him of her love and the glory he deserves.

Throughout history, the People of God who are the Church have had to struggle to fulfill their mission. Some succumbed to the temptations of the journey and hindered the spread of Christ's message. Many Catholics, however, have endured the symbolic dragons, monsters, allurements, and shipwrecks along their journey—and have remained faithful. They keep alive the hope that Christ's message can be brought to every age in history, and they merit the glory that comes with remaining faithful to the quest. They are *The Hope and the Glory of Catholic History*.

Glossary

abbot: a name derived from the Hebrew word Abba, meaning father; the title given to the superior of the monks.

Act of Supremacy: declared the king the only earthly head of the Church in England.

age of discretion: the age at which a child is able to distinguish ordinary bread from the Eucharist; a child of this age is able to receive the Eucharist, this usually occurs when a child is seven years old.

Albigensians: a heretical group stemming out of Manichaeism; used two gods to explain the existence of good and evil.

Americanism: a phantom heresy resulting from the false interpretation of the French translation of the biography of Isaac Hecker.

anchorite: a person who lives a life of solitude and penance.

Anglican Church: the Church in England.

Anglicanism: the Reformation in England.

Apologists: the educated Christians of Justin's era; justified their beliefs by explaining them to unbelievers in philosophical language.

apostate: someone who denies the Christian faith after having once professed it.

asceticism: comes from the Greek and has its root in the idea of training; those in the ascetic life dedicated themselves to lives of hardship and sacrifice as a form of prayer.

Augsburg Confession: the teachings of Luther as presented in Augsburg by Philip Melanchthon.

benefice: the gift of land given to a bishop when he was appointed bishop.

Biblical Commission for the Catholic Church: established by Pope Leo XIII in an attempt to give the Catholic Church a better understanding of the relationship between Scripture and science.

bishops: successors of the office of the apostles; in governing a diocese a bishop has the responsibility of teaching the faith, celebrating divine worship, and guiding his parishes.

bourgeoisie: a new class which emerged when trade began to flourish; the name means "those who live in the city."

Breviary: the prayerbook used by presbyters and monks; revised by Pope Pius V.

Caesero-Papism: the custom of the emperor giving himself rights that belonged to the Church, and especially those rights which belonged to the pope.

cenobites: comes from the Greek word meaning common; term used to describe monks and nuns who lived within a community.

Christ: a title; the Greek translation for the Jewish word Messiah, also translates as the anointed one.

Cistercian: a movement, started by St. Robert of Molesme in Citeaux, which worked to bring the

Benedictine ideals back to monastic life; named after Cistertium, the Latin name for the town Citeaux.

Civil Constitution of the Clergy: put the clergy under the rule of the government, and gave the people the right to select Catholic bishops and other clergy for their area.

Code of Canon Law: a listing of all decrees of the popes, past and present.

College of bishops: the group of bishops that help govern the Church; they report directly to the Pope.

Company of the Blessed Sacrament: one of the first missionary groups to serve the Catholic population of Canada; also known as the Recollects.

conciliarism: a heresy, proposed at the Council of Constance, that taught that councils were a higher authority than the pope.

Concordat of Worms: an agreement, made in 1122 between Pope Calixtus II and Emperor Henry V, that gave the pope the exclusive power of appointing bishops; the bishops chosen were required to pledge their allegiance to the emperor.

congregational parish: a parish run by the laity.

Council of Constance: declared John Huss a heretic and ordered him to be burned at the stake.

Council of Jerusalem: the first council of the Church; established that Gentiles would not be required to be circumcised or accept the dietary restrictions of the Jewish faith.

Council of Nicea: (325) first ecumenical council of the Church; called by Constantine to resolve the Arian heresy crisis; resulted in the composition of the Nicene Creed.

curia: the offices that assist the pope.

cyrillic alphabet: the alphabet which Cyril, and Methodius constructed and used to translate parts of the Bible, the liturgy, and several other books into the Slavic language.

deacon: developed to assist the bishop in caring for the needs of the poor and outcast; today a presbyter first shares in the office of deacon on his journey toward ordained priesthood.

Deists: the enlightened thinkers who believed in an unconcerned and distant God.

Diaspora: Jewish groups living outside Palestine.

Diet of Worms: a meeting, called by Charles I of Spain, in which Luther was asked to recant his beliefs.

diocese: large area covering a number of towns, cities, and rural areas which contains many parishes; governed by a bishop.

Discalced Carmelites: the nuns of St. Theresa's order; literally means "barefoot" Carmelites.

Donatism: a schism in the Church resulting from the teaching that a minister in sin did not have the power to confer a valid sacrament.

Donatist heresy: taught that the validity of a sacrament depended on the worthiness of a bishop.

double monastery: a monastery for both men and women.

ecumenical council: a council involving all the bishops of the world.

Enlightenment, The: a movement, beginning toward the end of the reign of Louis XIV, which placed reason above faith.

excommunication: highest form of penalty in the Church; cuts a person off from the community of the Church.

feudal lord: a tribal king or wealthy noble owning a large area of land.

feudalism: a system which landowners developed as an attempt to protect their land.

First Lateran Council: first ecumenical council held in the West; called by Pope Calixtus II to ratify the decisions of the Concordat of Worms.

Five Pillars of Islam: what the Muslims grounded their faith upon; one God, dedication to prayer, fasting, almsgiving, and a commitment to visit Mecca at least once.

flying buttresses: provided support by reaching out from the top to the lower roofs of the structure; derived from the image of flight through air.

Four Gallican Articles of 1682: a list of judgments which King Louis XIV and a group of clergy decided upon in regard to the pope's power.

Friars Minor: name, meaning "Lesser Brothers," given to the group founded by St. Francis.

Gallicanism: the idea that the Catholic Church should be ruled by the nation, rather than the pope.

God-fearers: converts accepted by the Diaspora Jews.

Gothic architecture: a form of architecture which depended on a framework of arches and columns for support; had a soaring quality that made for higher and thinner-appearing churches.

hermit: a person who cuts him/herself off from society to live in solitude; has its roots in a Greek word meaning desert.

high priest: the major religious leader for the Jews; appointed by the Roman emperor.

homily: a message which applies the readings of the day to situations in our lives.

Immaculate Conception of Mary: a mystery of the Catholic Church teaching that Mary was free from original sin from the time of her conception; introduced to the Catholic Church by Pope Pius IX, it was the first infallible teaching of the Catholic Church.

infallibility of the pope: a Church decree that teaches that the pope cannot teach error in matters of faith and morals.

Inquisition: forum established by the Fourth Lateran Council as an attempt to discover and punish heretics more effectively.

Inquisitors: Franciscans and Dominicans who formed a traveling tribunal with the mission of exposing and punishing heretics.

Islam: a word meaning surrender or submission; religion, led by Muhammad, teaching that there was only one God.

Jesuits: the followers of St. Ignatius; also known as the Society of Jesus.

Jesus Christ: an expression meaning that Jesus is the Christ or Messiah.

Justinian Code: a set of laws that Justinian established in an attempt to unite his empire; although, the code was intended to offer Christians directions for living one's daily life, it presented some practices which today would be clearly contrary to Christianity.

Knights Hospitallers: a nursing group who cared for the pilgrims in Jerusalem; originated before the crusades as the earliest foundation in about 1023.

Lateran Synod: decreed that only a cardinal could be elected pope, and that laypeople no longer had a vote in the elections.

lay investiture: the ordaining and presenting of the bishop with the signs of the office—a cross and ring.

Liberation theology: a theological movement that attempts to apply Christian principles to the needs of the poor and oppressed.

Lutheranism: the religious movement which evolved as a result of Martin Luther's teachings.

Manichaeism: founded on the belief that one god created good, and a second god created evil; taught that an avoidance of all pleasure was necessary in order to avoid sin.

monasticism: comes from a Greek word which means to live alone; those choosing to live a monastic life were called monks/nuns.

Monophysitism: a heresy which taught that Jesus was only divine, and not human.

motherhouse: the central house of an order, often the house of origin.

Muslims: followers of Muhammad and the Islamic faith.

nepotism: the practice of lord's appointing relatives to Church offices, especially to the office of bishop.

Oath of Supremacy: an oath supporting an act which declared anyone refusing to support the new title of the king, as head of the Church, guilty of treason.

Order of Preachers: the official name of the Dominicans, founded by Dominic; lived a communal life of prayer and study; introduced the practice of allowing the community to elect its leadership.

Organic Articles: introduced by Napoleon; decreed that all representatives of the pope must receive permission from government before entering France; reintroduced the Gallican Articles into all French seminaries.

Our Lady of Guadalupe: the name given to image of Mary which appeared on Juan Diego's cloak.

Papal States: the additional territory, in Italy, that Pepin gave to the Church; also referred to as the *Donation of Pepin*, and the *Patrimony of St. Peter*.

Passover: a religious feast recalling God's liberation of the Israelite nation from the slavery of Egypt and the Israelites' eventual escape to the Promised Land.

Pelagianism: the heresy initiated by the British Monk, Pelagius; taught that God help was not needed in achieving salvation, and denied the effects of original sin on salvation.

Pentecost: (a Greek word meaning fifty) a feast which celebrates the fiftieth day after the liberation of the people from Egypt, when their leader, Moses, received the commandments in their name, as their part in the covenant with God.

Pharisees: laymen dedicated to adapting the religious law to the everyday life of the Jews.

Poor Ladies: the name of the order founded by St. Clare, later known as Poor Clares.

Poor Men of Lyons: followers of Peter Waldo; practiced great poverty and sacrifice, excommunicated by the pope because of their preaching; later became known as Waldensians.

Pope: a word meaning father; originally used as a title of respect for bishops and prebyters; now the exclusive title of the bishop of Rome.

Pope: the successor of Peter and the visible leader of the Catholic Church.

predestination: the belief, taught by Calvin, that God had chosen only an elect few for salvation.

Presbyterianism: Calvin's Protestant tradition.

Pueblo Indians: the Native Americans encountered by the Spanish explorers, in the southwestern portion of the United States.

pueblos: the Spanish name for village; where the Native Americans, living in the southwestern portion of the United States, lived.

Puritans: group in England who championed the Calvinist movement in its purist form.

Qur'an: a sacred book in which the Muslim's gathered Muhammad's revelations.

reign of God: the presence of Jesus and his message of love of God, neighbor, and self.

religious pluralism: different religions existing side by side within the same country.

Roman Catechism: introduced by Pope Pius V as a summary of the teachings of the Council of Trent.

Roman Missal: first published by Pope Pius V in Latin; book used in all Catholic churches throughout the world.

Romanesque: a heavy, stone style of architecture which dominated the style of church buildings before the year 1000.

Rule of St. Benedict: monitored the daily life of monks, placing special emphasis on moderation and balance; founded by St. Benedict.

Sadducees: a priestly class centering their authority on the Temple.

Sanhedrin: a powerful religious group, led by the high priest, consisting of seventy men chosen from among the Pharisees and Saducees.

schism: a term used to signify a break in the Church.

secular: a group that is not bound by rules or vows.

semi-anchorite: person who lives alone, but also meets with other hermits for prayer and support.

Septuagint: Greek word meaning seventy; the Greek translation of the Bible.

simony: the practice of selling spiritual offices or spiritual powers, oftentimes for a high price.

Supreme Pontiff: the title that Leo the Great chose for the papacy; at one time it was the title used to designate the head of the pre-Christian religion in Rome.

synod: a gathering of Church leaders with the task of resolving or advising on matters concerning the Church.

Templars: a group dedicated to the medical field; their red cross on a white field is a universally recognized symbol of mercy.

totalitarian state: a state in which only one political party exists; its position is maintained by force.

trustees: a board of lay people that help in the administration of the parish.

vassal: appointed by the feudal lord to administer to his land; this person paid taxes to the feudal lord, and provided a regiment of soldiers to protect the land; the serfs referred to this person as lord.

Viking: name given to the Scandinavian invaders from the north; the name means people who roam the sea.

Western Schism: the era where two popes and two sets of cardinals reigned, Clement VII in Avignon and Urban VI in Rome.

Zealots: a fervent group of Jews within Palestine that believed that God wanted them to fight to regain Jewish control of Palestine.

Index